OUR ALBERTA HERITAGE

OUR
ALBERTA
HERITAGE

By Jacques Hamilton

Illustrated by Tom Nelson
and Dianne Bersea

COMMISSIONED BY CALGARY POWER LTD.

CALGARY, ALBERTA, CANADA

People

First Printing, May, 1971,   25,000
Second Printing, July, 1971,   25,000
Third Printing, March, 1972,   25,000
Fourth Printing, July, 1974   25,000

Places

First Printing, May, 1971,   25,000
Second Printing, July, 1971,   25,000
Third Printing, March, 1972,   25,000
Fourth Printing, July, 1974,   25,000

Progress

First Printing, May, 1971,   25,000
Second Printing, July, 1971,   25,000
Third Printing, March, 1972,   25,000
Fourth Printing, July, 1974,   25,000

Mountainmen

First Printing, September, 1975,   37,000

New Pioneers

First Printing, September, 1975,   37,000

Our Alberta Heritage
(Hardcover version of all five books)

First Printing, June 1977,   10,000

INTRODUCTION

It is not unusual that Calgary Power should have a deep interest in the events that have shaped Alberta. Because, in a sense, we have played a significant role in the province's history. It has not been without a certain sense of duty that the company has undertaken, for many years now, the task of recording some of Alberta's historical events. It began with a series of radio vignettes, and has expanded into the volume you are now reading.

It was just over 65 years ago when a small generating plant, 50 miles west of Calgary, began delivering power to a few customers in the Calgary area. That plant, Horseshoe Falls, was owned and operated by Calgary Power Company Limited, the forerunner of what is now Calgary Power Ltd. Since that time the company has been intimately connected with Alberta and its heritage.

From that modest beginning in 1911, Calgary Power has expanded, with the growth of Alberta, to become Canada's largest investor-owned electric utility. Of course, we hope to continue growing with Alberta, providing the electric energy that is needed to light the lights, spin the wheels of industry and contribute to Alberta's modern lifestyle.

The compilation of volumes in this book began as a 60th anniversary project for our company. We commissioned the research and writing of the books back in 1970. You will notice in the reading that we have not attempted to present a detailed chronology of Alberta. We leave that to the scholars. Rather we have attempted to capture the spirit of Alberta through a series of anecdotes and stories about the people who lived, worked and died in Alberta.

The stories between the covers of this book are filled with happiness and sadness, hardship and reward, triumph and failure. At the same time they are all laced with the determination and ambition that gave Alberta pioneers a special place in Canadian history.

We at Calgary Power trust that you will find the same enjoyment in reading these stories as we have experienced in finding and recording them.

A. W. Howard
Chairman of the Board
Calgary Power Ltd.

PROLOGUE

The reader will find this book is really five books. Originally Calgary Power produced three softcover volumes, and two years later published an additional two.

Each of these volumes was published under the title *Our Alberta Heritage*, and each had a separate sub-title: PEOPLE, PLACES, PROGRESS, MOUNTAINMEN and NEW PIONEERS.

Since these volumes have now been assembled in this one hardcover edition, the reader should note, before proceeding, that each small volume is page-numbered as a separate book. Therefore, when you find five page 47s, for example, simply remember that each belongs to a different book in the series.

The Table of Contents has been assembled to overcome any confusion.

Author's Note

It is impossible to name them all here, but we would like to express our gratitude to the hundreds of Albertans who so graciously gave their time, their help and their rare records to make this project possible.

—J. H.

CONTENTS

People

Places

Progress

Mountainmen

New Pioneers

PEOPLE

Our Alberta Heritage Series

CHURCHMEN

BEENY, DISCIPLE OF ZAZEEKRY . . . .

The first black-robed missionaries struggled westward to what is now Alberta in search of heathens to convert.

They found heathens, all right, but they also found a surprise waiting for them. Sheltered in the foothills of the Rockies, completely isolated from white men, they found a tribe of Indians practising a distorted but recognizable form of Christianity.

The missionaries heard of the Indians' god and Zazeekry — a figure astonishingly close to the Christian Christ. They heard of angels, of baptism, and they saw with their own eyes the cross that was the symbol of the tribe's religion.

And soon they heard the name of Beeny, the Indian seer who had brought his people this new religion and who was probably the west's first "missionary" — though hardly in the Christian sense of the word.

Stunned, the missionaries dismissed Beeny and his religion as tools of the "Dark Spirit". But, at the same time, goaded by curiosity, they investigated what they had found, and uncovered a story as strange as any to come out of the west.

The story they uncovered had begun some years earlier, during a snow-bound February.

Since fall, Beeny had hidden himself in his hunting lodge. He was said to be sick, but there were many of his tribe who suggested he was only sick with mortification at being put to shame by an arch-rival in the yearly witchcraft contest.

The rival, a sorcerer named Gustlee, had dumbfounded the gathered tribes by emerging from the earth as a ghost, accompanied by a dreaded monster, the Double-Headed-Snake. At his sudden appearance, a number of his followers had "fallen dead" with fear, and Gustlee had used his magic to bring them back to life.

The trick of "resurrection" was one Beeny had heard of, but had ne'er been able to master, and he could not bear the thought that his hated rival had managed to conquer its secrets.

Beeny's defeat at the hands of Gustlee had been a disgrace. It had shamed him before the assembled tribes, and Beeny had taken to the cedar mat inside his lodge rather than show his face in daylight.

Long before spring, however, those who had questioned Beeny's illness had cause to reconsider. Word had come from the seer's lodge that he was on the point of death.

"He has not long to live now," the messengers claimed; "a green fluid is streaming out of his mouth and he is unable to speak."

As the Indians told the missionaries years later, the ailment was strange indeed. Beeny had continued to waste away. After the green fluid had flowed from his mouth, he would be lifted into mid-air as if his body had become as light as a leaf. It was difficult at times to hold him down to his couch.

At nights, they claimed, Beeny would rise from the ground and walk along the walls like a beetle or under the roof like a fly.

In desperation, Beeny's tribe even summoned his hated enemy Gustlee to try to save him. Gustlee, however, was not even granted entry to the lodge.

Enraged, Gustlee warned the frightened gathering that "Beeny is too ill to recover. Shame and jealousy have gnawed at his heart. He shall die! That is what I have to say."

Gustlee's prediction soon came true. Or at least it seemed to come true.

One morning, the tribesmen discovered that Beeny had simply disappeared from his mat in the lodge.

Outside, there were tracks in the snow, leading off to the woods. The Indians followed the trail, but it gradually faded, disappearing entirely at a spot where dozens of trees had been violently uprooted, plucked from the earth and scattered as though by some giant hand in the sky.

In the remains of one pine tree, the followers found Beeny's clothes. "Strange," they muttered as they looked around fearfully, "he has died and gone up into the sky against his will."

There, but for Beeny's relatives, it might have ended. They, instead of accepting the seer's death, stubbornly insisted that "He is not dead, he has only gone up."

Refusing to go into the required deep mourning, they pressed on in the search for the missing Beeny.

Summer passed, then another winter, and a new spring, but still the relatives refused to hold the funeral rites.

Suddenly, in May, Beeny was found; apparently dead.

The women of the tribe had been out gathering pine sap, and had come to the edge of a clearing where it looked as though monsters had held a war. Holes had been torn in the ground and the forest was a jumble. Trees had been thrust, upside down, into the ground.

Horrified, the women fled back to the village and roused the men who snatched up weapons and raced to the spot.

Like the women, they hung back, terrified, on the edge of the clearing. Then, one of the men, squinting upward suddenly yelled: "Look! There is a body."

The rest of the men focussed on the tree. There was, indeed, something wedged in the fork high off the ground, but none could tell if it was human or animal.

Reluctantly, the men decided to chop down the tree.

As they began battering the base of the trunk with their stone axes, a board came clattering down; a piece of cedar covered with signs and scrolls in black and red.

Although uneasy, they chopped on and minutes later a white cloth decorated with shiny discs fluttered to their feet. None of the men had ever seen anything like it before.

The tree was on the point of falling when a ghostly, whistling voice was heard from overhead and the men dropped their axes and fled.

Some time later, when a trace of courage had returned, the men came back to the clearing. A body had fallen from the tree and was buried to its waist in the ground. Face and hands painted white, skin as dry as buckskin, it was the corpse of Beeny.

As soon as the body was laid within Beeny's lodge, mourning began. For three days, as the number of criers, singers and dancers grew, the camp was filled with the moaning funeral dirge:

"We are near the cave of the dead, the cave of the dead

. . . The trail is bad, we fear we are lost . . . Here we have come to the dark river . . ."

Then, on the third day, something strange happened inside the funeral lodge and the camp fell silent. Those beside the body had heard the scroll-covered board creak and sizzle, and had heard four distinct rapping sounds.

Just before sunset, a youth whose skin and hair had been white from birth crept into the lodge and sat beside the body. He stared at Beeny for a long time, listening closely. "I hear something," he whispered. "I hear him singing, inside his body."

No one else could hear anything. But the youth was insistent. "So it is, I hear his voice, I hear his song, Hahaee-he neebahu-dju tisnahay . . ."

Gradually, as time went by, others in the lodge began to hear the song coming from inside Beeny's lifeless body. The song grew steadily louder and more distinct.

The youth began to hum the song vibrating in the corpse, and soon others were humming as well. Then the youth began to sing Beeny's song and, in minutes, the whole camp was singing in unison. "Hahaee-he neebahu-dju . . ."

In the hours that followed, the amazed watchers saw faint stirrings in Beeny's body, saw him begin to breathe. Slowly, as the spectators gasped, Beeny sat up. Then he stood.

Beeny had come back to life; he had resurrected himself.

Up to this point, the story of Beeny did not alarm the skeptical missionaries particulary. It was clearly just a case of a skilled sorcerer taking much time, and going to great lengths of trickery, to outdo a hated rival.

But as the story continued, the missionaries found much to disturb them:

Beeny, when he opened his mouth to speak, dumbfounded his listeners. His words were like nothing they had ever heard before. They could not understand him at all.

But the sorcerer had anticipated the problem. Beeny drew the white-haired youth to him, pressed a bone in each ear and rubbed saliva on the boy's brow.

Beeny had given the youth the power to understand him, and from that point until Beeny "relearned" his own language, the boy would be his disciple and interpreter.

Beeny and his disciple went outside the next morning to face the hundreds of Indians who had gathered from near and far to see him. As the youth interpreted, the seer told his story:

"My body was sore to the point of crumbling away many moons ago. Then I saw a ladder alongside my body, a ladder reaching up from my cedar mat into the sky. A voice at the top called me up; that is why I started to climb.

"When I looked down I stood at the tree tops. I tried to touch them with my right hand; that is how the trees were pulled out of the ground. Brothers and friends, have you seen the trees uprooted?"

There was a murmur of acknowledgment from the people before him. Beeny continued.

"I dropped my raiment, I dropped it and it fell upon the limbs of a tree. Was it lost or was it found?"

"We found it on the limbs of a tree," one of the crowd replied.

Beeny nodded. "I climbed the ladder for a night and a day. It was only my shade that was climbing, for my body was left behind. It fell between the forks of a tree. It was dead.

"I could not get into the sky all at once, only little by little. My shade pierced the sky vault slowly, slowly, even as a new-born child comes slowly into this world. When I was half-way above, I beheld the four corners of Heaven.

"At the point where the sun sets was a very old man, as tall as a tree, as white as snow. Many, oh so many people, all pale-faced, sat everywhere, but they were all like wood carvings, mute and motionless. No one took any notice of me.

"Then I turned to the east and beheld the spirits with white garments who stood near the opening where the sun rises every morning. They alone in sky-land moved their hands, their feet, their faces and their bodies as we do. In their hands they were beating skin drums while they danced in circles and sang, 'Sun, good Sun, when is it that you be-gan to rise and set in the sky?' "

Beeny paused to rest, and, when the sun rose, continued his story.

"This is the second day of the shortest span of time (the week)," Beeny said. "I shall tell you of the two head-chiefs of the Sky, the Father and the Son.

"The name of the Father is Old Man. He has always been, he is as ancient as the world. Yet he cannot die, for he is a manitou, the oldest sky manitou.

"Listen to his song, brothers and friends. It is a wonder-ful song, the song of the Old Man: 'Since the world first grew I have lived until now. Old as I am, I remain strong. The manitous of the mountain peaks, the manitous of the canyons, the manitous of the wind, the manitous of the trees and the waters are all in me. From them, from all nature, I am strong, I am everlasting. I can give life again. Those who sing my song shall stand up from amongst the dead, . . .' "

The crowd, excited by the words of the song, began to hum, then to sing.

As they sang, Beeny retired to his lodge and resumed his trance.

The next morning, however, he appeared again. On his left arm he carried the white cloth with the shining discs. At his feet lay a horn bowl filled with clear water.

"This is the third day of the short span," he said, then touched his forehead with his right hand, then touched each shoulder and his breast. Everyone in the crowd imitated him in making the Sign of the Cross.

"Listen," Beeny continued, "my dream now was of the Son, Zazeekry, who stands next to Old Man among the Sky manitous, and holds a tree (the cross) and a bowl of water in his hands. This is what the manitou Zazeekry told me, 'Very soon a great plague shall visit your people. The earth shall crumble to pieces and fire shall leap out of the ground, and the big sky monster shall swallow the sun and the moon. Darkness and smoke shall prevail everywhere.

"'Go and tell your people! They are all sinners. They are not baptized, they know nothing of my Cross, they do not marry in the proper way, and when they die, their bodies are hung in the trees, then burned to charcoal on the pyre. 'Your people are bad, they are heathens. That is why the earth shall break up and burn to cinders.'

"Then Zazeekry poured the water of baptism from his bowl on to my head, and he said, 'Beeny — Mind-all-over-the-world — this shall be your name, for you are the first to discover who I am.

"'You must go down the sky-ladder and return to earth, to save your tribe, your tribe and all the tribes that welcome the Truth. Baptize the people, give them new names, tell them to repent and show them the right way.'

"Then I travelled all around the sky. I stood at the four corners of the world and learned the new ways of life. The time came for me to return to you, my people. I sang the song of Old Man, the song of life, Hahaee-he neebahu-dju . . ."

All through the following days of the "short span" (the Christian week), the people of the tribe and of tribes all around rushed to Beeny to be baptized. And to listen as he continued preaching the message of Zazeekry:

"You shall not kill, you shall not lie, you shall not steal, you shall not have more than one wife, and you shall observe deemawse (dimanche, Sunday)."

Beeny also showed his followers the three "magic" gifts he said he had brought back from the sky.

The first was the white cloth he had carried on his arm while preaching. "This," he explained, "is the white cloth of Heaven. It is a blessing, for it shall cure diseases and drive away the big plague."

The second was a small board covered with peculiar colored signs. "Now behold the prayer board! Here are the seven notches, the days of the short span. You shall work six days and rest on the seventh. That is what Zazeekry does. So you must do.

"Here are the signs (the Scriptures). You shall look at them, for you must all pray and be saved from the big fire."

Then Beeny pulled out a small spruce tree carved to represent a cross. "This is the Cross of Heaven, the Cross of Penance. When you see it you must repent, you must do penance. A ten days' fast, that is what you must observe before you begin the big Indian dances."

Beeny's religion caught on quickly among the Indians of the mountain tribes. Even traditional enemies — thanks to

Beeny's ability as a magician — were converted. In one case, Beeny used a convenient eclipse of the sun to make such a tribe see the light.

But Beeny and his growing number of disciples became too lavish in their claims of the power of the new religion. As years went by, the Indians were encouraged to abandon hunting and gathering berries in favor of continuous worship.

Inevitably famine struck and, with it, disenchantment. Encouraged by Beeny's enemy Gustlee, among others, thousands turned their backs on the faith of the Sky People, and returned to their old beliefs.

Beeny himself lived long enough to hear condemnation of him by the first missionaries as "a juggler, an imposter, a servant of the Evil Spirit."

Broken-hearted, the old sorcerer died a few weeks later.

This time for good.

Historians, like the early missionaries, have always been at a loss to explain the uncanny accuracy of Beeny's visions of Christianity. Perhaps the most plausible explanation is that offered by Marius Barbeau in his book, Indian Days in the Canadian Rockies:

"The wonder of it all is that this event antedated the labours of missionaries, even the appearance of the earliest white men along the perilous trails of the northern uplands.

"How could a seer like Beeny, in the vastness of his remote country, dream of heaven, baptize neophytes and establish pseudo-Christian ethics in a manner which reminds one more of a Catholic missionary than a pagan of the mountains?

"Time rubs off many connecting links, distance obscures our perception, and it is not possible yet to unravel the puzzle.

"Beeny, in his prolonged absence after his disappearance, may have travelled to some distant point, though not as far as the trade outposts. From the very impurity of his mystic notions, from his tale of marvels, it seems more likely that in the beginning at least, he laboured under the delusions of hearsay.

"Many stories from the lips of other Indians, of catholiciz-ed half-breeds from the east — Cree or Iroquois — and of French coureurs-des-bois may have reached his ears, pos-sibly through the 'free hunters' who resorted by the score to the Rocky Mountains even before the time when Thompson, in 1807, first wintered at Lake Windermere.

"A stimulus once provided, his imagination may also have elaborated other themes about the coming of the white people — 'the sky beings' as he called them — which must have filtered through the mountain passes at a very early date."

Whatever the source of the vision, and however sad its failure, even the early Jesuits acknowledged that it eased the way for true Christian teaching among the Indians.

And so Beeny, that wily and misguided sorcerer, earned his place in history as Alberta's first missionary . . .

* * * *

THE "BIG CHIEF OF THE PRAIRIES" . . .

It was 1852, and Chief Factor Rowand — volatile chief of the Hudson's Bay post at Fort Edmonton — was leading a string of loaded York boats west.

In the party, keeping well out of Rowand's way, was a young French-Canadian priest who was to become the resi-dent churchman in the western post.

The priest, still a stranger to the west, was filled with

sympathy for the voyageurs whose unhappy task it was to haul the York boats upriver by brute strength. Strapped into harness like dray horses, they scrambled over rocks, through swamps and sometimes waded up to their armpits in the icy water.

As a French-Canadian himself, the young priest became close friends with many of the suffering boatmen.

Suddenly, one day, the young priest made an infuriating intrusion on the chief factor. One of the voyageurs, the priest informed him, was sick and barely able to stand in his harness. The man should be allowed to rest and should be given proper food.

Rowand's Irish temper boiled. How dare this callow priest

interfere with his party? And how dare one of his men complain of illness?

Those within earshot of the argument that followed were astonished to find the young priest every bit as stubborn as Rowand, and finally to hear the factor grudgingly give way.

"Give him some of your food if you must," Rowand snapped, "but he needs no rest. Any man who is not dead with three days' illness is not sick at all."

Many days later, in Fort Edmonton, Rowand had cause to recall that argument and his angry words.

Rowand had injured one of his fingers painfully and had gone to the priest — the closest figure the post had to a doctor. The priest did what he could, then sent the factor back to his own quarters with the comment: "You are not suffering, Rowand!"

Three days later, with Rowand still in agony, the priest paid him a visit. As he wrote later:

"I had to say what was in my mind, though I feared trouble might come of it. I had to touch that man of iron.

"I went to him and said — not that I was sorry, but — 'You will understand what I mean, my friend, when I tell you that you are not sick. Three days have passed now, and you are not dead. So of course you are not sick; it is all imagination.'

"His face took on an awful cloud. If I had not been his friend and a priest, I believe he would have struck me. Hah! He was like a can of powder, that little man!"

It was Rowand's first encounter with Father Albert Lacombe, that gentle but stubborn priest destined to become one of the greatest — if not the greatest — figures in Alberta history.

The little "black-robe", with the blood of an Ojibway

chief and of the voyageurs in his veins, symbolizes — more than any other man — the history that turned Alberta from a raw wilderness to a modern province.

Father Lacombe created a Cree dictionary, a Blackfoot dictionary. He built the first bridge in the west, and the first flour mill. Single-handedly he broke the transportation monopoly of the Hudson's Bay Company and introduced the Red River Cart as the main method of moving goods across the prairies.

Time and again, all alone, he stepped in to stop the carnage of the never-ending war between Cree and Blackfoot. Alone, on one occasion, he saved Fort Edmonton from an overwhelming Indian attack.

Alone, during the nightmare days of the Riel rebellion, he was able to keep the Blackfoot at peace, and thus save Alberta's white pioneers from what might have been terrible slaughter.

Without complaint, he undertook the pride-crushing task of begging through eastern Canada, the United States and Europe for the money needed to keep the vital western missions going.

The same audacity that led him to the confrontation with Rowand led him, in later years, to take on the Canadian Parliament and the Quebec press over the issue of separate schools. Once, it led him to brusquely interrupt a conversation between an archbishop and the Emperor of Austria — a diplomatic blunder that no one but Father Lacombe could have got away with.

It would be futile to attempt here the biography of this great man. That task has already been lovingly accomplished by Katherine Hughes in her book, "Father Lacombe, The Black-Robe Voyageur".

Instead, we offer a glimpse of the "Big Chief of the

Prairies" at his bravest and most-loving.

It was 1865, 13 years after Father Lacombe had first come to Alberta. All those long years he had labored among the Cree, bringing them religion and a sense of civilization.

For his efforts, he had earned the undying respect of these northern Indians. And from them he had earned an Indian name: Kamiyo-atchakwe — The Man-of-the-Beautiful Soul.

Now Father Lacombe was about to move on a more dangerous mission; to the Blackfoot whose fierceness and hatred of the white — including missionaries — was legendary.

Father Lacombe, however, didn't put much stock in legend. Particularly legend about the Blackfoot. Had not their leaders already approached him several times with an invitation to visit their people? And had they not told him that he would need to carry only a white banner emblazoned with a red cross to guarantee his safety throughout their lands?

All that summer he labored among the nomadic tribes. In one sense, his labors were discouraging. Although he made many friends, he made few converts.

Proud and stubborn, the Blackfoot refused to turn from their old beliefs — particularly not to a religion that taught the subservience of man, and that demanded the unthinkable sacrifice of abandoning the harem in favor of life-long devotion to one wife!

It was a depressed Father Lacombe who, on a December night that year, dropped off to sleep in the lodge of the Blackfoot chief Natous.

Pressed by the scarcity of food in their own territory, Natous and other Blackfoot leaders had led their people northward — dangerously close to the dividing line between their territory and that of the Cree.

Late that night, as Natous and Father Lacombe lay

asleep in their thick cocoons of buffalo robe, the Blackfoot camp was suddenly torn by the wild shrieks of war cries and by a hail of Cree bullets and arrows.

Father Lacombe, shocked awake, lay in rigid disbelief as he heard the night echo with the deadly struggle outside.

Most of the Blackfoot warriors were away hunting for game, and it was a pitifully small force that was left to withstand the large force of Cree and Assiniboine bent on slaughtering the camp.

Father Lacombe was jarred to his feet when musket balls tore through the chief's lodge and snapped two of the supporting poles.

Hastily, he threw his black robe over his buckskins, grabbed the cross of his order and his red-cross flag, and rushed outside.

Father Lacombe wasn't afraid. He was enraged. Feeling certain there were some Christians among the Cree attackers, he yelled repeated commands to them to stop their treacherous attack.

Fortunately for Natous and his braves, the echo of the gunshots had carried to the other Blackfoot camps. Hurriedly, hundreds of warriors — the fiercest the west has ever known — were grabbing weapons and leaping on horseback.

The Cree and Assiniboine had already overrun most of the camp, and had begun looting, when the Blackfoot warriors fell on them.

The Cree party retreated, but only to the cover of a nearby hill. Three times that night they mounted fresh attacks on the Blackfoot.

By dawn, both sides were dug in and exchanging a steady hail of musket fire.

With the coming of light, however, Father Lacombe decided it was time to call a halt. Raising his crucifix in one hand and his red-cross flag in the other, he called on the Blackfoot to stop firing.

The Blackfoot complied, then watched astonished as the little priest deliberately marched out into the middle of the battlefield and the rain of Cree musket balls falling through the morning mist.

The Blackfoot could not believe his bravery.

"Here, you Crees!" Father Lacombe yelled at the unseen enemy. "Kamiyo-atchakwe speaks!"

The Cree could not see him in the mist. Nor could they hear his voice over the gunfire.

The Blackfoot, realizing his peril, begged the priest to turn back.

Suddenly, horrified, they watched a musket ball hit the frozen ground and rebound up into Father Lacombe's face. The priest staggered and fell.

The Blackfoot could not know that the ball had only scratched his temple. To them, it seemed that the hated Cree had killed their friend, the powerful white medicine man who had nursed their sick and wounded, and whose bravery seemed a hundred times greater than their own.

An unbelievable anger swept over the Blackfoot, and the warriors leaped to their feet as one, charging past the fallen priest to the heart of the Cree position.

The Cree, suddenly smothered by Blackfoot, broke and ran. For hours, from hill to hill and coulee to coulee, the retreat continued. With every cover, the Cree would turn and fight, only to be forced to run again.

It was during one of these lulls, while the Cree lay in cover, that they heard the scorning yell of a Blackfoot warrior:

---

where in these books, the reader will meet John a personal role in ending the era of the whiskey who controlled most of southern Alberta for nearly e. He will meet John again as he witnesses the birth rt that would grow to be the modern city of Calgary, will watch him play a vital part in shaping an Indian o bring lasting peace to Alberta.

n Rev. George McDougall arrived in Edmonton in a decade after Father Lacombe, he found only a small post and a handful of tumble-down shacks. But he omething more as well; a vision of the future.

e wind, he confided quietly to his wife, he could hear und of that advancing multitude which will soon fill rairies . . ."

determined Methodist missionary then set out to pre- e west for that vision.

Dougall's first mission was 70 miles from Edmon- Victoria (now Pakan). It took him a year to build it was the summer of 1863 before he could bring e to her new home. With her came her two sons, nd David, her daughters Flora and Georgina, and wife, Abigail.

six years, the Victoria mission would be a bustling, place as the McDougalls worked ceaselessly to trust of Cree and Blackfoot, and to convert them to religion. John worked at his father's side in the ary endeavors, while David chose to follow a career der.

ress in the mission was rapid. George quickly gained m affection and trust of powerful chiefs. Young John as skilled with words as his father, but he had a keen and some talents that made him the favorite of young- ns.

"You have killed your blackrobe, dogs! Have you not done enough?"

The message swept through the ranks of the startled Cree. Was it true? Had they really killed their friend, their man of prayer, their honored Kamiyo-atchakwe?

Terrified and ashamed, the Cree and Assiniboine lost all will to fight. What had, up to now, been a retreat became a rout.

A few days later Father Lacombe, wounded and desperately ill, left the Blackfoot for a period of recuperation at Rocky Mountain House.

Despite his physical condition, Father Lacombe left with a strong feeling of satisfaction. He had earned the faith and friendship of the Blackfoot; a faith he was rightly confident would pay off in conversions later. Also he felt — again rightly — that his intervention in the battle had planted the seeds for a negotiated peace between the traditional enemies.

And, to his lasting honor, he left these fierce, proud people of the plains with a second Indian name: Arsous-kitsi-rarpi, "The-Man-of-the-Good-Heart."

Of all the tributes that would come his way during his long missionary life, this Blackfoot name would always be among those he cherished most.

* * * *

THE MAGIC MCDOUGALLS . . .

Thousands of people a day stream by a small wooden building in the heart of modern Edmonton. Few give it more than a passing glance, and fewer still know the proud story that lies sleeping behind its doors.

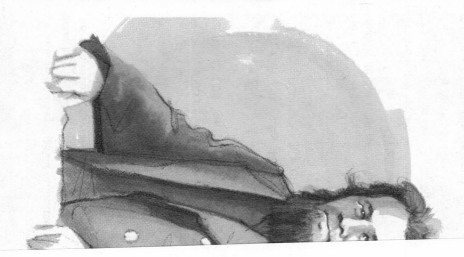

The small building, near the and First, is McDougall Church — Alberta's first white family, and of trade of missionaries who brought peace a frontier.

No one, except perhaps Father L frequently in the pages of our earl and John McDougall.

It was these younger Indians who gave John his first Indian name — one that meant "the winner". He earned it by proving himself the fastest runner in the west, consistently beating every man, white or Indian, who raced him.

Never one given to modesty, John used to point to a high hill north of the mission and claim: "Over there, I ran down the hill, across the valley and up another hill, faster perhaps than any man ever did — and not because a buffalo was after me, either!"

By the fall of 1869, the McDougalls had every reason to consider their work at Victoria a success. The mission had grown to include a school, and Indians were flocking to Victoria in such great numbers that the Hudson's Bay Company had opened a post by the mission.

Then, a few months later, disaster struck. A smallpox epidemic swept the west, killing thousands of people. All around the mission were camped dying Indians.

All the McDougalls, except George's wife, were infected, and Mrs. McDougall was left to stand by helpless as both her daughters, and John's wife, died of the dreaded illness.

The McDougalls never spoke of their grief, but its depth can be measured even today. Every female descendent of the family has as her second name "Victoria", in remembrance of the unhappy settlement.

By spring, the McDougall men had recovered well enough to try to re-establish the shattered mission. But, though they struggled for a year, persistent flare-ups of smallpox defeated them.

Finally, in 1871, they gave up and returned to Edmonton which, thanks to the quarantine precautions of the Hudson's Bay Company, had escaped the epidemic entirely.

George McDougall built a new house on a hill east of the

Fort, then built the church that now stands in downtown Edmonton. His wife, burying her sorrow, began teaching school to the children of the Hudson's Bay men — no easy task since she spoke English and they Gaelic.

From Edmonton, the sturdy McDougall missionaries, father and son, spread outward. Soon all Alberta felt the influence of their religion, their firm ethics, and their warm concern for their fellow man.

John, more than his father, took eagerly to the rough and tumble of pioneer life. Often dressed in Indian buckskin, he would use his famous speed and, rifle in hand, take off on foot after buffalo and moose.

By 1875, the McDougalls had built a new mission headquarters at Morley, west of Calgary. In 13 short years, they had gained so much respect that there wasn't an Indian lodge or pioneer cabin that wasn't open to anyone with the McDougall name.

Even the American whiskey traders, whom John and Father Lacombe were working tirelessly to drive out, liked and respected the young Methodist. Alone and unarmed, John was a frequent and welcome visitor at their forts — a venture that would, for most men, have resulted in a quick trip to the graveyard.

Fortunately, for the student of Alberta history, John McDougall turned to writing in his old age. His journals provide a rare and detailed picture of life here during Alberta's first years, and a portrait of this unusual man.

Recently Calgary's Glenbow Foundation found and published the last of John McDougall's journals. Although he died before he could finish it, the slim volume offers some of his most exciting writing.

One chapter in particular is as vivid a picture of frontier life as has ever been painted. And it shares with its readers

John's painful memories of the second great tragedy of the McDougall family: the death of George McDougall.

"It was now December, 1875," McDougall writes, "and in taking stock of our provisions we found the supply was limited. Accordingly my brother David and I arranged to strike out for a buffalo hunt.

"Gathering up our horses we pushed out to the big open country to the east. Our objective point was down into the Rosebud region north-east of where Calgary now lies.

"After scouting in several directions and finding no game, and as the cold was intensifying, we concluded to fall back on our dried provisions and possible cattle at home for another month or two. We were now as a hunting party down to starvation conditions.

"I well remember one very cold evening as we went into camp my brother shot a coyote. When he had taken off the pelt it looked like good meat.

"Our boys and men soon had it cleaned and roasting by our lodge fire. In a little while morsels of this coyote meat, so attractive in appearance, were being passed around. As my share came to me I fully intended to eat it, but in lifting a little of the roast to my mouth I caught its odor and my stomach revolted. I at once concluded to fast awhile longer.

"While we were away on this trip father and mother had gone down to the mouth of Highwood River where my sister Mrs. Wood and her husband were wintering. They planned to spend Christmas with them and also to visit the Blackfeet in that vicinity.

"New Year's eve father returned alone and brought word of buffalo coming up country between the Bow and Red Deer rivers. He had seen them moving westward and he advised me to make a break for meat lest the herds might soon be driven back again by hunters onto the plains.

"The buffalo were still, even as they had been for many years, our main food. To obtain a supply of meat was very essential, for our settlement was growing. In our mission party, permanent and transient, there were all told twenty-three souls. In my brother David's family were five. In the home of the one stockman there were two. In a lodge of French mixed bloods, four.

"On the second of January I began to make ready for a fresh meat hunt. I hired the one mixed blood to go with me and had my young cousin Mose as my third man.

"When ready and about to start, my mixed blood came to tell me that he could not go as his wife was seriously ill. Then my father volunteered to take his place and, while I was most reluctant to agree, there did not seem to be anything else for us to do.

"Behold us then starting out to make the trail and hunt buffalo. Father drove a four horse team hitched to a home-made ironless pair of bob sleighs. Mose and I followed with a string of single-horse flat sleds and the saddle and buffalo-running horses."

(McDougall notes at this point the party was swelled by an Indian friend, Hector Nimrod, and his 10 year old son.)

"We left the valley of the Bow soon after we had crossed the Ghost River, and we struck out into the country north of where the City of Calgary is now located.

"By Friday night we had about half loaded our sleds with meat. This I had done by stalking the buffalo, as there had not been a favourable chance to run them. That night I decided, with father's consent, to fall back west to the last willows as our stock of wood was nearly exhausted.

"Saturday morning we loaded up and travelled some ten or twelve miles back and camped on the bank of a small creek at the foot of a knob of hill which became a first class lookout for us.

"Monday morning we were up and ready for the hunt long before daylight. By sunrise we were near to the spot I had in view, and I had barely time to gather up the horses, give them to father to hold, catch up and saddle one of my runners, when a bunch of buffalo came cantering on towards us. These I tried to run but, as the prairie was frozen hard and glassy and the snow was piled here and there in drifts and also hard on the surface, my unshod horse would not run.

"In vain I tried to spur him on. He very rightly judged that he had enough to do to keep on his feet. However, I picked a good animal and, jumping from the saddle, I made a long, dead shot.

"Straightening out No. 1 in position for skinning, I galloped back to father and put my running pad on another horse and waited for another bunch to appear, which it did shortly. Again I made an attempt to run, but this horse was even more wary of a fall than the first one. Again I sprang from the horse and, making another long shot, brought down my second cow.

"I now made up my mind to take my old war horse Tom out of the shafts and try him once more for a run. Tom had been a famous buffalo horse and was full of pluck. I very soon had my pad on him and, as father and I talked for a few minutes, there appeared another bunch of buffalo over the hill.

"I sent old Tom after them. He, as I hoped, went at his work with all his heart and it was now my turn to feel nervous as, regardless of ice and sharp turn, Tom gathered up speed. Soon we were near the buffalo and I was busy looking for the fat ones.

"I had barely placed a good animal when out from under him went Tom's four feet and down we went, rolling over and over. My gun was thrown one way and Tom in another and my lariat was almost uncoiled to its extreme end before we stopped.

"I was pretty well shaken, but I jumped up and was glad to see old Tom rising to his feet. He seemed to say, 'Hurry, jump on and we'll try again.' Running for my gun and coiling up my lariat, in a moment we were off again.

"Now the situation favoured us, for here was a big dry swamp. The buffalo had eaten off the grass and, in doing so, had left a stiff short stubble which gave Tom firm footing. Soon we were in the herd and I caught sight of four fine farrow cows running in a bunch.

"Tom brought me jump by jump nearer to them and I began to shoot. In a little while the four splendid animals were stretched on the frozen prairie.

"Father and I moved down to my last kill and, beginning at the first, skinned, cut up and loaded it on the sleds. The day was now well spent, and it behooved us to hurry.

"We had finished two and were at the third when I suggested to father that he make a fire with a little bundle of wood we had brought along, melt some snow and make a cup of coffee.

"I well remember that we had five small biscuits. Father insisted that I should eat three of them, while I said I was satisfied with two. Finally, he split the odd one in half and we ate and drank and were greatly refreshed and soon again at work in the dark.

"Just as we were through with the third animal, Hector and his boy came to us with the two sleds and we moved over to the last cow. Hector and I made quick work of this one, and in due time we were ready to start for camp.

"When about two miles from our camp we came to the valley of the west branch of Nose Creek and here, as there was a long incline, Hector, who was leading his horses in front, started into a run.

"With a crack of my whip I sent my four horses after him and thus, for some time, I was parted from father. After we had crossed the creek, pulled up the further bank, and were beginning the long slow ascent up to our lodge, father cantered up.

"He rode to one side and said, 'I will go on, see about Mose, and help him to have supper ready when you come.' Pointing to a bright star ahead he remarked, 'That star is right over our camp John.' I looked and answered 'Yes,' and on into the darkness of the night he rode away.

"I little dreamed that I would never again in this world look upon my living father.

"Presently we were at the dark and silent lodge and I could not imagine what had happened to father as the land marks were extremely good and the night not very stormy.

"I opened the door of the lodge and called, 'Father, Mose; father, Mose,' but there was no answer. In the dark I felt around the inside of the lodge and stumbled over the boy buried under a pile of buffalo robes, sound asleep.

"When he was sufficiently awake to understand, he said he had not seen father. I jumped out and grasped my rifle, which I had fastened on one of the sleds, and fired several shots in rapid succession. I had the Indian shoot off his old flint-lock with heavy charges of powder. Then I said to myself, 'How foolish to make such a fuss. Father may have missed the spot a little, but he will be in before I can get the horses unharnessed. Perhaps he has ridden out to hunt up our horses left here today.'

"With these thoughts I unharnessed the horses and disposed of them for the night. We fired more shots from time to time. We made a beacon light on the summit of the hill, but the long night passed and we still had no clue.

"Hector and I each wore out two horses that next day in riding the country in every direction, but night came and we had not even found a trace. The moving herds of buffalo blotted out other footprints. This condition, with the drifting snow, made it impossible for us to track anyone, experts though we both were at such work.

"We planned to start for home with the early morning. About midnight, however, a wild north-east storm set in and, by morning, thick swirling snow was in full possession of the plains, making it impossible to safely venture out. We waited impatiently for the storm to let up. This did not occur until night again came upon the scene.

"Bright and early Thursday morning we started for Morley. As soon as I got our party over the worst hill and fairly on the road, I left them to come on and hurried home, reaching there late at night. But alas father was not there, nor had anything been heard of him since we had left for the hunt.

"As quickly as we could Friday morning, my brother David, Kenny McKenzie and I started down the Bow valley searching and making all enquiries possible, but without any clue until Saturday morning.

"When near the spot where our hunting lodge had stood, we came upon the track of a horse dragging a long lariat through the snow. We surmised this to be the horse father had with him. Tracking him, we soon came upon him with a little bunch of horses.

"Continuing our search all day, we found ourselves after dark at a native camp. These people had no more tidings for us so we determined to go into Fort Calgary and there obtain all the help possible from the North-West Mounted Police and cover a still wider stretch of country.

"We arrived there through a wild night at one a.m. We roused the police and resident traders, trappers, hunters and arranged for a large search party. Early next day, Sunday, in intense cold, we were away and, spreading out within call of each other, searched all day but in vain.

(The diary records the intensifying search and the final, tragic, result.)

"The following Sunday morning, while searching some brush in a coulee, my cousin Capt. George McDougall who was next to me in line of search, called, 'They are making signs to me over yonder.' I mounted and, as we approached the congregating party, my brother cried, 'Oh John, father is dead. They have found his frozen body.'

"A half-breed who was not with us in the search had, while out hunting buffalo, come upon my father's lifeless body. He had put him on his sleigh and taken him back to his camp and sent us word. The kind native woman had spread her shawl over the lifeless form.

"When I lifted the shawl and saw the position in which he had frozen, I felt whatever may have happened to father toward the last he was conscious and, feeling that death was upon him, he had picked a spot as level as he could and laid himself out, limbs straight and hands folded . . ."

Rev. George McDougall was buried near the mission at Morley. The words with which his son laid him to rest were simple: "His work was finished but will never be forgotten. A faithful son, a true husband, a fond parent, a real patriot, a devoted pioneer missionary. Such was our father."

A visitor to that little wooden building near the busy corner of Jasper and First in Edmonton will find inside old beams hewn with a broad-axe.

Some of the deepest marks in those beams were made by George McDougall. But none of them are as deep as the mark he made on Alberta history.

CHARLES MCKILLOP, THE "FIGHTING PARSON" . . . Southern Alberta in the late 1800's was filled with hard-drinking, hard-fighting cowboys, and any churchman bent on taming this wild flock had to have more than his share of faith and determination.

Charles McKillop arrived in Lethbridge in 1886 with faith and determination aplenty. And with a solid right arm that would leave a lasting impact on many an unruly "heathen".

* * * *

If Rev. McKillop had any romantic illusions about the task that lay ahead, they were dispelled the moment he stepped off the train in Lethbridge. As he wrote years later:

"No welcoming hand took mine as, tired and travel-stain-ed after a journey of two thousand miles, I stepped out on the platform of the depot. I felt as a stranger in a strange land. I lifted my heart in prayer to my Master to give me courage and wisdom for my work.

"That night, under the pilotage of a Presbyterian whom I had met on the street, I 'roosted' under the roof of what was then known as a hotel.

"The minister's room was one of two directly above the barroom. One layer of inch flooring was all that separated him from the scenes below.

"I went to sleep with the clinking of glasses, bits of ri-bald song, fierce oaths and a jumble of talk all mingled in my ears. In the middle of the night I was awakened by the sound of a number of shots fired beneath.

"In alarm I jumped out of bed, dressed, and hurried downstairs. The manager, who had heard my moving about, met me on the stairs and said, 'Don't be alarmed, it's only the boys shooting for drinks. Come in and look on!'

"On doing so I found a number of men, seemingly in the best of humour, shooting at cards tacked to the wooden walls of the room. 'Only our western way of doing things,' remarked the manager. 'Not bad fellows, perhaps a bit rough'..."

When McKillop left the hotel in the morning, he was met by startled stares and suppressed laughter. Innocent in the ways of the west, the 38-year-old minister was turned out in a very proper black, broadcloth Prince Albert coat, clerical collar and tall silk hat.

As he quickly discovered, it was the fine "topper" that was attracting all the attention. In the west of that time only Indian chiefs wore top hats — and they usually cut holes in the crown for ventilation.

The social error, however, was about to lay the foundation of McKillop's reputation as the "fighting parson" of Alberta.

"While going about my pastoral duties," he recalled later, "I had occasion to pass the window of a certain office ... I was attracted by a loud tapping on the panes. I stopped, looked back and saw a number of grinning faces behind the glass. On a sudden impulse, I quickly stepped into the office, which was a few feet above the level of the street.

"A young lawyer, who has since become a very notable figure in western politics, and who was evidently ring-leader and spokesman on this occasion, remarked in his drawling manner, 'Mr. McKillop, we merely wished to know where you got that hat?'

"'Well, gentlemen,' said I, very pleasantly, 'if you will

permit me to put my hat and coat on this shelf, I will give you an answer that perhaps will be satisfactory.'

'Having rid myself of my coat and the obnoxious hat, I turned and faced the half-dozen young men who formed the gang, none of whom seemed formidable, and said, 'Gentlemen, for answer, I propose to pitch you all out of this office.'

'A chorus of jeers greeted this statement. Like a whirl-wind I turned myself loose, as we say in the west, and in a few minutes — the job was done!

"As I stood on the doorstep looking at the sprawling figures, I quietly asked, 'Do you desire any further informa-tion, gentlemen, about that hat?'

McKillop, the citizens of Lethbridge respectfully noted after that incident, was no ordinary minister.

"The lawyer, who is a good fellow and a humorist, said, as he was dusting his coat, 'Mr. McKillop, I am very sorry to say that I seem to have lost all interest in that hat.' "

What he had grasped right from the start was that, on a frontier where might was still right, it was going to take at least a measure of might to bring peace and civilization.

McKillop was uniquely well-suited for the task. He had come to the ministry late in life. In the years before he assumed the clerical collar, he had trained as a boxer and a wrestler — and polished his fighting skills in the rough and dangerous logging camps of northern Ontario and Quebec.

He never lost his interest in hand-to-hand encounter and, two years before his death, the aging McKillop proudly mas-tered Ju-jitsu and was giving free demonstrations to anyone foolhardy enough to take him on.

Only once did Rev. McKillop come close to earnest

combat — and that was the result of a misguided practical joke.

McKillop had been giving instruction in Latin and Greek to a young student in the Methodist ministry who informed his teacher that he understood a new family of Presbyterians had arrived in town and told McKillop where to find them.

The next day McKillop went out to visit the family. Fortunately, before going up to the house, he stopped in next door to visit a parishioner.

He asked the mother of the house if she knew anything about the strangers as he had heard they were Presbyterians.

"Oh, mercy no!" the startled woman replied. "They are dreadful people; you mustn't call there as they'll kill you."

"I'm not in the least afraid," the minister said and, now forewarned, he went next door. The front door of the cottage was ajar and he could hear the sound of hammering inside. McKillop knocked.

The response was a gruff male voice telling him to "Get to hell out of here."

McKillop immediately threw open the door, and stepped inside to see a huge man on knees, nailing down flooring with the back of a broadaxe.

"What do you mean by talking to me like that?" the minister demanded.

The man jeered. "What business have you preachers to come around here when you think that the men-folk are away at their work?"

"None of your vile insinuations, or I'll give you a lesson you will not soon forget." McKillop strode over to the man and commanded; "Put down that axe."

The man put it on the floor and the minister kicked it into the corner.

"Now get up and sit on that chair," he ordered. Taken aback, the man complied. "You're a pretty like-ly-looking fellow," he said, staring at the minister.

"I've licked far better men than you," McKillop pointed out grimly. Then he noticed a girl peering at them through the open back door. "Is that your daughter?" he asked.

"Yes, that's Rosie."

McKillop beckoned to the girl. "Come in, Rosie, and sit beside your father, as we're going to have worship."

In minutes, the astounded father and daughter found themselves kneeling in prayer.

When they arose, Rev. McKillop's tone was soft and friendly. Shaking hands with both of them, he invited them to attend church services the following Sunday — which, to the pleasure of the minister, they did.

As the years went by, Rev. McKillop, to his satisfaction found fewer and fewer occasions when he had to display his might. The congregation of Knox Presbyterian Church grew steadily, and Lethbridge nights were no longer inter-rupted by the sound of gunshots.

But even though he was well into his 50's, the fighting parson had lost none of his keen enjoyment of the wrestling ring.

One morning, not long after he had mastered Ju-jitsu, he was sitting at his front door when Charlie Hyssop, the town's waterman, arrived carrying his huge buckets of water.

Charlie was a giant of a man, well over 250 pounds, and a keen student of wrestling.

Waterman and minister were soon cheerfully debating the merits of a famous wrestler who had died not long before.

"Well," said Charlie, "what do you say to trying out your pet system of wrestling against mine?"

The two, stripped to shirtsleeves, squared off. Before Charlie knew what had happened, he found himself sailing over the minister's shoulder, through the open door, and onto the lawn.

Mystified, the waterman leapt to his feet and jumped back inside. A few seconds later he found himself once again sailing towards the lawn.

Utterly humiliated at being tossed about by an aging man barely half his size, Charlie made good his escape.

The match, however, was to be Charles McKillop's last.

A few months later, he was felled by a stroke and, on August 20, 1907, he died.

There were some, even in his own day, who criticized him for his reputation as the fighting parson. But there were more, many more, who saw him as a man with the right qualities for the temper of a raw frontier.

Charles McKillop was a soldier of the Lord. And he knew, better than most, that sometimes a soldier has to fight . . .

PIONEERS

Alberta is, in many ways, still uniquely a frontier. Ask any farmer. Ask any lineman slashing a narrow trail through the trees on the east slope of the Rockies. Ask, for that matter, any city dweller who stops his car on a rural road and steps out to let his eyes search the rimless prairie.

So the title "pioneer" is one that has to be used carefully in this province. And only time will tell if the few people whose stories follow are any more deserving of it than the bearded man in Peace River country carving a homestead out of virgin land and reading this page today by the light of a coal-oil lamp.

* * * *

Looking back into history at our earlier pioneers, the ones we recall best are those who were particularly brave or particularly colorful. Or the ones who had the strangest stories to tell.

One of the most unusual stories has to belong to a man whose name we don't know — and who we can only guess came to Alberta.

The man was a sailor on a British privateer, part of the era before English seamen took on the Spanish armada and won. The man was part of an expedition trading by force in the West Indies when this side of the world still belonged to Spain.

The man, and dozens of his shipmates, became mutinous and were forcibly marooned on the coast of Mexico.

Somehow this sailor managed to walk from Mexico, clear up North America and be rescued off the coast of Canada's maritimes.

Fragments of the story he carried back to England have survived. He described the Great Lakes to listeners who still thought America was only a sliver of land, separating the Atlantic from the China seas.

Most importantly to us, he described the prairies, and the great hump-shouldered "buffes" running across the grass in thousands.

And he described something else — something plains Indians tried to tell our first white settlers about years later — and left historians with a puzzle they still haven't solved.

This unimaginative seaman described an elephant, long-tusked and covered with shaggy hair, and claimed he'd seen it on the prairies. If he was telling the truth — and if the drawings Indians made years later are to be accepted — the Hairy Mammoth was wandering Alberta a thousand years after the civilized world considered it extinct.

* * * *

Then there was Nigger Molly, the Medicine Hat washer-woman who proudly claimed she was "the first white woman in the west." And there was her arch-rival, Irish-born Slippery Annie.

For years, it was even money which of these two hard-drinking, hard-fighting women would come out the winner in their never-ending battle.

But it was Slippery Annie, finally, who carried the day with as unusual a wedding as the west had seen.

The good Annie found herself a diminutive French-Canadian from Quebec and pointed him towards the church.

The whole town turned out to see Annie in purple dress and fine linen, and her groom-to-be in his frock coat, white vest and silk hat.

Unfortunately, both bride and groom were in an advanced state of inebriation. Once inside the church, Annie commandeered the organ and turned loose with "Pop Goes The Weasel" and "Gin a Body Meet a Body Comin' Through the Rye" and other entertaining — but singularly inappropriate — songs.

The minister tried in vain to bring the concert to a halt. Finally, losing all patience, he ordered Annie out of the church with instructions to come back when she and her beaming boy friend were both sober.

Annie, however, changed his mind with a simple, tearful truth. "The trouble, yer riverence, is he won't come back when he's sober."

* * * *

And there is Billy Henry who, close to a hundred years old, spent one night in an old-folks home then stomped out and went back to his own cabin near High River. He couldn't stand the institution, he told the relatives who finally found him, "because there are too many old people in there."

The stories go on and on. These are the people who haven't just earned a place in our history. These are the people who are our history.

* * * *

THE "SMOKED IRISHMAN" . . .

John Ware was a big man, a solid man.

And he was a dark man.

One summer Saturday in 1970, more than 200 people went to the quiet valley outside Millarville where John Ware built his first home in Alberta. They came to picnic and to laugh and to exchange stories about the Negro cow man who was born into slavery in the southern United States and rose to become one of Alberta's most honored pioneers.

There were old people in the crowd — people who had known John Ware as a neighbor, and who had respected and liked him. And there were youngsters there, playing along the banks of the creek that had once provided the Ware cabin with water.

The four surviving Ware children were on hand. Janet — "Nettie" — to shake her head at the playing children and remember that: "Lord, I don't know as how we didn't drown in that creek a dozen times. We were playing there all the time."

Grey-haired and cheerful, she pointed out, over and over again, the pine tree on the hillside where the cellar of the old Ware cabin used to be.

Her sister, Mildred, huge-eyed and shy, just listened and shook her head at questions. "You'd best ask Nettie. I was too young to remember anything from then."

Bob and Arthur Ware, grey-haired and solemn, circulated through the crowd, exchanging memories with the men and women who had known their father.

Bob Ware frowned when someone asked him why the family had objected, finally, to the "Nigger John" name by which his father was known until a few years ago.

"There were lots of kinds of men who settled this country. Some was Irish and some German and some half-breed Indians.

"I don't remember anybody being called Half-breed Sam or German Joe."

Then he stared, unspeaking, until the embarrassed questioner turned away.

"Anyway," one old-timer commented, "no one would have called him Nigger John to his face, I'll tell you."

John Ware himself had always jokingly called himself a "smoked Irishman". Anyone who dared to make any less flattering reference to his color was in for a thumping from the powerful cowboy. Indeed, on one occasion, John Ware threw a man through a hotel window for making a rude reference to his color.

Lazily, with big rough hands wrapped around homemade sandwiches and cakes, the men chuckled and exchanged stories about John Ware.

One man recalled the time John showed up at the edge of Calgary with a herd of cows he wanted to drive east across the Elbow Bridge. The town fathers refused to let someone clutter up their streets — even if they were mostly mud — with a bunch of dirty steers.

John Ware hadn't argued. He'd just waited until midnight and drove the herd through anyway. By the time the town fathers woke up, the deed was done, and John Ware was politely tipping his hat to them from the far side of the Elbow.

Nettie remembered a night when the Ware cabin got flooded out and her dad had plunged into the stream to rescue his wedding certificate. Then he'd hurried the family up the hill and, in his haste to build them a warming fire, accidentally hit his wife on the head with the back of an axe.

Nettie giggled, then pursed her lips. "A man just has one of those days every so often."

In time, when the picnic had ended, Lt. Governor Grant MacEwan arrived, granddaughter in lap, behind a pair of mules.

Then, to the sound of the creek and the playing children, the lieutenant-governor told the story he has told so often about his favorite pioneer.

About how John Ware was born in slavery. How he couldn't read or write and had no shoes until he was 20. How John Ware signed on, in Texas, with a cattle-drive north and was given the worst horse and the worst saddle and left to ride "drag" — eating dust all the way to Alberta.

About how, when John Ware asked for a better horse, he was given an outlaw — and broke both it and the prejudice against the color of his skin.

Grant MacEwan, like Nettie, pointed to the pine tree on the hill and talked about John Ware building his home and bringing his new bride there.

Then he talked about how John Ware died, too young, 65 years ago when his horse stumbled in a gopher hole and rolled on him.

(At John Ware's funeral, the minister had said: "John Ware was a man with a beautiful skin. Every human skin is as beautiful as the character of the person who wears it. To know John Ware was to know a gentleman, one of God's gentlemen.

"Never again will I see a colored skin as anything but

lovely. He leaves me with the thought that black is a beautiful color — one which the Creator must have held in particularly high favor because He gave it to His most cheerful people.

"Make no mistake about it, black can be beautiful.")

Then the lieutenant-governor found the words the old-timers had been looking for all afternoon.

"John Ware was a good neighbor, and he was a good friend."

The lieutenant-governor stepped over and uncovered the plaque on a rundlestone memorial the Millarville Historical Society had found near Canmore and moved to this spot in memory of John Ware.

Anyone can go and see that memorial any time. It is a big stone and it is a solid stone.

And it is a dark stone.

* * * *

BUFFALO BUD . . .

Time does funny things to a man. It would seem reasonable that anyone who was riding the Alberta range in 1906 would now be content simply to find a warm spot in the sun and sit there.

But E.J. "Bud" Cotton is, well, just plain getting younger and more active all the time.

Which is a very fortunate thing, because Bud Cotton is a pioneer with a rare and valuable set of memories to share. He's one of the last Albertans to know intimately the age of the buffalo.

Actually, the buffalo age he knew wasn't the first — the one that littered the prairie with bleached bones. It was the second age, the one that wouldn't have happened if the federal government hadn't, at the last possible moment, decided it might be worth saving a few of these mighty animals.

Young Bud Cotton was cowpoking on the Pat Burns spread when the government opened the Wainwright National Buffalo Reserve in 1909.

Four years later, through some set of events he still can't comprehend, he turned his back on the Herefords and signed to ride herd on the buffalo; a career he followed until the reserve was turned into an army base in 1940.

Today, Bud Cotton lives in Calgary where he carves exciting things from wood and from words, and where he is always available to reminisce about a way of life that will never be again:

"You ask, stranger, what it was like when the buffalo ran wild in the big park at Wainwright. Well, there were miles of rolling prairie, clumps of poplar and willow in the low spots and around sloughs, high ridges of sandhills, here and there a bunch of buffalo grazing contentedly, a few elk standing silhouetted against the skyline, and along the side hills and brush patches, a group of deer nervously browsing or nibbling at a juniper.

"It was a great life riding the buffalo range. I'll never forget my first day. It was early in the spring of 1913 that two cow-waddies, Ed and I, first were introduced to the buffalo.

"We had been riding the range in central and southern Alberta. Now we were given the opportunity to ride in the Wainwright Buffalo Reserve. Here was something different, with a promise of unknown excitement — certainly a change from the cow-camp!

"Upon reporting for duty, we were given a couple of saddle horses. We supplied our own saddle gear and bedrolls as was the custom in those days. Then we were told to try and get a count on the buff herd and check for casualties.

"Nine hundred or more buffalo had been turned loose in the reserve — 200-odd square miles of rolling prairie, sand brakes and river coulees. It took a lot of riding to locate and check on the herd of now approximately 2,200 head that had ranged free and unbothered for four years in this large brush-covered terrain.

"We had lots to learn about our new woolly pals. Lucky

for us the saddle horses were good and buffalo-wise. The one I was riding was a big rangy bay named Frost. Ed was atop a slick chestnut gelding called Nick.

"Now buffalo are funny critters and we had to learn the hard way. Here were two well-intentioned cowpokes just wanting to ride around and do a little counting, peaceful-like.

"In cowland tallying, saddle strings were used, tying a knot to represent 50 or 100. But the new boss, apparently with little faith in our cipher education, gave us two punch clocks. We'd squeeze a little gadget for each 'buff' seen, and up popped the totals.

"We drifted towards a bunch of buffalo, and they promptly broke into a run, scattered, and disappeared into the willows and muskeg. Well, no count!

"'There's some big ones over here,' yelled Ed.

"Twenty head of old bulls for the tally clock! They too drifted into some timber, and to make sure we had 'em all, we moseyed in too. The bronc didn't seem to like this. Suddenly we realized why: One old bull that had been standing, backed up against some brush with his tail straight up, gave a grunt and charged straight at us.

"The wise saddle horse had apparently known just what to expect. Both ponies wheeled and got out of there pronto. I lost my hat as my spine hit that saddle cantle with a tooth-rattling jolt.

"The bull only charged about 40 yards, but oh boy, could he come fast! Again no count — forgot to punch the tally gadget!

"Riding over a knoll we spied quite a little herd grazing along the shores of a small lake. It looked as if our count could really start now. But the unpredictable buffalo fooled us again.

"We had approached them through a ravine that was apparently their chosen way out, and out they came! There seemed to be buffalo everywhere, all travelling fast: so we travelled fast too. No count! And lesson number three: Don't try to figure out which way a buff will run.

"One more try that day sent us back to the bunkhouse disgraced with our luck and in disgrace with our saddle broncs. I could tell it by the way they wagged their ears and shook the bit chains.

"It had happened this way. While we were circling a lovely lake, sandy beach, coves and all, a good place to water the horses and relax awhile, we saw them. There were only a dozen or so of the old buffalo cows and their cute little newborn calves, apparently feeling quite sociable, just standing there looking us over as we rode along the water's edge.

"I noticed the old saddle horse roll his eyes as we passed the closest cow and he acted as if he hated to turn his rump to the old lady. I figured he was just acting gentlemanly.

"Then there was a snort and Mrs. Buffalo charged right in under the bronc's tail, circled back and got set for another run. However, taking the hint, the broncs were out belly-deep in that lake.

"Every time we forced the horses toward the shore, that vengeful old cow would charge us. Cussing did no good, so with the best grace possible two cowpokes went across that lake.

"I told Ed to punch 10 cows and 8 calves on the tally clock, but in the excitement he had lost it in the lake. No count! Four runs — four errors!

"No wonder our broncs took a dim view of us, but despite that I gradually grew to respect and admire those shaggy beasts.

"'God's critters.' That's the right name for the buffalo. Some folks call them ugly and ungainly brutes, but I always see them as a majestic animal, big and powerful, kings of the North American rangeland.

"In the days when our wild life ran free and unrestricted, they dominated the range. Even the old grizzly bear thought twice and had to be mighty hungry before he tried for a buffalo steak.

"Don't let me throw a scare into you about the buffalo though. They are not vicious. You could ride the buffalo range for weeks and watch them as they roamed there — hundreds of them contentedly grazing or streaming along the old buffalo trails to some waterhole or new pasture.

"It was only when those things on horseback came around trying to corral them and interfere in their way of life that they really got peeved and riled up and certainly made life interesting and miserable for those same pests of buffalodom — the riders.

"The buffalo herd bulls generally ranged in bunches of a couple of hundred or so and did not mix with the cow herd. The cows roamed in family groups, just mother, junior, and her two and three year olds, with perhaps a granddaughter or so in the herd.

"June and July is the mating season. The hills and flats resounded to the roaring challenge of the mating bulls. Here nature demonstrates her code of 'the survival of the fittest'. In buffalo land that means 'might is right'.

"The bull fight is really a spectacle of sheer brute strength and tenacity, coupled with the urge to kill. Two tons of infuriated buffalo meet, out for murder, all for the favor of a sloe-eyed buffalo heifer who, by the way, usually calmly wanders off with another gentleman during the fight.

"There are very few preliminaries in the battle. It's a crash-bang, head-on affair with flying dirt and hair as these mighty animals meet with 'no holds barred'. Action is unbelievably fast as each exerts every effort to get a horn into the other's side, groin, or flank, and when this happens it's generally finis — a buffalo doesn't hook. The horn goes in and then, with an upward rolling swing of that mighty head, the horn tears its way through hide and muscle.

"With a ghastly wound like that, especially in the side or groin, it's only a matter of days before the vanquished fighter's carcass is found in some isolated spot where the animal has crawled away and died — alone, with only the magpie's chatter and a coyote's howl as a farewell lullaby.

"Other bulls escape, crippled and soured on life in general, and pass the rest of their days in what we called the 'Outlaw Gang' — confirmed bachelors!

"Nowadays, when all the buffalo are confined to smaller fenced areas, I guess they could all be called imprisoned outlaw gangs of today's civilization, but to me when running free they were 'God's Critters'."

Many a man with Bud Cotton's memories would spend his time brooding about the "good old days." But not Mr. Cotton. Instead, with his carving tools, he carefully recreates in wood the scenes of a past too few are still around to recall.

Maybe that's the secret of growing "young" as a pioneer.

* * * *

THE VOICE OF THE PARK COUNTRY . . .

Red Deer's Annie Gaetz has never much thought of herself as a pioneer. Indeed, she is going to be pretty surprised

young Annie, worn-out and ill,
room to rest. But by 11 that morn-
washed and dressed and heading
Employment Agency" building
on platform at dawn.
r that, yes, he could fix her up
place outside a little town called

l, and then he told me that they'd
keep her there a month, because
but once a month.

could find a place to sleep —
otherwise anyway with no train

woman who'd let me rest in her
k everybody she saw if they knew
She tried real hard, and finally
I can come up with is the girl
itchen. She stays with her sister
he sister doesn't really have any
only has a kitchen, a bedroom
But she gives the girl two blankets
eep on the floor.

d they said if you can't find any-
there with her.'"

r gratefully and for the next three
he crowded house with the young

a man had arrived from Red Deer
ime and the new teacher.

day," Mrs. Gaetz remembers with
oad of lime. It was a double-box
before. The seat was way up an

to find herself singled out as one in these pages.

But then Mrs. Gaetz doesn't even think of herself as an author — despite the success of her book "The Park Country" — so maybe she deserves a few surprises.

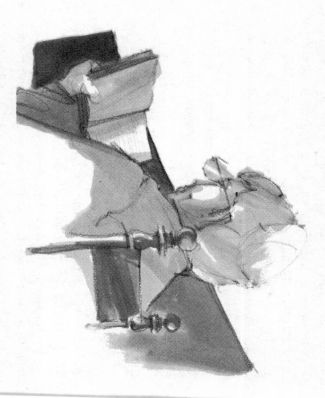

Mrs. Gaetz is 90 years old, and her eyesight has failed to the point where she can barely see to peck out a few letters on the keyboard of her typewriter.

But she's an energetic, bustling example of all the strength and determination Alberta's first women brought to a raw frontier.

She was 21, a product of solid United Empire Loyalist stock and a proud Nova Scotian, when fate turned her westward in 1903.

"I had a very bad cough," she recalls. "I went to see the doctor and found out I had tuberculosis. If I would stay

When the woman saw she let her use her own bed ing, Annie was back up, determinedly for the " she'd spotted from the stat

The man inside told h with a teaching job — at a Red Deer.

"I said I'd take the scho said if he got a teacher to nobody came in from ther

"So I said I'd stay if I didn't know what I'd do coming or anything.

"I went back to see the room, and she said she'd a where I might find a roo she said, 'The only one who works here in the k quite close to here, and room even for her. She and a small sitting room. and a pillow and lets her s

"'Anyway, I asked, a thing else you can go sleep

Annie accepted the offi weeks shared the floor of kitchen girl.

Finally word came that — to get a wagon-load of

"We went out on Satu a smile, "on that wagon- wagon. I'd never seen on calmly wanders off with another gentleman during the fight.

"There are very few preliminaries in the battle. It's a crash-bang, head-on affair with flying dirt and hair as these mighty animals meet with 'no holds barred'. Action is unbelievably fast as each exerts every effort to get a horn into the other's side, groin, or flank, and when this happens it's generally finis — a buffalo doesn't hook. The horn goes in and then, with an upward rolling swing of that mighty head, the horn tears its way through hide and muscle.

"With a ghastly wound like that, especially in the side or groin, it's only a matter of days before the vanquished fighter's carcass is found in some isolated spot where the animal has crawled away and died — alone, with only the magpie's chatter and a coyote's howl as a farewell lullaby.

"Other bulls escape, crippled and soured on life in general, and pass the rest of their days in what we called the 'Outlaw Gang' — confirmed bachelors!

"Nowadays, when all the buffalo are confined to smaller fenced areas, I guess they could all be called imprisoned outlaw gangs of today's civilization, but to me when running free they were 'God's Critters'."

Many a man with Bud Cotton's memories would spend his time brooding about the "good old days." But not Mr. Cotton. Instead, with his carving tools, he carefully recreates in wood the scenes of a past too few are still around to recall.

Maybe that's the secret of growing "young" as a pioneer.

* * * *

THE VOICE OF THE PARK COUNTRY . . .

Red Deer's Annie Gaetz has never much thought of herself as a pioneer. Indeed, she is going to be pretty surprised to find herself singled out as one in these pages.

But then Mrs. Gaetz doesn't even think of herself as an author — despite the success of her book "The Park Country" — so maybe she deserves a few surprises.

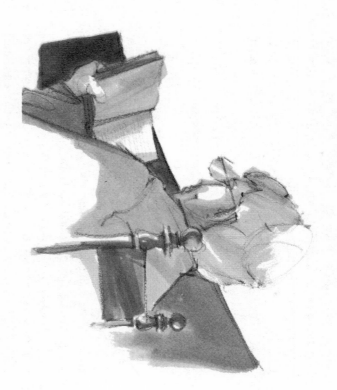

Mrs. Gaetz is 90 years old, and her eyesight has failed to the point where she can barely see to peck out a few letters on the keyboard of her typewriter.

But she's an energetic, bustling example of all the strength and determination Alberta's first women brought to a raw frontier.

She was 21, a product of solid United Empire Loyalist stock and a proud Nova Scotian, when fate turned her westward in 1903.

"I had a very bad cough," she recalls. "I went to see the doctor and found out I had tuberculosis. If I would stay home, and do nothing but look after myself, I might live for quite a few years.

"Well, that didn't suit me at all, and I thought that if I was going to die I might just as leave die out here as die there."

Young Annie had been trained as a teacher and she discovered that the prairies — in addition to being a good place for someone with a cough — badly needed teachers.

That combination was enough to make her bundle her belongings together and climb on a train west.

"When I came out, I came on a colonization train. All it had was those slatted wooden seats — not very comfortable, I'll tell you.

"I was on that train six days and six nights, and all it did was stop and start, stop and start. I got so train sick that I just couldn't stand it any longer.

"The next morning I got off the first time we stopped and took off all my things with me. The place was Woolsey and when I saw it I wished I'd had the courage to go to Moose Jaw, which is where my ticket was for. It was just a little place, with only a few buildings and a station.

"I saw there was a hotel right close by, and I went into the station and asked the agent when the hotel would be open. He said, 'It will be open at 8 o'clock, but you don't need to look for a room there because I know there isn't one.'

" 'Well,' I said, 'and where would I get a room?' and he said 'Nowhere that I'd know of.'

"Finally, he told me that a woman across the street kept a boarding-restaurant and her men left at 7:30 to go work on a construction project in the country, and they took their dinners and didn't come back 'til night. 'Perhaps if you ask her, she'd let you rest in one of their rooms.' "

When the woman saw young Annie, worn-out and ill, she let her use her own bedroom to rest. But by 11 that morning, Annie was back up, washed and dressed and heading determinedly for the "Employment Agency" building she'd spotted from the station platform at dawn.

The man inside told her that, yes, he could fix her up with a teaching job — at a place outside a little town called Red Deer.

"I said I'd take the school, and then he told me that they'd said if he got a teacher to keep her there a month, because nobody came in from there but once a month.

"So I said I'd stay if I could find a place to sleep — I didn't know what I'd do otherwise anyway with no train coming or anything.

"I went back to see the woman who'd let me rest in her room, and she said she'd ask everybody she saw if they knew where I might find a room. She tried real hard, and finally she said, 'The only one I can come up with is the girl who works here in the kitchen. She stays with her sister quite close to here, and the sister doesn't really have any room even for her. She only has a kitchen, a bedroom and a small sitting room. But she gives the girl two blankets and a pillow and lets her sleep on the floor.

" 'Anyway, I asked, and they said if you can't find anything else you can go sleep there with her.' "

Annie accepted the offer gratefully and for the next three weeks shared the floor of the crowded house with the young kitchen girl.

Finally word came that a man had arrived from Red Deer — to get a wagon-load of lime and the new teacher.

"We went out on Saturday," Mrs. Gaetz remembers with a smile, "on that wagon-load of lime. It was a double-box wagon. I'd never seen one before. The seat was way up and

I wondered how in the world to get up there, because there was no sidewalk or anything to help you up from the ground.

"And it was just time for the beer rooms to open, and there was a good order of men waiting for their morning refreshments — so I had lots of audience, I'll tell you.

"Anyway, with some help, I managed to get up on that seat, and we were on our way . . ."

Mrs. Gaetz talks without complaint of the year she spent in the one-room school, trying to instill a sense of learning in 31 restless children ranging in age from 5 to 16. She had no textbooks, no notebooks or pencils, no maps, no help. Just a cracked blackboard and some pieces of chalk and a lot of Nova Scotia determination.

Most of those school-hating children grew up to be her friends.

A year after she arrived in Red Deer, Annie married the son of Rev. Leonard Gaetz, one of the founders of the town, and assumed all the arduous chores of a pioneer wife and mother.

Year after long year, she watched the world growing up around her, and she remembered what she saw. One day, a relative suggested she write a little book about the Gaetz family, and she did. Then she wrote another little book and, finally, the big book that is the best history there is of the Red Deer district.

All this and much, much more Annie Gaetz told me one autumn day in the little house, in a quiet corner of Red Deer, where she lives alone.

To say that Annie Gaetz lives alone is somewhat less than the whole truth. She lives with a host of bright memories — memories intertwined in the rich fabric of Alberta's history.

* * * *

RIDERS AND ROPERS

It was 1912, the first year of the Calgary Stampede, and an eastern lady was sitting on a corral fence watching a cowboy saddle and board a bronc.

The woman's brow quickly clouded with indignation. "Oh, look at that pony jump around, and that brute of a man is kicking him in the tummy!" she exclaimed.

Then, as the pony did some real sunfishing, the rider lost his hat, then both stirrups, then was thrown looping over the pony's ears just in time to receive a hoof print "right where mother used to apply the cane."

He rolled to a dusty stop against the corral poles, then slowly picked himself up and gingerly poked all his aching joints to make sure he was still intact.

Satisfied, he ambled over to the still indignant easterner. "Sorry, ma'am," he apologized, "I didn't mean to hurt the little pony. I just had to get off to pick up my hat."

* * * *

It's easy to be a rodeo rider, as easy as falling off a horse — which is probably where the whole thing started.

The sport of rodeo may not have been born in Alberta, but it sure did its growing up here: to a stature unequalled anywhere else in the world.

The basic rodeo skills of riding and roping and wrestling were the natural product of cowboy life. Every working cowhand had to be able to ride a horse that didn't want to be ridden, and able to persuade stubborn cattle to do what he wanted them to do.

The point, of course, was that some men could do these things better than others. And there were others who thought they could do them even better still. And with that attitude around, it was only a matter of time before these skills were pitted in competition.

Indeed, by the time pioneer cowboys were moving into the short-grass country of southern Alberta, it was no longer enough for a man just to be a "good" rider and roper. He had to be an outstanding one.

It was no accident that John Ware, the famous Negro cowboy, first had to "prove" himself by boarding and beating one of the meanest broncos available. And it was no accident that his success was followed in short order by promotion from riding "drag" (in the dusty rear of the herd) to foreman of the Bar-U Cattle Co.

The cowboy competition of rodeo has always been a natural as a spectator sport, with highly-skilled men pitting their talent against the determination of wild and powerful animals.

Thanks to the foresight of a handful of men, and the outstanding ability of Alberta cowboys, Alberta has grown to become the rodeo centre of the world. Of the 26 rodeos authorized by the Canadian Rodeo Cowboys' Association, for example, 18 are staged in this province.

Today, of course, with thousands of dollars in prize money at stake, rodeo is no longer a place for casual cowboy competition. Rather, the men who compete at the Calgary Stampede and other big shows are skilled professionals who make their living by being consistently the best in the world.

But the basic quality of rodeo is still — and always will be — the same as it was the first time a determined cowboy climbed aboard an equally determined bronc.

* * * *

THE GREATEST RIDER IN THE WORLD . . .

Alberta is the unquestioned home of rodeo greats. Year after year, our cowboys and cowgirls bring home the top honors and the championship saddles.

With so many greats, it is easy to understand why today only a few people still remember a little cowboy from Pincher Creek who proved himself the greatest rider in the world and, in a few short minutes long ago, gave the sport of rodeo its greatest glory.

It was Winnipeg in 1913 and the announcement had just been made that Emery La Grandeur had won the title of World's Champion Bronco Rider, with a gold medal and a cash prize of $1,000.

As the crowd clapped and cheered, everyone thought the Winnipeg version of the late Guy Weadick's "Stampede" had come to an end. Only Emery La Grandeur knew different.

"While the announcements regarding winners in other events were being made," Weadick recalled later, "Emery

La Grandeur approached me and asked me if I would do him a favor.

"Sure, I'd be glad to do anything I could for him.

"He then asked me if I would have the big sorrel bucking horse named 'Red Wings' brought into the arena as he wanted to make an exhibition ride on him.

"For my part I had seen about all the bronc riding I cared to during the past week, and told him so, also suggesting that considering he had ridden several top horses during the week — and had been fortunate enough to win the money, title, etc. — it was beyond me why he wanted to prolong the performance fooling around with this 'Red Wings' which, by the way, was an outstanding bucking horse of the Ad Day string.

"'Never will I forget the earnestness in his voice nor the almost pleading look in his eyes as he replied, 'Doggone it Guy, don't turn me down in this. I sure want to take a sittin' at that sorrel, and I know the audience will be glad to see one more final bronc ride after the last announcement has been made.'

"Then he continued, 'Go ahead Guy, have them bring him in. You know old Joe Joe La Mar was a friend of mine, and I'd hoped all week that I'd get to draw this Red Wings. Let me take a ride at him, Guy; I want to kinda square things up for old Joe.'

"His eyes sorta filled up as he looked at me — and I, I turned away feeling a little softened up myself. I ordered the sorrel to be brought into the arena at once.

"Emery's eyes sparkled as he heard the order given. 'I'll be right back,' he called over his shoulder. 'Goin' to get my saddle.'"

The attendants brought the big bronc into the arena and snubbed him up to a saddle horse. As Emery was saddling him, an announcement was made that turned the inside of the arena silent as a tomb. The new world champion bronc rider was going to give an exhibition ride on the noted outlaw 'Red Wings' — the horse that had killed the champion's best friend, Joe La Mar, at Calgary the previous year.

In the stands, La Grandeur's wife Violet turned pale and held their infant son a little closer to her.

The area inside the arena fence was cleared, and every man who had competed in the week-long Stampede gathered at vantage points along the rail.

Picking up Guy Weadick's description again: "The saddling finished, La Grandeur climbed up on the bronc, settling himself in the saddle with both feet set in his stirrups. He quietly told the man on the snubbing horse to take the dallies off his saddle horn and pass the halter rope over to him.

"When that had been quickly and quietly accomplished, Emery reached over and unbuckled the halter, stripping it off the horse's head.

"He straightened back up in the saddle and swung the halter in the air — bringing it down between the horse's ears with a resounding crack.

"As the snub man loped out of the way, La Grandeur tossed away both halter and shank and shouted: 'Bow your head bronc, and do your best!'

"Raising both hands high in the air above his head, the reckless rider planted both spurs high in the horse's neck and raked him with both feet from there clear back to the cantleboard of his saddle.

"As the big sorrel plunged forward he really turned on the juice. Not a sound was to be heard from the spectators in the seats nor the contestants encircling the arena, but gradually — it seemed almost unconsciously — all rose to their feet in spell-bound silence; everything forgotten but the drama that was being enacted out there in that long, tan, bark-covered arena.

"Red Wings had a reputation as a top bucking horse, and that August night in 1913 he sure lived up to every bit of it.

"With his big head free and no restraining rein, either to hold him back or to assist the rider in steadying himself, the sorrel really demonstrated that his bucking propensities had not been over-estimated by the many who had touted him as a hard horse to ride.

"He ducked, he plunged, reared, sunfished, leaped high in the air, swapped ends and hit the ground repeatedly like a ton of brick.

"In fact he opened up his entire bag of tricks as he bucked this way and that, zig-zag across and down the long arena.

"The sorrel did everything in his power to unseat the reckless, cool and calculating cowboy astride him — who was still holding both hands high in the air . . .

"And La Grandeur, instead of doing anything to restrain the bucking horse, urged him to still further 'turn it on' by playing a spur tattoo, scratching him continuously high, wide and handsome from shoulders to flanks.

"There was no time limit set to the ride. Nothing had been said as to when the horse was to be picked up, and after Red Wings had bucked the entire length of the arena he swapped ends and started his dizzy waltz back toward the upper end, seemingly getting tougher with every jump.

"Emery still continued to work on him — all the time holding both hands high above his head.

"Suddenly the horse threw up his head and his tail. He broke, and started to run like a race horse.

"The pick-up men immediately started to close in on the fleeing animal and, as there was no halter or halter shank on the horse, they decided to crowd in on him from each side and pick off the daring rider.

"Before these good intentions could be carried out La Grandeur nimbly quit the running horse and landed safely on both feet. The ride was over."

For almost a minute, there was nothing but stunned silence in the arena. Then, suddenly, the crowd went wild. They cheered and shouted in a non-stop tribute to Emery La Grandeur.

La Grandeur struggled through the crowd of contestants trying to congratulate him and made his way to his wife's side.

"You made a fine ride, Emery," she said with a quiet smile.

La Grandeur fumbled in his shirt pocket and pulled out the cheque for the $1,000 prize money and his gold medal.

He handed the cheque to his wife. "Violet, here's the money, it's yours, get what you want with it."

Then he pinned the championship medal on his shirt and commented softly: "It's a purty medal, ain't it?" Violet only nodded.

On the arena floor, one of the top riders in North America, Clay McGonagil of Texas, looked up at the still-cheering crowd.

"All these folks here," he said to a champion, "may live till they're old and greyheaded but they'll never see a bronc ride like that again . . ."

With so many greats, it is easy to understand why today only a few people still remember a little cowboy from Pincher Creek. But it is a little sad, too.

* * * *

THE $100,000 DREAM . . .

Around Stampede time in Calgary every year you can find a few sentimentally superstitious cowboys who'll claim they've seen a grey ghost prowling the grounds by dark of night.

It's not a frightening ghost, they'll assure you. Far from it. It's just Guy Weadick back to make sure his dream is still doing well.

The dream of the Calgary Stampede was born in 1908 when the young Wyoming cowboy pulled into Calgary as a performer with the 101 Ranch Show.

Guy Weadick took one look at the bustling frontier city and decided it would be the perfect place to stage the western show to end all western shows — the greatest rodeo and fair in the world.

Weadick managed to infect one of his fellow-performers — a young cowboy named Tom Mix — with the dream, but everyone else around seemed totally immune to Stampede fever.

Everywhere he turned, Weadick found his dream of a show offering unheard-of prize money, a publicity campaign stretching to Mexico, and brand-new facilities, rejected out of hand.

When he approached E. L. (Ernie) Richardson of the Calgary Exhibition, Richardson turned the mad young cowhand down with a flat "No thanks".

Harry McMullen, a former cowman who had taken over the job of general livestock agent for the CPR, was sympathetic to the idea, but he argued that Weadick was "premature" with his dream. Calgary just wasn't ready for the greatest outdoor show in the world.

Discouraged, Weadick left town. A few months later, his prospective partner Tom Mix abandoned the scheme and headed to Hollywood to become the greatest cowboy hero of silent films.

Weadick and his young wife turned to the vaudeville and rodeo circuits with a popular show of tricks and talk — "Wild West Stunts" or "Roping and Gab" or "Weadick and la Due" (Mrs. Weadick's stage name was Flores la Due) depending on where they were playing.

It was three years after his trip to Calgary, in 1911, and

the Weadicks were playing the music halls in England when Guy received a letter from an almost-forgotten Harry McMullen.

The railroad agent's letter was a strong appeal to Weadick to bring his idea back to Calgary again. There was a land boom on and the city was bursting with money and enthusiasm for new ideas.

It was all the encouragement Weadick needed. In early 1912, he was back in Calgary again. On the way, he had stopped in Medicine Hat for a long talk with rancher Ad Day — who assured Weadick he had enough stock "to supply a hundred rodeos" and who hinted that Weadick should try to sell his idea to the "big four" of Alberta ranching: Pat Burns, A. E. Cross, George Lane and A. J. McLean.

Harry McMullen, who Guy looked up as soon as he'd checked into Calgary's Alberta Hotel, shared Day's view that the Big Four were the logical backers of the show.

Weadick decided, however, to have one more try with the managers of the Calgary Exhibition. Again, however, he was turned down flat.

That interview over, Weadick was walking through the lobby of the Alberta when a man stepped forward to intercept him — Alec Fleming, foreman of George Lane's Bar-U Ranch. The message was simple and exciting. George Lane wanted to talk to him about this wild idea he had for the greatest outdoor show on earth.

When Weadick appeared for the interview, he found himself facing not just George Lane, but Pat Burns and A. E. Cross as well.

Weadick's enthusiasm was catchy. Before he knew what had happened the three cattle kings were at the point where they were asking simply how much it was going to cost. Guy, probably with an eye to dividing things by three, suggested $60,000. In a matter of minutes he was on his way to the bank with the trio, and listened amazed as they set up a credit of $100,000 for him. Archie McLean, the fourth of the Big Four, had simply been written in as a backer without his knowledge — a fact he accepted coolly when he heard about it.

What the Big Four realized, perhaps better than Weadick himself, was that they'd found the right man with the right idea at the right time.

Their judgment was sound. As it turned out Weadick did so well on advance ticket sales that he apparently never had to touch a cent of the $100,000 credit.

The name Weadick picked for the show was "Stampede"; chosen because it had never been used before, and because of its descriptive and publicity powers.

Weadick's only instruction from his backers was to make the show "the greatest thing of its kind in the world," and he set out to follow it.

The Stampede was scheduled for the week of Sept. 2. At Weadick's instructions, Victoria Park was invaded by carpenters who constructed thousands of bleacher seats. Weadick, meanwhile, was busy recruiting riders and ropers from all over North America and building a publicity campaign to drag in visitors from thousands of miles away.

As Stampede time drew near, excitement in Calgary built to fever pitch. The city fathers suddenly realized that even if all the 40,000 people to fill the new seats in Victoria Park didn't show up, there were still going to be more visitors in town than could be handled.

With the show still more than two weeks away, The Calgary Herald reported:

"Mayor (John W.) Mitchell has sent all over the Do-minion asking about tents in which to accommodate the

Stampede crowd next month. He is now receiving wires and letters and expects to secure all he wants.

"It is proposed to make the tent city across the Elbow on the property which the Great Northern bought from Dr. Lindsay. It will be fitted up specially and those who secure accommodation there will be just as comfortable as they would be in hotels."

At the same time, The Herald noted an undesirable, if inevitable, result of the Weadick publicity campaign:

"Warnings from an under-ground source which convey to the police inside information have been sounded. Reports from 2,000 miles away have reached Chief Cuddy regarding the advent of dangerous crooks who are coming for the Stampede. From all over Canada and the northern States talented pick-pockets and confidence men are planning a sortie.

"The chief has been warned in time. When the Stampede opens half a dozen of the most astute sleuths in the employ of the Pinkerton Detective Bureau will be in Calgary to assist the local detectives in rounding up the bad men."

Not all press reports were so ominous. A few days later Harry McMullen, who Weadick had recruited to help manage the Stampede, was quoted in The Herald as saying: "The pageant on opening day will be the biggest that was ever seen in Canada.

"There are now in the city waiting for the competitions, cowboys and cowgirls from Texas, Colorado, Utah, Montana, Idaho, New Mexico, Washington and Oregon."

Then, on Aug. 31, The Herald reported that: "One special train to the Calgary Stampede left Spokane today and a second will follow Sept. 2. The first started from Cheyenne and the second will be made up at Pendleton.

"By Monday the heart of Calgary will be a blaze of brilliant colors, and when His Royal Highness, the Duke of Connaught, arrives the city will be in the vortex of the greatest celebration that has ever taken place in the West."

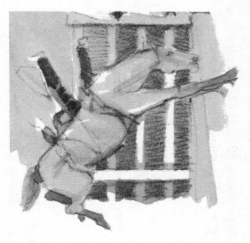

To open the Stampede, Weadick had hit upon the idea of a massive parade. And when that parade moved onto the streets of Calgary Sept. 2, Weadick had immediate confirmation of the soundness of his dream.

In Calgary, a city with a population of 61,450, an estimated 75,000 people were packed along the parade route.

Mindful of his directive to create "the greatest thing of its kind in the world," Weadick had spent months of careful negotiation with every Indian tribe in Alberta. Those negotiations paid off in the parade as more than 2,000 painted and feathered Indians rode the streets of the city.

Moved almost to literary frenzy, a Herald reporter wrote of *"the wonder of the spectacle of 2,000 western Indians, smeared with paint and decked in the attire of ante-civilized years, who passed through the streets of Calgary yesterday morning.*

"*Authentic and seasoned opinions would have it that, never in all the world, since the red men became dominated instead of a dominant influence, has there been such a gathering of the picturesque aborigines who, a few short years ago, roamed these western foothills, unmolested by the white man.*

"*Verily, it was a spectacle that money could not present. Mayhap, never again will those who watched yesterday's procession have a similar opportunity afforded them.*"

When the parade was over, a crowd of more than 50,000 crushed into Victoria Park. Once he'd got them that far, Weadick could relax a little and leave the rest to the talent in the show. And what talent it was!

The first of the two special trains from the United States had brought in George Drumheller of the big Drumheller Ranch in Washington and 15 of his best riders — including 1910 world champion Bert Kelly.

Already on hand were virtually every top rider on the continent. There was Joe Gardner of Texas, Ed Echols of Arizona, George Weir from New Mexico, Tex Macleod from San Antonio, Harry Webb from Wyoming, Art Acord of Portland, Otto Kline of Montana, Charlie Tipton from Denver, 'Doc' Pardee and O.K. Lawrence from Oklahoma. There was also a large Mexican contingent headed by Senor Estevan Clemento.

Among the female competitors was the good Mrs. Weadick — registered under her professional name of Florence la Due — who was destined to win the trick and fancy roping crown.

In all, there were 150 competitors.

Ad Day, true to the promise he'd made to Guy Weadick in Medicine Hat months earlier, was on hand and determined to make the competitors work for their prize money. Ready to go into the chutes was the biggest herd of outlaws — from wild and rangey Texas long-horns to top bucking broncs — ever assembled in Canda. And to try the stuff of champions, Day had waiting the greatest bucking horse in the world; that jet-black terror called "Cyclone."

If Guy Weadick thought he had it made at the end of that first day, he learned differently the next morning when he woke up to meet the demon that has plagued so many Stampedes — bad weather.

Rain was falling in sheets, and so was attendance, as riders struggled in an infield that was a sea of mud. Wednesday, the third day of Stampede, was no better. Nor was Thursday when the Royal party arrived.

Also adding to Weadick's worries was the fact that Calgary's hotel and dining facilities just weren't up to the crowd.

Like many others, Weadick had seen the article in Tuesday's Herald noting: "It is estimated that up to 20,000 visitors are already in Calgary. Yesterday was the busiest day that restaurants and hotels have ever had.

"From 6 until 9 o'clock last night it was impossible to get into a restaurant and at 9 o'clock many of the waiting hundreds were saddened when the proprietors opened their doors and announced that every digestible had been consumed."

Nevertheless, the show went on.

Thursday, when the Duke of Connaught and Princess Patricia arrived, the Royal party had hardly settled in its box before the rain poured down again.

Weadick quickly decided to move the show into the Victoria Park arena, and soon thousands of people were inside, scrambling for seats.

Watching the show, the Duke was so delighted he decided to make an unscheduled return to the grounds the next day.

The decision seemed to mark a turning point for the show. By Friday morning, the rain had stopped and the crowd was swelling again.

By the time the Stampede ended, Weadick could justifiably claim it had been a success.

Thanks to bad weather and inadequate facilities, however, it wasn't an unqualified success.

In 1913, even though the show had made money, Calgary was unreceptive and Weadick had to take his Stampede to Winnipeg.

Then the war years came and put an end to any such shows in Canada. Weadick made one try to stage the Stampede in the United States in 1916, but it was a financial flop.

It wasn't until 1919, again with the backing of the Big Four, that Weadick and the Stampede returned to Calgary. That year the weather co-operated and the so-called "Victory" Stampede was an enormous success. Finally, in 1923, the Calgary Exhibition had a long-awaited change of heart about Weadick's show, and the amalgamation that followed made the Stampede a permanent part of the Calgary scene.

Weadick was the Stampede's master-mind until he retired as arena director in 1932.

In 1952, he was on hand to present the prizes to the victors in the 40th Calgary Stampede.

Then, the following year, Guy Weadick's career came to an end as a riderless horse, boots reversed in stirrups, led his body to a cemetery.

At least, it seemed to end. It remains a little hard to

account for the grey ghost that wanders the Stampede grounds, smiling contentedly at a dream that came true . . .

* * * * *

TAMING THE CYCLONE . . .

The first Calgary Stampede in 1912 was seven days of thrills and spills — with most of the thrills and spills being provided by a snorting, spinning, wild-eyed bundle of black dynamite called "Cyclone".

Cyclone had come to the Stampede as the best bucking horse in the world, and as the show moved into its final day, his record was intact. A total of 129 men had tried to mount him and stay on him, and 129 men had ended up in the dust.

The only man in the world anyone rated as having a chance to beat Cyclone was a young Indian cowboy from Macleod, Tom Three Persons.

But as that closing Saturday dawned, Tom Three Persons wasn't available to take on the horse. Tom, lamenting his fate, was under lock and key in the Calgary jail, and staring vainly through the bars at the distant Stampede grounds.

In Victoria Park, the finals in the bucking horse contest were about to begin, and Cyclone's record of 129 to 0 was about to permit him to withdraw from the competition the undisputed champion.

But an Indian agent named Glen Campbell wouldn't hear of it. Red-faced with anger, he kept insisting that Tom Three Persons should be given a chance at the beast.

Somehow, word got to the Mounties, and they evidently agreed that a little thing like a jail sentence shouldn't keep an Alberta cowboy from showing a crowd how to ride.

With the finals already underway, a cash bond was posted and Tom Three Persons was rushed to the grounds.

A surprised crowd cheered when the announcer gave the word that Tom Three Persons of Macleod was about to ride in the finals. But the cheers gave way to apprehensive groans when the announcer added that Tom would be climbing on the back of Cyclone. Even the other competitors looked sympathetic.

Indeed, the only person who didn't seem worried about it all was Tom himself. As The Calgary Herald recorded the scene:

"The horse thrown to the ground, Tom jumped across him, placed his feet in the stirrups, and with a wild 'whoop' the black demon was up and away with the Indian rider.

"Bucking, twisting, swapping ends and resorting to every artifice of the outlaw, Cyclone swept across the field. The Indian was jarred from one side of the saddle to the other, but as the crowd cheered themselves hoarse he settled every time into the saddle and waited for the next lurch or twist.

"His bucking unable to dislodge the redskin, Cyclone stood at rest and reared straight up. Once it looked as though Tom was to follow the fate of his predecessors. He recovered rapidly and from that time forward Cyclone bucked till he was tired. The Indian had mastered him.

"The thousands created a pandemonium of applause that was not equalled all week. The Princess Patricia and the Duke (of Connaught), who were in the Royal box, leaned far out over the railing, laughing and applauding at the Indians in the enclosure to the north.

"It was a thrilling moment and in it Tom Three Persons had captured the championship of the world for himself and for Canada."

Even though Tom had to return to jail for a while, he emerged as the pride of Alberta's Indians — the only Indian to win the bronc riding championship of the world. Even today, more than half a century later, his picture hangs in the Blood reserve community hall at Standoff; a permanent tribute to a man who walked out of a jail cell to tame a Cyclone.

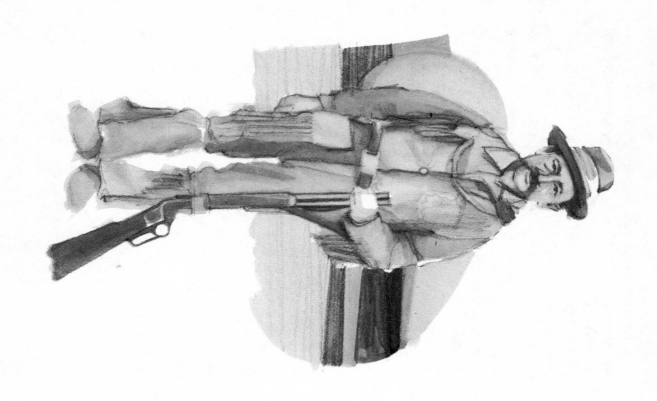

LAW MAKERS & BREAKERS

OF LAW AND JUSTICE . . . .

The temptation to think of Alberta as part of the "wild west" is strong. Indeed, over the years, many story-tellers and — yes — even responsible journalists have given into the temptation.

It's a puzzling business, because the ingredients for these "wild west" stories are just plain missing.

"Oh, it's true enough that Alberta had its share of murderers and rustlers and rum-runners and con men. But it never had them in the legend-inspiring quantity we've been led to believe.

The simple, unromantic truth is that all the gunslingers and organized gangs belong to another part of the west — the part just across that thin line of cairns and steel posts that marks the boundary between Canada and the United States.

Even the young man named Harry Longbaugh spent his time in Alberta busting broncs, and made it a point to go back to Montana before he started work on building his reputation as the Sundance Kid.

This doesn't mean that the story of law-enforcement in Alberta isn't an exciting one. It is exciting — in many ways more exciting than the story south of the border — because, thanks to a laconic half-breed and a pitifully small number of red-coated men, the word "law" in Alberta has always meant the same as the word "justice."

The mating of those two words is one of the proudest events of Alberta's heritage.

* * * *

WHISKEY & WOLFERS . . .

The laws of the Young Dominion of Canada always did apply to the territory that was to become Alberta. The only problem was that there was no one around to enforce those laws, so a lot of people just calmly broke them.

Right into the 1860's, the years of Confederation, the territory was open prey to any brute or opportunist who felt like moving in.

The business of flaunting the law reached its peak in the late 1860's when American traders poured into southern Alberta to use rot-gut whiskey to part Indians from fur and buffalo hides. And when cold-blooded "wolfers" all but took over the plains in search of bounty; poisoning wolves and Indians with equal unconcern.

It was one of these unnamed wolfers who committed the most horrible crime in Alberta history. Enraged by the death of a partner in a fight with some Indians, he went south into the United States, to a town hit by a smallpox epidemic, and brought back hundreds of infected blankets wrapped in oilcloth bundles.

Carefully, he scattered the bundles across the plains of southern Alberta. As he anticipated, the Indians found the bundles, broke them open, and took the blankets back to their camps.

In exchange for his partner, the wolfer collected the lives of thousands of innocent Indians — and went unpunished.

But when another group of wolfers rode into the Cypress Hills and coldly slaughtered a band of helpless Indians a few years later, they enraged a nation, forced the birth of the North West Mounted Police, and rid the southern plains of wolfers and whiskey-traders forever.

* * * *

THE BOW-LEGGED SCOUT . . .

In the fall of 1874, the first small, exhausted force of mounted police was limping into Alberta.

No one could have cared less about that force — or about southern Alberta for that matter — than Jerry Potts.

Jerry Potts, sitting in Fort Benton, Montana, had already had his fill of whiskey traders and wolfers. For the past five years, he had worked as a hunter, providing food for virtually every one of the infamous whiskey forts north of the line.

Fed up with the excesses of the traders and sick of the depredations visited upon the Indians, he had gone south and taken a job for the respectable I. G. Baker and Company.

But, unknown to Potts, two tattered mounties were already riding south to Benton to find him and coax him into a place in Alberta history.

There probably wasn't a man in the west better-qualified for western glory than Jerry Potts.

Potts was born in 1840, the son of a Scot father and a Blood Indian mother. The year Jerry was born, his father was killed by an Indian who had mistaken him for someone else.

Fatherless, Potts was raised for the early part of his life by Alexander Harvey, one of the most notorious and vicious traders on the upper Missouri. By the time he was five, young Jerry knew intimately the pattern of villainy and cunning he would encounter later. This knowledge would, on many occasions, save his life.

When Harvey fled the Missouri to escape assassination by some of his fellow-traders, Jerry was adopted by Andrew Dawson, a gentle Scot, who taught him to speak English, to be a clever fur-trader and — most importantly — to be a just and honorable man.

The mixture of the legacies left him by his two foster-fathers and by his mother would set him apart for the rest of his life.

By the time he was in his late teens, Jerry had taken on the mannerisms of the frontier. Drifting back and forth between the white world and the lodges of his mother's tribe, he developed a passion for whiskey, a way of dressing that was white from the waist up and Indian from there down, and a code of justice as fairly divided between white and Indian as his clothes.

Jerry Potts killed his first man when he was 23, forced to shoot in self-defence during a quarrel with a drunken trader named Antoine Primeau. It was his first, and only, battle with a white.

Potts' warrior skills, when combined with his passion for drinking, sometimes led him into strange escapades.

One old-timer recalls how Potts and a half-breed friend named George Star used to get thoroughly drunk then stand 25 feet apart and try to trim one another's moustache with bullets from their six-shooters. Somehow, although they performed the trick dozens of times, both survived.

So it was Jerry Potts, now 34 and the veteran of Indian wars and whiskey posts, whom the mounties looked up as soon as they got to Fort Benton.

The situation the two red-coated officers outlined to the reluctant Potts was desperate.

The force of 150 men was stranded in southern Alberta. Their guides were unreliable, food was running out, their horses were dead or dying, and winter was only a few weeks away.

Potts listened and pondered. Then, with a grunt he accepted the position of police scout to the North West Mounted Police at a wage of $90 a month.

For that salary, he undertook to guide, interpret, advise — and generally nurse the new force to maturity.

Although he didn't realize it at the time, he had also undertaken a job he would keep to the end of his life.

The two grateful mounties led Potts north that same day to begin his new job. To see how he tackled it, we turn to, Jerry Potts, Plainsman, an excellent booklet by Hugh Dempsey of the Glenbow Foundation.

"His first assignment," Mr. Dempsey records, "was to lead the Mounted Police to Fort Whoop-Up to attack the American whiskey traders. Potts tried to explain that the traders had fled to Montana but, not trusting their new guide, the police forced their crippled horses and tired men on towards the fort. Under the able guidance of the little mixed blood, they travelled across the short grass country from Milk River Ridge, passing buffalo bones bleached in the sun and huge herds of the shaggy beasts grazing like domestic cattle.

"'He won the confidence of all ranks the first day out.' recalled Sam Steele (one of the party of police), 'and when morning came he rode boldly in front of the advance guard. It was noon when the party reached Milk River and found him there sitting near a fat buffalo cow which he had killed and dressed for the use of the force. To those new to such life he appeared to know everything.'

'It was during this trek that the Mounted Police noticed their guide did not waste words. When they found the riddled body of a dead Assiniboine Jerry was asked to explain the probable reason of the killing. 'Drunk,' he muttered.

'After burying the body, the police continued the journey over the monotonous terrain. Finally, one officer of the force, hoping that Whoop-Up was only a short distance away, rode up to Potts and asked: 'What do you think we'll find on the other side of this hill, Jerry?'

'Nudder hill,' replied the laconic guide.

'When they reached Fort Whoop-Up, the Mounted Police found they did not need their two nine-pounder field guns and two mortars. With the exception of an old trader the fort was deserted.

'It was then early October and Col. Macleod, seeing the need for immediate quarters, urged Potts to lead them to a suitable site for a fort. Guiding the tired caravan of redcoats, winded horses, Red River carts and wagons across the rolling prairies, the scout followed an Indian trail westward until they arrived at a large island on the Oldman River. Here was a site that offered natural water protection, abundant cottonwoods for construction, and was on a well-travelled route.

'While Fort Macleod was being built, Potts travelled among the Blackfoot of the area, explaining the presence of the red-coated strangers and gaining promises of nonviolence. Late in October, he reported that whiskey was being sold at Pine Coulee and guided the police to the illicit post where the five men were apprehended. This was the first successful raid by the force since arriving in Blackfoot country."

Mr. Dempsey records a trip early in 1875 in which Potts displayed his remarkable sense of direction.

"The trip occurred in March when Col. Macleod, three policemen, and Potts started for Helena, Montana, three hundred miles away.

"When well out on the plains a wild blizzard struck, forcing the men to camp beside a cutbank for two days. When the food and fuel supplies were exhausted, Potts suggested travelling thirty miles south to Rocky Springs where proper shelter was available. Onto the plains of swirling snow the men followed their guide and, within an hour, everyone but Potts had lost his sense of direction. There were no landmarks and weakened men and horses stumbled in exhaustion.

"Finally, after several hours Potts dismounted and led the men into a narrow protected valley. It was Rocky Springs. Later, when everyone was settled before a roaring fire, the police were dismayed to learn that Potts had been almost completely snow blind during the final part of the journey."

In those first six months, Jerry Potts had made himself a legendary figure to the force. It was a legend that would continue to grow and expand for the next 25 years — and that would let Jerry Potts get away with behavior that no one else among the strictly-disciplined mounties would even dream of.

On one occasion, a group of starving Indians appeared at Fort Macleod and their chief treated the police to a long and urgent speech — of which Col. Macleod couldn't understand a word. Potts was called upon to translate, and the long speech was boiled down to three short words: "He wants grub!"

Another time, several Blackfoot chiefs appeared before the colonel and made a round of speeches. Potts, looking magnificently bored, followed his usual habit as an interpreter: he didn't say a word.

Macleod caught one or two words he thought he recognized. "Napi-okee" or whiskey. "Napi-kwan" for white man. He surmised that the chiefs were expressing their gratitude to the mounties for riding the plains of the whiskey traders.

He turned to Potts for his translation and the little guide just shrugged his shoulders.

"Dey damn glad you're here," he assured his colonel.

Even more troublesome to the mounties than his failings as an interpreter was Potts' appetite for whiskey. He would drink anything — from first-class alcohol to rot-gut trade whiskey with equal enthusiasm.

Sometimes Potts had to be tied up until he slept off a violent drunk. Once he almost shot a mountie when he mistook him for an old enemy.

One policeman recalled that the scout had "an unquenchable thirst which a camel might have envied."

Hugh Dempsey records one occasion when Jerry Potts' drinking habits sorely tried the loyalty of his mountie employers. Word had been received that a suspicious wagon had crossed the border from Montana.

"The scout and two constables were sent to investigate the nocturnal traveller and intercepted the wagon after a day's ride. The owners had goods and whiskey in their load so they were arrested and handcuffed together in the back of the wagon.

"One constable took the reins, the other took charge of

the saddle horses, and Potts was placed in the back to guard the prisoners.

"Upon arriving at Fort Macleod a constable discovered that Potts had broken into the whiskey supply and the three men had drunk themselves into an unconscious stupor. The liquor was consumed and the evidence was gone."

Despite incidents like this, Potts never lost the respect of the mounties. Drinking, after all, was a common fault among the men who braved the rough frontier of the west and, in the case of Jerry Potts, the fault was more than offset by his honesty, courage and devotion to the force.

Right to the end of his life, Jerry Potts went on doing the job he undertook that October afternoon in Fort Benton — and doing it well.

Time and again, in his later years, the officers of the Mounted Police would pay tribute to his skill, his faithfulness to the force, and to the diplomatic talent that bonded Indian and mountie in friendship.

When, on July 14, 1896, Jerry Potts died, the Fort Macleod Gazette summed up the feelings of all who knew him:

"Jerry Potts is dead. Through the whole North West, in many parts of eastern Canada, and in England itself, this announcement will excite sorrow, in many cases sympathy, and in all, interest.

"His memory will long be green in the hearts of those who knew him best, and 'faithful and true' is the character he leaves behind him — the best monument of a valuable life."

* * * *

"COMPETENT HORSEMEN OF SOUND CONSTITUTION" . . .

On a warm May 23rd in 1873, word finally reached Ottawa of the infamous Cypress Hills massacre. The reports were wildly exaggerated, but they were all that was needed to sweep Parliament into a frenzy of legislative action.

Before the day was over, His Excellency the Earl of Dufferin, Governor-General of Canada, had given Royal Assent to the bill that brought the North West Mounted Police into existence.

The new force specified by Parliament was to be a semi-military body, the immediate objectives of it being: to stop the liquor traffic among the Indians, to gain the Indians' respect and confidence, to break the Indians of their old practices by tact and patience, to collect customs dues, and to perform all duties such as a police force might be expected to carry out.

As for members of the force, only competent horsemen of sound constitution, good character, and between the ages of 18 and 40, were to be enlisted. All had to be able to read and write either French or English. The command was to be divided into troops. The commanding officer was to hold the title of "Commissioner". Service was to be for at least three years.

Parliament set the size of the force at 300 men. But it was decided, for the time being, to form only three troops of 50 men each.

These men, at the advice of those with experience in the west, were to be clad in red tunics. Blue, the color first considered, would be associated by the Indians with the uniforms of the United States cavalry — a force the Indians hated with a passion that would appear later at a place called Little Big Horn.

By fall, the 150 green recruits had expanded to a force of 300. A year later, exhausted, starving, and with their red uniforms in faded tatters, they finally rode onto the plains of southern Alberta.

In all, 274 men — including guides and drovers — had reached their destination, and began the staggering task of policing 300,000 miles of virgin territory, peopled with a handful of whites and more than 30,000 potentially-savage Indians.

In truth, the commanders of the new force had never really wanted to pit their green troops in open battle against the cunning and dangerous plainsmen of the whiskey forts and wolfer parties.

So, through missionaries and friendly Indians — and through co-operative members of the International Boundary Commission then marking the 49th parallel — the traders and wolfers were barraged with fearsome rumors.

Although the Americans scoffed in public, in private they became increasingly disturbed by the conviction that what was on the way was a hardened army, bristling with cannon and gatling gun.

As the force drew nearer and nearer, the invaders, one by one, then by the dozen, and finally en mass, fled back across the Montana border.

The mounties had won their first battle without firing a shot. When they rode up to the gates of Fort Whoop-Up (which the whiskey men had turned into a fortress they'd sworn to defend to the death), the gates were opened to them by a friendly Dave Akers, the only occupant of the Fort.

The way in which the problem of the wolfers and whiskey men was "solved" was probably the most important single factor in the success of the NWMP in Alberta.

The Indians were awe-struck. None — not even the

proud Blackfoot — wanted to do battle with these mighty men in red who had rid the west of the invaders without firing a shot.

Gradually, as the mounties began to work among them, the Indian feeling of awe was replaced with respect for the fairness with which the redcoats dispensed justice and help to Indian and white alike.

Time and again, in the years to come, that respect would save the west.

* * * *

SITTING BULL & THE STUBBORN MAJOR . . .

Within months of arriving on the plains, the mounties had the business of law and order in Alberta effectively under control.

Everywhere, from one end of the territory to the other, Indian and settler could see the red-coated rider — usually alone — who meant that the peace was being kept.

It was one of these redcoats, face wind-burned and pill-box hat askew, who directed the main body of Mormon settlers to their destination of Cardston.

And it was another, a canny, stubborn major named J. M. Walsh, who calmly controlled the frontier's biggest crisis.

Two years after the NWMP entered Alberta it was still only 250 strong. But it had spread its slim resources carefully and — in the case of the 75-man detachment at Fort Walsh in the Cypress Hills — luckily.

On Sunday, June 25, 1876, at a spot on the Wyoming-Montana border called Little Big Horn, 2,000 Sioux under Chief Sitting Bull wiped out a force of 250 cavalrymen.

Within weeks, with the U.S. army snapping at their heels, the entire Sioux nation — nearly 6,000-strong — was fleeing north across the Canadian border and into the waiting arms of James Morrow Walsh of the North West Mounted Police.

In two years in the west, respect for the fairness of the NWMP had spread to Indians on both sides of the border. Sitting Bull was counting on this fairness, and on the strength of the force he had at his back, for protection from the pursuing American forces.

As soon as Sitting Bull's tribes had made camp around Fort Walsh, the old chief discovered he would get fairness all right — but on James Morrow Walsh's terms, not his.

Walsh, on that particular day, saw his tiny garrison surrounded by thousands of Sioux still flushed and cocky with their bloody triumph over the cavalry, and knew that it was up to him to quiet them down in a hurry.

Never a cautious man, Walsh slapped his braided cap on his head, grabbed a sergeant, three constables and two scouts, and galloped off to find Sitting Bull.

Right in the middle of the Sioux camp, with his tiny escort doing their best not to look nervous, Walsh stuck his jaw out and informed Sitting Bull point blank that he would have to behave himself in Canada and would only be tolerated here as long as he remained peaceful.

It was a remarkable bit of bluster for a man who couldn't have mustered many more than 200 troops in all Alberta, but it worked.

Sitting Bull quietly agreed to all the conditions the red-coat imposed.

So impressed was the chief by Walsh's courage in this first meeting that only once in the four years the Sioux remained in Canada did Sitting Bull try Walsh's patience.

The Sioux were hungry and restless, their warriors spoiling for a fight, and Sitting Bull and a force of his braves rode into Fort Walsh. Sitting Bull was shouting unreasonable and threatening demands when Walsh stormed out of his quarters and across the parade ground.

Jabbing his finger at the astonished chief, Walsh grimly reminded him that he was not a Canadian Indian and Canada owed him nothing but hospitality — and only as much of that as the Sioux were prepared to earn.

And furthermore, he continued, if Sitting Bull and his braves did not behave and stop stealing horses he, Walsh, would arrest them and personally place Sitting Bull himself in irons.

It was a much subdued Sitting Bull who led his warriors back to camp again.

Walsh, fortunately for the west, was much more than a courageous man. He was a skilled diplomat, and it was he, finally, who negotiated the agreement that returned Sitting Bull and his people to the United States.

Walsh was unknown before those four years, and dropped out of historical sight soon after they were over. But those years were long enough to earn him his place as one of the greatest heroes of the plains.

* * * *

CROWFOOT, KEEPER OF THE PEACE . . .

"It was at this time that Crowfoot, head chief of the Blackfoot, paid us a visit. He was full of questions regarding the future. I took time to explain to him the history of Canada's dealing with its Indian peoples thus far and assured him that I expected in due time treaties would be made and a settled condition created in this country wherein justice would be given to all concerned.

"The chief expressed himself as delighted with what I had told him and said that he was much pleased with the change that the coming of the Mounted Police had brought in all the west. He also told me that he would depend upon

me to inform him of anything in the future that would be of interest to him and his people.

"When Crowfoot left me that August day of 1875 I felt encouraged and was thankful . . ." (from the journal of Rev. John McDougall).

All the efforts of the North West Mounted Police, and all the skill of the missionaries and of Jerry Potts, would have come to nothing had it not been for a great man named Crowfoot.

Time and time again, this man who was undisputed leader of the fiercest Indian tribe in the west, and spokesman for the strongest alliance in the Indian nation, single-handedly kept peace in the west.

In 1876, only a year after the conversation recorded in John McDougall's diary, the Blackfoot leader's loyalty to the new order was put to the test.

To Crowfoot's camp in southern Alberta came emissaries of the Sioux, begging the Blackfoot to join them in a daring undertaking.

In the south, the mighty Sioux nation was gathering under Sitting Bull, preparing for final battle with the white man. If the Blackfoot would join the war, it could easily be won.

Join us, the emissaries said, share in the booty, then we will all sweep northward, wipe out the redcoats and settlers, and be rid of the white man forever.

Many of the lesser Blackfoot chiefs were excited and eager to join the Sioux. But Crowfoot stood firm. He spurned the offer, and when it was made again and again, he spurned it again and again; firmly avowing allegiance to the "Great White Mother".

Finally, angry, the Sioux threatened to invade the Blackfoot country. Crowfoot remained adamant, and the Sioux gave up and went home.

In time, Col. Macleod of the NWMP heard of the incident. The relief he felt at Crowfoot's stand was overwhelming. Better than most, he realized how great the power of a Sioux-Blackfoot alliance would have been, and how deadly to the whites.

Macleod sent a message to the chief, promising that if the Sioux attacked the Blackfoot, the Mounted Police would come to Crowfoot's aid.

Then Macleod sent another message, this one to the east, and in time Crowfoot received a letter of gratitude from the "Great White Mother", Her Majesty Queen Victoria.

Again and again, in the months and years that followed, Crowfoot came to the forefront in efforts to keep peace between Indian and white. He even led efforts to negotiate peace with the Blackfoot's traditional and hated enemy, the Cree.

In 1885, Crowfoot's strength and loyalty received its greatest test.

The Metis, under Louis Riel, had taken up arms and rebelled against the new dominion. The Cree had joined them, and strong pressure was on all the Indians of the west — many of them embittered by broken white promises — to join in the rebellion.

All through Alberta, as the rebellion grew in strength and ferocity, Indian agents, missionaries and red-coated mounties struggled to hold the plains Indians in check.

It was a tense situation. There was no question of how Crowfoot himself felt, but the great chief was now aging, and the young sometimes will not heed the words of the old.

Then, in Parliament on April 12, during debate on

the rebellion, the prime minister Sir John A. Macdonald rose to speak.

"I have received a telegram signed by Crowfoot, which I will read.

It is not in Blackfoot:

"From Blackfoot Crossing, via Gleichen, N.W.T., 11th April, 1885:

"On behalf of myself and people I wish to send through you to the Great Mother the words I have given to the Governor at a Council here, at which all my minor chiefs and young men were present. We are agreed and determined to remain loyal to the Queen. Our young men will go to work on the reserves and will raise all the crops they can, and we hope the Government will help us to sell what we cannot use . . .

"Should any Indians come to our reserve and ask us to join them in war we will send them away . . .

"The words I sent by Father Lacombe I again send: We will be loyal to the Queen whatever happens. I have a copy of this, and when the trouble is over will have it with pride to show to the Queen's officers: and we leave our future in your hands . . .

"Crowfoot."

Once more the prairie leader had succeeded, and once more he had prevented an alliance that would have taken a bloody toll of Alberta's white people.

Crowfoot, chief of all the Blackfoot and keeper of the peace. A man who made one promise — "We will be loyal to the Queen whatever happens" — and never broke it.

* * * *

EMPEROR PICK, THE BOTTLE KING . . .

By 1916, despite the sorrow of the war in Europe, Albertans had every reason to be pleased with the quality of law and order in their province.

The mounties had done their job well. No one worried any more about Indian problems or unrestrained violence or wolfers from the Montana side of the border.

And in town after growing town, municipal police forces were building a system of law enforcement that would preserve the redcoat traditions of justice.

But then, on July 1, 1916, all that changed. Prohibition came to Alberta and, within months, Alberta would be caught up in nightmare — sometimes tragic and sometimes comic — that would shatter the peace for six long years.

It was a strange world, filled with reckless men racing big black cars across the prairie nights, with rural milkmen whose big cans gurgled with something that was decidedly not milk, with box cars filled with "pickled pork" — hog carcasses stuffed to the snout with bottles of bootleg booze.

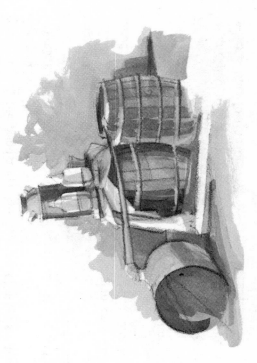

It was a world where even the janitor of a respectable Baptist church in Calgary thought nothing of converting the building's basement to a distillery.

Everything seems to have gone just a little crazy. When, a matter of months after that July 1, the mounties withdrew their protection from rural Alberta and the short-lived Alberta Provincial Police force took over, people just shook their heads philosophically.

Even when the battles between bootlegger and police began to cost lives, Alberta people could not shake the feeling that it was all not quite real, that it was just a weird game soon to be called on account of foolishness.

"I've been drinking beer since I was old enough to jump over a miner's lamp," a boozer named Joe Perotte had announced on the eve of prohibition, "and I'm damned if I'm gonna stop now." There was many an Albertan who felt the same way.

For the police, it was the worst of all possible situations. No matter how talented they were, or how devoted, there was just no way to enforce impossible laws — particularly when most of the population was bent on obstructing the enforcement of those laws.

Which brings us to Emperor Pick, a man whose story sums up all the unreality and tragedy of those unreal and tragic years.

Every age in history seems to create a man especially suited to it — and Emilio Picariello was the ideal man for the age of prohibition.

Born in Sicily in 1875, the big, smiling Italian came to Canada at the turn of the century. After working in the east for a few years — and getting married — he came west, settling first in Fernie, B.C. and finally in Blairmore as owner of the Alberta Hotel.

Prohibition seemed to Picariello to be the chance of a lifetime. In Fernie, in addition to building up a legitimate business in macaroni and ice cream, he had become the local distributor for a wine company. He had also begun the strange occupation of collecting bottles.

Hiding behind his smile, Mr. Pick had quietly cornered the market in bottles. On Sept. 22, 1916, he advertised the astonishing fact he had 27,000 bottles for sale: quarts 40 cents and pints 22 cents a dozen.

Before long every paper in the Crows Nest Pass was carrying another Pick advertisement that read: "E. Pick, the Bottle King, requests that all persons selling bottles hold them until they see E. Pick, who pays top prices."

Within weeks, most breweries were relying on Pick's efficient bottle-gathering system rather than trying to collect their own or buy new ones.

Looking over the prohibition scene, Pick made the purchase of the Alberta Hotel in Blairmore. Then he negotiated a deal that made him sole agent of Lethbridge Brewery products in the Crows Nest and began advertising "temperance" beer — a product that looked like beer, even tasted vaguely like beer, but that sure wasn't beer in any real sense of the name.

The combination of hotel, bottles and near-beer gave Pick the "front" he wanted. He was ready to go into the bootleg business.

Late in 1918, he bought a fleet of Model T Fords, and fitted them with barrier-busting bumpers made from steel pipe filled with concrete.

In the basement of the Alberta hotel, he dug a small room in one wall, then extended a tunnel from this room out under the roadway. The entrance to the sideroom was covered with a rough curtain of burlap, in front of which were

stacked huge barrels of his famous 40-ounce bottles.

The bottles in the barrels were empty, but the ones packed into the hiding place on the other side of the burlap screen were not.

Pick's favorite method of bringing in supplies was to use truckloads of flour. The outer layers of sacks contained flour — in case of a search — but all the rest of the sacks were filled with bottles of booze.

The police were on to Emperor Pick — as he was becoming known — right from the start. But they couldn't catch him. His hiding places were too good, his operation too well set up. And the people of Blairmore were bent on protecting him.

The last fact was due to Emperor Pick's growing reputation as a philanthropist. Partly because he really was a kindly man, and partly because he was a shrewd businessman, Pick devoted himself to good works. He subscribed for $50,-000 in Canadian Victory Bonds, he gave freely to the poor at Christmas time, and he was always there with an open pocket when someone needed help.

On the rare occasion when a police raid on his near-beer warehouse turned up a keg or two that was over-strength, Pick went to court and paid his fines without a whimper — and with a bow of acknowledgement to the talent of the police.

Emperor Pick might have survived the prohibition era — as did some other Alberta bootleggers — and become a "respectable" businessman.

But, on Sept. 21, 1922, fate dealt Pick a cruel hand, and justice finally caught up with him.

On that day, Const. R. M. Day of the provincial police at Blairmore was tipped-off that Mr. Pick was going to Fernie, B.C. for a load of whiskey.

About 4 o'clock, an A.P.P. officer named Steve Lawson and Police Chief James Houghton watched Pick's cavalcade of three cars come along the main street of Coleman. At the wheel of the first was the emperor's mechanic, J. J. McAlpine; driving the second was Pick's son, Steve, 19. The emperor himself drove the third.

Word was flashed to Sgt. James Scott at Blairmore. He and Const. Day were waiting at the Alberta Hotel when Pick's party arrived.

Mr. Pick was walking up to the hotel when the two officers appeared and served him with a search warrant. Pick turned abruptly and dashed for his car. He jammed down the horn in a warning signal and the police saw young Steve roar off in his souped-up McLaughlin.

Sgt. Scott rushed for his car and gave chase. But by this time Mr. Pick was also on the road, blocking Scott as he tried to catch up to young Steve.

Time and again Scott tried to pass, and time and again was cut off by Mr. Pick's swerving car. Scott finally had to abandon the chase.

In Coleman, warned by phone that Steve was on the way, Const. Lawson was waiting in the street to stop him. Steve, however, didn't stop. He swerved by the waiting policeman and Lawson began firing at the car. One shot hit Steve in the hand, but he kept going and made good his escape towards Michel.

By the time he returned to Blairmore, Mr. Pick had learned of Steve's wounding. Met at the hotel by Sgt. Scott, he is said to have grinned and remarked: "I saved my load, anyway, and I don't care how many times I ditch you. It was lucky for Lawson that he did not kill my boy, or else I would kill him."

Later that night, Pick learned Steve had been arrested. For some reason, he decided to go to Coleman and confront Lawson.

With him he took Florence Lassandro, the 22-year-old wife of a friend.

Pick stopped his car in front of the police barracks and Lawson came out. The policeman stood, with one foot on the running-board, talking to Pick.

Mrs. Lassandro later reported that Pick told the officer, "You shot my boy and you're going with me to get him." An argument followed and, for some reason, Pick drew a gun.

In the struggle several shots were fired, tearing through the windshield and dashboard of the car.

At one point, the muzzle swung towards Mrs. Lassandro, who had drawn a gun of her own by now. In a panic, she fired. Lawson fell to the road and was dead in a matter of minutes.

Pick and Mrs. Lassandro were arrested at Blairmore the following day.

The two were tried for murder, found guilty and, on May 3, 1923 — barely a year before the repeal of prohibition — they were hanged at Fort Saskatchewan.

Today, every so often, one of Mr. Pick's famous green 40-ounce bottles will turn up. Not much of a monument for an emperor — or an era.

* * * *

THE GREAT DEFENDER . . .

Bob Edwards, editor of Calgary's famous Eye Opener, once described Paddy Nolan, K.C., as "one of the seven wonders of the world."

There's no question that he was that and — in terms of Alberta justice — maybe more. Paddy Nolan was the greatest, and wittiest, criminal lawyer in Alberta history; possibly in Canadian history.

The facts of his life are straightforward enough. He was born Patric James Nolan in Limerick, Ireland, on St. Patrick's Day, 1864.

Educated in law, he practised in Ireland and in England before coming to Alberta — then simply the North West Territories — in 1889.

He had the unique distinction of having been admitted to three bars: the Bar of Ireland, the Bar of England, and the Bar of the N.W.T.

But here is where Nolan himself takes over. Once, when

reference to his triple admittance was made, Nolan solemnly assured his audience that the reference was an understatement. "In fact," he beamed, "I've made it a point to be admitted to every bar that would open its doors to me — and it was more than three I assure you!"

Paddy Nolan was a man who inspired stories by the dozens and hundreds and many of these stories have survived.

So here, in the hope they may contain a trace of quicksilver, are a few of the more famous stories about Paddy Nolan.

* * * *

Of all the breeds of law-breakers, none was closer to Nolan's heart than the cattle rustler. And when someone was close to Nolan's heart, as his records show, that someone usually got acquitted. Indeed, so good was Paddy at defending rustlers that the Stockmen's Association tried to hire him as their special prosecutor — just to have him on their side for a change.

On one occasion, Nolan was defending a man accused of stealing a steer from the ranch of W. R. Hull, a wealthy cattleman who lived in Calgary and had his spread 70 miles away in Claresholm.

Hull knew nothing of the details of the case. He had been called by the Crown simply to prove his ownership of the animal.

When Nolan rose to cross-examine, he nodded politely to Hull and asked: "I believe you are one of the largest ranchers in Alberta, Mr. Hull?"

"Yes, Mr. Nolan, I believe I am."

"And where are your headquarters, Mr. Hull?"

"In Calgary, Mr. Nolan."

"And where are your hindquarters, Mr. Hull?"

"In Claresholm, Mr. Nolan," Hull responded before he could stop himself.

"Well," said Nolan drawing back to beam at the jury, "if your headquarters are in Calgary and your hindquarters are in Claresholm, you are certainly the very largest rancher in Alberta!"

* * * *

Nolan's client was a poor Calgary widow who, being left penniless, had tried to raise a few dollars by raffling off her late husband's watch — and suddenly found herself charged with conducting a lottery.

Nolan knew, according to the letter of the law at least, the woman was guilty. But he was incensed at the injustice of the situation.

So, a few days before the case was to come to trial,

Nolan went to visit the judge who was to try the woman — with the full knowledge that the judge hadn't yet been informed he'd be hearing the case.

Nolan poured out a tale of woe about the woman's pitiable condition and the judge, moved to compassion, bought two raffle tickets which Nolan just happened to have with him.

Later, the squirming judge listened as the prosecution proved its charge beyond any shadow of a doubt, then listened as the twinkling-eyed Nolan summed up his arguments for the defence:

"Your Honor knows full well the danger of these lotteries, and how even the best-intentioned people in the community fall victim to them and, out of sheer sympathy for their object, commit offences by buying tickets in them — as no doubt Your Honor has done on occasion yourself."

The woman was given a suspended sentence.

* * * *

For all his talent as a lawyer, Nolan didn't win all his cases — nor did he expect to. But he suffered one legal defeat he never forgot — in a murder trial that is still one of the most famous and controversial in Alberta court history.

It was the trial of a young man named Ernest Cashel.

Cashel was a Wyoming cowboy who had fled to Alberta with a posse at his heels. Arriving in Red Deer, he made friends with an old homesteader and arranged to spend the winter with him.

One day, Cashel appeared at a bank in Red Deer and had a hundred dollar bill changed into smaller bills.

There was a peculiar blue smudge on a corner of the bill, and the teller recognized it as one he'd paid out to the old homesteader some weeks before.

"Where'd you get this?" the teller asked, more curious

than suspicious. Cashel responded simply that he got it from a man with whom he was staying.

Shortly after, Cashel disappeared from Red Deer. He appeared in Calgary and passed a bad cheque; an act that brought him to the attention of the police. A warrant was issued and the North West Mounted Police caught up with Cashel in Moose Jaw.

As Cashel, under guard, was being brought back to Calgary, he jumped through the window of the train and escaped.

In Red Deer, meanwhile, some neighbors had discovered that the old homesteader was missing, and had informed the police.

As the search was going on, the teller who had changed the bill for Cashel opened a copy of The Calgary Herald one day and discovered a picture of the man and the story of his daring escape from the train.

The teller immediately hurried to the police with his story of the hundred dollar bill and the searches for both Cashel and the old homesteader were intensified.

The police found the body of the old man when the spring break-up came. There were marks of violence on the corpse. A warrant was sworn out for Cashel's arrest on the charge of murder.

Cashel was finally found on a ranch in Saskatchewan, and brought to Calgary to stand trial.

Nolan undertook the defence. The case was circumstantial, but it was damning — particularly in the light of Cashel's reputation and his previous escape.

Those who were at the trial claim that Nolan never worked harder at a case in his life, but it was all in vain. Cashel was found guilty and sentenced to hang.

Nolan was a stubborn Irishman. Determined not to give

up, and with the hanging only days away, he hurried to Ottawa to appeal to the justice minister for a new trial.

Nolan had already started the interview with the minister when a telegram arrived for him. He read it, then crumpled it in a ball, and heaved a sigh of defeat.

"Never mind the new trial," he said. "My client has escaped."

The night before, Cashel's brother had smuggled two guns into the death cell and, holding three guards at gunpoint, Cashel had got away.

It took time, but Cashel was eventually caught, and with Nolan now powerless to help, duly hung.

To this day, there are those who argue that Cashel was innocent, and that Nolan would somehow have proved it if his client hadn't made that escape from the death cell.

There is no doubt how Nolan felt about it. The night Cashel was executed, Nolan was playing a gloomy game of billiards in the Royal Hotel in Calgary when the hangman accidentally walked in.

Enraged, Nolan took off after him with a billiard cue and only the efforts of the bystanders spared the executioner from a savage beating.

But the story of Paddy Nolan shouldn't end on so angry a note.

When Nolan died in 1913, at the too-young age of 49, The Calgary Herald found a much more fitting way to bring his story to a close:

"*His remarkable skills as a barrister, his marvellous and never-failing wit, his pungency of criticism and his warmth of praise, have been known those many years. Stories were told of him around the world, each one testifying to the breadth of his Irish kindness, and to the marvellous flow of his Irish humor . . .*"

* * * *

ONE LAST WORD OF JUSTICE . . .

Inevitably, in the history of every place, there is one incident, sometimes small, that sums up the worth of its system of law and justice.

In Alberta, the incident came in 1899 when three Indians from Lesser Slave Lake were arrested and brought to trial for murder.

The case, from both the Indian and white points of view, was simple. To the Indian mind, the three had done a duty to their people. To the white, it was a case of cold-blooded homicide.

An Indian named The Pheasant had run amuck in his tribe's camp, threatening to kill and eat anyone who crossed his path.

This sort of thing had happened before, to other men, and the Cree believed that The Pheasant was possessed of a cannibal spirit known as the Witigo which prompted him to eat his own kind.

The medicine men of the tribe tried to drive the spirit out, but to no avail.

Finally three executioners were chosen, and they cut The Pheasant down with their war axes, then opened his body to let out the evil spirit.

When the Mounted Police heard what had happened, they arrested the three and took them to Edmonton to stand trial.

A missionary working among the Cree, Father Falher, saw the extenuating circumstances of the case and wrote to Father Lacombe, asking him to plead the Indians' case to the courts.

This he did. It says something important about the humanity of justice in Alberta to record that all three were released and allowed to return to their own people.

* * * *

HEALER & HELPER

"In 1880, he heeded the call of the west, joined the North West Mounted Police force with a group of other young men from the east, and was sent to the North West Territories. They travelled via the U.S. on flat boats up the Missouri River to Fort Benton, thence on to Fort Walsh . . .

"At Fort Benton, an amusing incident occurred. All the boys were broke. Fort Benton was then a frontier town with few service facilities. One resourceful young chap, who was a barber by trade, put up a chair on the sidewalk and a sign nearby that read BARBER. Soon he was very busy, and the money began to roll in.

"Not to be outdone, Fred Shaw put up a sign on the sidewalk reading DENTIST, set out a chair and soon the extracted teeth were strewn about the board walk." (A pioneer's recollection of Dr. Frederick D. Shaw, first registered dentist in Alberta.)

* * * *

FRANK MEWBURN, SURGEON . . .

Of all the great medical men who came to frontier Alberta, one is consistently singled out as "the Alberta doctor".

It's not that Dr. Frank Hamilton Mewburn was the best surgeon in the world, or that he headed off some grave epidemic.

It's just that, in this frail little doctor, strength, compassion and humor were blended in exactly the right proportions to let him face harsh and primitive conditions, and triumph.

The Lethbridge that Dr. Mewburn found in 1885 was about as primitive, in the medical sense, as he'd ever seen.

All medical care was being provided by the town druggist, who would examine patients, carefully write out a list of the symptoms, then mail the list to the NWMP doctor in Fort Macleod for a diagnosis!

Fortunately, as nearly as we can make out from history, all the patients were hardy enough to survive the wait.

Needless to say, everyone — particularly the druggist — was delighted to have Dr. Mewburn in town. The delight persisted even though the new doctor somehow managed to lose the first patient he treated.

The patient, a Swedish miner, had complained vaguely of some internal disorder which Dr. Mewburn couldn't pin down. The next morning, the miner was found dead in his bunk.

The man's superintendent tried to soothe Mewburn by pointing out that: "Well, doctor, we all must die sometime or another, and some pass away no matter how we may try to prevent it.

"It cannot, therefore, be avoided, so there is no use worrying over it."

To which Dr. Mewburn responded with an explosive "Doesn't that beat hell!"

The new doctor, people gathered, had a philosophical streak in him.

One of the biggest tests the pioneer doctor faced was the treatment of Indian patients. It wasn't just a problem of overcoming their primitive fears; it was also a problem of persuading them to part with a fee.

Dr. Mewburn met both problems almost right away, and solved both — with a little help — just as quickly.

The first Indian patient he treated was a man from the Blood reserve who arrived at his surgery surrounded by a flock of worried relatives.

Mewburn quickly diagnosed the man's condition as a severe goitre, and he knew he'd have to operate. He turned to face the Indian's relatives and delivered a solemn speech: "I shall have to make a big cut. If you all do as I tell you after the big cut is made, this man may get well, but I cannot tell for sure until I have made the big cut, and then if he does not get well, and if he should die, you must not blame me.

"What do you say? Shall I make the big cut?"

His audience — including the man who would have to undergo the "big cut" — all grunted eager agreement.

The operation was a success and the man recovered completely. From that point on, Mewburn had the total trust of the Indians and the Bloods, and every other tribe in the Blackfoot confederacy made a point of bringing all their seriously ill people to him for treatment.

The second problem — that of collecting fees — was solved with the kind assistance of the Indian agents.

One day, an aged squaw appeared in Mewburn's office

with a little girl — and a note which she handed to the doctor.

The note read: "Dear Dr. Mewburn; This old woman has a little girl with her who has a large lump on her neck, which she would like you to remove. Also, the old lady has in her pocket a lump of twenty-five dollars which she would like to have removed at the same time." The note was signed by an Indian agent.

Both operations were performed successfully.

Dr. Mewburn would treat any kind of ailment, but his real love was surgery. And it was in the operating theatre that he created his reputation as one of the west's most volatile characters.

Indeed, the only time he was ever known to take an operating-room incident calmly was a day when all the lights went out during an operation. As the nurses and assistants winced and braced themselves for the inevitable outburst, all they got was the gentle protest that "I can't do the subject justice."

That occasion, however, was the exception. Once, for example, Mrs. Mewburn tried to telephone him while he was in the operating room.

Mewburn stormed out, had a nurse hold up the receiver so he wouldn't have to touch it with his sterilized gloves, and yelled: "Is that you, Louise? Go to h—!!" He then returned to finish the operation.

Probably the most famous illustration of Mewburn temper is the one recorded by John Higinbotham in his book, When the West Was Young:

"During a 'Mission' at which a number of the Roman Catholic clergy, bishops and priests, from various parts of Alberta gathered at Macleod, one of the visiting fathers, who was over eighty years of age, was suddenly stricken with a strangulated hernia.

"Dr. G.A. Kennedy was called in, but feared to operate owing to the patient's advanced age. He telephoned to Lethbridge for Dr. Mewburn and the latter immediately responded by Mounted Police conveyance.

"He decided to operate at once by local anaesthetic and arranged that one of the bishops (Legal, I think it was) should read to the patient and thus divert his mind during the operation.

"In the midst of the clinic a fly entered the room and buzzed so close to the operating table that it got on Dr. Mewburn's nerves. His lips began to move convulsively yet he continued with difficulty to work without exploding.

"Finally, as the objectionable intruder persisted in annoying him, he looked at Dr. Kennedy, who shook his head as a warning to the 'Chief' to contain himself, and said, 'Kennedy, kill that fly or put the bishop out, I don't give a damn which, as I can't hold myself any longer.'

"I never learned whether the fly was swatted or the bishop made his exit."

Mewburn was a tireless worker. At no time in his life was he ever known to refuse an appeal for help, no matter what the weather or time of day. Nor was he ever known to make any distinction between rich and poor. He treated both alike, and never pressed a man for payment. When the Galt Hospital was opened in Lethbridge, Dr. Mewburn became its first superintendent.

And, for all his legendary temper, Mewburn was basically a gentle man. When, in 1929, he was in a hospital bed dying of pneumonia, one of the last things he said to his nurse was:

"I hope my going won't give you too much trouble . . ."

As we said at the beginning, it's not that Dr. Frank Hamilton Mewburn was the best surgeon in the world, or that he headed off some grave epidemic.

It's just that, well, he was "the Alberta doctor".

* * * *

The history of Alberta is filled with the names of helpers. On the frontier, everyone was everyone's neighbor, and his sole protection against the dangers of a new land.

Help took many forms. In Red Deer, for instance, it was four young bachelors who raised the first building there — then cheerfully went to work to help every new arrival raise a home for himself.

Or it was a handful of boy scouts who cornered and captured a bank robber and held him until the police arrived. One of those boys, by the way, was a youngster named Roland Michener — who went on to become our Governor-General.

Once it was Father Lacombe, who nearly died when he chose to starve rather than keep his slim provisions from 18 dying Indians.

And once it was John Ware, the pioneer rancher, who demonstrated that "help" doesn't always turn out to be what you might expect.

Ware had ridden out one day to see a neighbor on business. He reached the house to find the man away — and his wife in the midst of having a baby.

Ware had no choice but to roll up his sleeves and help. When the immediate crisis had been handled, Ware rode back and fetched some female assistance for the new mother.

Then he rode into town to "break" the news to the new father.

He found the man propped up at the bar, having a few to steady his nerves.

"I'm going to teach you your duty to your family," Ware informed him grimly, then gave the man a sound thrashing.

The unhappy gentleman carried around the bruises of Ware's "helping hand" long enough to make sure that he became one of the most devoted of husbands.

But there were just too many helpers, and too many occasions on which they helped, to tell the whole story. So, instead, we'll tell just two stories — one of a little man and one of a little girl — and hope they'll show how many things the word "help" can really mean.

* * * *

THE "WORTHLESS" ONE . . .

His name was Henry Collins and he lived 86 years. In his prime, he weighed more than 180 pounds and was so strong that he lifted a 400-pound bale of goods.

But Henry Collins was only four feet tall, a dwarf, and the name given him by his Cree mother's people was "Muchias, the Worthless One".

No name was ever further from the character of the man who carried it.

Even in Edmonton, where there are still some who remember Muchias by sight, it may come as a surprise to think of him as a "helper".

But he was a helper, one of the finest on the frontier. Orphaned at the age of nine, Muchias was adopted by John Walter of the Hudson's Bay Company, and came with the Walter family to the tiny settlement of Edmonton.

If anyone was inclined to feel pity for Muchias when they saw him first, Muchias quickly disinclined them. He had a ready grin and the ability to laugh at himself. And, as he used to point out, he was really only a dwarf from the hips down. The rest of him was full-sized. He used to brag that, if it weren't for his legs, he'd be seven and a half feet tall.

Into the harshness of frontier life, Muchias injected a valuable commodity — laughter.

And, right from the first, Muchias was convinced that his role in life was to help those around him. He became Edmonton's water man, beaming out from under a white stetson and carrying heavy pails into every kitchen in town.

If there was a woman who needed wood chopped, Muchias would appear out of nowhere and chop it — without asking for so much as a thank-you. And if a man had a heavy load to move, Muchias was there to help move it. He helped put houses up and, in time of flood, he helped chain them down. He hunted and fished, and shared what he got with anyone who needed it.

And more than all this — much more — he helped the children of Edmonton.

Muchias was child-sized and, at a spot close to where Edmonton's high-level bridge now stands, he created a child-sized house and opened its doors to all the children in town.

For a generation of Edmonton children, chafing in the confinement of a rough settlement, Muchias became the magic guide to a magic world.

As Tony Cashman, author of The Edmonton Story, put it: "The house of a friendly dwarf, set in the woods, something right out of a fairy tale."

Child-like himself, Muchias loved the children. He let them run free in the house, and they marvelled at the miniature furniture and utensils. When they were tired, they'd sit with Muchias and tell him stories, or listen to the stories he had to tell.

With his busy hands, he made miniature bows and arrows for the boys, and carved toys and trinkets for the girls.

Muchias gave a strong and helping hand to a city, and brought laughter and magic to a generation of children for whom laughter and magic were scarce and precious.

There are still a lot of grey-haired "children" in Edmonton today who are grateful to the "worthless one" for that.

* * * *

THE FROST-BITTEN "FEAT"....

"Heroism may be found anywhere," the Pembina News Adviser noted on Jan. 6, 1965.

It wasn't meant as a belittling statement. Far from it. It was an awed tribute to a 4½-year-old heroine named Doris Pollard.

The ultimate of help is always heroism and, in this sense, Doris represents one of the ultimate helpers.

Doris, a two-year-old brother, a three-year-old brother, and a nine-month-old baby sister were alone in their farm home near Chip Lake one morning just before Christmas.

Doris' parents were in the barn with a veterinarian, discussing the condition of a sick animal.

Doris was in the kitchen, drying a dish, when the stove that heated the farm house exploded and filled the house with flames.

The little girl ran into a back room where her younger brothers were playing. She grabbed their hands and led them through the flames to the farm house, drying a dish, when the stove. Sharon was sleeping. Doris pulled up a stool and, stretching, reached in and lifted out the baby.

Then, carrying Sharon in her arms and herding the two boys ahead of her, she struggled out of the house.

Behind her, as she waded bare-foot through the snow, the farm house was already an inferno. In a matter of minutes, even before her parents could run up from the barn, the house was destroyed.

Doris ended up in Drayton Valley Municipal Hospital with frost-bitten feet.

She didn't stay there long. And, in a matter of a few months, she was receiving a tribute to her courage.

For saving the lives of the three children, the Alberta Weekly Newspaper editors had named her the winner of a special award for heroism — the only special award ever — and named her the youngest Alberta Junior Citizen of the Year in history.

It could be that award was the first document in a new and exciting chapter of our Alberta heritage . . . .

PLACES

Our Alberta Heritage Series

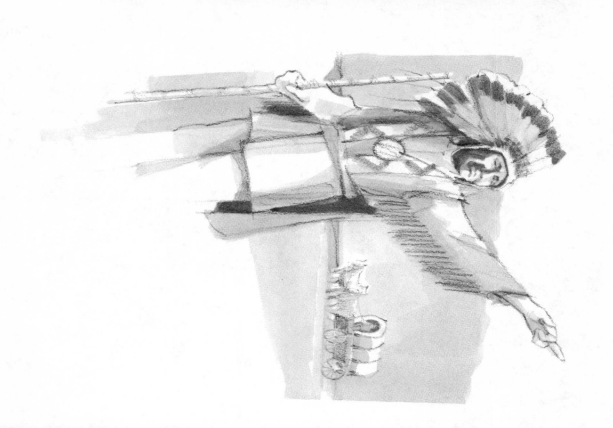

THE LEGEND

"NOT THE END, BUT THE BEGINNING!" . . .

It was 1650, a winter of bitter cold and famine, and inside a lodge of the mountain tribes the two greatest medicine men of the Rocky Mountains were in bitter contest.

Beeny and Gustlee had each had a vision, a vision of white-skinned people. To Gustlee, on one side of the smoking lodge fire, these white-skins were the Kannawdzets —vicious dwarfs who would tear the tribes of the mountain limb from limb.

To Beeny, they were the Sky People, and they would bring with them peace and prosperity.

"Our lives shall be a blessing," Beeny shouted over the taunts of his opponent. "Hard work shall be unnecessary, food shall always be plentiful."

Gustlee scoffed and the wise men of the mountain tribes, sitting to either side of the medicine men, swayed with Gustlee's scorn. But Beeny was not to be silenced.

"In my dream I saw the things which are slowly moving towards our country: the dogs of the sky (horses) that will come across the flatlands and over the mountain passes.

1

Though large as moose, they are gentle, docile; the horn of their feet is not cloven, but all one.

"They drag loads after them, and live among the people as our dogs do.

"I saw the goats of the sky (cattle) living in herds near the villages, whose flesh is used in the place of salmon.

"I saw strange people walking on earth, people almost like ourselves, whose bodies are covered with tight-fitting clothes, whose faces and hands are white like those of ghosts, and whose power is as great as that of manitous. I saw . . ."

Gustlee broke in. "Those strange beings are the Kannawdzets, the Kannawdzets I have seen at the mountain tops, the dwarfs that cause death whenever they are seen!"

Beeny ignored the interruption and went on:

"The white Sky-people I have seen in my dream will soon be coming to our country. The time is at hand when they will make life easy for us.

"They will show us how to cook in solid pots, without boiling boxes, thongs and red hot stones that burn our hands.

"Their axes cut the trees in four blows, their long sticks (guns) cast thunderbolts and kill the game a long way off.

"Their houses, two stories high, are warm in the winter, and the fire always stays invisible within a black box (stove) in the centre.

"They sow in the ground outside seeds that grow into plants, and the plants feed them when the cold moons return.

"The people, the ghost-like people are coming, I tell you, my friends! And those shall be the good days that change our lives and our ways, the days that Zazeekry is bringing from the eastern sky-land to the land of our forefathers . . ."

Gustlee, arms folded, stood grimly shaking his head. "Those ghost-like beings," he argued, "are nothing but the Kannawdzets I have seen up the crags. Beware, my friends! They can do no good, they mean only harm, death. If they come to us, the end is near."

"No! No!" screamed Beeny, eyes glazed with his vision. "Not the end, but the beginning!"

Neither man emerged from the medicine lodge that night the victor. And the wise men, shivering back to their own lodges, shook their heads in confusion at the words of the medicine man Beeny.

It was, after all, a curious vision for the 1650's. Especially for isolated mountain Indians who knew nothing of the Europeans gathering at the eastern end of the Great Lakes; Europeans for whom the Canadian west was still an undrawn map.

What was it Beeny had said? "Not the end, but the beginning . . ."

TRADING POSTS

With all our modern pre-occupation with oil and cattle and grain, it's easy to forget what really started the move to settlement of Alberta — a soggy, rather dumb little animal with protruding yellow teeth and a furry hide. Castor Canadensis; the beaver.

Until the 1700's, the Alberta beaver led a tranquil existence. It was a simple round of building a dam here and a lodge there, and mooring a few choice young willow and aspen branches in the mud for winter snacks.

The only human threat was that of the occasional Indian hunter who had the unfriendly idea of converting the beaver's coat into a coat of his own. It was an idea the beaver did his best to discourage.

In 1690, a man named Henry Kelsey followed his curiosity west. The visit, the first to Alberta by a white man, didn't make much of a stir in beaver circles.

But a hundred years later that visit was going to have the beavers fighting — literally — for their skins.

What excitement was generated by Kelsey's reports of

his western explorations — including the report of the presence of beaver — was short-lived.

Game in what is now Ontario and Quebec provided more than enough fur to meet the demands of the time. And people were still too busy trying to "civilize" the east to think seriously of doing the same thing for the west.

But, as the 1700's moved on, feelings changed. The east was getting crowded and — much more importantly — something was happening on the European fashion scene.

Ever the dictator, fashion had decreed that no English gentleman was complete unless properly topped by a beaver hat.

English gentlemen, being no slouches in the fashion department, immediately set up a loud and passionate cry for beaver toppers.

Being good businessmen they also set up the machinery to make sure that what went on their heads did something to fatten their purses as well. The great fur game was on.

Dueling their way across the continent, the Hudson's Bay men and the Nor'westers stitched the northern prairies together with trading forts. In Alberta alone, 42 forts went up between 1778 and 1864.

Then, stung by the impudence of John Jacob Astor who was coolly creating an American fur monopoly on the coast of British Columbia, the Bay men and Nor'westers pushed on to break the barrier of the Rockies.

Those first trader-explorers — men like Peter Pond and David Thompson — were hardly settlers. (Unless "settling" in one spot long enough for a hurried meal or a few hours sleep qualify.)

No, it was those who followed — the sharp-penned and careful merchants who manned the posts — who really started settlement in Alberta.

Not that these "gentlemen-traders" were the mild-mannered merchants one sees today. Far from it. With Hudson's Bay and Northwest posts usually set up in sight of one another (and once or twice inside the same stockade) so that each side could keep track of the competition, the early traders had to be wily and tough and ready for anything.

Indeed, it was to be expected that when a post was doing too much better than the competition, chances of a sudden fire of "mysterious" origin became astronomically high.

The competition was guaranteed to show up a little too late with an offer of help. And to cluck sympathetically over the ashes. And, far from incidentally, to remind Indian customers that business was going on as usual across the street.

Fire sales weren't quite the same thing in the 1700's as they are today.

Indian customers, of course, were stirred to great heights

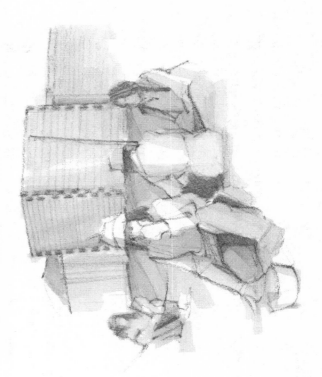

of activity by the sudden interest in fur. For enough fur — preferably beaver pelts — an Indian could get virtually anything he wanted: knives and hatchet-heads and blankets and colored cloth and ribbons and beads. Even tobacco and tea.

And the bargains! Why, all an Indian had to do to buy a Hudson's Bay rifle, for example, was match its height in beaver pelts.

So enthused were the Indian customers by bargains like these that sometimes the same customer would show up two or three days in a row — equipped every time with a pile of pelts that bore a curious resemblance to some that had disappeared from the post the night before.

All the trading clerk could do under the circumstances would be to offer a dry compliment on the trapper's ability. And all the Indian could do would be to shrug modestly — and wonder how soon the supply of padlocks would arrive from the east.

And all the beaver — who started the whole thing — could do was huddle in his lodge and hope fervently that the spotlight of fashion would shift from him to buffalo coats or something . . .

* * * *

MEANWHILE, DOWN AT THE BORDER . . .

It was the summer of 1874 and Rev. John McDougall, a missionary at Morley, was on his way to pay a social call — to the notorious whiskey fort, Fort Whoop-up.

"Crossing the Belly River," he wrote later for posterity, "we rode up to the fort. We found the gate shut and very little sign of humanity around. But presently the gate opened to us and we entered.

"Joseph Healy was in charge and had but one man with

him, for at the time the others were away interviewing members of the Boundary Commission, which was now about finishing the work of survey to the foot of the Rockies. Both countries interested had troops of soldiers and engineers working together determining the 49th parallel from Red River to the mountains. These had been at work since 1872.

"Healy told us he expected the Whoop-up contingent back any minute and asked us to make ourselves welcome in the fort and, as his man was more or less under the influence and he himself pretty well braced, he set to work preparing a meal for our party.

" 'Unbuckle and lay off your armoury for the moment, Parson John,' was his kind injunction to myself, and while we were at lunch he discussed the situation from his standpoint.

"There was not much need for government intervention in this country. He and his friends had been able to and kept the rougher element out.

"For instance, there was So-and-so. He came in and was going to run things. He lies under the sod at Standoff. And there was So-and-so. He had aspirations and we stretched him beside the first. And there was So-and-so. He went wild and we laid him out at Freezeout. And some more at Slideout.

"These bad men could not live in this country. We simply could not allow it. 'No, Parson John, we did not let any really bad men stay in this Whoop-up region' . . .' "

A visitor to Lethbridge today — if he's hardy enough — can wade through some rapids to the remains of a shallow well and a battered cairn that mark the spot where the conversation recorded by 'Parson John' took place.

Or he can drive to a historic site south of the city and trace the deep ruts cut a century ago by the bull-trains that led to Whoop-up from Fort Benton in Montana.

Or he can do what thousands of others have done and visit the excellent replica of Whoop-up the Kinsmen have erected in Lethbridge's Indian Battle Park.

Whichever place he chooses, if he spends a few minutes considering Joe Healy's fervent reassurance that "we did not let any really bad men stay in this Whoop-up region," the visitor will have to conclude that old Joe wasn't a strictly truthful man.

Because, for the most part, the American free-traders who created Whoop-up and Standoff and the other whiskey posts were indeed "bad" men.

With few exceptions, they were outlaws who cheated, stole, and murdered. Some of their excesses outraged a whole country and one — the so-called "Cypress Hills massacre" — was the main reason for the birth of the North-West Mounted Police.

But, ironically, it is these same "bad" men who have to be given most of the credit for opening southern Alberta to settlement.

By 1869, decades of fur-trading activity had given a start to the settlement of northern Alberta. Posts like Fort Edmonton and Rocky Mountain House were gradually becoming the centres of small villages.

But south of the fur posts, Alberta was still largely a grassy and silent wilderness. It would take the whoops of the whiskey men to break the silence.

* * * *

OHHHH, GIVE ME A HOME . . . .

It was December, 1869, in Montana Territory, and two free-traders were brooding over the injustices of federal government. So upset were Joe Healy and A.B. Hamilton that they were drowning their grief in their own whiskey — a sure sign that things must have been very bad indeed.

"Things," Healy ventured bitterly, "are just gettin' too civilized around here." Hamilton nodded sad agreement. It was all too true.

Fort Benton was turning into a regular town. Women were talking about Paris hats and men about ranching and it was getting so a man couldn't sleep for train whistles and church bells.

Worse than that, government control had arrived — with federal marshals and federal troops to enforce it. Which, for free-traders like Hamilton and Healy, meant an end to ignoring the silly law that said you couldn't trade whiskey to Indians.

Indeed, some of those federal marshals weren't above shooting a trader who was doing no more than help an Indian customer to a friendly drink or two. Montana, definitely, was getting to be an unhealthy place to do business.

Beyond the Canadian border, on the other hand . . . Hamilton and Healy were suddenly struck by an idea and they stared at one another. Then they leaned back and started to laugh and laugh and laugh.

* * * *

"LET'S WHOOP UP" . . .

Fort Whoop-up, at the junction of the St. Mary's and Belly river (now the Oldman River) started out in 1869 under the respectable name of Fort Hamilton. When the first crude fort burned down in the spring of 1870, its replacement was again named Fort Hamilton. How the name was changed has been the subject of many stories; all contradictory.

The most popular story of the origin of the name is that

a man who had returned to Fort Benton told people there that they were "really whoopin' it up" at Hamilton and Healy's post.

The most likely explanation is the one that was offered in The Lethbridge Herald in 1912:

The naming of Fort Whoop-up is traceable to a Frenchman named Charles Choquette, who freighted from Fort Benton to what was then Fort Hamilton. Choquette did not know much English, and whenever he learned a word he had a habit of repeating it over and over. There was an eighty-mile barren stretch between Fort Benton and Fort Hamilton, and it was a dread to the outfits that made the trip. One night Choquette was drawing near to the fort; his outfit was tired and lagging, and the others were complaining, including Charlie. Finally, someone said: "Let's whoop up and get to the fort." This struck Charlie as a good phrase, and he kept repeating it now and then. As they neared the fort he yelled "Whoop Up", and it became a byword.

* * * *

How the second-most famous whiskey fort, Fort Standoff, got its name is no mystery at all.

It earned the name for the biggest bluff in Alberta history.

Hard on the heels of Hamilton and Healy came dozens of other Montana free-traders, among them two men named Joe Kipp and Charlie Thomas.

The pair, however, faced a tougher escape from the United States than did the Whoop-up duo. It was now 1870, and Montana had a marshal whose name was Hard and whose reputation was harder still.

Marshal Hard was determined to keep Montana dry. He'd already confiscated several stocks of liquor at Fort Benton.

And he'd warned the free-traders that any wet goods found in the Indian territory — which included Benton and several hundred miles of country around it — would be seized.

Kipp and Thomas knew the marshal meant business, but they also figured that they had a scheme to outwit him.

They'd simply go outside Indian territory and buy a large quantity of liquor and race it across the line into Canada — cutting off the Blackfoot trade that had been going to Benton.

Kipp headed for Helena, Montana, to start the plan rolling. But, riding right behind, was the ever-suspicious Marshal Hard.

Kipp knew the marshal was behind him. In Helena, he managed to dodge his follower long enough to buy 75 cases of high-proof liquor and arranged to have it delivered, secretly, to a spot on the Missouri River just below the town.

There Kipp hurriedly built a raft, loaded the cases aboard, and floated off to the mouth of the Sun River (the present site of Great Falls).

Waiting for him was Thomas with three four-horse teams and a hired man.

Knowing that the persistent marshal couldn't be too far behind, they threw cases onto the wagons and took off, heading straight north to the Canadian border as fast as they could travel.

Three days later, just after fording a river, Kipp looked back and saw a lone rider hot in pursuit.

Kipp didn't have to guess who it was.

"It's the marshal," he muttered to his partner, "and right here is where we stand him off."

The triumphant marshal reined in and ordered Kipp to turn his outfit around and head back to Benton.

"Turn back?" Kipp was wounded. He shook his head. Then, slowly, a grin spread over his face and he leaned back.

"You know, marshal, you're just 20 minutes too late. We cross the boundary line at the North Fort back there."

The marshal exploded. He ranted. He raved. He threatened.

Kipp grinned. He yawned. He scratched his chin. He winked at Charlie Thomas.

Finally Marshal Hard stopped for breath — and to think the situation over. Kipp might be right. At least, he certainly seemed to think he was. And then there was the matter of three guns to one.

Hard took one last, regretful look at the wagons and their gurgling loads. Then he wheeled his horse with a curse and headed back to Benton.

Kipp never forgot the encounter. When he and Thomas built their fort on the Belly River, they named it after the confrontation.

Kipp re-told the story hundreds of times, but never with quite as much delight as he did right after the International Boundary Commission, turned in its report in 1874.

It seems that when the marshal caught up with them, Kipp and company were still 300 yards within the confines of the good old U.S. of A.

* * * *

"WE HAD A FEW GOOD YEARS" . . .

The era of the free-traders in southern Alberta lasted a short five years. And the first few of those years were a lot more peaceful than many would like us to believe.

The real failure of the whiskey forts was their success.

Kipp and the Standoff crowd had figured to cut off the trade to Benton. They succeeded admirably. During their first spring, they were able to ship south more than 3,000 prime buffalo robes and 2,000 small furs while Benton went bare. And other traders were doing just as well or, in the case of Fort Whoop-up, even better.

But what the free-traders didn't realize was that they were having even more of an effect on the fur-trade to the north.

Before the invasion of the free-traders, the merger of the Nor'westers and Hudson's Bay Company had created an enormous fur monopoly. The Whoop-up crowd had broken the monopoly, and the Hudson's Bay Company wasn't going to let them get away with it.

Almost from the moment the free-traders crossed the border, Ottawa was subjected to a barrage of complaints and exaggerated reports — virtually all from the Hudson's Bay Company, or inspired by them.

By 1871, these reports were taking on a serious tone:

"Indians visiting the Rocky Mountain House during the fall of 1870 have spoken of the existence of a trading post of Americans from Fort Benton, upon the Belly River, sixty miles within the British boundary-line. They have asserted that two American traders, well-known on the Missouri, named Culverton and Healy, have established themselves at this post for the purpose of trading alcohol, whiskey, and arms and ammunition of the most improved description, with the Blackfeet Indians; and that an active trade is being carried on in all these articles, which, it is said, are constantly smuggled across the boundary-line by people from Fort Benton."

The next year, Col. Robertson-Ross, head of the Canadian Militia, submitted an even more ominous report:

"Beyond the Province of Manitoba westward, there is no kind of government at all, and no security of life and property beyond what people can do for themselves. Serious crimes have been allowed to go unpunished. . . .

"When at Rocky Mountain House I was informed that a party of American smugglers and traders had established a trading post at the junction of the Bow and Belly Rivers, about 30 miles due east of the Porcupine Hills and 60 miles on the Dominion side of the boundary. This trading post they have named Fort Hamilton, after the mercantile firm of Hamilton, Healy and Company, of Fort Benton, Montana, from whom they obtain their supplies. It is believed that they number about 20 men, under command of John Healy, a notorious character . . .

"It is stated on good authority that, in 1871, 88 of the Blackfeet were murdered in drunken brawls."

It's significant that both reports originated from Rocky Mountain House — a Hudson's Bay post.

These reports, however, were being supported by others of unquestionable sincerity — from the missionaries working among the Indians.

"Since last autumn," lamented Father Lacombe, "the process of demoralization has, alas!, made very considerable progress; the disorders of all kinds which have taken place among the savages and these miserable traders of rum are frightful.

"We have done our best to inform the American Government of these unhappy infringements of its laws; while on the other side the government of the Red River has made a very severe law prohibiting intoxicating liquors throughout these territories.

"But while we await the coming of some impressive force to compel the fulfilment of this wise law, we suffer unceasingly."

The combined pressure of military, church, and the biggest mercantile empire in Canada couldn't be ignored in Ottawa. Soon the government was stirring into action.

If the free-traders hadn't been aware of the Hudson's Bay Company when they crossed the border, rumors of the reports to Ottawa had them conscious of them now. And the Bay men were threatening to make the presence felt in a more direct way as well.

When Hamilton and Healy rebuilt Fort Whoop-up in the spring of 1870, they spent $20,000 turning it into an armed fortress. Modelled on Fort Benton, Whoop-up bristled with cannon and was fully stocked with grape and cannister shot.

They took all this trouble not because of hostile Indians, but because of threatened attack by the Hudson's Bay Company.

Hamilton and Healy may have wondered, uneasily, why their powerful enemies never bothered following up the threat.

Unknown to the free-traders, their posts — particularly Whoop-up — were creating scandal on both sides of the border. The public was turning strongly against the practice of trading rot-gut liquor to Indians. And the American newspapers were having a field-day painting pictures of horror at the border posts.

Years later, Fred Kanouse, a veteran of the Whoop-up era, could see all too clearly what none of the free-traders had been able to see at the time.

"The source of Whoop-up's reputation as a rendezvous of bad men," he told an interviewer, "is traceable to a San Diego, California, newspaper. The story must have been more than a column, and was about as lurid as imagination could make it.

"It is said that Fort Whoop-up was the rendezvous of the bloodiest band of cut-throats that ever went unhung, including escaped convicts, murderers, renegades, and that ilk, who pillaged and murdered Indians, stole horses and cattle, and did many other things equally as bad.

"It is true that there were such men along the border at that time. But they were not a part of those who made the fort their headquarters.

"At no time were there more than sixty men at the post, and in most cases five or six traders was all that remained when the trappers and wolfers were out seeking pelts.

"In those days it was policy to be on good terms with

the Indians, as we traders were doing a good business and desired that friendly relations remained unbroken . . .

"There were stirring times along the border about that time, and many men who were not willing to have their past investigated, but contrary to popular belief, Fort Whoop-up was not the gathering place for them, but the home of traders and trappers."

Kanouse, of course, was inclined to lean a little to the generous side in his recollections.

* * * *

IS THERE A DOCTOR IN THE HOUSE? . . .

Perhaps the fairest description of the men of the whiskey forts came from the pen of Morley missionary Rev. John McDougall, who was trusted and respected by virtually all of them.

At one point, Rev. McDougall was paid a visit by the Rev. Laughlin Taylor, general secretary of the Methodist Church. When it came time for Dr. Taylor to leave, McDougall decided to take him home via Fort Benton.

The first stop was Fort Kipp, one of the smaller whiskey posts, where the party picked up some tinned fruit (which Rev. McDougall had never seen before) and an escort of drunken, boisterous free-traders.

Dr. Taylor, who had previously visited the Holy Land, did his best to offset the effect of the escort by lecturing the whiskey men on "The Land of the Bible."

McDougall prudently doesn't record the audience's reaction to the lecture.

"On to Whoop-up," his chronicle states. "Across the Belly at Fort Kipp, and up the big hill, and out across the wide upland, and with our wild, uproarious, heavily armed escort whooping and yelling and cursing, we drove and rode and wondered what might come next.

"Presently we looked down upon the junction of the St. Mary's and Belly Rivers, two deep valleys; quite well timbered with fine bottom lands of prairie intersecting . . . Here was the fort, strongly built of cottonwood and poplar logs, and further down was another post . . ."

McDougall and Dr. Taylor spent a few pleasant hours at Whoop-up, chatting with friends of the Morley missionary. Then, rid finally of their Kipp escort, they headed towards Fort Benton.

On the east bank of the St. Mary's River, they decided to stop and eat their tinned fruit. Just as they'd begun, they heard a terrific racket coming from the west.

McDougall writes: "Around the woods came a troop of horsemen, a wilder, swearing, whooping lot seldom could be seen. They were after us for some reason, that was plain, and they were evidently wild with whiskey. Right into the river they plunged, and never let up until they had surrounded our party.

"It had come to pass that almost immediately after we left Fort Whoop-up a party had come in from the northeast. These had been fighting with the Indians, and one man was brought in all 'shot up'.

"Then the rumor had gone out that a doctor had just passed through; so this party gathered up to come after the doctor.

"We had a time explaining to them the difference between medicine and divinity . . ."

* * * * *

THE GREEN RIVER RENEGADE

Had the free-traders been alone in coming to Alberta, they

might have hung on in the border country a little longer. But they weren't alone.

Trailing behind, and soon outnumbering them, were the wolfers.

Not satisfied to rely on rifles to hunt, they coldly poisoned game across the plains.

These wolfers were the real-life counterparts of the rumoured "murderers in the south." Most of them thought nothing of killing a man who crossed them. Human life was absolutely without value. And they considered the Indian even less than human.

It was one of these wolfers, Thomas Hardwick, known as the Green River Renegade, who finally brought the Whoop-up era to an end.

In 1873, Hardwick was 29 and the acknowledged leader of the Alberta-Montana wolfers.

Born in Missouri, he'd served in the Confederate Army, and traded among the Indians in Wyoming during 1869 and 1870.

At some point in his life, he'd acquired a fanatic hatred for Indians and, while in Wyoming, he was captured twice by tribes bent on punishing him. He managed to escape each time.

Moving to Montana, he was involved in several fights with Indians. In February, 1871, he is known to have murdered one Crow Indian and wounded another.

The next spring, he was wolfing in the Sweetgrass Hills of Alberta; setting out poisoned buffalo carcasses to kill the wolves. His party had already had one or two run-ins with Peigan Indians, and shortly after sunrise on April 5, 1872, Hardwick spotted a party of Indians on a nearby hill.

The Indians were Assiniboines, but Hardwick took them for Peigans or Bloods. Without warning, he opened fire.

In the fight that followed, four Indians were killed and ten others wounded.

Then, in May, 1873, Hardwick was leading a group of wolfers back to Fort Benton from a successful winter on the plains around Calgary.

Cree Indians ran off their horses near Benton. Hardwick's party rushed into Benton, grabbed new horses, and set off in pursuit.

Days later, on Battle River in the Cypress Hills, the trackers located a camp of Assiniboines. The Indians weren't the horse thieves, but the enraged Hardwick — again without warning — opened fire. The rest of his party followed suit.

Minutes later, between 30 and 80 Indians — men, women and children — lay dead.

News of the massacre reached Ottawa in a matter of days — exaggerated to the point where parliament was told that "more than 200" Indians had been brutally slaughtered.

Ottawa, already goaded by three years of increasingly disturbing reports from the west, acted immediately. On May 23, 1873, only three weeks after Hardwick opened fire, the North-West Mounted Police force was created, with orders to tame the west and drive out the whiskey traders.

Late the next year, Col. James F. Macleod led his red-coated force up to the gates of Fort Whoop-up.

But news of his arrival had travelled ahead of him. Most of the wolfers and traders had fled back to the U.S. (Hardwick, for example, was never punished, and ended his days in 1901 as a prosperous businessman in Missouri.)

The gates of Fort Whoop-up were opened by Dave Akers, the only one of the traders to remain behind. Friendly in the extreme, he showed the colonel his vegetable garden (but not the whiskey kegs buried under it), and communicated

Healy's offer to sell the fort to the mounties for $25,000. Col. Macleod rejected the offer as too high. Then he ordered his men to tear down the free-trader flag over Whoop-up, and had them raise the Union Jack.

With its raising, the Whoop-up era came to an end.

And, today, standing between the well and battered cairn, the visitor can almost hear the earnest assurance of Joe Healy that:

"No, Parson John, we did not let any really bad men stay in this Whoop-up region . . ."

PIONEER HARDSHIPS

No one can say honestly that he knows why they came. But they came.

Perhaps it was the lure of the legendary Chinooks or tales of grassy plains that had never known a plough. Or perhaps it was just the dream of a frontier.

They pushed north from Montana behind bawling herds of cattle, or west from Winnipeg in wagons loaded with household effects and brave women and crying children.

And even when the Chinooks proved only rare respites from the bitterness of winter, and even when their ploughs turned nothing but dust, they stayed on.

It was a desperate fight, but slowly — furrow by furrow — they won it. Sometimes the price of winning was bitter. In every churchyard in Alberta there are graveplots, some only two feet long, that count the cost they paid.

And on headstone after headstone is carved the one-word epitaph that is the proudest any Albertan can earn: "Pioneer."

* * * * *

The Whoop-up era was dead, but as the last three decades

of the 19th century spun away it was obvious that what had started with Whoop-up wasn't going to end with it.

In 1870, a young American named Nicholas Sheran had come through Whoop-up on his way to search for gold. Instead of gold, however, he found coal, and by 1874 he was busy chipping away at exposed seams on the Belly River — and unknowingly digging the foundations of Lethbridge.

The North-West Mounted Police, having torn down the Whoop-up flag, were now 30 miles west; building Fort Macleod and the core of what would be Alberta's first true "town."

In the open space between the fur posts and whiskey forts, wagon ruts were beginning to replace the snaking trails of Indian travois.

At Red Deer Crossing, four young bachelors had already raised a few crude log huts and new arrivals, many of them families, were beginning to build near them.

Legitimate trading companies, like the I.G. Baker Co., moved in to take the place of the whiskey traders. On their heels came smaller traders, often one-man operations, to fan out and give budding settlements their first "stores."

In Fort Benton, Montana, in 1877, readers of the fort's newspaper, The River Press, noted with interest a small announcement:

"Joseph McFarlane and Miss Marcella Sheran were married at Fort Whoop-up, N.W.T., on the fourth of July last. Father Scollen performed the ceremony and the happy couple received the salute of six guns from Fort Whoop-up. After the ceremony, they were escorted to the McFarlane home by their friends. This is the first marriage of a white couple recorded at Whoop-up. Such is the progress of civilization."

THE BREATH OF OUR BEAUTIFUL CHINOOK . . .

Many Alberta pioneers, right into the 20th Century, were brought here, literally, by the wind.

If Alberta has a magic word, it's "Chinook"; the word for a west wind that sweeps down from the Rockies, raising temperatures as much as 45 degrees in 12 hours and melting a foot of snow and ice at a time.

Indian legend has it that Chinook was a beautiful maiden who wandered into the mountains of the southwest and was lost. For days and weeks, warriors searched for her without success.

Then, one day, a soft and warm breeze blew from the west. The elders of the tribe nodded their heads wisely. "It is the breath of our beautiful Chinook," they said, and the warriors searched no more.

The legends Alberta's early pioneers created weren't as beautiful, but they definitely rated higher in entertainment value.

There was hardly a prospective settler who hadn't heard of the man who'd driven his team into town in a blinding blizzard and hitched it to a pole — only to wake up the next morning in a Chinook and discover his team hanging from the top of the church steeple.

And the insistent claim of the trapper who said he'd raced ahead of a Chinook with his lead dog lost in driving snow and the runners of his sleigh kicking up a cloud of dust.

Lost alongside these tall tales was another Indian warning; one that held an ominous message no one heeded.

When winter passed without a warm wind, snow stayed and food supplies could not be replenished, and people died.

The Indians had a word for that death: a word that meant "no-wind."

* * * *

A LIGHT IN THE WINDOW . . .

Perhaps no story illustrates the meaning of the word better than that of Lee Brainard; a man who ended his days equating the word "Chinook" with the worst curses that man has devised.

Although the story took place in 1906, it is a vivid example of what happened to so many earlier pioneers who followed the wind and ignored good advice when they came to Alberta . . .

Lee Brainard was 47 years old, a widower with a teen-aged son, and a successful rancher in Montana. But he was tired of the work of gathering winter feed, and tired of ranching on over-crowded, over-grazed range.

Often, from wandering cowboys, he'd heard stories of the legendary Chinook belt where cattle could graze freely all year round.

It was, he'd been told, a country where a man with a stake could carve himself out a cattle empire.

The stories were attractive — and persistent — and Brainard finally decided to follow them to Alberta.

It was mid-summer when he, his son Albert, and an old hired hand named White set out. They had two covered wagons and a herd of 700 head of cattle; 450 yearlings and adults plus calves. They also had more than 100 horses.

With the occasional help of hired riders, they drove the herd northwest and across the Canadian border. Skirting the western fringe of the Cypress Hills, they pushed on to the valley of the South Saskatchewan and the young town of Medicine Hat.

In Medicine Hat, restocking supplies, Brainard came to the attention of the Mounted Police who heard of his plan to go into new country at the end of the summer with no feed supplies and no buildings put up for shelter.

The police were on the point of prohibiting him from going on, but decided instead to let him go with warnings of the dangers that lay ahead.

Brainard chose to ignore the warnings, and headed for the government land office.

There, to his disappointment, he found that all possible sites for a large spread along the South Saskatchewan, the Bow and the Red Deer rivers were already taken.

Brainard perked up, however, when the helpful agent pointed out that there was still a large expanse of land north of Red Deer with only a few scattered claims marked on it.

What the agent didn't tell Brainard, possibly because he assumed he already knew, was that the northern land was outside the Chinook belt.

Ignorant of the danger, Brainard, Albert and White restocked the wagons, rounded up the herd and headed north.

Days later, they forded the Red Deer and pushed up a large creek to a spot about three miles north of where the town of Richdale stands today.

Brainard thought he'd found the answer to his dreams: miles of open grassland, a creek for water and willows for shelter and fuel.

The trio lifted one of the wagon boxes from its chassis to serve as a home. Then they gathered a small supply of wood and chips for fuel, far too small a supply to meet the needs they had yet to learn existed.

Secure in the belief they were in the Chinook belt, Brainard's party spent most of their time exploring the new country around them.

On one of these rides, about 40 miles from camp, Brainard came upon the ranch of the Hunt brothers. The Hunts, finding out what position Brainard was in, urged him to bring all his calves and yearlings to them for wintering.

Brainard, being a stubborn man, refused.

One morning in mid-October, the Brainard party awoke with a shock to discover the ground covered with snow.

Brainard reasoned, however, that since it was still early in the year a Chinook was bound to come along and clear the snow away.

But there was no Chinook. Just snow and more snow.

Finally, the party moved its camp and the herd to hilly country near Dowling Lake where there was some shelter, and where the wind kept some of the ridges free of snow so the stock could get grass.

But with only the wagon for shelter, their plight was desperate. Week after week, the cold and storms continued. Christmas came and passed without a break.

January brought blizzards and temperatures that averaged 30 to 40 below zero.

Some of the cattle were already dying, and if it hadn't been for the horses pawing through to the grass, others would have perished.

Day after day, the three men grew weaker; huddling in the bitter cold of the wagon and eating nothing but skinny beef.

Brainard, tortured constantly by the cries of his dying cattle, bitterly regretted his stubbornness in ignoring the Mounties at Medicine Hat and in turning down the Hunts' offer to winter his stock.

His only hope was for a change in the weather; a break that would let him make a dash for the Hunts' and save part of the herd and their own lives.

On January 29, the break finally came in the form of a Chinook so warm the three were working in shirt sleeves before the day was out.

In a race against time, they gathered what cattle still had strength to move and shot the rest. They hitched Brainard's stallion and another horse to the covered wagon.

By dawn they were on their way, the rest of the horses being pushed ahead to break trail in the deep and soggy snow.

It was almost impossible going. They had to stop frequently to rest the lathered horses.

But, by noon, they had made a dozen miles. If the Chinook would hold another day, they'd make it to safety.

It was dead calm, and Albert and White made a small fire of willow twigs and roasted some fresh beef. They would eat and rest, then push on to the Hunts' ranch.

Suddenly, young Albert turned around and leapt to his feet. "For God's sake," he yelled. "Look what's coming!"

From the northwest, a towering grey wall of cloud was swirling down on them, kicking up writhing eddies of snow. In a moment the sun was blotted out.

Floundering through the snow, the three made a desperate attempt to catch their saddle horses, but all except Brainard's stallion got away as the storm struck.

They tried to take shelter in the wagon, but the wind tore through it in paralyzing blasts. It grew colder and colder until they could stand it no longer, and they had to get out and exercise to keep from freezing to death.

All night, with Brainard goading, the three marched round and round in a circle. Every so often they'd try to make a fire from willow twigs, but the flames would be torn away by the wind or buried in drifting snow.

By dawn, they were like statues of ice, floundering in a whirlpool of wind and snow. They could hardly breath and their legs were failing.

Finally, inevitably, the aged White stumbled. Young Albert grabbed him under the arms and yelled to his father. Before Brainard could reach the pair, White had gone limp and slipped from the boy's grasp to the ground.

Father and son worked feverishly over the man who had been their companion since Albert was born. But, long minutes later, they realized that White was dead.

With White dead, the boy seemed to lose all will to live. Brainard pummelled him with his fists, screamed, pleaded, but the boy wouldn't fight on. Finally, Brainard picked the boy up and struck out in the storm.

Even with all the strength of his fury, it was too much of an effort for Brainard. A bitter half-hour later he was back to lay the corpse of his son gently by that of his old friend's.

Brainard cut loose his stallion to give it a chance for survival. Then he explored the area around the wagon and found some of his cattle frozen upright in the snow.

Taking an axe from the wagon, he chopped pieces from them and ate the meat raw.

Then heading directly into the wind, he struggled towards the Hunts' ranch.

Hours later, delirious, he thought he saw the figure of a long dead friend walking towards him. He tried to pull off a mitt to shake the hand of the apparition before him, but the blast of the wind on his wrist snapped him back to sanity.

Still hours later, he bumped into something and collapsed in a faint.

But then he was conscious again, and realizing that what

he had fallen over was a fence.

No longer able to stand, he crawled alongside the wire on his hands and knees. He passed the feed corrals and came at last to the Hunt brothers' shack. He fell against the door.

Jack Hunt thought it was a steer at the door. "Get to hell out of there!" he yelled.

"I won't get out," was the weak response on the other side of the door and the startled Hunt brothers were immediately on their feet.

Dragging Brainard inside, the Hunts rubbed his frozen face, hands and feet with kerosene.

But the three brothers were virtually helpless. Brainard needed a hospital but the storm, distance, and his condition all conspired against moving him.

In the end, despite the efforts of the brothers, Brainard lost all but one of his toes. It took months for his face and hands to heal.

Brainard was eventually taken out to civilization and shipped to a hospital in Montana.

As soon as the storm eased, one of the Hunt brothers had gone out and covered the two bodies with snow to protect them from coyotes. So severe was the winter of 1906-7 that it was May before the Mounted Police could come out and move the bodies to Stettler.

Later the next summer, a partially recovered Brainard returned to try to find what was left of his herd. Of the 600 head he'd arrived with, he found only 15. Others of his animals, cattle and horses, continued to turn up — some in remote parts of Saskatchewan and Montana — for seven years afterwards.

Ruined and alone, Brainard went back to Montana to make a fresh start.

But he didn't go back to Montana to stay. Brainard still had the courage and determination that had carried him through the storm to Hunts' door. And he still had the dream that had brought him to Alberta in the first place.

Years later, remarried, he again headed north. This time he put wisdom to work and made it, living and ranching here until his peaceful death in 1938.

Lee Brainard was never known to talk of the storm that had cost him his only son and his old friend. But he had one eccentricity that proved the storm was never far from his thoughts.

To the end of his days he never allowed a blind drawn on any window in his home. He wanted his lights to shine out at all times as a guide to safety for anyone lost in darkness or a storm . . .

* * * *

THE GREAT TREK . . .

Even for the well-prepared, the trip to Alberta was filled with hardships. And no one could be better prepared than the 12 Mormon families who followed Charles Ora Card north to Canada in 1887.

They were no tenderfeet. They had pioneered once already, to carve out homesteads in Utah.

They knew the hardships of the trail, and they had no illusions about Chinooks or any other break that nature might offer.

In choosing to follow Charles Ora Card north, they knew they faced long weeks and months through dangerous country. And they knew that even when they reached Canada, it would take years to regain even the little comfort they had created in Utah.

Why did they come?

The reason is probably much simpler — and much more complicated — than religion alone can explain. Perhaps, as the words of a song written by one of those who made the trek suggests, it was simply that they were pioneers:

"I am just a pioneer —
Landed in the eighties here;
And the trail seemed long to Canada by team.
When I hear the coyote howl, and
The hooting of the owl,
Then I dream again my early manhood dreams . . ."

Card was a cautious man. Before proposing the trek north, he made a long trip of exploration and chose a spot by the side of Lee Creek, just south of the huge reserve left to the Blackfoot Indians by Treaty Number 7. On his way back to Utah, Card carefully mapped a route to that spot; mapped it so carefully that not one of the lonely wagons was lost for so much as a day.

In 1960, two of the last survivors of that trek, Jane Eliza Woolf Bates and Zina Alberta Woolf Hickman, wrote their memories of the famous trip:

"To us, the younger ones of the party, the coming trip was hailed as a challenging adventure. To our elders, who had been pioneers or the children of pioneers of Utah, it was a huge undertaking.

"They knew that the greater part of Idaho and Montana through which we were to travel was wild, Indian infested, unsettled country for the most part, with rugged mountains and turbulent rivers to cross. The roads were poor at the best, often cut through forests, and were sometimes only narrow trails.

"Our outfit, the Woolf's, consisted of father, mother, six children, two wagons and Henry Matkin, aged twelve, who helped drive the cattle and horses. There were thirty-six head of stock in the two outfits.

" . . . We had two good teams of mares, other horses and cows and a white pony called Peter that all except the youngest child could ride when he was not otherwise on duty. One of our two wagons had a set of bed-springs fitted to an extension on the double-bed wagon box. This was for mother and the children.

"Aunt Zina's wagon was arranged the same way. All the wagons had two boxes and were well packed. These extension wagons carried prepared sandwiches and rusks in case it was necessary to satisfy our hunger while still driving to find camping places and water for the horses. They also carried changes of clothing, extra bedding and other emergency or needful commodities.

"Fastened on the back, outside of the two extension wagons were mother's rocking chair and Aunt Zina's camp chair. Our second wagon held bags of oats, flour, potatoes, and other vegetables, packed trunks of clothing, wooden wash tubs and wash board, and such things as hand plow, camp stove, shovel, axe, wrenches, wagon grease, pewter and tin table utensils, candle molds, bullet molds, nose bags for feeding oats to the horses, cooking pots and utensils, all of iron; tea-kettle, bake oven, frying pans; a rack made at one stop to accommodate a new-born calf which during the crossing of one very steep river had to be taken into the front of the wagon.

"Most of the towns we had looked forward to visiting were disappointingly small. I remember Camas, Swan Lake and Pocatello. The last was a small place which seemed to me to be surrounded by Indian encampments. I remember being impressed with the clean, bright appearance of the Indians, Bannocks, and of their surroundings. They seemed to be different and of a higher class than the Indians I had seen at home. We had no difficulty with them but kept careful watch over our stock.

"There were endless miles of sage brush, rough roads and often mud holes from which it took four and sometimes six horses to drag us.

"When Johnny was needed to assist others, or find fords, Mamie or I cared for young Joseph while his mother drove team and Sterling drove cattle.

"The cows sometimes became lame with cracked hoofs or with gravel in them. At such time two or three days' stop-over was necessary. The hooves were washed clean of gravel, filled with tar and wrapped with gunny sacking.

"During the layovers the women did the necessary baking and cooking, washing and mending. This also was the time when Aunt Zina and mother made as many light loaves of bread as was possible; and for bathing in the front of the wagons, with washtubs replacing the spring seats, and with covers drawn. . . .

"Wagon wheels scretched and groaned and bumped along over long stretches of prairie when prairie dogs came out in numbers and barked at the intruders as we passed. A lone wolverine drank without fear from a stream that we crossed. There were many coyotes and badgers.

"From now on there were no roads, only old trails with ruts, stones, stumps and tree roots to keep us bumping. There were often stormy days with both snow and rain to add to the discomfort.

"It was often so cold the wagon covers had to be drawn tight and smooth over the bows and made close at the back. Often blankets were hung at the front, back of the driver, as well as at the back, to keep the cold and the driving rain and sleet out.

"What a happy relief when the sun shone and the front cover could be thrown back so we could feel the warmth! How pleasant to be able to see where we were and to look for something besides snow, mud and sage-brush! What an extreme joy we felt when we camped in the mountains where the steep slopes were covered with towering pines from which the boys brought us pine nuts!

"Weather permitting, we spent our evenings around the campfire. Sitting on spring-seats from the wagons, on packing boxes or fallen logs we listened to the sweet strains of the mouth organ played by Will Rigby and Brother John. One of the favorite songs of all was 'Hard Times Come Again No More', though often we sang hymns such as 'All is Well', and 'Oh Ye Mountains High, Where The Clear, Blue Sky Arches Over The Homes of The Free'. After prayers of praise and thanksgiving and petitions for continued guidance we retired to rest as best we might in cramped and crowded spaces.

"On reaching Helena it was found there was not enough water for bathing purposes so the children were bathed in skim milk.

"We made butter by tying the jar containing the cream to the back of the wagon. By night the jolting of the wagon had produced a nice pat of fresh butter, and the buttermilk made a refreshing drink. Carrying the milk had been a problem. At Helena mother purchased a tall tin dasher churn in which more butter at a time could be made. The milk was placed in covered pans and jars at night, the thick cream skimmed into the churn, and all the milk that could not be used or given away was thrown away. We could not permit the cows to go unmilked or they would dry up.

"There had been on our trip, no serious accidents, but two very close ones and in one mother was the victim.

"An axe in the hands of one of the young men chopping wood had flown off the handle and struck mother on the side of the head and she had fallen, fainting. The spot over her temple was very painful and she suffered from headaches. But she had good care and soon recovered.

"A horse kicked the Farrell driver, George Thompson, on the leg, but he too had good care and was soon able to take over his job again.

"The pioneers knew what to do in almost every case of accident or sickness, whether travelling or at home.

"Another near accident involved both mother and Wilford. While camped on Boulder Mountain a sudden dynamite blast from railroad workers sent a shower of rocks down the side. One huge boulder bounded down close to Wilford and just missed mother where she was dipping water from the stream. Camp was hastily moved to a safe distance.

"On the ninth of May, President Card and company,

travelling south, met the first advance company headed north for the new colony. By horse Brother Card travelled on to meet his family.

"Johnny, as usual driving the lead team, spotted the lone khaki clad rider approaching. The man alighted, tied his horse to a post of the wire fence along one side of the road and started for the wagon train.

"Johnny kept his eye on him, and as he stopped Aunt Zina's team, climbed in her wagon and kissed her, Johnny shouted to father who drove the team just behind him, 'Pa, that old galoot is getting in Aunt Zina's wagon . . . He's kissing her!'

"Father had recognized his bewhiskered friend, C.O. Card, and gave the go-ahead sign and the wagon wheels rolled along.

"It was a joyful camp-making near Little Boulder Range that night. Brother Card recorded in his journal, 'It was a happy meeting to join my family and friends who had toiled through weeks of cold, stormy weather, over snow-capped mountains, hills and bleak plains. I found them in good spirits for they had leaned on the Lord.'

"The next morning, May 13th, we awoke to find six inches of snow on the ground and still snowing. There was poor food for the stock and no wood here, so we hitched up without breakfast and drove on about ten miles to within three-quarters of a mile of Little Boulder Mountain. Here we found plenty of water and snow-covered grass.

"However, the men borrowed a large tent from nearby railroaders, cleared away the snow, set it up, cut pine boughs to spread over the floor, spread horse blankets over them and made big fires without, and in the camp stoves within the big tent.

"The women cooked, the children played, the men talked with their leader and exchanged experiences. We ate together but slept in our wagons and were warm and comfortable. The next day the weather cleared and we drove on to the north side of Big Boulder Mountain . . .

"Occasionally we saw ahead of us a long mule or ox-team with several wagons drawn close together and an equal number of teams in front with the driver walking beside them cracking a long black whip over their backs. We never did get close enough to hear the language they used, though the ferocity of their voices left no doubt as to its meaning.

"From this point on near Choteau we had to start night-herding the horses. Brother Card took the first part of the night to 1 A.M. and father took the balance of the night. We were nearing Indian country and must be careful.

"We camped about six miles south of Dupuyer near a beautiful spring of water on May 27th, and on the 28th we camped on the north bank of Birch Creek on the Peigan

Reservation. Our wagons were growling in the congealed hub grease.

"On the next day we drove to the Indian agency to procure lumber to build a boat as the streams were swelling with the melting snow from the mountains. We waited for the stock and the men who helped to get them across Badget Creek, then drove to Medicine River which was very high.

"An Indian named Peter was engaged for the price of $2.50 to guide us to a safer crossing. About one and a half miles on, a place was found where the river had spread. Up-rooted trees and much debris had been carried down stream on the muddy waters. On examination it was found the approach to the river had been washed away and a new one must be dug out.

"While the new approach was being made ready, three Indian Police brought a note into camp written by the agent, Mr. W.D. Baldwin which read as follows:

May 29, 1887, To Whom It May Concern: A white or gray horse in your outfit is claimed as the property of one of the Indians belonging to the Agency. You will at once return to the Agency and account for same. The bearer is one of our Indian Police, the Captain of the force. Very truly, W.D. Baldwin.

"Peter, our white horse which we had brought from Hyde Park with us, was the horse in question.

"Henry Matkin had been riding him as he drove the cattle when the Indian claimed him. Henry refused to give the horse up or even to dismount, so the Indian had led him into camp by the bridle. Father, accompanied by his friend Brother Farrell, returned to the agency at Dupuyer and during the examination by the agent, the Indian was asked if there were any identifying marks by which he could prove his ownership.

"The Indian pointed to black spots on the pony's legs and another Indian swore this was true.

"Quietly, father took out his jack knife, opened it out and cut the spots away. Mr. Baldwin said, 'Take your horse, Mr. Woolf and go.'

"A few nights before, the boys had gleefully held a pail of wagon grease while Johnny decorated Peter with buttons, gaiter-like, from hock to fetlock.

"But Peter the pony was kept near the wagons at nights from now on, and the wagons night-watched constantly.

"The Indians were very unfriendly and the chief sent word that our stock must be taken off their grazing lands at once. They were told that we intended to move as soon as a suitable crossing to the river could be made, but this did not satisfy them.

"Soon we could see them coming, headed by their chief, all in war paint and feathers.

"It was suggested that now would be a good time for the men to clean their firearms. Father had a pistol, relic of Indian troubles in the early days of Utah. Sterling Williams and Johnny each had a shot gun and there were one or two others in camp.

"The Indians came, but they made no trouble after looking the situation over and seeing that we were able to defend ourselves. However they made frequent visits while the work was in progress of making an approach to the river crossing.

"None seemed friendly or would give information as to the best place for the approach to be made.

"A gravel bar had been located by Johnny under President Card's direction. One of father's wagons was in the lead with two teams of horses attached. Johnny rode one horse of the lead team while father handled the lines.

"There was much debris, and occasionally an uprooted tree came down the muddy stream, but it was not known that the treacherous waters had undermined the river bank at this point causing a jump-off for the horses, and a sudden drop-off for the front wheels.

"The sudden plunge caused an empty two-gallon stone jar in the back of the wagon to fly out at the front, grazing my head and striking one of the horses. There was no time for inquiries or explanations as the hind wheels quickly followed with a jolt.

"Those behind watched with apprehension and all were greatly relieved when the opposite side was reached in safety.

"It was June 1st, at 10 A.M. when Brother Card stopped his team and helped Aunt Zina to alight over the wagon wheel. They stood by a pile of stones. He waved his hat and shouted something which none could hear but all understood.

"Wagons were drawn up while smiling occupants climbed out over the wagon wheels and gave their heartiest salutes: 'Hurrah for Canada!' 'Canada or bust!' 'Three cheers for Canada!'

"Laughter and gladness on every side: Snatches of songs were sung. Each then selected a stone which was added to the fast growing mound which marked the boundary line.

"We had reached the new home land. We were nearing the end of the trail. The new land was indeed an ever-growing source of wonder and delight.

"Sagebrush had been left behind. Instead were wide, rolling prairies covered with tall, waving prairie bunchgrass and wild flowers in profusion — bluebells, yellow sweetpea, Indian paint brush, cranebills and buttercups.

"There was one thing resembling home — the Rocky

Mountains — a wondrous range, with majestic, square-topped Chief Mountain stationed in front as if to give strength and courage to our undertaking.

"There was the morning sun coming up out of the prairie, the lone days, numerous lakes dotting the landscapes, and teeming with a variety of wild fowl.

"We drove north as far as Willow Creek and camped about 2 P.M. at a spot where the Taylorsville school house now stands. Johnny shot two wild ducks. What a welcome change to the bill of fare! It began to rain as soon as camp was made and kept it up all night until about noon on the following day.

"Thursday, June 2nd, was Fast Day; accordingly, fast meeting was held and special prayers offered for our continued safety, especially in crossing the swollen waters of the St. Mary's River. Some Indians had recently drowned in the treacherous and ever-swelling stream.

"Works must ever accompany the faith of these hardy pioneers, so after the prayer meeting they immediately set to work to build a flat-bottomed boat to aid in the crossing. The lumber they had bought was soon converted into a boat.

"On arising at 3 A.M. the following morning, June 3rd, President Card was delighted to find there had been a severe frost during the night. Arousing the camp, an early start was made.

"They were met at St. Mary's River by Sergeant Brimmer of the North-West Mounted Police, who informed them that because of the frost the water had fallen eighteen inches, and that it would not be necessary to use the boat. This word was received with great relief and gratitude, for all felt that an answer to their prayers had been graciously granted by Providence.

"On his excellent mount, Sergeant Brimmer very kindly gave the men all possible assistance.

"The wagon boxes were tied down so they could not float away. Even so, the water ran in, soaking everything. With the sergeant piloting the way, several trips were made with double team each time, crossing and recrossing, until the seven wagons were safely across as well as the stock and drivers. The crossing had been accomplished in four hours at ten A.M., when they were across, it began to rain again.

"They later learned that by sundown of that day the St. Mary's was again at its former high level.

"On they went joyfully, for travelling in the rain was no hardship now as they looked forward to the last lap of the long journey. No more rivers to cross; no more mountains to climb; peace and rest from weary travel was soon to be had for all, after an eight weeks' trip.

"Lee's Creek was just ahead.

"There was now talk of home. 'We'll be home tonight.' 'How good it will seem to be home.' 'Just wait 'til we get home . . .'

"On arriving at the location in the rain, with the long, sodden grass lying flat, the trees drooping and dripping, one wagon box in sight on the ground, on the east side of Lee's Creek, Wilford, aged four, clasped his arms about mother and looking into her face, said woefully, 'Ma, you said we'd be home tonight.'

" 'Yes, dear,' she said. 'This is home from now on.'

" 'With quivering lips and brimming eyes he asked, 'If this is home, where's all the houses?'

"Mother gazed around too, who can tell with what longing, but bravely and cheerfully she reassured him with promises of a home and happiness until all felt that spirit.

"A new country to subdue, wet weather overhead and

underfoot could not dampen the spirits of that dauntless company . . ."

* * * *

They are gone now, every one.

And on headstone after headstone is carved the one-word epitaph that is the proudest any Albertan can earn: "Pioneer."

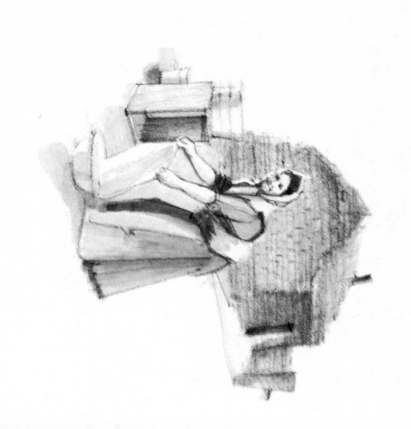

LIVING CONDITIONS

"I do not remember living in a tent, as the first year we were here father built a small 2 room log cabin with dirt floors and sod roof with a quilt hung up for a door.

"Conditions were not ideal, but we were very happy."

— Mary Amanda Anderson Layton, pioneer

* * * *

BE IT EVER SO HUMBLE . . .

Weeks and months of hardships on the trail were bad enough, but they were only beginning for the Alberta pioneer.

Starting with only land and water and sky — and the meagre supplies packed in his wagon — he had to plunge immediately into a struggle for survival.

If he came to ranch, there was a herd to tend day and night; protecting his cattle from wolves and fighting his animals' instinctive tendency to drift back to their old homes again. And he had to persuade the Indians that, despite superficial resemblance, domestic cattle weren't just another breed of buffalo and it wasn't considered good form to hunt them.

If he came to homestead, there was the desperate rush to turn the soil, plant and harvest, so that there would be crops to turn into cash, and food to feed his family.

And, always, the pioneer was goaded by the knowledge of winter's inevitable sweep from the north.

With so much to tend to at first, the pioneer rarely wasted much thought on the issue of a home. A tent or, failing that, the wagon he came in would serve well enough until the pressure was off.

But, sooner or later, the pioneer husband would return to the supper campfire to face a determined wife, pot in hand, wanting to know when she was going to get a house to live in.

Given her determination (and the fact the pot was solid iron) the husband usually found it wise to promise an immediate plunge into the construction industry.

On open prairie, however, it was easier to promise a house than to build one.

For one thing, wood — the key ingredient — was almost always missing. Scrawny willow and aspen were fine for firewood, but they weren't the stuff of the building trade.

So the pioneer wife with visions of a gabled roof and sweeping porch was in for an unpleasant surprise.

If there were a hill somewhere around, she could expect to make her first home in a dug-out: a shallow, man-made cave extended outward with a few poles and a little canvas.

To get house-sized logs usually involved a long trek, hard hauling, and time the pioneer didn't have. Lumber was even harder to get — assuming there was a sawmill around at all — and it cost cash he couldn't afford to pay.

Inside, a low platform raised the bed from the dirt floor. There'd be a crate for a table and an oil lamp for light. An open fire still served as both furnace and cooking range. Where there wasn't a suitable hill around, the usual alternative was a sod shack.

Foot-thick strips of sod were cut from the prairie, then stacked in a square the way a child makes a tower of blocks. When the shack was high enough, poles were laid across the top and shingled with still more sod. The only openings, usually, were for a door and crude chimney.

Interior furnishings differed little from those of a dugout. The only likely addition was a square metal stove.

The sod shack's efficiency as a house was summed up wryly (by a woman, of course) in 1884:

"On this first visit, Mrs. Shaw laughingly told of waiting in Mr. Barker's cabin with an umbrella held over her to keep dry until the storm subsided.

"The rain inside, under the sod roof, often continued after the storm outside was over . . ."

There is hardly a pioneer wife in Alberta who doesn't remember at least one winter day in a sod shack, with frozen dirt underfoot and frost seeping in the walls. With smoke swirling from the stove to sting her eyes and a pail of snow waiting to melt.

Wondering, over a coughing child, if freedom doesn't sometimes have too high a price.

* * * *

LACE-TRIMMED CURTAINS COVERED THE WINDOWS . . .

Sooner or later, the pioneer wife got the house she'd asked for in the first place. It often took time — a year or two — and the arrival of enough neighbors for help in its construction. But the day would finally come when she could leave the sod shack behind — maybe stopping long enough to help push down its walls before she did.

One of the best descriptions we have of these first true "houses" comes again from the written history of early Cardston:

"The first homes were alike, built to the square, the gable ends with beams and floor joists. The roofs were covered with rough lumber, tar paper and squares of sod placed closely together.

"The chimneys were five-gallon coal-oil cans fitted in a square hole in the roof through which the stove pipe was thrust.

"The walls were chinked with split timber and plastered inside and out. The floors were made of rough lumber either

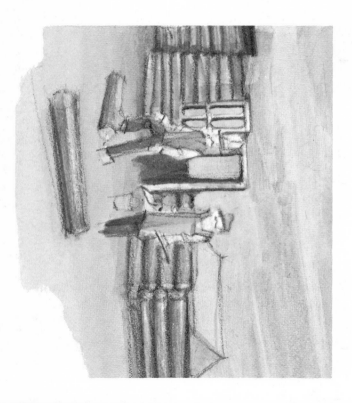

sawed with a whipsaw or hauled from Lethbridge with the doors, windows, nails and tar paper.

"The whipsaw was set up on a steep bank on the J.A. Hammer lot. A pit was dug, a log was marked with a string dipped in flour or charcoal and flipped along the length of the log.

"One man operated his end of the saw by standing in the pit, another handled his end from the bank above. Lumber soon began to pile up when it was found that the boards brought from Lethbridge did not suffice.

"All of the men could do carpentering of a sort . . .

"None had reason to be ashamed of his house or furniture, all were so nearly alike and the best to be had at the time — homemade tables, benches, stools, wash benches and corner cupboards nailed to walls.

"For the beds, short lengths of small peeled logs or poles were nailed to walls and floor at the proper height for beds. Poles were fitted and securely nailed to these and bed springs placed on top.

"Where there were not sufficient feather beds or mattresses, bed ticks were filled with straw or hay, placed on the floor at night, or on low trundle beds which were pushed under the stationary bed at night, or on top of another bed.

"For a dressing table three coal-oil cases were used. Two, upended with shelves and with a third laid on its side across the top, left a space between where another small box could be placed.

"Half of the top box had a hinged lid. Covered with curtains and a lace-trimmed scarf, these could be made to look very dainty and were exceedingly useful. Candles, coal oil lamps, and various toilet articles were put on top and a mirror hung on the wall above.

"Nearly every family had brought with them engraved

or enlarged family portraits, daguerrotypes and tin-types of family and relatives left behind. These were hung on the walls or placed on the improvised dresser tops. Some brought their choice hair flowers in shadow-box frames to decorate the walls.

"The floors were covered with home-woven rag carpets over layers of clean wheat straw, and those lucky enough to obtain buffalo robes from the Indians spread these on the floor on which children could tumble about. These were also used as laprobes in the winter.

"Homespun, lace-trimmed curtains covered the windows. All the lace was hand-made.

"Wood-burning stoves had four holes, a wide removable hearth in front which hid the ashes from view. The oven doors swung outward and were fastened with a latch. There were no reservoirs or warming ovens.

"These were soon replaced with coal ranges and new utensils replaced the heavy iron pots, bake ovens and skillets, the brass buckets, and wooden tubs."

* * * *

BEHIND EVERY WELL-FED MAN . . .

"*The women were all experts at making a variety of breads such as salt-rising, graham gems, cornmeal Johnny cake, pancakes and biscuits made with buttermilk and soda, and now that the potatoes were dug and stored they once again had their delicious potato-yeast bread.*" (*Recollections of a pioneer — female*)

"*The bread was fried and, of course, it was as hard as wood. After setting until the next meal, it was so hard you could knock a cow down with it." (Recollections of another pioneer — male)*

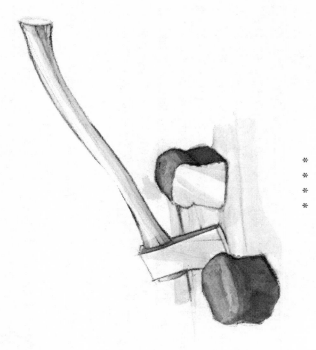

* * * * *

A WORD FROM THE KITCHEN . . . .

Pioneer women sometimes complain that historians (male historians, that is) give the impression that the west was won by man alone.

Not so, argue those like Dora Trew of Lethbridge. If the man was in front, she claims, the woman was never more than a step or two behind — and usually dragging a stone-boat to boot.

Discussing the life of the pioneer woman, she paints a fascinating picture of domesticity in a growing Alberta:

"A typical kitchen in those days centred, of course, around the cooking range with its warm-air oven above, its tank of hot water attached to one side, its coal-bucket close by. Coal was not too hard to find in the south; it sometimes could be dug out of the side of a coulee, or obtained around the vicinity of Lethbridge. If the bucket was empty, one could go out onto flat prairie and gather 'buffalo chips'.

"Nearby was the big table with its chairs or benches and beside the door, because it was handiest for filling, stood the barrel of water with its long-handled dipper. There was the broom, the big tin tub, the laundry wash-boiler hanging on the wall, and the modest coal oil can, its long spout stopped with a small potato.

"There was usually a cot or bed squeezed in somewhere. In one corner stood the triangular shelf with its wash basin, beside it the roller towel, that handy, rolling symbol of a heroic age, that played such an important part along with the canned tomato and dried apple.

"If the women lived on the prairie as most of them did in the beginning, the water usually had to be hauled from a river or well on a stone-boat.

"This was a contraption with a flat platform on heavy runners, that did double duty by hauling away stones when clearing the land. It was dragged easily enough over the prairie grass, but where would you find a place for it today?

"Water was so valuable that it was mostly used for cooking and drinking, though of course one had to wash occasionally.

"For the family laundry the housewife had the pleasure in winter of hauling in snow and melting it in the big copper boiler where the clothes were boiled, and afterwards scrubbed on a washboard. However, these clothes flapping on the line (or on the fence) were something to be admired.

"In the small towns that grew up there developed the 'water-man' who hauled water from the river in tanks. In Lethbridge, for instance, it was delivered three times a week at a cost of $2 per month.

"In winter he seemed a replica of the modern Wizard of Oz as he staggered up the yard, a pail of water in each hand, making a silken rustling sound as he walked. From his coat and elbows hung snapping icicles and the drips from his pails froze instantly into little round balls.

"Finally he would reach the back door, sloshing into the kitchen with a big blast of cold air, spilling as he went, and always with a cheery word for everyone as he turned away.

"But of course all this improved as time went on. Finally came the waterworks in small towns. In Lethbridge it appeared from the taps in the spring break-up as a sort of thin mud. It was cleared for drinking by settling with alum, then boiled to settle the germs, and by this time was nasty enough to settle anyone but an old-timer.

"I can recall the horrified expression on the face of an aunt from England when mother nonchalantly turned a thick, steaming mass of this gruel into the bathtub.

"At about this period our waterworks became out of order until an enterprising plumber found, and removed, from the tank, the remains of a fish.

"Pioneer white women did not have too much to do with that horror, pemmican, but some of them had their experiences with the unpalatable stone-like bun called 'hardtack'. It was made of flour, water, and salt, fried or baked, and, like pemmican, was sometimes served with an axe. There were such luxuries as beans and 'larup', a sort of light molasses which provided sweetness, and occasionally there were dried fruits.

"However, after the early days of buffalo meat, there were many splendid dishes made savory by being cooked in iron utensils.

"The cellar was usually well-stocked with foods by autumn. In our home, we managed to get rid of a whole ton of potatoes, not to mention two barrels of apples, which around 1900 were sent out yearly from 'down east'. Eggs were preserved in big crocks of lime or dipped in boiling water, wrapped and stored . . ."

* * * *

MEANWHILE AT THE COSMOPOLITAN . . .

If the Alberta pioneer ever found home fare dull, well, he could always take a run into a town like Medicine Hat, tie up at the Cosmopolitan Hotel, and have a meal that would — judging from the Christmas menu that follows — more than satisfy any appetite.

Russian Caviar on Toast

Chiffonade Celery   White Onions

Green House Lettuce   Queen Olive

Sliced Tomatoes   Sliced Cucumbers

SOUPS

Potage Alexandrine   Consomme Renaissance

FISH

Boiled B.C. Halibut and White Sauce

Boiled Columbia Sole and Genoise Sauce

(Wafer Potatoes)

SWEET ENTREES

King Apple in Sponge Ring

New York Chocolate Eclair & Rignet Sauce

Rabbit Cutlets Breaded and Calf's Head Sauce

Young Pigeon, aux Gelee

Broiled Oysters, Maitre de Hotel

BOILED

Sugar Cured Ham and Champagne Sauce

Sheep's Tongue au Gelee

Boiled Chicken and Almond Sauce

ROASTS

Young Alberta Turkey, Marjral Dressing
and Cranberry Sauce (Weaners)

Tenderloin of Beef and Yorkshire Pudding

Suckling Pig and Sauce Pomme

Spring Chicken and Bourginotte Sauce

Mallard Duck and Crab Apple Jelly

Roast Goose and Walnut Dressing

COLD MEATS

Turkey   Chicken   Goose   Duck   Ham

Ox Tongue

VEGETABLES

Steamed Potatoes   Lyonnaise Potatoes

Mashed Potatoes

French Green Peas   Wax Beans

SALADS

Russian Salad   Shrimp Salad   Hamard Salad

Fruit Salad

RELISHES

Lee and Perrin's Sauce   Mixed Pickles

Sweet Pickles   Chow Chow

Tomato Catsup   Pickled Beets

Pickled Walnuts

PUDDING

English Plum Pudding with Cognac or Hard Sauce

COLD SWEETS

Fruit Trifle   Fruit Pudding

PASTRY

Deep Apple Pie with Whipped Cream

Boston Cream Pie   Hot Mince Pie

Citron Tart

For those hardy enough to continue, the menu goes on to list 11 varieties of cakes, six varieties of jellies and a whole host of "desserts."

The wine list includes Champagne (Mumm's Extra Dry), Claret (Julien), Port Wine, Dry Catawba and St. Augustine. The Cosmopolitan's price for permission to tackle the feast was one slim dollar. Wine (and bicarbonate of soda) extra, of course.

* * * *

For most of the earlier settlers, of course, a feast at the Cosmo — even at $1 — was a luxury hopelessly out of reach. Many didn't have a dollar, and even those who did couldn't leave ranch or homestead untended that long.

So it was left to the ingenuity of the prairie wife to make a feast of what could be grown or hunted. Sometimes, as the following ditty of the period illustrates, she didn't succeed:

"Rabbits young, rabbits old
Rabbits hot, rabbits cold
Rabbits tender, rabbits tough
Thank you Sir, I've had enough"

* * * *

*

LONELY TIME, PARTY TIME . . .

Sen. F.W. Gershaw, recalling the lives of the pioneers, paints a bleak picture of conditions in early Alberta:

"Married men usually went alone, and got their families out when they had some accommodation. There were many difficulties. Water was scarce, the flies were bad, stores were far away and money was scarce. The roof often leaked and wood or coal was very hard to obtain.

"The settlers were lonesome and often discouraged. The women in particular deserve great credit for the heroic way they lived. They kept the homes, managed to prepare food and taught the children. They read the Bible and tried to maintain their religious beliefs. They would walk miles to help a neighbor in trouble.

"Some of the bachelor homesteaders developed mental trouble. Loneliness, poor food, worry and lack of cleanliness on account of water being so hard to get, in some cases, caused a departure from the normal way of acting.

"It was a hard life . . ."

Oh, it was a hard life all right. But not so hard, as Sen. Gershaw acknowledges, that a man forgot how to laugh.

And there wasn't a man or woman in pioneer Alberta

whose toe didn't start tapping to the sound of a fiddle, or who wouldn't struggle into a boiled shirt or a thick layer of petticoats at the prospect of a party.

And early Albertans could turn anything from the opening of a church hall to the raising of a barn into a party.

"They'd come from as far as 50 miles away," muses one pioneer, "with bull teams, buckboards, prairie schooners, buggies, or on horseback.

"Max Broulette fiddling away; John Smith, master of ceremonies calling out his hoarse commands from a point of vantage on a packing box.

"Many of the men were married to Indian women; the women arriving in their best print dresses, on their backs the babies which were blanketed and stowed away under seats or benches.

"It was not an uncommon joke for some of the young cowboys to change the wrappings on these bundles of young natives and when the mothers returned home they would discover they had the wrong offspring!

"The big social event of the year was the military ball given by the NWMP, attended by people from all over Alberta.

"The ladies, fashionably dressed in their silk gowns, and the red-coated Mounties in full dress, made a gay sight as they danced the lancers, the military schottische, the ripple waltz, mazurka or three-step . . . ."

* * * *

SO I SAYS TO THE QUEEN . . .

Pioneer Albertans had dozens of ways to entertain themselves in the inevitable intervals between dances, but no way was more popular than story-telling.

Probably the undisputed champion in this department was Fred Stimson, owner of the famous Bar-U Ranch in High River.

In 1887, it seems, he went to London to attend the celebrations connected with Queen Victoria's Jubilee:

"Well, boys," Fred said, propping his feet up on the bunk-house stove, "on my arrival in London I went straight to the Hotel Cecil and had scarcely got nicely settled in my quarters when a bellhop came and said I was wanted on the telephone.

"I went at once to the booth and took up the receiver. A sweet-voiced woman said, 'Is that Mr. Fred Stimson, of High River, Alberta, Canada?' to which I replied that my name and address were quite correct.

"I nearly dropped dead with surprise when I was next informed that it was Queen Victoria speaking. I was 'so flabbergasted that I could only say: 'Oh, your Majesty! I have often heard of you.'

"But she put me quite at ease by saying, 'And I have very often been informed of you and your doings in the far West, Mr. Stimson. I hear that you are stopping at the Cecil?'

" 'Yes, your Majesty,' I replied, 'and I am very comfortable.'

" 'No doubt you are, Mr. Stimson, but I should like you to visit us at Buckingham Palace, and as we have rooms to burn here, I shall send the carriage for you.'

"With this she rang off. I knew of course, that a royal invitation was a command and I had scarcely got my traps together when I chanced to look out of the window. My heart nearly stopped beating when I saw the royal coach drawn by four white horses with outriders and postilions standing in front of the hotel.

"You should have seen the flunkies of the Cecil dance

attendance on me — they took me for some pumpkins, I can tell you.

"We drove at once to Buckingham Palace, and who should meet me at the door but Queen Victoria herself. She told off a couple of servants in livery to convey my luggage to a suite of rooms reserved for me.

"You ought to have seen the wonderful paintings and Oriental rugs that you sank into when you walked on them, and a bed with a canopy over it and all of the other gorgeous things that you see in a palace.

"Well, boys, it was all very fine for a time, but after a while it began to pall on me so I went down town to see the sights and falling in with some Canadian visitors in London, I stayed out pretty late.

"Next morning at breakfast the Queen, who had come to know me pretty well by this time, said, 'Fred, you were a little late in getting home last night.'

"'Yes, your Majesty,' I said, 'I met in with some western friends and — ' but she cut me short with 'Oh yes, I understand, boys will be boys, but for your convenience I shall see that you are supplied with a latch-key.'

"Well, I received the key and carried it about with me, but a few evenings later, when strolling down Picadilly, I ran into a bunch of Alberta boys and we made a night of it. I got back to Buckingham at about three a.m. and fiddled around with the latch key for a time.

"Presently I heard a window overhead go up and a soft voice called out, 'Is that you, Fred?'

"Recognizing it at once as that of the Queen, I replied, 'It is, your Majesty, I have the latch-key all right, but I can't find the keyhole.'

"'Never mind,' said she, 'just wait until I put on my crown and I'll come down and let you in.'

"And sure enough," Fred concluded with appropriate solemnity, "she did."

* * * *

THE DECEASED CAME TO HER DEATH . . .

If some men were good at telling a story, there were others who were just as good at providing the real-life material for one. Such a man was Jack Symonds, one of the early members of the North-West Mounted Police.

John D. Higinbotham of Lethbridge writes of running into the good Mr. Symonds at Wood Mountain detachment in the early 1880's.

"Jack," explains Mr. Higinbotham, "acted as cook and batman for 'Paper Collar Johnnie,' as Inspector A.R. Macdonnell was irreverently nick-named, and took fearsome liberties with his master's food.

"Whenever beefsteak was to be cooked for breakfast Jack usually prepared (?) it by tossing it upon the kitchen floor and jumping on it with his long boots, and then throwing it against the walls or ceiling before putting it in the frying-pan.

"These culinary liberties, or eccentricities, were, fortunately for Jack, not reported to the Inspector or solitary confinement on bread and water might have been his portion."

Jack Symonds brought his cooking career to its climax in an incident that made him story-material all over Alberta — and came close to costing him his neck.

It was touched off by the sudden death of an Indian woman on the Blood Reserve, and the verdict handed down by the coroner's jury. The written decision tells the whole story:

"That the deceased came to her death . . . by poison ad-

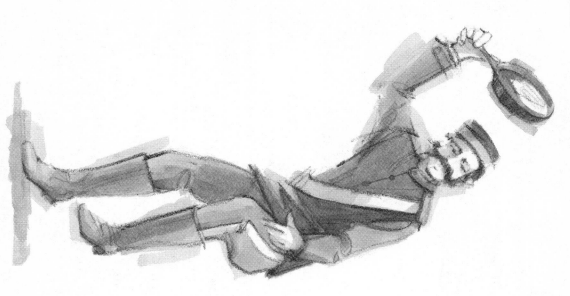

ministered by John Symonds, of the North-West Mounted Police, OR ELSE by eating too large a quantity of sour beans."

Although there were some who grumbled that Jack's cooking made the first alternative more than likely, the verdict's "or else" saved his skin.

* * * *

And, of course, there was many a green-horn or remittance man who went away convinced by the solemn assurance of an Alberta pioneer that the rags hung on fences by survey teams were really large handkerchiefs for the cattle to blow their noses.

Oh yes, this new land of Alberta was tough country all right. And the people who tamed it had to put up with leaky cabins and poor food and every other variety of hardship.

But they never forgot how to laugh.

RANGE RIDERS

PISTOL PERSUASION . . .

John Ware, the famous Negro cowboy and foreman of the Bar-U Cattle Company, was away when the two strangers rode onto the spread.

The pair found owner Fred Stimson and demanded the return of a horse they claimed they had raised, but which now bore the brand of the Bar-U.

Stimson, a deceptively mild-mannered man, was enraged at the suggestion he was a horse thief, but he chose not to show it. Instead he decided to try the course of sweet reason, and listened politely as the two armed and angry men described the animal they had come to get.

Finally, Stimson saddled up and led the two out to where the ranch horses were grazing. He sat quietly as his visitors again laid adamant claim to a white gelding, then just as quietly pointed out the animal's mother which, like the gelding in question, had been raised from birth on the Bar-U.

The strangers, growing uglier by the minute, insisted they were going to take the horse anyway.

At that moment, John Ware came riding up. Stimson turned to him:

"John, you know this gelding we call Billy?"

Ware nodded. "Yes sir, I sure do. We brought him up from a colt. What of it?"

"Well, John, these two gentleman claim that he belongs to them. What are we going to do about it?"

Ware's hand blurred across his holster and before the two startled strangers knew what had happened they were taking turns looking down the barrel of the foreman's .45 Colt. There was an ominous click as Ware cocked back the hammer.

"Shall I kill 'em now, boss," Ware asked softly, "or will I wait until they take the horse?"

Not anxious to hear Stimson's answer, the strangers abruptly wheeled their horses and fled in a cloud of dust.

* * * *

WITH HOPE AND A REPEATING RIFLE . . .

The age of the open range in Alberta didn't last that long — only the 32 years from 1880 to 1912 — but it lasted long enough to create the particular stamp of outlook and temperament that marks an Albertan today.

Determination and self-reliance are still important qualities, and big factors in a province that hasn't stopped changing and growing.

But in 1880, determination and self-reliance weren't just important. They were vitally necessary if a man was going to survive in Alberta.

In Montana and Texas, by 1880, civilization in its least desirable forms was beginning to catch up with the cattleman. Precious range land was being cropped bare by flocks of sheep, and it was being cut away by the fences of newly-arrived farmers.

It seemed there just wasn't room for a rancher in the U.S.A. anymore.

More and more, cowmen found themselves staring northward to the rolling grasslands of southern Alberta. And, more and more, they were deciding to "try their luck" in an unsettled land.

It was a tempting gamble. And, thanks to Chinooks and good grass — and a healthy injection of British capital — it was going to pay off.

In 1880, of course, no one knew anything certain about any pay-off. All they knew about was the gamble itself.

Sure there were Chinooks. But Chinooks — in those areas where they came at all — were still only intervals in cold and stormy winters. And even good grass dries out in summers when there is no rain.

Nor was nature all that the pioneer rancher had to worry about. Open range land was an invitation to rustlers and horse-thieves, Indians had been made hostile by whiskey traders and wolfers, and police were few and far between.

It was the era of Mutiny Fleming; of young Jack De-Haven, rifle in one hand and pistol in the other, fleeing the law on both sides of the U.S.–Canadian border; and of Kid Currie on his blueberry roan — wanted for shooting the sheriff of a Montana town.

And, in 1891 at High River, Harry Longbaugh — the Sundance Kid — was breaking horses for a railroad contractor, and getting occasional visits from a friend by the name of Robert Le Roy Parker, alias Butch Cassidy.

The "law" of the range was a set of quick wits, a repeating rifle, and a fast hand with a Colt pistol.

* * * *

RANCHING THE BORDER COUNTRY . . .

Unlike most of the other pioneer ranchers in the border country of southeast Alberta, Bill Mitchell didn't speak with the twang of Montana or Texas. Rather, he spoke with the soft burr of his Kippen, Scotland birthplace.

Bill was a boy of 10 when he and his family had their first taste of Alberta ranching at Elkwater Lake in 1888. There the youngster quickly learned how dearly pioneer ranchmen paid for their gambles in the unknown of the border country.

Years later, he could still recall the prairie fires that threatened to destroy the ranch time and time again. He remembered the timber wolves that prowled the calf sheds, and he remembered the bear-mauled carcass of a doe whose fawn he carried home and fed from a baby bottle.

Most vividly of all, he remembered the winter, one of his first in Canada, when hundreds of cattle perished in the deep snow. In the spring he watched the cattle that survived buckle under their own weight and lie helpless until ranch hands could come and put them out of their misery with rifle bullets.

Bill Mitchell watched carefully and learned, better than most, the lessons nature was teaching.

He was also quick to learn anything the shrewd cowboys on the ranch had to teach him.

"When I was 14," he recalled in an interview a couple of years before his death in 1946, "I'd ridden with Michel Quesnel (a former NWMP scout working as a horse-breaker at Elkwater) after Indians who'd run off with a bunch of the horses.

"Michel lost no time, and he knew his business. When we were leaving father told him to notify the Willow Creek detachment.

"Michel grunted a reply and we started up the old mill road behind the house, although the tracks showed they'd gone west toward the Medicine Lodge.

"He never intended going near the detachment, but rode straight south. We picked up their trail in Willow Creek and started crowding them hard.

" 'Indian cayuses have bad time driving that bunch,' he chuckled. 'We catch up leetle while now. They see us, then vamoose.'

"He was right. They only got away with two gentle saddle ponies they were able to catch. We rounded up the others under a cutbank and Michel roped two with a new rawhide lariat I'd helped him plait, and we started for home on fresh horses.

" 'Never waste time notifying police — git goin' your-self,' was his advice then, and I decided to follow it . . ."

Bill Mitchell was a good student. At 17, he staked squatter's rights on Willow Creek and was in business as owner of the LA Ranch — right in the middle of the best winter-grazing land in Alberta.

Three years later, Bill's father died, and left him heir to the Elkwater ranch, and heir to the responsibilities of caring for a large family of younger brothers and sisters.

Remembering the fate of the cattle at Elkwater, Bill moved all the stock to Willow Creek and turned the old ranch into a feed operation.

The Willow Creek ranch quickly became the rendezvous of cowpunchers for hundreds of miles around.

He remembered thousands of cattle grazing the hills and coulees. They came in from as far north as the Bow River. Many were "drifted" in by Montana ranchers who had been "sheeped out" and were poaching on the rich Canadian grass and winter range.

Everywhere, Mitchell recalled, you could see long-legged Texas steers with the horn-spread of a moose. Wild and wily with age, they were almost impossible to catch as they raced off at the first sight of a man on horseback.

Roundups were massive affairs, and cowboys criss-crossed the territory with pack-horse, branding iron and lariat — branding the calf crop where they found it.

Maverick cattle were considered the property of the first man to run a brand on them. Usually they were slaughtered for the chuck-wagon or sold to help defray operating expenses.

Cattle rustling, brand-working and butchering were all considered a form of free enterprise as long as they were confined to American stock. "After all," Bill Mitchell said explaining the rationale behind the practice, "ain't we feedin' the critters — thousands of 'em — free?"

The NWMP took a different view, but in so large a territory enforcement was all but impossible.

American beef finished on Canadian grass, grinned Bill Mitchell, "was shore toothsome."

And, as he pointed out, it wasn't all one way. Montana outfits were just as handy at drifting Canadian beef across the line during their fall round-ups.

The rugged border country between southeastern Alberta and Montana was ready-made for cattle rustlers and horse thieves.

Very often, Bill Mitchell explained, the Montana rustlers had confederates on the Canadian side of the border — "Sometimes they turned out to be fellows who had their feet under your table most of the time."

What made the situation intolerable for Alberta ranchers was the attitude across the border. In Montana there was a vigilante committee that "strung up" anyone preying on

Montana ranchers. But as far as the U.S.A. was concerned, rustlers had a free hand on the Canadian side of the line and once cattle had crossed the border there was little chance of recovery.

The NWMP, on the other hand, was diligent about returning any stock rustled from the U.S. side.

The policy of the Alberta rancher faced with a case of Montana rustlers, explained Mitchell, was "git after them yourself."

Not long after he started the LA Ranch, Mitchell was raided by horse thieves and, remembering the advice of old Michel Quesnel, he put the "git after them yourself" philosophy into practice.

He had a hunch the thieves were a Montana bunch known as the Bear Paws' Gang, and he rode hard to a cabin he knew they used. It was dark when he arrived.

"The lamp was lit when I rode up to the door. I recognized one of the men and walked in.

" 'I've come for my horses,' I told him. His eyes fairly popped. Then he shrugged, 'All right, kid, you win. They're in the corral and damn tired — the wild buggers.' "

It wasn't to be the last time Bill Mitchell would have to step boldly into possible trouble with outlaws. But, as he recalled years later, it wasn't outlaws who were responsible for the only two times in his life he was in serious danger; it was the weather.

The first time had come when he was only a boy and he and his brother had nearly perished in a blizzard. They survived only by the accident of running into a haystack in the storm.

The second time came years after his run-in with the Bear Paws' Gang.

Mitchell was riding along the Milk River alone when he

went snow blind. With all sense of direction lost, he had to trust his life to the instincts of his horse. On open range, a horse given his head would head home or to a place where he'd been frequently stabled.

Mitchell hoped fervently it would be the latter. The LA Ranch was 40 miles away.

"I tied a knot in the lines, and hung them over the pommel, giving my horse his head.

"For a long time he didn't go off a walk, but I could tell by the way he was feeling his way we were in rough country. Probably in the badlands and headed for the detachment at Pen d'Oreille — or maybe Spencer Bros.

"Then he started hazing along at a steady walking trot. He was evidently on a bare ridge, and from his blowing snorts I knew he was contented, and was on his way to stable and oats.

"After a while he slowed to a walk, stopped, snorted and turned back. When it happened a third time I figured he was looking for a way down a cutbank. I was right, and it was surely steep.

"Next there was a yelping of many dogs. Indians, b'gad! I picked up the lines and turned him toward the barking. A strong Indian lifted me off and helped me into a teepee. It was warm and smelled of kin-a-kin-ic and wood fire.

"I knew a little Cree and was able to make him understand to bring in my saddle. He spread my saddle blanket over me. It was still warm.

"The woman gave me a can of what tasted like sage tea, and put a warm pad on my eyes. It smelled like soaked buffalo grass and sure felt good.

"I drank a lot of the tea but I couldn't bring myself to the dog mulligan. Not for a long time. But finally I grew such an appetite I'd have eaten the old buck himself if he'd been in the pot.

"The morning I left I gave him what money I had — $7 or $8 maybe. Not much for all their care and kindness, but it bought a lot of flour in those days.

"Oh, yes, I was covered with fleas all right, but rearin' and prancin' like a grain-fed bronc.

It was no wonder that Bill Mitchell always fought the theory that wandering bands of Indians were to blame for killing beef. He always maintained that the real culprits were white men hiding behind the plight of hungry natives.

And to the end of his days, Bill Mitchell was always arguing — with a grin — that dog mulligan was "dashed good eating at that!"

* * * *

Not even so serious a business as rustling can keep the western sense of humor hidden for long.

Again it is Fred Stimson of the Bar-U who proves that even a court of law isn't immune from frontier wit.

Stimson's Bar-U was prosecuting a man for misbranding one of their cattle, and the defendant had hired walrus-shaped Paddy Nolan (the Alberta lawyer who was one of the best criminal lawyers in Canadian history) to act for him.

Stimson, as chief witness for the Crown, was in the witness box:

Mr. Nolan: "Your name is Frederick Stimson, I believe?"

Mr. Stimson: "It is, sir."

Mr. Nolan: "You spend most of your time riding the range, do you not?"

Mr. Stimson: "No, sir, I spend most of my time in bed."

Mr. Nolan: "You are very short-sighted, I believe, Mr. Stimson?"

Mr. Stimson: "No, sir, I am not."

Mr. Nolan: "Then why do you wear glasses?"

Mr. Stimson: "Oh, just for effect."

Mr. Nolan: "Now, Mr. Stimson, you claim that my client misbranded one of your cattle?"

Mr. Stimson: "I do, sir."

Mr. Nolan: "Please describe the animal to the Court?"

Mr. Stimson: "Well, it was an ordinary, everyday steer with a leg on each corner."

Mr. Nolan: (disgusted at not making any headway with the witness) "I believe, Mr. Stimson, that you regard yourself as something of a smart aleck?"

Mr. Stimson: "I am also informed that you do a little smart alecking yourself."

Mr. Nolan: (thoroughly exasperated) "That will do, Mr. Stimson. Your Lordship, I am through with the witness."

* * * *

NOW, ABOUT THAT DRINK....

Cowboy humor was honed in that toughest of arenas, the bunkhouse. And unfortunate indeed was the greenhorn who set himself up for a sample of it — particularly if the greenhorn was one of those frontier rarities, a travelling salesman.

The travelling salesman, stiff-collared and perspiring, was hanging over the bar and holding forth with excitement at seeing his first herd of buffalo.

Trying to stir some enthusiasm in his straight-faced cowboy audience, he offered to set up the drinks if anyone present had seen more than 100,000 buffalo at one time.

One of the audience, a famous joker, promptly volunteered the information that he had seen "a hundred million billion blessed buffalo at one time."

The salesman demanded details, not noticing the other cowboys were red-faced with the strain of not laughing, and the joker was delighted to comply.

He spun a tale of horror in which he and a troop of 50 men had been caught for five days in a buffalo stampede and each man fired his rifle steadily during that time to keep the troop from being run over.

"And finally," he told the pop-eyed drummer, "there was a break and we got across a river and up on a hill.

"It was a good job we did, because from there we could see the main body of buffalo coming."

* * * *

GOT EWE! . . .

Occasionally, if we can believe yet another cowboy tale, the greenhorn didn't always come out second-best in exchanges of humor with ranch hands.

Even though one can't help but be a little suspicious when the victim is a sheep rancher, the following story at least suggests the westerner was prepared to laugh at himself now and then:

The sheep rancher, despite grave misgivings, had broken down and hired a young British remittance man to work as a hand on the ranch.

Determined to test the foppish young gentleman early, the rancher assigned him the chore of rounding up a flock of sheep about a mile from the ranch house.

The young man seemed hesitant, and when pressed, admitted he didn't know what a sheep looked like. The rancher, rolling his eyes, pointed out that sheep are white and fuzzy and "Maybe I'd better send another man and a dog out with you to make sure you get them in."

The remittance man drew himself up to full height and thanked the rancher coldly, but added: "Won't really be necessary, sir. Quite capable of handling the little blighters myself. At Eton I attained some fame for my fleetness of foot, etc. and I'm sure I am quite capable."

The rancher pointed his new hand in the right direction and sat back to wait for results.

Hour followed hour and still the young man did not return. Finally, with the sun about to set, the rancher grew alarmed and prepared to set out in search of the greenhorn.

Just then, the remittance man, bedraggled and panting, stumbled in the door.

"I did my best, sir," he told the astonished rancher with visible anguish, "but try as I might I could only run down half a dozen of the little devils."

And, with that, he handed the rancher six struggling jack rabbits.

* * * *

HERE, PRINCE . . .

Western hospitality is legendary — almost as legendary as western informality.

It is doubtful that in any part of the world but Alberta would one illustrious newcomer have been given quite as casual an introduction:

"Prince, meet Billy-the-Buster. Billy, meet Prince."

"Howdy, Prince."

"Good afternoon, Mr. Billy-the-Buster," responded His Royal Highness, Edward, The Prince of Wales, with a bare-ly-suppressed grin.

* * * *

ROUND-UP DAYS . . . .

Most of the old cowboys are gone now. Only a few remain who can feel the warm tug of recollection when someone like the late Bill Mitchell writes of the bunkhouse where Michel Quesnel would wring lively French-Canadian tunes from a battered accordion while his saddle-mates plaited lariats, filled cartridges and moulded bullets in preparation for another day on the range.

One of the last survivors of that era is Bud Cotton, who now lives in Calgary. A talented wood-carver and a literate writer, Mr. Cotton is filled with chuckling memories of the years when he rode "night hawk", herding the saddle horses through the hours from dusk to dawn, on the Pat Burns spread.

"During the fall roundups," he explains, "on a real frosty morning, those cow ponies always had a hump in their backs, and no matter how hard you hauled up on the old latigo strap (the strap for tightening the saddle girth), the saddle seemed never to lie down.

"The cowpoke, with the chill of dawn in his bones and kinks in his frame from bedding down on the hard prairie, didn't feel at all anxious to fork old Dobbin, who was watching his every move with a malevolent eye.

"Sometimes, talking sweet nothings in the bronc's ear and easing gently into the saddle, you could coax·him out of camp without getting the coffee and bacon riled up too bad. Camp scenes at dawn were always interesting at any time of the year.

"The summer of 1912 found us camping at the Indian Head spring on the Blackfoot reservation. It was one of the P. Burns outfits, with Jack Monahan as wagon boss.

"There were 75-odd head of saddle broncs in our string and about 25 head of a rep string which brought the cavvies (saddle horses) up to a hundred, including the old bell mare.

"The chuckwagon was manned by our prize cook, Lee Quong. Don't know where Jack Monahan picked him up, but Lee sure was a good cook. He had been with the outfit for years. Many a hunk of pie and swig of java he has left out for me, the night hawk, in case it should be possible for me to slip in during the long night of riding herd on the wandering cavvie.

"Ask any of the old cowmen and they'll tell you, 'Sure we knew Jack Monahan.' He had been with the Burns outfit for over 30 years and to me, then a young punk, he was one of the best.

"Dawn would just be creeping over the ridges with wisps of fog still hanging around camp as I ran the cavvie into the rope corral strung up from the camp wagon. Jack would be waiting there with his rawhide coiled, and despite the fact that he had lost one hand in an accident, he would rope out the saddle string for the day's ride with never a miss.

"Sometimes I'd get in late with the bunch — and when I say late I mean about 6 a.m. — noticing I'd lost four or five head during the dark hours. On dark wet nights especially, it was hard to keep track of the cavvie. They roamed all night, and that meant sitting in the saddle and drifting with the bunch until daylight. By then you might be miles from camp. It was a case of rounding up what horses you had and hitting it for camp pronto, as the boys would be waiting.

"Jack would just seem to glance over the cavvie. 'Now where in hell is that J Flag bay? You been sleeping again, boy? Well, you brought in that old bell mare anyhow. You get some grub from Lee and hit out and hunt those lost horses.'

"The cow waddies (cow-punchers) that were on Jack's crew that summer, Sam Brown and Phil Bozart — Missouri — were top hands. Also included were Scotty Ross, Clem Hanson, Powder River and Jim Finch. Art, a Yank from Fort Worth, wrangled the horses during the day and an Indian by the name of Red Blanket also rode with the outfit — that is, when he and Jim Finch were not too busy trading horses and camp bacon.

"I remember it was that summer we had to ford a bunch of cows and calves across the Bow, the ferry having gone out during the high water a few days before, and we were having one hell of a time trying to get them started, for the calves would balk at the water's edge and mother cow would run back.

"Missouri, on a bet, chucked his clothes and swam across the cold, swift-running Bow, which was nearly half a mile wide at this point and tough swimming too. He was carried downstream quite a way but made it and brought back an old rowboat.

"This we loaded with some of the bawling calves. Their frantic mammies edged into the river trying to reach their infants and were soon swimming out and acting as leaders. We had the whole outfit swimming across the Bow.

"I can still remember how cold the water was, and how scared I was as some of the cattle, turning in the swift current, had riders and doggies all mixed up in the churning mess as we landed on the south bank.

"Another good cowpoke was Powder River — I never knew his real name — a local cowpoke, happy-go-lucky as they make them and always in trouble.

"I remember the morning I had brought in the saddle bunch and corraled them. Jack Monahan, roping out the mounts, snaked out a big wild-eyed black and turned it over to Powder River, then went into his pup tent.

"Mornings were chilly and the saddle just stuck cantle-up on that black's kinked back no matter how hard Powder pulled on the latigoes. You could tell by the look in the black's eye that he did not feel like working for any ornery cowhand that day.

"Powder's horse had loped into the camp just before dawn so I knew he had been in town pretty well all night and was feeling none too gentle about life in general.

"So here was a real set-up for action. Two ornery critters, cowboy and bronc, open range; no stampede rules; no holds barred.

"The bronc bucked through his repertoire. There were times that too much daylight was showing under Powder's pants, but he stuck, and the Black seemed to be determined not to be ornery, so he bucked through the bunch in the corrals, round the wagons and over tent ropes, and finally into and Over Jack Monahan's sacred tent.

"From Jack's remarks it looked as if Powder's days on the NL wagon were done. Jack figured Powder had done it on purpose and steered that bucking black into his tent just to be ornery. But by the next day it was all forgotten.

"Jim Finch was another of the boys—an old cow waddie from Amarillo, Texas way; old but awfully tough, with tales of long trails and gunsmoke in the southwest.

"Jack Monahan once sent Jim into Gleichen for a side of bacon when Lee, the cook, was short, figuring that Jim was a staid old puncher that could be trusted, and not like us unstable punks.

"Jim came back into camp that night wearing a grin, but no bacon tied to his saddle. It would be in the next day he said, but this happened three days running.

"Jack got suspicious and decided to take a trip into

town himself to investigate. He learned that Jim, the trust-worthy, had left town each day with a side of bacon but en-route had traded off the bacon for jugs of Red Eye.

"Red Blanket, the Indian who was a day wrangler, found one of Jim's cached jugs, sampled it, and that afternoon tore through camp like a howling dervish, horse cavvie and all, uttering wild war whoops until he fell off and went to sleep.

"Jim stayed with us, but he hated anyone who mentioned bacon. Red Blanket was sent home to his hogan in disgrace."

Bud Cotton sighs and shakes his head. "Gone are those old cow wagon days," he muses. "Gone, too, the old open range where we used to roam the tough, rough old cow trails of yesterday . . ."

* * * *

*

THE BIG GAMBLE OF 1903 . . .

It was the winter of 1902-1903 and, even though the era of the open range had only nine years left to run, Alberta ranchers were convinced it would last forever.

As winter broke into an early spring, ranchers — with unconscious unanimity — decided to stake everything they had on the biggest gamble of their lives.

Had the gamble paid off, who knows what Alberta's ranching industry would be like today.

But it didn't pay off. In a tragic seven days in May, Alberta cattlemen lost virtually everything they had, and ranching here changed forever.

Never before had the range been as green in the short grass country of southern Alberta as it was that early spring. The grass rolled on endlessly, as far as the eye could see — hundreds of thousands of acres of it still unscarred by barbwire fences and untouched by plough.

Everywhere, springs bubbled full, sloughs and water-holes were filled to overflowing.

Grass and water, slough hay, an early spring and expanding markets. It was a rancher's paradise — and it was all free.

It was the ranchman's chance to make a killing. The country was opening up. Division of the North West Territories into provinces was a foregone conclusion now, and a great development period loomed ahead for the west.

There would be legislative buildings going up, railways and roads to be built, settlements and schools. Beef and more beef would be in demand for construction crews and new immigrants.

It was the hand cattlemen had been waiting for.

Year after year, the rancher had gambled his whole herd on the unpredictable mood of the elements, playing close to the table. But when the spring of 1903 rolled around, he decided the cards were finally stacked in his favor and threw in everything he owned for the big win.

Even the banks felt the fever, advancing loans at 10 per cent, throwing up new branches, and sending out their managers to stalk the streets for customers.

The stock boom, which had begun with the Klondike gold rush in 1898, was well under way by 1903. Thousands of range-bred steers were trailed in across the Montana border; thin animals from the over-grazed, sheeped-out U.S. range.

Prices were on the upswing. Big American outfits were establishing ranches on the Canadian side of the border, bringing in huge herds to grow fat on free Canadian grass.

Money was easy — too easy. With pockets full, Alberta ranchers decided they could afford the big gamble of speculating on cheap, farm-bred yearlings from Quebec, Ontario and Manitoba.

Speculation on eastern yearlings spread like wildfire, and by May 19, 1903, trains loaded with thousands of them were on the rails west.

The ranchers were taking a terrible chance. Open-range cattlemen of that day provided feed only for bulls, weaning calves, and saddle horses — and there was absolutely no precedent for supposing the eastern cattle would be able to acclimatize themselves well enough to rustle for forage on the open prairie when winter set in.

Ranchers knew the score, but they were betting everything on the hope for a mild winter. None of them, in those hot first days of May, realized he might better be praying for a mild spring.

On May 19, from all parts of the short grass country, ranchers and round-up crews gathered along the CPR tracks, listening to the far-off whistles of train after train loaded with eastern yearlings.

Unknown to them, miles to the west, a 16-year-old boy named Henry Cavan was staring upward at a whirling cauldron of grey cloud sweeping in across the Rockies. The boy shivered, pulled his jacket around him, and started to run eastward to shout warning.

The storm, too fast for his legs, raced past to announce itself.

It started with rain that lashed the traffic jam of trains and turned stockyards into seas of mud. As hours went by, the temperature dropped steadily and the rain began to have the sting of ice.

By the 20th, the rain had turned to snow, a raging blizzard with the temperature at 10 above zero and dropping steadily.

Inside the packed stock cars, yearlings were trampling one another to death, or simply perishing from the severity of cold they had never experienced before.

Desperate train crews and ranchers were throwing animals from cars so that still more trains could move into place and unload.

When stockyards grew too full, the yearlings were driven out, bawling and stumbling, to fight for their lives on the open prairie. It was a fight most of them lost.

Like everyone else, young Henry Cavan worked 20 hours a day during the seven days the storm lasted. There was no way to brand any of the calves, he recalls, and he and the other cowhands ended up simply tying rag identifying bands around the animals' necks before driving them out into the storm.

The storm finally broke on the morning of May 27. But its effects — two-foot deep snow and drifts too high to ride a horse through — would linger until the end of June.

Unable to paw through to the grass under the snow, the yearlings continued to perish by the hundreds.

Grim-faced ranchers began the chilling task of counting their losses.

Dan Hamilton: 2,500 lost of 6,500 head. Spencer Bros. of Milk River: 1,200 lost of 5,000. Albert Desbrisay, Sage Creek: 500 lost of 1,000. Western Pack Company: 1,500 lost of 3,500.

And on it went. By the time the count was over, the short grass ranchers had lost 50 per cent of the eastern yearlings during the storm alone.

Desperately, ranchers tried to strengthen the survivors during the remaining weeks of summer. But winter came too soon and too hard, and outfit after outfit was wiped out completely.

Cresswell and Day, for example, had saved close to 4,000 of the 8,000 yearlings they had on the doomed trains — only to lose them all to the onset of winter.

It had been a great gamble, a great adventure — the last fling for the short grass rancher.

As one recalled defensively later: "Why, doggone it, a man couldn't associate with himself no more if he threw in a hand like that."

In the aftermath of empty range and 10-percent loans that would lead to foreclosure, rancher after rancher went out of business.

Those who were left, like young Henry Cavan, found themselves turning reluctantly to a new way of ranching: digging irrigation canals and becoming half farmers to grow winter feed.

They themselves finally put an end to open range, helping to string the barb wire ranchers have always hated.

Today, of course, those like Henry Cavan realize the changes were inevitable; the spring blizzard of 1903 only hastened the process.

And today they are the first to acknowledge that the results — in larger, better-managed ranches and more efficient handling of cattle — have given Alberta ranching a stability it would never have had otherwise.

But, sometimes, they can't help but wonder what would have happened if the biggest gamble in ranching history had somehow paid off . . .

SOD-BUSTING

"On our way back, we passed by Charlie's place and got treated to an astonishing sight. There was old Charlie at the plough, dressed in nothing but his underwear and boots and covered with dust from head to foot.

"As he passed us, urging his ox on with oats and a stick, I demanded: What are you doing out in nothing but your underwear, Charlie?

"'Well,' he answered, not stopping, 'it makes more sense than getting my clothes dirty, doesn't it?'

"Unable to think of a suitable reply, we just sat and watched this unusual spectacle until the hour forced us to shake up the team and get on back to Diamond City."

* * * *

*

A FAIR GROWTH OF PLANTS & FLOWERS . . .

Most people today — even in Alberta — take the province's prominence in the field of agriculture pretty much for granted. It wasn't always so.

In 1859, at the request of the British government, Captain

John Palliser was exploring what is now southern Alberta. One purpose of the trip was to fill in blank spaces on the map of Canada.

But the main purpose was to report back on the resource and agricultural prospects in the unknown west.

Palliser's report on southern Alberta wasn't encouraging:

"The whole region as far as the eye could reach was at times covered by buffalo in herds varying from hundreds to thousands. The grass was eaten off the earth as if the place had been devastated by locusts."

Describing the areas as unfit for agriculture, he sent in his report and a map that identified the treeless grassland as "arid plains".

Only a few years later, however, a botanist travelling through the same country sent a different report back east. It spoke of ample rainfall and of "a fair growth of plants and flowers".

What the botanist had encountered, of course, was only the freak of a wet year. But he and the people who read his report didn't know that.

By 1880, prospective homesteaders in eastern Canada and Europe were being urged to the Canadian west — a land where it took only the turn of a plough to uncover security and happiness — and thousands of sod-busters were eagerly pursuing the dream.

None of the newcomers knew about the Palliser report, of course, But it wasn't too long before those who turned the soil of southern Alberta found themselves writing "arid plains" on the bitter, personal map of experience.

It would take long years of struggle and the irrigation talents of the Mormon pioneers at Cardston to turn those arid plains into the "garden" of the prairies.

* * * * *

AND APPLAUSE OF THE SPECTATORS . . .

The rush of homesteaders to Alberta, which started in 1880, continued almost unchecked until well past the First World War. Dazzled by the promotion efforts expended on them before they came west, most settlers were unprepared for the hardships of the land. And fewer still were prepared to handle the surprising amount of trouble it sometimes took just to get into the land office.

The following account, from the Lethbridge Herald of June 6, 1910, illustrates the point all too clearly:

"What is supposed to be an organized gang of 'bull-rushers', as they are known to the police, land office officials and others, received a setback this morning when they endeavored to turn the well known trick of ejecting by brute force the man holding first place at the land office in the rush for a homestead thrown open for settlement.

"This morning it was land situated near Grassy Lake that became open. It was previously owned as a pre-emption by William C. Llewelyn but he having recently sold his homestead, by the regulations the pre-emption automatically became vacant.

"Llewelyn, however, had the right to purchase a homestead and thus he was attempting to apply on this quarter this morning.

"According to a land office official, at half past eight there were only two or three men present, Llewelyn and one or two others, who had been there since Friday or Saturday.

"Two or three minutes before nine o'clock, however, a gang which had operated at numerous other rushes, drove up in a couple of automobiles and immediately made a set at Llewelyn and forced him and his friends away, taking possession of the steps.

"A number of spectators assembled and sided immediately with Llewelyn, with the result that a sort of Donnybrook fair scene was enacted. Someone ran for the police and Constable Taylor arrived and later Sergt. Lamb.

"They stopped the fighting but there their powers ceased.

"Agent Stafford, who had witnessed the whole affair, however, came out and asked them to eject off the premises the whole crowd with the exception of young Llewelyn.

"This action was taken amid the cheers and applause of the spectators."

This particular story ends happily. But there was many a newcomer — particularly among those who spoke no English — who fared far worse than the lucky Mr. Llewelyn.

* * * *

THE COURTSHIP OF VERA . . . .

With so many hardships to overcome in wresting a living from the land, Alberta's early farmers had to depend heavily on enterprise and ingenuity.

This enterprise and ingenuity often paid off — even, as a young man named John Jackson discovered, in the romance department.

The young Mr. Jackson was unlucky enough to have a homestead right in the middle of Captain Palliser's dreaded triangle. But he was lucky enough to have a best girl named Vera, and he was determined to win her.

John was tireless in his courtship of Vera; more tireless it turned out than the battered buggy he used to make the long trips back and forth between her home and his.

Punished by the rutted trails, the buggy just plain gave out, one wheel threatening to come right off the hub.

With no new wheel available — and with no money to buy one even if it was — it looked for a few gloomy days like the end of a beautiful romance.

John, however, was in love, and he wasn't about to let some fool buggy stand in the way.

One afternoon a startled Vera rushed outside to find a grinning John driving up to the door in a squealing apparition.

On the hub where the ailing wheel had been, John's buggy now wore the bottom of a wooden tub.

John had come to ask an important question and, faced with so much determination, how could a girl say no?

The 'tub-buggy', incidentally, held together long enough to carry the blushing Vera 50 miles to Medicine Hat and back again to begin a happy new life as Mrs. John Jackson.

* * * *

WOOING THE DUST BOWL . . . .

There were probably few places in the country in 1880 that could match southern Alberta as a frustrator of farmers.

At first glance, the area seemed to be a wonderland for homesteading. It was relatively easy to accumulate large parcels of land for virtually nothing. There were no trees to clear away and few rocks. And the soil itself was rich, sandy loam.

All that was missing was water. There wasn't enough rain, and what little there was didn't fall at the right time. It takes 30,000 gallons of water to raise a bushel of wheat, and 500,000 gallons to raise a ton of hay.

The homesteaders, whose large holdings earned them the title of Canada's wheat barons, tried anyway. Their ploughs ripped up the centuries-thick buffalo grass to expose the rich soil for planting — and trouble.

Although the homesteaders couldn't realize it, the buffalo grass was all that was holding southern Alberta down. By stripping away the grass, the homesteaders had simply turned the earth over to the prevailing west winds.

Dismayed homesteaders stood by helpless as wind erosion blasted great craters in the unprotected soil, tore loose precious seed, and created dust clouds that turned high noon as black as night.

Size was no protection. The late Charles Noble, after whom the village of Nobleford is named, was one of the biggest of the "wheat barons". He measured his holdings in townships, but went broke twice.

It was only his ingenuity that kept him from going broke a third time — and that gave the farmer one of his most valuable tools. Realizing his enemy was the wind, Noble invented a device called the Noble blade; a sub-soil tiller that leaves trash cover to hold down the surface of the soil.

The invention became world-famous, but even with it, Noble could count on no more than two or three good years in ten because of the lack of moisture.

Noble himself managed to struggle on. Most of his neighbors weren't able to.

As years went by, the concerned federal government and the CPR, which was bringing homesteaders west, realized that irrigation was the only answer if southern Alberta farm land was going to produce.

Fortunately, the irrigation expertise they needed was already in Alberta, in the small Mormon settlement at Cardston. The Mormons had raised irrigation techniques to a fine art during the long years in their old home of Utah, and they were using it to keep their Alberta holdings green.

Indeed, one of the first projects of the colony had been to dig irrigation ditches to tap the precious water of the St. Mary's River.

Industrialist C.A. Magrath (later to become mayor of Lethbridge) was one of the first to approach the Mormons. He offered Charles Ora Card 30,000 acres of land at a dollar an acre if the Mormons would dig an irrigation canal through it.

Card wouldn't commit his people to the $30,000 purchase, but the offer finally led to the Mormons undertaking to build the canal under contract.

Work started in August, 1898, and was finished two years later. Precious water was flowing from the St. Mary's River all along the Milk River Ridge toward Lethbridge. An extension of the irrigation canal brought water into the city itself.

Soon Mormon experts were being called to Ottawa to advise the federal government, and soon the CPR committed itself to the long, slow job of watering Palliser's dust bowl.

In 1935, the federal government stepped into the act directly with the formation of the Prairie Farm Rehabilitation Administration.

Today that irrigated area — only four percent of the province's worked land — produces twenty per cent of Alberta's agricultural output.

Through construction of the St. Mary's Dam, and the St. Mary–Milk Rivers projects, water is being tapped and fed into a system that irrigates more than a million acres of southern Alberta.

Where Charles Noble once struggled to survive, 7,500 irrigation farmers are now producing nearly $170 million in cereal and specialty crops and livestock.

It took more than a century, but the Alberta farmer has finally erased "Arid Plains" from Captain John Palliser's warning map.

* * * *

HOW SWEET IT IS . . .

Ever since a homesteader named Francis Willock found a few heads of Golden Chaff in his jacket pocket and planted them in the soil near Pincher Creek, Alberta has been known as wheat country.

Not without justification. Even in a modest crop year, enough Alberta wheat is harvested to feed 6 million people.

But wheat isn't the whole story of Alberta agriculture. Indeed, it wasn't even the beginning of farming here.

If legend is to be believed, farming in Alberta started with a fur-trader's liking for potatoes. Whether or not Peter Pond (one of the original partners in the North West Company) actually did start the whole thing in the 1700's with an addiction to spuds is impossible to prove.

But whoever started it, today more than half a billion dollars a year in field crops comes from the successors to Alberta's early kitchen gardens.

There are apples in Edmonton, strawberries at Morrin,

and red currants at Beaverlodge.

And from thousands of Alberta acres comes the sweet success of the sugar beet.

Driving the highway between Lethbridge and Medicine Hat in the fall, the motorist soon begins to think the whole world is filled with sugar beets. In field after field, farmers are pulling the brown-skinned vegetables. Every few miles, by the sides of the road, the motorist can see huge piles of millions of the beets.

And ahead and behind him roar big trucks loaded with still more beets. Beets bounce on the road, lie in the ditch — seem almost to fall from the sky.

It all started through a man named Jesse Knight founder of the town of Raymond), and as an off-shoot of the irrigation program in southern Alberta.

As the present century started, the first irrigation scheme was well underway. Men like Jesse Knight realized, from the start, that the only way to make the relatively small irrigated area turn a profit was to come up with some high-yield crop for which there was a ready market.

The sugar beet was a natural, and Jesse Knight had little trouble interesting C.A. Magrath, manager of the Canadian Northern and Alberta Railway and Irrigation Companies, in the scheme.

Magrath, in turn, soon had the federal government interested.

By 1902, Magrath and Knight had stirred up enough official interest to start a beet sugar factory at Raymond.

The factory wasn't built as a commercial enterprise so much as a service to the settlers of the area.

According to the contracts involved, the plant was to be kept in operation for 12 years.

But, right from the day it opened, the beet-sugar business

at Raymond was in trouble. The biggest problem was one that the planners hadn't foreseen — lack of interest by the farmers.

Oriented to wheat and livestock, and unfamiliar with the process of raising the beets, the farmer just stayed away.

Faced with a shortage of beets, Knight appealed to the federal government for assistance. The government, which looked on the plant as potent development force in the province, responded with a bonus scheme.

The bonus paid 50 cents a hundred pounds of sugar, the amount to be divided equally between farmer and plant.

And, to further bolster the operation, the government eliminated all taxes on the plant for the 12 years of the contract.

The action by the government was enough to keep the plant going for the 12 years of the contract, but it did little to overcome the problem of farmer disinterest. It would take a streak of bad luck to do that.

Shortly after the contract had ended, Knight and his associates closed the Raymond plant and moved the operation to Cornish, Utah, where the sugar beet was an established crop.

If the Alberta farmer didn't miss the plant right away, he did in a few short years. With the ending of the First World War, the grain farmer was hit by drought and falling prices.

Forced to find another crop, he rediscovered the sugar beet and was soon clamouring for a new sugar plant. But the clamour went unheard and farm after farm went under, abandoned to the weeds.

The CPR colonization office found itself with hundreds of parcels of land — many of them irrigated — turned back by discouraged or destitute owners.

In the small communities of Raymond and Magrath, the boards of trade set up a committee to try to persuade some beet processor to set up the desperately-needed plant in the area.

Soon the committee was concentrating on one company in particular, the Utah-Idaho Sugar Company, a firm which was already interested in entering southern Alberta with a factory.

It was 1922 before the negotiations paid off.

The sugar company, before agreeing to come to the area, demanded some specific evidence of good faith to make sure they didn't suffer the same fate as the earlier operation.

The primary conditions were that farmers would grow trial plots in all areas in 1923 so that yield could be measured; that 6,000 acres of good land would be summer-fallowed to company standards and irrigated in the summer of 1924; and that provisional contracts be signed to guarantee the growth of 6,000 acres of beets in 1925.

It took a great deal of scrambling, but the committee managed to meet the conditions, and by 1925 a new plant was going up at Raymond.

For miles around, farmers were turning the country into an enormous beet patch; meeting and overcoming all the inevitable problems involved in handling a new crop.

That first year, 1925, was the critical one if the industry was going to survive, and somehow the farmers made it — despite an almost-fatal last-minute blow from nature.

Early in August, with harvest approaching, the area was lashed by heavy rains that continued, with few respites, until the end of October. And, on Sept. 25, a storm piled 16 inches of snow on the beet fields, making harvesting almost impossible.

Somehow or other, the farmers managed to harvest anyway. They cleared 5,394 acres and poured almost 42,000 tons of beets into the new plant.

From that point on, despite occasional problems, there was no looking back. The Raymond plant has long since closed, but new companies are in operation at Picture Butte and Taber.

They stand today in lasting vindication of Jesse Knight, who history proved didn't have the wrong idea. Rather, he just had the right idea a little too early.

* * * *

ALBERTA'S MR. AGRICULTURE . . . .

The changes in Alberta's agricultural industry in the past 60 years have been phenomenal — so phenomenal that the farmer's biggest complaint today is his ability to grow too much.

It's a complaint the early sod-busters would have been glad to make.

Mechanization has replaced the old scythe, rake and threshing flail with huge, rumbling combines that can do in minutes what once took days and weeks.

Perhaps more important than mechanization, however, are the radical improvements in growing-techniques themselves.

And that's where we come to the late Dr. William Fairfield. From 1901 on, whether he was inoculating an alfalfa field or urging his staff on in efforts to find new strains of wheat, Dr. Fairfield held the prime place in Alberta's agricultural revolution.

The Ontario-born agriculture expert first came to Alberta to operate a demonstration farm outside Lethbridge for the Canadian North-West Irrigation Company.

In August, 1906, the Canada department of agriculture decided to establish an experimental station at Lethbridge, and Bill Fairfield was chosen to run it.

Dr. Fairfield attracted attention in agriculture circles right from the day he arrived in Alberta.

A missionary for better farming, he preached his theories, then put them into practice so well that farmers all over the province were imitating him.

Soon Bill Fairfield was the man to see if you had a farm problem.

Even Mormon leader Charles Ora Card, something of a farming wizard himself, went to Fairfield for advice.

Card's problem was alfalfa; the foundation crop of irrigation farming. Although Card had been able to grow alfalfa in Utah, he just couldn't make it come up in Alberta. Already Card's colonists at Cardston had written off the area as "just not alfalfa country," but Card himself wasn't convinced.

Nor was the young Dr. Fairfield. Intrigued by the puzzle, he recalled he had read somewhere that alfalfa seed needs inoculation so that it can take nitrogen from the air. Maybe, he wondered, this could be the problem.

To test the theory, he sent to Wyoming for a bag of soil in which alfalfa had been successfully grown. When he sprinkled the soil over a spindly field, he delighted Card and astonished the whole countryside.

The alfalfa responded almost immediately, and grew a lush crop the next year. Soon his "inoculated" alfalfa was an important part of the farming scene. Indeed, Dr. Fairfield always maintained that it was the alfalfa discovery that was his most important contribution to Alberta agriculture.

It was only one contribution of hundreds, however. Under his careful supervision, a network of agriculture research stations was set up in the province, farmers were being taught vital lessons about erosion-prevention and fertilization.

Under Fairfield's guidance, researchers began producing new strains of plants specially suited to conditions in Alberta.

Marquis wheat, produced under his program in 1910, is still the standard by which wheat quality is measured.

Strains resistant to sawfly — Rescue, Chinook and Cypress — followed. Chinook, in particular, has won the World Wheat King title for several Alberta farmers.

The list goes on and on: Galt and Betze barley, Winalta winter wheat, Beaver alfalfa, Chinook potato . . .

All Alberta today is a living, growing tribute to the work he started and carried through.

But perhaps nothing pays better tribute to Dr. William Fairfield than the trees he urged on southern Alberta.

When he arrived, the prairie was bare. Today thousands of trees stand as his monument, and as the symbols of the Alberta farmer's hard-won victory over a demanding new land.

EARLY SETTLEMENT

BONNET FOR A CHIEF . . .

Although his audience was only a few white men, Thunder Bird, the mighty Cree chief, told his story with care and skill:

"Twenty-one winters ago Red Deer, a chief of the Crees, was camped with his tribe where the river that bears his name joins the swift flowing water.

"In one of his teepees lived a beautiful maiden that I loved, Silver Rose by name. Her voice was soft and sweet as the brook rippling over the sun-kissed pebbles and her eyes when she smiled shone with a love that would endure as long as the stars kept watch.

"Red Deer, although he already had four squaws, forced her against her will to marry him and live in his teepee. When I heard of this I rode with two of my swiftest cayuses to his camp and eloped with her. We fled to the great bend in the river where it runs nearest to the Cypress Hills.

"The action caused Red Deer and his braves to go on the warpath and, for a time, civil war threatened among the Crees.

"Silver Rose, however, knowing of Red Deer's love of display and showy feathers, sent me to shoot a number of eagles nesting on the high cut-banks along the river.

"From seven of the best-matched of these, she selected the finest tail feathers and wrought them into one of the most beautiful bonnets any chief ever possessed.

"When this bonnet was presented to Red Deer as a peace offering it caused such a remarkable change in him that our people, being very superstitious, attributed the change to magic or medicine possessed by the bonnet or hat, hence it became known as The Saamis. Consequently the place where the hat was made became known as the place of The Saamis — the Medicine Hat."

The chief, his story finished, waited in expectant silence. One of the white men stirred and, clearing his throat, leaned forward.

"That hat," he told Thunder Bird, "must have possessed wonderful medicine to appease the wrath of the irate chief. I, therefore, shall in honor of your noble squaw who has played such an important part in these events name the place Medicine Hat."

The speaker was Sir William Van Horne of the Canadian Pacific Railway. And, as anyone visiting southeastern Alberta today knows, he kept his promise to Thunder Bird.

* * * *

WHERE THERE'S SMOKE . . .

Further north, other white men were listening to another Indian story that would give birth to a modern Alberta community, the community of Wetaskiwin.

The story is set more than a hundred years ago, when the Cree and Blackfoot were still fighting, raiding north and south across the Red Deer River that separated their territories.

A party of Blackfoot had pushed north across the river, following the buffalo on their summer migration — and taking the opportunity to raid Cree camps for ponies and scalps.

The Blackfoot party, late in the summer, were camped on the banks of Pipestone Creek. The Cree were out for blood and had rushed a large force south to cut off the retreat of their enemies.

All day the Blackfoot sat in council of war, listening to the muffled drums of the Cree.

If the Blackfoot were worried by their position, there was nothing in their council of war to show it. Far from mapping out escape plans, they were hatching a scheme to raid the Cree camp by night and return home with even more horses and scalps.

It just wasn't Blackfoot nature to avoid a fight.

At that time, each of the tribes had a powerful young chief rising to leadership: Little Bear for the Cree and Buffalo Child for the Blackfoot.

When the Blackfoot were ready to scout the Cree camp to make the raid, it was Buffalo Child who was sent on the mission. By coincidence, the Cree were in the process of doing some scouting of their own, and Little Bear was doing it.

Being talented scouts, both men wanted to find the best vantage point from which to spy on the enemy's camp. Only, as it turned out, the best vantage point for both sides happened to be the same hill.

The two young chiefs stole up opposite sides of the hill at the same time and, with a shock, suddenly found themselves face to face.

The two froze in their tracks, recognizing one another instantly. For a full minute they glared at one another, then Buffalo Child threw aside his rifle with a scornful smile.

"Dog of a Cree," he taunted. "See, I throw my gun away. I do not need it. With my bare hands I will break you in two."

With equal scorn, Little Bear tossed his knife aside. "No Blackfoot with the heart of a woman can get the better of Little Bear."

They circled warily, looking for an opening, spitting insults at each other. Then, like two great cats, they sprang and grappled.

The two were almost a match for size and strength and neither could gain an advantage. Locked in one another's grasp, they swayed and struggled. First the Cree would go down, then the Blackfoot, but neither for long enough to give his enemy victory.

For almost an hour, as the sun slowly set, the two struggled on in silence. Then, as though by mutual consent, they drew apart, panting, and exhausted.

"You are a stout fighter," the Blackfoot admitted as he gasped for air. "Let us rest awhile and, later, we will renew the struggle."

Little Bear grunted agreement, and the two squatted, facing one another. The fierce hatred in their eyes was now mixed with something almost like respect.

Buffalo Child fumbled at his belt and pulled forth a pipe and tobacco from a beaded bag. Little Bear followed his example, but found his pipe had been broken into three pieces during the fight.

Frustrated, he threw the clay fragments aside, then sat back enviously to watch his enemy smoke.

Slowly, the Blackfoot filled his pipe, lighted it, and began to puff complacently.

The sweet smell of 'kinnikinic' smoke almost drove Little Bear wild. He smouldered with rage at his enemy's enjoyment of a pleasure that was denied him.

All this was not lost on Buffalo Child. It was a form of torture which an Indian could appreciate. He watched Little Bear with amusement. Suddenly, perhaps to heighten the torture, he held the smoking pipe out to his Cree opponent.

Before he could pull back his hand, Little Bear had snatched the pipe free, thrust the mouthpiece between his lips, and inhaled deeply.

Abruptly, he stopped with a strangled cough and stared at Buffalo Child. Buffalo Child, equally aghast, was staring back, mouth open with consternation.

An incredible thing had been done. Impulsively, through an act of fate, they had accidentally smoked together the common pipe.

It was the sacred pledge of amity and peace, made so by immemorial tradition, as unbreakable to them as the most solemn vow.

Finally, the Cree spoke. "My brother," he said softly, "we did not mean to do it, but we have smoked the peace pipe together. Henceforth we must be friends, and because we are chiefs of our tribes, our people also must be friends and think no more of war. Is it not so?"

Reluctantly, Buffalo Child agreed. He rose to his feet. "We must go back to the lodges of our people," he said, "and tell them of this thing we have done." He shivered in the growing darkness.

"I cannot understand it, but some great medicine must have been at work. Undoubtedly it is a sign; it must be the will of the Manitou. Let us go."

They turned on their heels, two dejected and bedraggled

figures, and silently parted in the dusk.

The following morning, runners were sent from the camp of the Crees to summon the Blackfoot to council. During the night, on both sides, the older chiefs had listened gravely to the incredible story and shaken their heads in puzzlement. But all admitted that what had been done could not be undone.

Tradition could not be overridden lightly. And, without a doubt, it must be a sign from the Great Manitou.

In early morning, the council assembled on the hilltop where the struggle had taken place. Four chiefs of the Blackfoot and six of the Cree sat in solemn circle and passed the pipe of peace from hand to hand.

There were pledges of eternal friendship and peace, and the hatchet was buried with appropriate ceremony.

Ever since, outwardly at least, Cree and Blackfoot have respected the vows they exchanged.

And ever since, the hills outside one of Alberta's bustling communities have been known as "Weteskewin Spatinow" — the place where peace was made.

* * * *

"People are gregarious and life is too short to spend years in isolation" — Sen. F. W. Gershaw

LET US GATHER TOGETHER . . .

At first, the Alberta pioneer called the isolation of the prairie "freedom", and revelled in it.

But soon he was calling it "loneliness", and he was suffering from it.

It was no accident that those who had known pioneer life before — like the Mormon settlers at Cardston — built their community outward from the nucleus of a town.

They knew that illness and injury were risks too high to run alone, and silence too great a burden to bear in isolation.

Certainly most Alberta towns and villages began for economic reasons; as centres of transportation or trade. But what made all of them grow was a pressing need for community. The rest came naturally.

* * * *

AT THE MOUTH OF THE ELBOW . . .

Rev. John McDougall, who had seen Edmonton change from trading post to town, who had seen Whoop-up go up and come down, was in southern Alberta in the summer of 1875 in time to witness the birth of what would be Alberta's giant city of the south.

Reading his journal of the events of that summer and fall when he was clearing land to raise a home and a mission, one can't help but wonder if he didn't have a slight premonition of things to come . . . .

"It was sometime in September that I was putting on the first shingled roof in Alberta south of Edmonton when some Indians reported that a company of white men were at the mouth of the Elbow River and acted as if they were going to build and winter there.

"What did I know about it? I told them I did not know that such was the case but that I would soon find out.

"As I thought over this report, I remembered having very strongly commended this very spot to Col. Macleod as a suitable centre for a police detachment. I had pointed out that it was on the direct line from Fort Macleod to Edmonton House, also that there were at that time several frequented passes across the mountains by way of the Bow and Kananaskis rivers. In addition, all the balance of the country was easily accessible from this point, thus it was from every viewpoint strategic. So I thought it possible Colonel Macleod might be acting on my suggestion. Therefore I determined to know as soon as possible.

"Immediately after dinner I changed my clothes, saddled my horse and galloped down the valley of the Bow, and in the waning of the day came into sight of the mouth of the Elbow.

"Here, sure enough, was an encampment of a company of Mounted Police. As it was near dark I did not want to make the ford that night. Looking around I saw a solitary lodge on the flat on the north side of the river.

"Riding over to this I found it belonged to an old acquaintance of mine, a French mixed breed of whom I spoke in the volume preceding this as the man who smuggled whiskey into our fort on the hill in 1873-4. He and his wife welcomed me to their lodge.

"I noticed that they were somewhat embarrassed in so doing and while I was tethering my horse I saw disappearing over the hill a man who doubtless had crawled out the rear of the lodge as I came to the front.

"Then I recollected it was one of the sons of this man who had stolen my horse the season before and now I was sure this was the thief who was running away.

"While the man and woman were preparing some supper and making me comfortable I told the father to go out to the hill and signal to his son to come in and to assure him that I did not intend to lay any charge against him, indeed I had absolutely forgiven him the theft.

"This the father gladly went and did and before my supper was ready brought in the young man and presented him to me as the boy who had brought shame upon his people by stealing the horse from such a person as I was. I gave the young fellow some advice and cautioned him as to the future.

"After an early breakfast I forded the Bow and presently was welcomed into the camp by the police. Here I soon learned that my surmise was correct.

"This spot had been selected and here was a full company of police for the building of a fort. Already up on the Elbow was a gang of men under Mr. Davis, one of my quondam friends of the Whoop-up scenes, taking out timber for this purpose. The contract for the building had been given to the I.G. Baker & Co. of Fort Benton.

"Captain Brisbois, the commanding officer and myself, rode up the Elbow that same morning and dined with Mr. Davis and his men at their timber camp.

"That night I slept in one of the officer's tents and the next day rode back to Morley and told the Indians what was being done.

"Some were quite indignant that another post was being placed, as they said, right in the path of the buffalo. This would entail hunger and possibly starvation to the Indians. In addition, what right had the white man at this time to establish centres without the government conferring first about it with the Indians?

"I explained, apologized and sought to give them assurance. At the same time I told them that the days of the buffalo were being numbered, that no earthly power could stay the change that was coming.

"I reminded them that both my father and myself had told them the truth about these changes ever since we had come into the western country. I concluded by stating that the presence of this post at the mouth of the Elbow would be the best guarantee of peace, both with Indians and white men, we could have.

"Many of the head men acquiesced in this but a number were sullen and disgruntled because of this new move. We had therefore to intensify our efforts along the lines of conciliation and education. Many a prolonged night council I held at that time and for years afterwards.

" . . . Immediately following our making known the fact that the police were establishing themselves at the Elbow, the Hudson's Bay post master moved down there from Ghost River and commenced to build beside them. I.G. Baker and Company also started to build in the vicinity.

"Thus in a few weeks the mouth of the Elbow became a busy scene of government occupancy and trade development . . ."

That "busy scene of government occupancy and trade development", of course, was the beginning of Fort Calgary. The old fort has long since gone, but a few years ago it provided a rare glimpse at how close Alberta's past really is to the present.

A team from the University of Calgary was digging in the downtown area in a bid to find the foundations of the old fort. As they dug, they attracted many spectators — including a handful of old-timers who kept insisting they were digging in the wrong place, and who urged them to try another spot they described.

The university team, of course, had worked out its calculations well and were sure they were in the right place and weren't about to take advice from sidewalk engineers.

When, months later, the team had to abandon the search site, someone remembered the advice of the old-timers and the team decided to give it a try.

At the new dig, right where the old-timers had said, was the foundation of the fort.

ON MY BACK PORCH

ON MY BACK PORCH . . .

"... for the new settlers in their humble homes inconveniences did everywhere abound. It was the day of the tallow candle and the coal-oil lamp. It was the day of slab and tar-paper shacks.

"Mail was something one did not expect until it arrived. There was no certainty nor regularity in its delivery, whether by stage-coach or by train.

"All these things were part of the heavy curtain of silence and far distance that cut off the adventurous souls who had come from their dear ones left behind in other lands.

"Then, too, the uncertainties of a rigorous climate made it impossible for a traveller to know whether his journey would take him days or weeks. Because of the scarcity of stopping-places along the way there was a real danger in the matter of blizzards while on the trail. So travellers, except in the warmest season, usually were muffled to the ears in warm clothing . . .

"Over against this, what do I see today?

"A man slips on a light coat or sweater over his suit,

puts on light rubbers (or maybe none at all) and jumps into a warm luxurious car or on a plane. In a matter of hours or even minutes he has reached his destination, be it a hundred miles or a thousand.

"Besides the daily mail he has hourly broadcasts of the world and home news by radio and TV.

"On my automatic dial telephone I talk to my daughter in Montreal in a matter of seconds. All, rich or poor, have electric lights in their homes, and many running water. Gone is the day when we depend on wood and coal for our fuel, with abundant supplies of fuel oil, propane and natural gas available.

"If I ride by night in the country districts, I find the whole scene lit up through the wonders of rural electrification. The neon lights of the small village on the west spread their beams to encircle my home grounds.

"I no longer look out on a dark wide world when I step on my back porch."

* * * *

There are hundreds of Albertans who, like pioneer writer Evangeline Warren, remember an Alberta far different from the one in which we live today.

They came to an untouched land. To the east and south it was a grassy plain slashed with coulees and cutbanks — the home of the buffalo. In its centre lay the badlands. To the west, forming an unpenetrated wall, were the mountains. To the north, it was forest and desert and a tangle of wild rivers plunging to the arctic.

Today, the buffalo are gone and the plains are a quilt of grain fields and grazing land. The mountains are safely tied down with ropes of rail and road.

The north, slowly, is giving up its secrets and its riches. Even the badlands turned out to be not so bad after all.

And Evangeline Warren, in the introduction to her book "Seventy South Alberta Years," spoke of the trucks that now wakened her in the nights . . .

PROGRESS

Our Alberta Heritage Series

TRANSPORTATION

"... *without taking the harness off the dogs (we) un-fastened them from the sleds, and pitching them into the water, pelted them with pieces of ice, so that they swam to the other side of the river.*

"*We then got off the edge of the ice ourselves, and found the water took us above the waist, and getting the sleds, loads and all on our shoulders, waded through the rapid, which was about one hundred yards wide, and so reached the left bank.*

"*The wind, which had changed at sunset to N.E. was bitterly cold, so that the plunge into the water felt warm at first, but on re-emerging, we at once stiffened into a mass of ice, for as I found half an hour afterwards, the thermometer stood at −15 degrees.*" (from the records of a trip through the Alberta Rockies in 1858 by Sir James Hector)

* * * *
*

Travel in Alberta, as recently as the turn of the century, was something a person didn't undertake lightly. The roll of the prairies is deceptively smooth. In fact it is a spine-jarring bed of coulees, sloughs and gopher holes, criss-crossed with steep-banked and treacherous rivers.

In the north, it is thick trees and muskeg. And in the west . . . well, the excerpt above from Sir Hector's journal tells all too well the special challenge of daring the Rockies.

Even the most routine trip in pioneer Alberta could be shattered by tragedy. There is no more horrible illustration of such sudden tragedy than that offered by Rev. James Morrow in his history of the Medicine Hat area.

It was the fall of 1876 and two men, a NWMP constable named Mahoney and an unidentified half-breed freighter, were driving a string of bull-teams west. They came, finally, to the routine obstacle of the Saskatchewan River.

"In crossing the Saskatchewan," Mr. Morrow records "the boat capsized about forty feet from shore. The moment they touched bottom the half-breed instinctively knew he was in quicksand and, as the water was only a little over two feet deep, instead of wading ashore he threw himself flat on it and struck out for land. This undoubtedly saved him.

"However, Mahoney, who was 6 feet, 2 inches in height and weighed over 200 pounds, started to wade out of the river.

"The bottom of the river was no longer sand; it was like muddy glue. Suddenly he sinks in. His feet have disappeared!

"He pulls his foot out and throws himself to the left. The sand comes up over his ankles! He pulls himself out and plunges to the right. Worse! The sand is up to the calf of the Mounted Police boot.

"Then Mahoney recognizes, with unspeakable terror, that he is caught in quicksand and that he has beneath him the fearful medium in which a man can no more walk than a fish can swim. Quicksand to right and left. Quicksand all round him.

"He throws off his load, belt and revolver, and like a ship in distress tries to lighten himself. It is already too late. The sand has climbed above his knees.

"Meantime the breed, like a crazy thing, is running around hunting for a lariat or rope. No use; they are on the other side.

"Poor Mahoney is condemned to that appalling burial, long infallible, implacable, impossible to avoid or hasten, which endures for an hour or two, which seizes a man erect, free, in full health and strength, by the feet and, at every attempt he makes, at every shout he utters, drags him a little deeper, sinking slowly but surely in the bottom of the river bed . . .

"A hand comes to the surface, moves, shakes, disappears, then the current of the Saskatchewan rolls on silently and relentlessly as before Mahoney went to a living death."

A horrible example, true; but one that makes the point.

* * * *

THE FIRST TRAIL . . .

It began at Fort Benton in Montana and snaked northward 200 miles into Canada. Soon it would push west to Fort Macleod, then north to Fort Calgary, and finally it would drive north to the settlements at Red Deer and Edmonton.

It was Alberta's first "highway system", and the first part of it — the 200 miles from Fort Benton — was one of the most important, and most notorious, features of pioneer Alberta.

The name it bore was the "Whoop-Up Trail" because its northern terminal was the infamous whiskey-trading centre of Fort Whoop-Up.

Even today, more than a century later, a visitor to the Lethbridge district can see the deep ruts cut in that trail by loaded ox-carts and, if he has a mind to, he can follow that faint trail southward.

If he does, 66 miles south of Lethbridge at the border town of Coutts, he'll find a cairn and a plaque that gives a valuable clue to the meaning of the Whoop-Up Trail for Albertans.

The plaque reads: "Until the building of the Canadian Pacific Railway across the prairies in 1882 and 1883, the most practicable route to Southern Alberta and Saskatchewan was by the Missouri River to Fort Benton, and thence northward by the Fort Benton (Whoop-Up) trail. This crossed the international border about seven miles west of Coutts. By it came most of the travellers, mail and supplies for the region."

The whiskey traders who pushed that trail north from Benton weren't concerned about anything as noble as the welfare of "travellers, mail and supplies for the region". But, albeit unwittingly, those traders did perform the people of Alberta a service. The heavy traffic they generated, moving hides one way and trade goods the other, pounded a trail into a road of sorts, and gave Alberta its first real transportation link with the rest of the world.

Mind you, our first "highway" was no route for the impatient. Even under the best of conditions, it took two to three weeks to make the 200 mile trip from Benton to Whoop-Up.

The trail, quite apart from giving access to Alberta, also introduced a new form of transportation — the bull train.

Until the 1860's, the main ways to move goods across the plains were still the canoe, dog-team and pack-horse — all, in terms of capacity, expensive methods of carrying freight.

But now, snorting up from Benton, came the bull train to change all that. Those trains were an impressive sight. The average one would consist of three huge wagons, spaced with stub tongues, and hauled by as many as six to 12 yoke of oxen. Eight to ten of these would travel as a unit, the air above them alive with flies, cracking whips, and enough profanity from the drivers to turn a grown man pale.

In time, the bull trains would be overtaken by fast mule teams, harnessed by sixes and eights, which could cover the distance from Benton to Whoop-Up in half the time of the lumbering oxen (a decided boon for whiskey men trying to keep a jump ahead of the law).

And, still later, the trip would be cut to four to six days by the introduction of the horse-drawn stage coach.

Before the Whoop-Up Trail finally died, with the arrival of the Canadian Pacific line in 1883, it would become a busy route indeed. Even in 1882, the Fort Macleod Gazette recorded that: "There are one hundred teams of all kinds on the road between here and Benton."

* * * *

EAST THEN NORTH . . .

The coming of the CPR killed the Whoop-Up Trail itself, but not its Alberta extension.

The North West Mounted Police had come to Alberta and closed down the whiskey posts in 1874. That done, the force moved west and established a base at Fort Macleod. Soon, however, their patrols had created a road between the fort and the whiskey country around Lethbridge.

Then, as the Mounted Police expanded their network, a road opened between Fort Macleod and Fort Calgary.

The same year the NWMP reached Calgary, 1875, the first crude highway opened between that post and the fur-trading settlement of Edmonton.

Most of the credit for creating the Calgary-Edmonton Trail has to go to pioneer missionary John McDougall — who seems to appear everywhere in the pages of Alberta history.

It was McDougall who cut out the northern half of the route in 1873, to create a cart road between Fort Edmonton and his mission at Morley. The road followed an old Indian trail past the Bear Hills, across the Battle River at Ponoka, over the Red Deer River west of the present city, and turned west at Olds to make a bee-line for Morley.

When the Calgary post was established in 1875, the road was branched at Olds and driven south through Nose Creek and on to the new fort.

By 1883, the road had improved to the point where it was carrying mail and freight and, near the end of the year, stage passengers.

Started by a man in Edmonton, the weekly stage service made the trip between Calgary and Edmonton in five days, with stops at all the settlements in between.

As realization grew that Calgary and Edmonton were probably going to be Alberta's two major communities, efforts to improve the road between them increased.

By 1886, professional surveyors were at work creating the route it would follow into the future.

The surveyor working on the stretch between Red Deer and Edmonton was George P. Roy, and he turned out to be something of a prophet.

"In view of the great traffic and immense travel which some day may be done this way," he wrote in the report of his survey, "my intention was to make the road as straight as the actual direction of the trail between the two extreme points, Red Deer and Edmonton, would allow."

As anyone travelling modern Highway 2 between those points today will agree, Roy was a surveyor who meant what he said.

* * * *

ALBERTA'S FASTEST RIDE . . .

In 1885, even before the surveyors had finished their work on the Calgary-Edmonton Trail, the 200 mile road provided the setting for one of Alberta's outstanding — and probably least-expensive — jobs of riding.

It was the time the Riel rebellion was brewing, and in both Calgary and Edmonton settlers were huddled behind barricades, fearful trouble might spread into Alberta.

In the tension, wild rumors were circulating — and growing wilder by the day. It was critically important that some way be devised to get accurate reports between Calgary and Edmonton so that trouble between white and Indian wouldn't be touched off by accident.

Standing by in both cities were couriers, ready to ride at a moment's notice. In Edmonton, the courier was a man named James Mowatt.

The first detailed reports of the rebellion in the east came in over the telegraph to Edmonton and Mowatt was sent on his way to carry them to Calgary.

Maybe Mowatt was inspired by the urgency of the situation. Or maybe he thought the hills were alive with hostile Indians. No one knows. But whatever the reason, speeding south on horseback, he made the trip that took five days by stage in an amazingly short 36 hours. And the reward for his historical ride was a slim $26.

* * * *

THE "SQUEALERS" . . .

All the time the route north through Alberta was being built, another route — this one west — was being carved out. Or maybe we should say "screamed out".

"The shriek of a single Red River cart," someone once wrote, "was enough to set tenderfoot visitors writing home: it was an experience of an excruciating kind.

"But when they went out a hundred or two hundred at a time . . . the uproar was beyond imagination. They came like ten thousand devils filing saws, like the Gadarene swine in their frenzy, like the shrieking damned . . ."

Or, as someone only slightly less colorful put it, "The Red River cart brigades never sneaked up on anybody. On a still day you could hear them coming for miles, and see the great cloud of yellow dust they raised.

"And if the buffalo of the plains did finally flee into holes in the ground as the Indians believed — well, it was no wonder."

The Red River cart, invention of the Metis of Manitoba, was as important to the Alberta settler coming from the east as the bull train was to the settler coming from the south.

Physically, the cart wasn't that imposing, but writing of it in the early 1800's, Alexander Henry was quick to spot its virtue:

"Men now go again for meat, with small carts, the wheels of which are one solid piece, sawed off the ends of trees whose diameter is three feet."

By the time the Red River cart pushed into Alberta, it had changed somewhat from the version Alexander Henry described. It had acquired hoops, like a covered wagon, and its wheels had become spoked and stood as tall as a man's head.

But in one way — noise — it hadn't changed at all. The axles were unpeeled poplar or cottonwood logs, and the wheels could not be greased because grease would have collected dust and frozen the hubs to the axles.

Those ugly, noisy carts did an important thing for Alberta. They opened its borders to immigration from the east — and to export to the east.

And if they did sound like "the shrieking damned", ah well, it was only the sound of progress . . .

* * * *

WANNA BUY A REDCLIFF? . . .

From the bumpy beginning of the Whoop-Up Trail, the network of roads in Alberta expanded steadily. By the early years of the 1900's there were paved streets — though not too many of them — and in a matter of a decade or two, Alberta was firmly into the automobile age.

It was so firmly into it, in fact, that it even had a car of its own. Well, it usually came out looking like either a truck or a bus, really, but it was still our own.

"We are the pioneer commercial car builders in western Canada," was the proud claim of Redcliff Motors Co., Ltd.

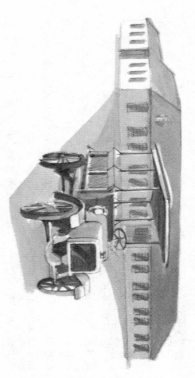

It was true. Indeed, as history would prove, Redcliff Motors would be western Canada's *only* commercial car builders.

Redcliff, today, is a sleepy little town near Medicine Hat. But for a few years in the 1920's (the exact dates weren't available), it was a thriving industrial community, and Redcliff Motors was its proudest achievement.

The fate of Redcliff Motors — why it went out of business in only a few years — is another of Alberta's historical mysteries. There aren't even any of the company's vehicles left for the historians to ponder.

But, fortunately, an early photographer snapped a couple of pictures of the Redcliff plant, with its trucks lined stiffly out in front of the building. These pictures have survived.

And, thanks to the enterprise of the Redcliff Chamber of Commerce in 1967, Alberta has access to reproductions of one of the company's sales brochures.

From the brochure we can obtain a wealth of technical specifications for their handsome vehicles, and discover that they were quite reasonably priced (by today's standards, at least). A 12-passenger bus, for example, cost only $4,500.

Most importantly, though, we find in the brochure a rare statement of the philosophy that was beginning to reach transportation-conscious Albertans of the day.

"Modern transportation without railroads would be a long stretch of the imagination," the brochure explains. "The common carriers have become absolutely essential to life. Modern industrialism is intimately related to transportation, and a study of transportation has developed many economies in handling materials.

"Yet the small manufacturer, the jobber, and the merchant, to whom economies are surely important, rely on the plodding horse to move their goods."

Time would soon see the manufacturer, jobber and merchant switch to trucks. But time would also dictate that it would be too late for Alberta's pioneering Redcliff Motors to supply those trucks.

* * * *

ALL THIS AND THE MINNOW TOO . . .

If there's anything one wouldn't expect to see sticking out of the prairies of Alberta it's the funnel of a steamboat.

But in the Alberta of the 1880's, that is exactly what was sticking out of our prairies.

Alex Johnson, president of the Lethbridge and District Historical Society, sums up the story in his preface to the book Boats and Barges on the Belly:

"From the beginning, the commerce of Canada moved along her rivers — starting with the epic canoe journeys of the voyageurs, who penetrated the length and breadth of the land.

"Southward, following the invention of the steamboat in 1807, the Mississippi, the Ohio, the Missouri and their tributaries blossomed with side and stern-wheelers that each year carried millions of tons of cargo. By 1873, steamboats had reached the Saskatchewan.

"Thus, in 1883, it was natural to think of steamboats and barges when coal from the Belly bluffs had to be moved to Medicine Hat.

Unfortunately, little was known of the variable flow of the Belly and South Saskatchewan Rivers and no one appreciated how dependent the flow was on snow melt in the mountains. From the outset, the use of steamers on the rivers of southern Alberta was doomed to failure."

There were three of them — all built in Alberta of wood from the Porcupine Hills.

The first, the Baroness, was 173 feet long, a stern-wheeler. She was launched at Coal Banks on July 2, 1883, and floated down to Medicine Hat where she was fitted with her machinery.

The second was the Alberta, also a stern-wheeler, and 100 feet long. She went in the water in 1884.

The third was the Minnow, more tug than steamer. Only 73 feet long and 10 feet wide, she started life as a stern-wheeler but was later converted to propeller. Like the Alberta, she went into service in the spring of 1884.

It didn't take Sir Alexander Galt, owner of the Galt coal mines at Lethbridge, and the instigator of the steamboat plan, long to discover his idea might not be as good as he'd thought.

"In 1884," he wrote gloomily "I waited at Medicine Hat for water till after the twenty-fourth of May, and by the twenty-eighth of June our boats and barges were tied up for the season."

The steamers had moved hundreds of tons of coal, but Galt realized the idea just wasn't going to work.

In 1885, Alberta's "navy" reappeared in the history books when they were pressed into service to help troops fighting the Riel rebellion.

Unfortunately, they proved no more satisfactory in this venture than in the coal business. Indeed, all three captains were written off by their military bosses as "incompetent".

In retrospect, that judgment was more than unfair. Even at the time, not all of the military men agreed with it.

By 1886, the Baroness and Alberta had both been beached and dismantled. The little Minnow survived until 1898, as a lumber tug, then she too was scrapped.

The remains of the Alberta clung to the shore of the river at Lethbridge for years.

For a while she was a playground for children, then

reduced to her ribs, a diving platform. Then she sank into the mud, and disappeared.

The idea of steamboats for Alberta was a bold one. And, in a period when so many bold ideas were paying off, it is rather sad that this one didn't.

* * * *

ONE HUGE MARSHALLING YARD . . .

The job of opening Alberta that started with the bull trains on the Whoop-Up Trail in the 1860's was finally completed by the arrival of the railroads in the 1880's and 1890's.

For a while, in the late 1870's, it seemed we might be in danger of having more railroads than people, and a province that was going to become one huge marshalling yard.

Fortunately for historians (and unfortunately for most of the Albertans who bought railroad stock), the early battle finally resolved itself with the Canadian Pacific winning out east-to-west, and the Grand Trunk — after some persistent fighting with Canadian Northern — winning out north-to-south.

It would be nice, here, to be able to tell the whole exciting story of railroading in Alberta. How Lady Macdonald, wife of Canada's prime minister, set off on a scenic tour of the Rockies with her chair perched on the cowcatcher of a speeding train. How Canadian Northern passengers would stand on the rear observation platform of the line's trains and watch, with a great deal of uneasiness, as the rails behind floated up and down like logs at sea.

And the proud story of how the citizens of Rimbey, when they decided they wanted a railroad, went out and built it — 35 miles of track and a train they called the "Peanut Special".

But it is simply too big a story. So, instead, we'll reach into the bag of railroad yarns and pull out just two small tales: of Edmonton's stuttering engineer and of a ghost train.

* * * *

*

D-D-DID I DO SOMETHING WRONG? . . .

Lin Bell was a big man — six foot three — and he was a railroad engineer. Indeed, if ever Alberta had an engineer who could be described as "the" engineer, Lin Bell might well be the man.

His story doesn't belong to the earliest days of railroading.

Lin started working for Canadian National out of Edmonton in 1916, and stayed with them until he retired in 1947.

And right from the first time Lin settled his 280 pounds behind the throttle of a CN locomotive, the company realized that the most anyone would ever be able to do to keep Lin Bell under control was to simply stay out of his way.

He could coax CN's startled old engines into feats of speed they'd never dreamed of — and broil a steak in the firebox while he was doing it.

Freight or passenger, he didn't care. As far as he was concerned, it was his heaven-ordained duty to get his trains where they were going in the shortest possible time.

On one early run with a passenger train, he had a conductor behind him who didn't like speed at all. Indeed, he got nervous if anyone even used the word.

So Lin pulled the train out of Edmonton and started to build up steam and speed. When Lin hit 72 miles an hour, the conductor's nerves finally gave out. The frightened man staggered forward through the coaches bobbing and weaving in the wake of Lin's engine, and finally made it to the front of the train.

Lin was waiting, and as soon as the infuriated conductor appeared, he shook his head sadly and pointed out: "G-G-George, th-th-there's no use asking me to go any faster. I'm r-r-running as fast as the engine will go."

As Lin's reputation as a high-baller grew, CN began making meek but persistent appeals for him to slow down. Lin would promise faithfully to do just that — then go out and move his trains faster than ever.

Hauling a freight to Edson one night, Lin had his old engine wide open when a car jumped the track and derailed 25 cars behind it. When everything finally stopped moving, the rest of the train crew came looking for Lin to point out the imminent possibility that his damn-fool speed was about to get them all fired.

They found Lin, wide-eyed, contemplating the wreckage. "S-s-say," he mused philosophically, "it's a good th-th-thing we weren't going very fast."

Probably the favorite Lin Bell story is the one Tony Cashman tells of the engineer in his book The Edmonton Story.

Magistrate J. W. McCulla and an Edmonton lawyer were standing on the station platform at Stony Plain when "A sound as of distant artillery, a singing in the rails, and a trembling of the platform signalled the approach of Lin Bell pulling freight. The roar increased and the train plummetted past the station.

"Well, it got halfway past anyway. Then a switch opened and the last fourteen cars ran off on to a siding and turned into a pile of wooden sticks of miscellaneous sizes. Lin got his engine stopped well on toward Edmonton.

"As he walked back towards Stony Plain he called out: 'D-d-d-did I do anything wrong?' "

* * * *

THE GHOST OF 1908 . . . .

Railroad men are a superstitious lot, and you can believe this story or not. But you won't be able to deny, as Ken Liddell pointed out when he recorded the story for The Calgary Herald, that "something strange happened" on the line between Medicine Hat and Dunmore in the summer of 1908.

"Bob Twohey was engineer and Gus Day the fireman on an engine travelling from Medicine Hat to Dunmore about eleven o'clock one night in June of that year," writes Mr. Liddell.

"At Dunmore they were to couple to the Spokane Flyer, which did not enter Medicine Hat, and take it west to Lethbridge and into the Crow's Nest Pass.

"They were two miles out of Medicine Hat when before them appeared a train approaching on the single line that wound around the cutbanks as it climbed a steep grade from the valley to the tableland of the prairie.

"As Gus Day recalled years later, the headlight of the approaching train seemed to be the size of a wagon wheel. The reflection ahead was as though the firebox was open on the locomotive of the approaching train.

"Day stood at the cab doorway and Twohey's hand remained suspended before the brake valve as a string of phantom coaches sped past. The coach windows were lighted and crew members waved a greeting from places where crew members would be expected to be found waving greetings as trains passed.

"And then the phantom disappeared. Twohey and Day each fearful of what the other may have thought had they expressed feeling, said nothing.

"Two weeks later, Twohey and Day met on a street in Medicine Hat. Feeling safer with the passage of time perhaps, they found courage to ask each other about what each had seen that startling night.

"Each was thankful to learn the other had witnessed the same sight and had experienced the same eerie feeling.

"But it worried Twohey. He told Day he had been to a 'reader', meaning a fortune teller, and had been told that he would die within the month.

"'I'm going to lay off for a couple of trips,' said Twohey. Day stayed on the job. A few nights later Day was on the same engine, going about the same duties. This time the engineer was J. Nicholson replacing Twohey who had booked off.

"At exactly the same spot the phantom train again appeared, headed toward them with whistle blowing and headlight burning. And again it simply evaporated into the darkness as its crew members again waved greetings from their positions on its engine and cars.

"On the morning of July 8, Day reported for duty and found he was assigned to yard service. H. Thompson took his place as fireman on the engine that made a morning trip to Dunmore to pick up the Spokane Flyer, but this time to take it east to Swift Current. The engineer was J. Nicholson. They left Medicine Hat and headed into the hills.

"About 100 yards from the spot where the phantom train had been seen on two different nights and by two different crews, another train appeared around the curve, headed straight for them.

"This time it was daylight and it was for real. It was No. 514, the passenger train coming in from Lethbridge. And the man at the throttle was Bob Twohey, who had overcome his fears and had returned to work.

"The inevitable happened. The outbound engine and inbound passenger train collided. The wreck took the lives of Twohey and Nicholson, the engineers, both of whom had earlier seen the phantom train at almost the same spot. It also took the lives of a fireman named Gray and a conductor named Mallett, on the in-bound passenger train, and seven of the passengers.

"Thompson, fireman on the out-bound engine, escaped by jumping. He recalled later that just before the crash he had seen a farmer standing on a hill, waving his arms. The farmer could see both engine and passenger train, and realized a crash was inevitable. Thompson had mistaken the farmer's frantic armwaving to be the usual friendly greeting . . ."

* * * *

Alberta's aviation age is still unfolding. But already it is building a history of its own.

And that history is accumulating as many legends as the railroads that came before.

It has a young woman flyer named Katherine Stinson giving Alberta its first airmail flight, from Calgary to Edmonton, in 1918.

It has Captain Fred McCall pioneering commercial aviation in the province when he flew a load of nitroglycerine in to help blow out an oil fire at Turner Valley in 1927.

It has Wilfred "Wop" May, one of the hardy breed of bush pilots who opened northern Alberta with their little airplanes. May himself made aviation history with a 700-mile winter flight to carry vital drugs to a stricken Fort Vermilion, and had a crowd of 2,000 waiting to cheer him when he returned to Edmonton.

But there is one story, unknown to most people in Alberta, that marked the real beginning of aviation in the province and that established the spirit of our growing air age.

* * * *

ALBERTA'S FORGOTTEN FLYER . . .

Ask most people when aviation started in Alberta and they'll guess somewhere after the First World War. And they'll be wrong.

It started in 1906, in the basement of a care-free Edmonton bachelor named Reginald Hunt.

Hunt was handy with his hands, and a bit of an inventor. Like most people, he'd heard of airplanes and was excited about the idea of flight.

And it didn't seem at all impractical to him to go one step further and create an airplane of his own.

It took him three years, but he did just that.

The first step, he decided, was to design a glider. With the help of a carpenter friend, and months of labor, he gradually created a monster of pipe and big flat wings and a tail-assembly that looked like a huge box kite. It had four bicycle wheels under it; two big ones under the wings and two small ones under the strange-looking tail.

And one day he ran the whole improbable contraption off a ramp and it glided gently through the air for a few feet. The blasted thing actually flew.

Most people would have been satisfied with that, but not Hunt. He wanted a real honest-to-God powered airplane.

What he needed was a motor, so he built one. It took a whole winter of effort, but he designed and hand-crafted an airplane engine.

Then he set to work and designed and hand-crafted a propeller. It had four blades and, as Hunt explained later, "I based my design on the fans that keep flies from sleeping in restaurants."

Hunt was still working on his flying machine when, on Feb. 23, 1909, James McCurdy made Canada's first recorded flight over the ice at Baddeck Bay, Nova Scotia. McCurdy had managed to stay in the air for about two minutes.

Hunt didn't pay any attention to the feat. He was too busy.

Finally, at two o'clock on the afternoon of Labor Day in 1909, Hunt was ready. He rolled his invention to a field in west Edmonton, strapped himself in, and . . . well, we'll let Tony Cashman explain what happened next:

"The engine started all right . . . he stepped it up . . . it turned faster and faster still running smoothly . . . the propellers hummed evenly . . .

"Hunt shut his eyes and opened the throttle wide. The plane lurched forward, and after a short run across the open field it was in the air. Hunt had calculated well. The controls worked just as he figured they would. The control surfaces were large and it was much like sailing a boat, only Reginald Hunt was sailing in a realm where no boat had sailed before, not in Western Canada anyway."

Hunt managed to keep his airplane flying, 35 to 50 feet above the ground, for an incredible 35 minutes — totally eclipsing McCurdy's record set six months earlier. This pioneer flyer spent years trying to interest backers in the idea of an aviation industry for Alberta. But people, even though he'd already proved otherwise, just said it "would never get off the ground."

So Reginald Hunt ended his days, a forgotten man, building boats in northern Alberta.

But what he did over Edmonton that afternoon in 1909 set the spirit of a transportation history that is still unfolding in Alberta . . .

* * * *

RESOURCE DEVELOPMENT

"The colonizers had brought with them their wood-burning cook stoves. Fuel was scarce. There were only a few cottonwood trees, willows and birch brush on the creek. Consequently, President Card, John A. Woolf and George L. Farrell set out to look for coal . . .

"A small vein of coal was found about three miles up the creek which was opened up on June 18th and which provided all with greater comfort." (Recollection of a Cardston pioneer)

BLACK NUGGETS . . .

It was 1870 and Alberta was still counting her natural resources in beaver pelts and buffalo hides.

Few of the traders gave much thought to the fact some of the more enterprising Montana ranchers were beginning to drift small herds onto the thick buffalo grass of the Alberta prairie. Fewer still knew that a settler named Francis Willock, at what would become Pincher Creek, had found a few grains of wheat in his pocket and — out of curiosity — planted them.

In the north, Hudson's Bay men simply shrugged off Cree stories of a sandy place where black tar seeped from the ground.

But, during that year of 1870, a young Irishman named Nicholas Sheran was plodding north on the trail from Fort Benton, in Montana, to the trading post of Fort Whoop-Up in southern Alberta.

Like so many other young men of the time, Sheran had the gleam of gold in his eye. He had visions of gravel bars in fast-flowing streams where a man could reach in and pull out shining nuggets, of swirling pans of sand that would yield rich flecks of yellow dust.

Like so many other young men of the time, Sheran would find his golden dream empty. But, unlike the others, he would stumble onto a dream to replace it, and start one of Alberta's major resource industries.

Even before he reached his destination of Fort Whoop-Up, Sheran had noticed black outcroppings along the shore of the Belly River. When he investigated, he discovered it was coal.

To a man interested in gold, however, coal isn't very exciting stuff. Sheran just filed the information away in his mind and pushed on north.

It took only a few months of prospecting to convince Sheran that southern Alberta wasn't gold country. But his prospecting trips hadn't been entirely a waste. All along the riverbanks near Fort Whoop-Up, Sheran kept on finding thick outcroppings of black coal.

Gradually, an idea took shape in his head. If a man could get a little backing, and was willing to work hard, it might be possible to mine that coal and ship it south to Fort Benton — which was becoming a main service and transport centre.

When Sheran approached some of the other prospectors about the idea, their comments were discouraging. Coal was nothing but hard work for little money. And anyway, no one could move enough wagonloads of coal along the rutted trail south to make it worthwhile.

Sheran was stubborn, but he was quickly running out of cash. So he built a crude shack near Fort Whoop-Up and began operating a ferry service across the Belly River.

Ferry traffic was light, and Sheran had enough time to continue probing the black outcroppings. Gradually he began building an operation to meet the heating needs of the fort and the growing number of settlers in the area.

For two years, Sheran struggled on. Then, in 1872, at a place later to be known as Sheran's Crossing, he discovered a new thick seam of coal in the side of a hill.

He began chipping away at the seam, following it into the hill. Almost unwittingly, Sheran was digging the first underground mine in Alberta.

The seam ran on and on. Soon Sheran's team of bulls were a common sight on the Whoop-Up Trail as they trudged south the 200 miles to Fort Benton with loads of coal.

Sheran coal sold at $3 a ton at the mine entrance, at $15 a ton in Fort Macleod, and at $22 a ton in Fort Benton.

Sheran, however, wasn't getting rich. He couldn't get the backing to make his mine — only half a mile from where Lethbridge's high-level bridge now stands — realize its potential.

All Sheran could do was struggle along, with hardly a cent in his pocket, and hope his luck would turn some day.

In 1882, it finally did, but it was a tragic turn for the worse.

Sheran was helping a party of North West Mounted Police to cross the flooding Belly River when his horse slipped and threw him into the water. He disappeared without a trace.

Sheran died a tragic figure. Even in death, he remained to his contemporaries "a stubborn Irish fool who didn't have the sense to give up."

Eighty-five years later, however, The Lethbridge Herald would remember Nicholas Sheran in another way:

"Sheran died a poor man, and like many others who have made great contributions to their country, failed to see the results or reap the rewards of his efforts.

"Little did he realize that he had pioneered an industry which was to form the backbone of Lethbridge."

* * * *

THE BIG DIG . . .

The real tragedy of Nicholas Sheran was that he died just a little too soon. By 1882, eastern capital was finally getting stirred up at the idea of a coal industry in the west.

The North Western Coal and Navigation Company had been formed, with Sir Alexander Galt — one of the fathers of Confederation — as its guiding force.

At his instigation, and that of his son, Elliot, the company sent two men named William Stafford and Capt. Nicholas Bryant west to look over the coal lands.

The two did extensive prospecting, and the reports they sent back excited the Galts. In a matter of months, the Galts were on the scene personally to check the finds.

Soon Sir Alexander was on his way to England to raise money, and Elliot was hard at work laying the foundations of the Galt mining empire that would give birth to Lethbridge.

William Stafford became the first superintendent of the operation, and it was he who persuaded the Galts to locate their mines on the east bank of the Belly River rather than the west shore that Sheran had been mining.

He knew that transportation of the coal was vital to the success of the enterprise, and that any mines operating across the river would face serious problems. There were no bridges and getting the coal to market would be an insurmountable problem.

At Stafford's advice, the miners went to work on the east side, sinking the first tunnel into the river bottom approximately where the high-level bridge now stands.

Originally, the Galts expected the settlers to be their main market, but the arrival of the trans-continental line of the CPR changed that.

The CPR tested the coal and found it excellent for use in their steam locomotives. North Western was given a substantial order — on the condition it would build a railway line to connect the mine with the CPR route.

This was done, and the narrow-gauge "turkey track", as it came to be called, was running tons of coal eastward by August, 1885.

The task of raising coal from the river bed was becoming increasingly difficult, despite construction of an inclined railway. The company turned to shaft mines. Galt No. 1 was followed in steady succession by Galt No. 2, then 3, 4, 5 and 6.

The hook-up with the CPR line, in addition to the direct business with the railway, opened all of Canada to the North Western complex.

In an effort to keep up with the demands, the Galts even tried the short-lived experiment of building three steamers to barge coal down to Medicine Hat. Impossible navigation conditions, however, soon put an end to the project.

The success of the Galt operation was drawing competitors by the score. Soon all Alberta was being probed for coal and mine after mine was opening. Almost overnight, there were strings of shafts all through the Crows Nest Pass, at Diamond City, and around the present city of Drumheller.

The western coal-mining business seemed to offer everyone a chance to make a fortune, so everyone came to make it.

But if the hastily-formed mining companies were developing one of Canada's major resources, they were also setting the scene for disaster.

* * * *

THE CRASH OF TURTLE MOUNTAIN . . .

The Galt coal-mining operation around Lethbridge was a carefully-engineered, safety-conscious operation.

Unfortunately, many of the other early operations were not. Reckless for profits, operators became reckless of lives, and they hurled miners into shafts that were poorly dug and poorly braced. Some of those shafts would have made better graves than tunnels. And some of them did . . .

The Indians always had a secret dread of Turtle Mountain in the Crows Nest Pass. They called it "the mountain that moves", and they would never camp at its base.

Unfortunately, Samuel Gebo and H. L. Frank didn't take Indian superstition seriously.

Coal had been discovered in Turtle Mountain in 1900 by a man named Henry Pelletier of Blairmore. Lacking capital, Pelletier had sold his claim to Gebo, a promoter with mining experience.

Gebo brought in Frank, a wealthy speculator from Butte, Montana, and by 1901, shifts of miners were burrowing into Turtle Mountain and a small town named Frank was taking shape at the foot of "the mountain that moves".

The objective of the mine was production of 1,000 tons a day, and the owners pushed their men recklessly to reach it. Sound engineering and safety rules were ignored.

By the spring of 1903, the miners had dug 5,000 feet into Turtle Mountain, ripping out seams of coal 9 to 12 feet wide in a long, upstretching tunnel.

It is easy, looking back, to gape in horror at the incredible stupidity building to a terrible climax in Frank. The men who climbed to the top of Turtle Mountain — and men did regularly — should have wondered at the long crack in the top edge of the mountain; a crack that was widening daily.

And the men working inside the mine itself should have wondered at the strange things happening there. There had been a minor quake the year the mine opened; there had been a series of small cave-ins. Two-foot timbers set one night would be found smashed to matchwood the next morning. Pockets of rock, emptied of coal, would be found mysteriously sealed a day or two later.

But, suddenly, it was 4 o'clock on the morning of April 29, 1903. Twenty miners were inside Turtle Mountain, a freight train was standing at the mine entrance, and more than 600 people lay sleeping in Frank. It was too late for wondering.

The engineer of the freight train, Ben Murgatroyd, and his two brakemen had just finished spotting a car and were preparing to leave the mine. They shouted farewells to the mine weighman and to two miners who had come out to the entrance to take a lunch break.

Then, abruptly, Murgatroyd heard a rock tear loose from high on the face of the mountain. He yelled a warning to the brakemen walking beside the engine and jammed the throttle wide open. The brakemen grabbed for the handrails and hung on desperately as the engine screamed down the grade from the mine and across a bridge.

Above them, they heard a terrifying roar as 70 million tons of rock — the whole face of Turtle Mountain — peeled loose.

In one minute and forty seconds it was all over. Everything was silent again.

Murgatroyd and his brakemen stood, staring in disbelief into the darkness. The bridge the engine had raced over, with sparks flying from its wheels, was gone.

The mine entrance was gone, and with it the three men who had been sitting there. Another 18 men were sealed inside the mountain itself.

In the valley below, most of the town of Frank, and the bodies of at least 66 men, women and children (the exact toll has never been determined), lay buried under a churning sea of rock.

In the hours and days that followed, the shadow of Turtle Mountain produced more heroes than any other town in Alberta history.

Men risked their lives to free those trapped in the

rocks that covered the town. Inside the mine, with the entrance and air shafts sealed, 18 gasping miners fought off deadly gas and dwindling oxygen to dig their way to freedom.

One of the brakemen, Sid Choquette, had run across the shifting rocks in utter darkness and successfully stopped the speeding Spokane Flyer, filled with passengers, before it could crash into the wall of rock across the main rail line.

But this isn't an account of heroism. It is an account of coal-mining and of an event that changed its shape forever.

Within a week of the disaster, investigators were pouring over the remains of Frank, demanding answers to questions of engineering and safety that no one could answer satisfactorily.

Samuel Gebo was ruined financially. H. L. Frank, haunted by the disaster, slowly went insane and died in a private sanatorium in 1908.

Unbelievably, the mine in Turtle Mountain was re-opened, but it was doomed. There were floods and fires, and Turtle Mountain continued to churn and heave.

Finally in 1910, after ownership of the mine had been sold to Canadian Coal Consolidated Limited, the Geological Survey of Canada warned that another slide could occur at any time. If it did, the government warned, the coal company would be held directly responsible.

Turtle Mountain, "the mountain that moves," was finally left in peace.

There have been other mining disasters, but the Frank Slide was the greatest single factor in creating the stringent safety regulations that forced so many opportunists to get out of the mining business.

And, inevitably, economic reality took over. The industry had seemed to offer everyone a chance to make a fortune, but the truth was that there is a limit to how much "fortune" there is in anything.

The remains of that shattered era are still there to see: at Frank, and in the tumbling mine buildings around Drumheller.

They can be seen, too, near Lethbridge in the grass-covered remains of Diamond City — of which The Lethbridge Herald said in 1911 that:

"There is probably no town or district in Alberta that has brighter prospects or greater resources . . ."

* * * *

THE STRUGGLE BACK . . .

The bad times that started with Turtle Mountain plagued Alberta's coal industry right up to the last decade.

In 1957, the last of the Galt mines closed. The Shaughnessy mines of Lethbridge Collieries followed in 1964. An effort to revive mining in Taber failed shortly afterward.

Markets for coal were shrinking as competition from oil and gas increased. The few coal companies still active were consolidating their holdings, closing down less profitable mines.

But, slowly, the coal industry has begun to climb back. Coal is, by a wide margin, the largest fuel reserve Canada has. As power and energy demands continue to grow, more and more industries are looking to coal to meet their needs.

Alberta power companies alone, for example, use more than 4 million tons of coal a year.

More important, possibly, than the increase in domestic demand, is the long-awaited breakthrough in export sales of coal.

For years, Alberta producers had fought to find a way to get to the enormous market in Japan. Finally, in 1969, the provincial government built a special spur of the Alberta Resources Railway to Grand Cache and in 1970 McIntyre Porcupine Mines Ltd. began shipments on a Japanese contract. The contract, to ship 30 million tons of coal over the next 15 years, is worth $450 million.

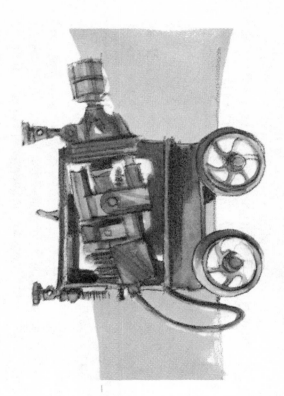

Which brings us back to Nick Sheran, chipping away at cutbanks on the Belly River with all the fury of his vision of a coal industry for Alberta.

It seems our coal industry has proved how right it was for him to be "a stubborn Irish fool who didn't have the sense to give up."

* * * *

Kootenai Brown was one of Alberta's most colorful explorers and characters; discovering among other things the scenic potential of the Waterton Lakes district.

But, for all that's known about him, few Albertans realize that he almost became our first oilman — all for the price of a horse.

Wandering the hills of southwestern Alberta in the 1890's, he and a friend called Lafayette French stumbled over a slough shiny with oil slicks.

Excited, they traded a horse for the rights to the spot and started drilling.

Unfortunately for Kootenai, the hole was dry. But the old explorer had started something: he'd started people thinking about oil.

* * * *

MEDICINE TO BURN . . .

A lot of people were talking about oil in the 1890's, but not too many were doing anything about it.

It took a stubborn old Waterton pioneer known as Uncle Bill Aldridge to really give the oil business its beginnings in Alberta.

The diary of one of the original Cardston settlers tells the story so well that it would be a shame to do anything more than pass it on the way we found it:

"Uncle Bill had heard of the oil seepage that was reputed to be somewhere in the vicinity of Waterton Lakes and he became determined to find it.

"One day in the summer of 1898 he and Oliver (his son) took their Winchesters, bedding, flour mixed with baking powder and salt, water pail and frying pan, and started from the cabin to find the oil. At noon they camped on Cameron Creek. Not far from the edge of the creek they kindled a fire and Oliver was sent to the creek for water.

"He was astonished when looking down at the edge, to see pools of what looked like black water, and called to his father come down and have a look at it.

"Bill came down, put his fingers into the black water, smelled it, tasted it and said, 'My gosh, boy, this is the ile we're lookin' for. Sure enough, it's ile.'

"He was then looking into what was later called Oil Creek, now Cameron Creek, and oil pools were lying in the wallows made by the bears when they came down to drink and rolled in the oil that seeped at the edge of the creek . . .

"Uncle Bill then laid a log across the creek to still the water and allow the oil to run out on top. To procure the oil, he laid gunny sacks on top of the water. The sacks absorbed the oil, which he then wrung out in buckets and barrels. Sometimes he boiled the oil to evaporate the water and to bring the oil to machine-oil consistency.

"This he carried in cans and barrels to Cardston, where he sold it to farmers to oil such conveyances and machinery as wagons, buggies, rakes, mowers and discs, and for other lubrication purposes. Sometimes he and his boys collected as much as 40 barrels a day from this seepage.

"For the Aldridge family, this crude oil had a medicinal value for such ailments as colds, pneumonia, sores, sunburn, blisters and 'the grip', by which name the flu was called in those days.

"At one time Uncle Bill became ill at the Hotel de Woolf. There was no doctor in town but nearly every family had a knowledge of the use of herbs and plasters with which to treat the sick.

'Mr. and Mrs. Woolf applied all their knowledge of herbs, plasters and nostrums to make him well, but nothing was of any avail.

'Finally, fearing he was going to die, Uncle Bill elected to be taken home where he could pass his last days with his family. The Woolfs, father and sons, made a comfortable bed of straw and blankets in the wagon bed, carried Uncle Bill there and snugly tucked him in, with a final warning to Oliver to drive slowly and carefully.

'When they reached the Belly River, 15 miles west of Cardston, Uncle Bill said, 'Boy, you'll have to stop. I can go no further.' Then he had an inspiration. 'Boy,' he said to Oliver, 'get me that bottle of ile out of the jockey box.'

'He tipped the quart bottle up and drank a half a pint of it. After an hour or two, with the oil acting as a purgative, he began to feel better. Oliver prepared supper over the campfire. His father ate hungrily and then said, 'Boy, hook up the horses and we'll go on home;' another 16 miles over rough roads.

"He then climbed to the spring seat beside Oliver and drove to his home where an anxious wife and children awaited him in alarm over his unusually long stay.

" 'That ile sure worked,' he said affectionately to Oliver in retelling the story to his family. 'It sure did,' said Oliver dryly."

It didn't take long for businessmen to hear of Bill Aldridge's oil find. Offers poured in, and finally, seven years after he found it, Uncle Bill sold off his Cameron Creek claim to the Vancouver Coal and Coke Company for $2,000 and 100,000 shares of stock.

The company drilled and struck oil at 1,100 feet. But they never were able to strike the main reservoir, and finally abandoned the project.

The rig burned down and the well eventually became a repository for garbage and junk.

But, at Cameron Creek, the oil still flows on the water. And, any time you want to, you can go down, stick your finger in the black water, smell it, taste it, and — in memory of Bill Aldridge — holler: "My gosh, boy, this is the ile we're lookin' for!"

* * * *

IT'S A GAS . . . .

Oil may have been what Uncle Bill was after, but across the province other exciting discoveries were being made.

So exciting, in fact, that the mayor of Medicine Hat forgot to put his clothes on.

In 1892, a CPR crew drilling for water 30 miles west of Medicine Hat was astonished when its well caught fire.

They had discovered natural gas.

Industry attracted by the find would make Medicine

Hat the Pittsburgh of the west, predicted the townspeople.

Under Mayor W. T. Finlay, the town council authorized the drilling of more gas wells.

But when the first well in Medicine Hat reached 1000 feet below the ground, all the money was gone — and still not a whiff of gas.

Mayor Finlay gambled and ordered the drillers to keep going.

Ten feet deeper, gas under great pressure blew the drill out of the ground with a mighty roar.

The blow-out occurred early in the morning while the mayor was dressing. He didn't bother to finish.

Braces blowing in the wind, he ran toward the hissing well.

The informally-attired mayor was soon joined by a throng of citizens celebrating the discovery of a resource that would soon make the town and the province famous.

* * * *

OLD GLORY AND OTHERS . . .

By 1908, the Calgary Natural Gas Company, under Archibald Dingman, had drilled a successful gas well on the Colonel James Walker estate in east Calgary.

Enough gas was produced to service some homes, provide a few street lights, and supply the Calgary brewery.

But this didn't satisfy Eugene Coste who acquired Dingman's company and, in 1911, founded the Canadian Western Natural Gas, Light, Heat and Power Company. Coste was determined his company would live up to its name.

Old Glory, a well on the Bow Island gas field, had blown in for Coste in 1909, earning him the title of "father of the natural gas industry".

Coste then undertook the mammoth task of constructing a 16 inch gas transmission pipeline from Bow Island to Calgary — a distance of 170 miles.

The pipeline — the third longest in North America, and the longest of its diameter — was completed in 86 days; good time even by today's standards.

Lethbridge, Calgary, Fort MacLeod, Granum, Claresholm, Nanton and Okotoks were connected with the main line, which became the backbone of the natural gas company's present operations in southern Alberta.

But the best was yet to come.

* * * *

*

SLICK BUSINESS . . .

For Albertans in 1914, the rainbow's end was Turner Valley.

Oil may not have the same aesthetic value as gold, but its value in dollars and cents was enough to turn Calgary into a city of lunatics.

"It was the wildest, most delirious, most uproarious, most exciting time that had ever entered into human imagination to conceive," exclaimed the Calgary Albertan.

Overnight, everyone became a "shareholder" — some filing claims in such unlikely spots as Bowness Park, now in Calgary.

And, just as fast, most of them went broke.

Five hundred "oil companies" sprang up instantaneously. Of the 50 companies that even made an attempt at drilling for oil, few were even mildly successful.

Within a few months, most of the big oil promoters had slunk away, their pockets bulging.

Calgarians had parted with more than a million dollars of their savings.

What they had to show for it were thousands of worthless share certificates — which some enterprising souls eventually used to wallpaper their homes and even a hotel lobby.

It wasn't that there was no oil at Turner Valley — but the excitement and speculation accompanying the 1914 discovery were out of all proportion to the actual find.

Even though Turner Valley was Canada's first commercial oil discovery in 50 years — and the first ever in the west — the field was producing a meagre average of less than 20 barrels of oil a day.

The man behind the hysteria over this comparative trickle of oil was a persistent optimist called William Stewart Herron.

Herron came from Ontario to settle on a farm in Okotoks in 1903.

Dreams of wealth nagged at the dissatisfied farmer. When the gas seep bubbling through Sheep Creek which flowed across his land turned out to be not marsh gas but petroleum, Herron was ecstatic.

After some shrewd property dealings, he had the money to secure oil leases in Turner Valley.

"I knew — or at least I thought I knew, which amounts to the same thing — that there was oil in the Valley," Herron was said to have remarked.

* * * *

PETROLEUM COMES OF AGE . . .

It was almost inevitable that Herron would get together with a man of equal ambition, Archibald Dingman.

In 1912, the pair formed Calgary Petroleum Products Company and agreed to spend $50,000 to drill a well.

Their decision couldn't have been more timely.

South of the border Henry Ford had begun to make automobiles in a big way. Throughout North America the need for new oil sources was far outstripping the supply.

The sun had risen on the petroleum industry.

But drilling for oil, Dingman and Herron discovered, was a tedious procedure.

Their "Discovery" well — the one that caused the furore of 1914 — was a teaser. It yielded a respectable amount of oil, but refused to come up with the "gusher" everyone was waiting for.

Dramatic reports of their progress, however, carried by Calgary newspapers, maintained a fever pitch of interest among the citizens.

Only a few saw through the frantic "get-rich-quick" schemes which had become the local obsession.

"The trouble with this oil situation at this formulative stage," Bob Edwards wryly suggested in his Calgary Eye Opener, "is that you are never sure whether the man you meet on the street is a multi-millionaire, or just an ordinary, common millionaire."

When Dingman and Herron's "Discovery" well made its modest debut May 14, 1914, the ordinary common millionaires were left out in the cold.

As the overnight oil companies faded away with fat wallets, and sadder but smarter Calgarians turned their attention to the coming of war, Dingman and Herron continued their search for the big gusher.

The Turner Valley story had just begun.

* * * * *

OIL TO BURN . . .

It was ten years before another major discovery was made in the valley, but between 1924 and 1936, 114 wells were drilled in the area.

Most of the natural gas was being burned off in enormous flares consuming 600 million cubic feet per day. The wastage was equal to nearly one third of Canada's natural gas consumption in 1969.

But what the early Turner Valley oilmen did not know was they were only skimming the surface.

Below the cap of gas they were burning off in vast amounts lay a pool of more than a billion barrels of crude oil.

Risking their combined life savings, three Calgarians, R.A. Brown, George Bell and J.W. Moyer, drilled the well which revealed this pool in 1936.

But the damage had been done.

Years of burning off the gas flares had dwindled away the gas pressure needed to bring the oil to the surface.

Petroleum engineers estimate that, instead of half a billion barrels, only 120 million will eventually be extracted from the Turner Valley pool.

It was a costly lesson for Alberta, but the mistake has not been repeated.

What of the two men who were in on the beginning of it all?

William Herron finally became a millionaire in 1926 when the Turner Valley leases he had clung to so tenaciously made good.

Devoted to his motto "Carry on; we want and need more oil," Archibald Dingman continued to make his living from small Turner Valley oil finds.

But Dingman died three months before the discovery of the huge Turner Valley oil pool in 1936, too soon to see the truth in his oft-spoken words.

* * * *

THE SEARCH GOES ON . . .

By the end of World War II, dreams of gigantic oil fields in Alberta were dwindling fast — as were the finances to support oil explorations.

After years of drilling with nothing to show but 133 dry holes, Imperial Oil decided to invest in one last try.

The company chose a location west of the Viking gas field, which supplies Edmonton with natural gas.

Imperial Leduc No. 1 got off to a discouraging start on the farm of Mike Turta.

But as the drillers reached the 5,000 foot level their hopes began to rise.

On February 3, 1947 oil squirted out of the well to a height of 70 feet, drenching the triumphant crew.

Imperial realized it had discovered the first oil in western Canada in 11 years.

Two months later, the company had an even bigger find on its hands, Leduc No. 2.

Just a mile and a half southwest of Number 1, the second well yielded the best pay section yet found in Canada.

* * * *

THE RICHEST SANDBOX IN THE WORLD . . .

Sidney Clark Ells set off on a 250 mile hike from Edmonton to Fort McMurray in 1913 and returned with samples of what would soon become the world's most valuable sandbox.

The Athabasca Tar Sands contain enough potential oil to meet Canada's needs for oil (based on 1969 requirements) for 700 years.

Suspecting the vast promise of the bituminous sands, Ells shipped out 60 tons of the tar sands from McMurray to Edmonton in the winter of 1915.

The sand was moved by horse team "in temperatures ranging from 20 to 50 below zero without tents for men or horses."

Ells' cargo was used to pave Edmonton streets — pavement which was still being used 50 years later.

But the dilemma posed by the tar sands was how to separate the oil from the sand.

In the decades that followed Ells' expedition, many schemes were tried without success.

It was not until 1962 that Great Canadian Oil Sands Ltd. won a government permit to start production from the sands.

They had the technical know-how. All they needed was the money.

With backing from Sun Oil, the company launched a project which would eventually cost them $250 million and produce 45,000 barrels of oil per day.

Five hundred government, oil industry and press representatives flew to the dedication of the GCOS plant at Fort McMurray in September 1967.

Already the plant was processing synthetic crude oil which would soon begin its journey along the 3,000 mile pipelines to refineries in Ontario and Ohio.

Seated at the head table among the dignitaries was Sidney Ells who made the first, most difficult journey to the Athabasca Tar Sands 54 years ago.

* * * *

With the promise of ample petroleum in the foreseeable future added to Alberta's other vital resources, economic progress in the province is assured for years to come.

Half of Canada's mineable coal exists in Alberta as well as abundant hydro-electric power.

The petroleum industry, through the development of an important fertilizer operation, has spurred the growth of agriculture.

Together, these two furnish the necessary ingredients for another boon to the economy: manufacturing.

The ups and downs of the oil industry have taken their toll on many Albertans.

Men lost their life savings.

Some, like William Herron, gained and lost several fortunes during the years of wild speculation.

Big oil companies invested millions of dollars in barren ground.

But, appropriately enough, the town of Leduc has coined the phrase which sums up the real story of oil in Alberta: "Oil's well that ends well."

* * * *

"In Lethbridge the housewife has the advantage of electricity at a low rate, and she may use it from early in the morning until midnight. She cooks, irons, sews, and can do a hundred things a day with its aid and it greatly lessens household duties" (The Lethbridge Herald, 1911)

* * * *

THE HARD DARK DAYS . . .

Alberta pioneers endured many hardships in settling the new land of the west; hardships that were compounded by isolation.

Well into the present century, settlers here were still far behind eastern Canada in many of the amenities we now all take for granted — mail, telephone and telegraph service, fashion, entertainment.

And if the settlers were being left in the dark in a cultural sense, they were being left "in the dark" in a literal sense as well.

In 1911, Albertans had electrical service in only the most rudimentary sense, and most didn't have it at all. A few cities, like Calgary, were using steam generators to bring a dim glow to life. In a few towns, enterprising individuals were using primitive equipment to offer a handful of customers sporadic "Saturday night and Monday morning" service.

But in most communities — and in all of rural Alberta — there was no electricity at all. These were the hard dark days. And for the farm family, because of sparseness of population and high development costs, the days would remain hard and dark for at least two decades longer.

Ten years ago, a writer named Mary Ellen Bradley painted a picture of a "typical" farm family of the era before power, and showed vividly how great a difference electricity makes to the quality of life:

"Mr. Farmer," she wrote, "started his day at dawn by hand-milking the five cows, feeding the pigs and horses. He separated the milk, using a hand-turned separator. Water for all the livestock had to be pumped by hand; though later a gas engine was purchased for the pump, but it proved unreliable and balky to start — especially on winter mornings.

"Meanwhile, the lady of the house had started her day, too. She was busy emptying ashes from the messy wood stove, carrying wood, building a fire to cook the meal and heat the house. Periodically the stove would refuse to burn the fuel properly, and smoke would fill the house.

"This was official notice that it was time to clean out the stove pipe, a major operation in any household. All the pipes would be taken down — gingerly handled, so as not to drop soot in the house — carefully carried out and away from the house, and then pounded to knock out the soot. In spite of the careful handling, when the job was done there usually would be a coating of dirty black soot over everything.

"Mrs. Farmer, among her many duties, assumed the responsibility of looking after the chickens; often as many as

200. Since a commercial hatchery was unheard of in those days, a small incubator, made of redwood, was kept warm by a coal-oil lamp.

"The eggs had to be turned every day, the lamp refueled, drafts screened off the eggs — and away from the lamp as well; of course, there was the constant danger of the lamp being blown out and the eggs ruined.

"When the small chicks were put in the brooder house a careful watch had to be kept on the heater — also non-electric — to see that it didn't become either too hot and smother the chicks, or too cold and allow them to freeze.

"When they first moved to the farm, Mrs. Farmer churned all the butter for the family with a dash churn. A few years later, the couple were able to buy a really modern convenience — a churn with a crank. So that she would not have to churn every day, she made a crockful of butter at a time, and put it into the well to keep it cool.

"Mr. Farmer had dug this well close to the house, about 25 feet deep, and 4 feet square. Food was put in pails or jars, a rope tied to the pail-handle or pail, or around the jar, and the whole thing was lowered into the natural 're-frigeration' of the well. It was only possible to keep fresh meat for a few days — butter and cream would keep for a few weeks.

"Keeping food, especially in summer was extremely difficult . . . Without home freezers, the Mason jar and canning kettles were part of the rituals of harvest.

"Mr. Farmer butchered the family's meat. Since a whole beef was too large for the family to use, half of the carcass was sold to a neighbor. (In some areas of the province, farmers joined in groups to form a 'ring', and butchered each others animals in turn for the group.)

"After the meat was butchered, Mrs. Farmer took over.

She cut the meat to fit into a quart jar, added salt, and secured the lid very tightly with a rubber jar ring. The jars were then put into a boiler or canning kettle and boiled for three hours.

"Preserving pork was quite a different process. First the meat was cured for three weeks in a brine made of saltpetre, salt, pepper and sugar. Then the pork was put into a wooden box to be smoked. A trench 8 to 10 feet was dug, a stove pipe laid along it and reaching into the box, a fire was built at the end of the trench about ten feet from the box. The smoke would draw through the pipe into the box where the meat was, giving it a nice smoky flavor."

Miss Bradley noted the difficulty of transportation, even for such routine matters as the weekly trip to the grocery store in town, then continued:

"Usually, after such a trip, they would arrive home much after dark and have to light the coal-oil lamps or lanterns. After all the rush and excitement to get away early that morning, it is quite possible the lamps had been forgotten, and would be out of oil. Then there would be fumbling in the dark until the oil can could be found, and further fumbling and spilling while filling the lamp.

"In the winter the lamps had to be filled every other day, or every day, depending on how early the family got up in the morning, and how long the lamps had to burn in the morning.

"Later, about 1928, a great improvement was introduced — the family acquired gasoline mantle lamps and a lantern utilizing the same principle. These gave off much better light than coal-oil lamps, but these also presented the same filling problem, complicated by the greater danger from the more explosive gasoline.

"And then, too, there was the exasperating problem of

delicate mantles which disintegrated when accidentally touched by clumsy fingers.

"One of Mrs. Farmer's most difficult chores was doing the family laundry. Her first washing aids were a wooden tub, a washboard and a hand-turned wringer. Then, several variations of hand-operated washing machines came on the market. Later, a washing machine with a gasoline engine was used. The water had to be hand-pumped and heated in a boiler on the stove.

"A sad iron — and they were properly named — was kept hot on the kitchen stove to iron all the clothes."

Given Miss Bradley's account, it is easy to understand why Alberta farm families chafed with impatience for the coming of electricity. And the account also provides a clue as to why so many farmers, even in the poverty years after the First World War, invested in the "extravagance" of a gasoline-powered generator.

* * * *

A FLICKER OF LIGHT . . . .

If the farm family was suffering from lack of power in 1911, his neighbor in town wasn't doing much better.

In most small communities in Alberta, it was the era of the single light bulb and of part-time electricity.

One man, or a group of men, would invest in a generator — powered by gasoline or natural gas or, sometimes, a steam boiler — and go into the electrical business. As mentioned earlier, it was the day of "Saturday night and Monday morning" service.

Power was supplied only twice a week; on Saturday night for shopping in the stores, and on Monday morning for the housewives to use new electric washing machines to do the family laundry.

Even that part-time service, thanks to the unreliability of generating equipment, wasn't consistent. As unhappy customers soon discovered, it could often be as dark on Saturday night and Monday morning as it was the rest of the week.

And, for this sporadic service, customers were paying 25 or 30 cents a kilowatt hour — 10 to 15 times as much as electricity costs today.

* * * *

AND THEN A GLEAM . . .

But, in 1911, in Calgary, something was starting that would change the electrical scene in Alberta for good.

Calgary, like many other cities, was trying to meet its own power demands. It had first got electricity in the late 1880's, and the city had been struggling ever since to meet the expanding power requirements of industry and an exploding population.

Population growth alone — from 4,091 in 1901 to 43,-704 in 1911 — demonstrates vividly why the city, despite unceasing expansion of generating facilities, just couldn't keep up with the hunger for electricity.

By 1911, after three or four years of debate, the city fathers were wavering between an all-out expansion of their facilities, and the alternative of turning the whole mess over to some private company.

As it happened — far from accidentally — there was a "private company" waiting in the wings, eager to take over the job from the city.

As early as 1906, the Calgary Power and Transmission Company — which had among its backers R. B. Bennett (later Viscount Bennett) and W. Max Aitken (later Lord Beaverbrook) — had been working on a proposal that involved constructing a dam on the Bow River for hydro-electric power to supply Calgary.

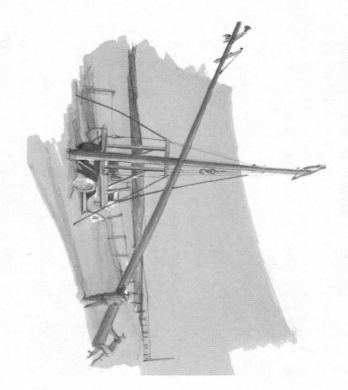

By 1909, this company in combination with others, had proceeded to the stage of acquiring the rights to 1,000 acres of land at Horseshoe Falls from the Stony Indian Reserve. It had also arranged for the lease of water rights from the federal department of the interior, arranged an industrial contract in Exshaw — and a contract to supply power to Calgary.

That year, in order to simplify what was becoming a corporate nightmare, the backers created a new company — Calgary Power Company Limited — to handle the electrical business. The new company was officially registered in March, 1911.

Soon all the necessary agreements were signed and Calgary Power was in the position — not as enviable as it might have seemed — of trying to meet Calgary's electrical demands.

The key to the scheme was construction of the hydro plant at Horseshoe Falls. Work on the project had started in 1909, even before Calgary Power had been incorporated.

The deadline for completion was April 1, 1911 — a critical date if Calgary Power was going to be able to live up to its agreement with the city. As it turned out, the contractor almost made it. He was a "mere" one month and twenty-one days late.

Calgary Power wasn't enchanted with the contractor, and the city fathers weren't enchanted with Calgary Power (nor would they be for many years), but the first hydro plant on the Bow was in operation, and the two tenuous wires linking Calgary to Horseshoe Falls would soon be woven into a web for a whole province.

* * * *

THE COWBOY LINEMAN . . . .

"I guess," grins Henry Bradley, "that you could say that I was sort of a cowboy."

Which, in a strange kind of way, is precisely true.

Henry Bradley, today safety supervisor for Calgary Power, is a veteran of a unique period in the history of electrical power in Alberta. He is part of an era when a handful of men made it their personal responsibility to see that — no matter how impossible the odds — the people of Alberta got consistent and reliable electrical service.

The confidence with which you flip on your kitchen light is the lasting evidence of how well they succeeded.

Henry was a lineman and, as he says, "sort of a cowboy."

"The reason for this," he explains, "is that, at that particular time, you patrolled lines on horseback. I did it out of Calgary.

"You hired on to be sort of a tough guy, see; the idea being that if you couldn't repair it any other way you could bend it or make it work somehow or other.

"Patrolling the line, you'd usually be out maybe a week. You'd get your climbing irons — we called them galloping irons — and safety belt and gloves and stuff, tie them on back of the saddle and off you'd go.

"You'd eat and sleep at farm houses along the way.

"Horses were used to ride the lines right into the 40's. It was an excellent method of patrolling, because your attention was not necessarily distracted by having to drive or anything. The horse just took you along and away you went — as long as you were sufficient cowboy to stay there.

"The chap I hired from here was kind of a bronc buster himself, and what he used to do was rent three horses to the company. There was always two available, and one he was breaking.

"And when he got them half-broke, he gave them to the patrolmen to ride, to finish off the job. Then he could sell them off as saddle horses broke to ride.

"I can remember one time on one of those horses when I made it just as far as 4th St. and 8th Ave., where Eaton's is now, and the horse started to buck.

"This may be all right during Stampede time, but any other time you sure attract a lot of attention. I'll tell you, I sure scattered a lot of people when that horse decided to stand up on his two hind feet!

"People were yellin' 'Ride him cowboy!' and I thought, Oh Lord, if you only knew how little cowboy I really am! Made the job interesting, all right."

"I remember the first time I had to cross the Bow River down here on patrol. I wasn't just sure where they crossed the river on horseback, and I asked one of the CPR maintenance men who was stationed down there if he knew where the power patrolmen crossed the river.

" 'Right across there,' he says. So I looked at the river and I thought, well, he should know, and in I went.

"It was a good job I had a horse that was a strong swimmer. I got across with him goin' hard as he could and me hangin' on to his tail.

"It was a cold day, and I remember winding up at my destination where I was staying for the night just about literally frozen to the seat.

"When I caught up with that guy later, all he did was laugh and say I should have had more sense. True, I guess. Sometimes you've got to learn the hard way; get your knocks."

Henry pondered for a moment. "Strange thing, you know. I don't know whether we were really more self-sufficient then or what, but you didn't much think about the risks, the chance-taking.

"It was a risk being out on horseback in some of the weather we had to face, and we did some mighty chance-taking, working on those lines alone.

"But you never much thought about it. And if you did it just seemed an additional challenge.

"It was a duty you had to perform. Power must go on. It had to be restored. This was the thing, no matter how you had to do it.

"And when you'd get it repaired, you'd be relieved, and you'd think, well, you'd given a service. And that's what it was all about."

* * *

THE FLICKERING YEARS . . .

For many long and difficult years after its birth in 1911, Calgary Power had to fight to survive. The reserves of water above the Horseshoe were far from stable. There was too much water in summer, and too little in winter. Even with the use of Calgary's Victoria Park steam generating plant, Calgary Power couldn't cope.

In winter, at Horseshoe, great slabs of ice would be sucked down and pinned against the intake, and the station would suddenly lose its generating load. Every available man on the staff would rush out with axes and poles and try to clear the obstruction.

Some of those men, in those trying days, found themselves with bundles of dynamite in hand and well on their way to becoming self-educated demolition experts.

The dynamite was for the ice, of course. But there were times, when Calgary's aldermen were complaining particularly loudly about flickering lights, that it was a sore temptation . . .

* * * *

GAHERTY TO THE RESCUE . . .

It was 1920, and Geoffrey Abbott Gaherty, chief engineer of Montreal Engineering Company Ltd., was on his way back to Montreal.

The owner of Montreal Engineering, I. W. Killam, had a small financial interest in an electric company called Calgary Power, and he asked Gaherty to take a look at the operation on his way back east.

Gaherty was the perfect man to "take a look at" a power company. Unlike most other engineers in Canada at that time, he had experience in the field. He'd been instrumental in Killam developments on Quebec's Gatineau River, and had done investigation work on the Nova Scotia Light and Power Company project.

Gaherty, as requested, stopped in Calgary to investigate the situation at Calgary Power. What he saw was hardly encouraging.

"At that time," as someone wrote later, "the company was in difficulty, power plants with no effective storage, producing unreliable power for only three customers, earning barely enough revenue to cover expenses, and its owners discouraged."

Gaherty, however, was interested in "potential", and he saw Calgary Power as a company with potential to spare. Back in Montreal, he had a long discussion with Killam, and Killam set to work to buy control of the ailing company.

As soon as he had it, he sent his chief engineer back to Alberta to bring Calgary Power to life.

It was Gaherty's engineering talent that inspired the projects that finally gave the company the generating reserves and stability it needed.

And, though few of those closest to him realized it at the time, Calgary Power was going to need amazing reserves and stability if it was going to live up to a dream Gaherty was nurturing.

Years later, a man who worked with Gaherty said that "he was a man who commanded admiration and respect from all who knew him."

It must have taken a great deal of both admiration and respect for those around Gaherty to accept the unbelievable targets he began setting in the early 1920's — a vastly-expanded generating network, an all-out bid to bring the majority of Alberta towns into a power system served by Calgary Power and, more astonishing still, an all-out bid to electrify rural Alberta.

It says something about the special quality of G.A. Gaherty to note that he wasn't immediately written off as insane. For "insane" is about the best word to describe the enormity — both financially and technically — of the projects Gaherty was proposing.

But those around Gaherty just said "Let's go," and the biggest gamble in Alberta history to that point (and possibly since that point) was underway.

Actually, Gaherty's plans were not as wild as they sounded. Technical improvements had now made long-range power transmission possible. Alberta's towns were beginning to grow, and with them their market potential — particularly since most towns were still suffering along with the

"Saturday night and Monday morning" quality of service.

If Calgary Power didn't reach out and make a try for the business, other companies might.

So, into the mountains of Banff late in the fall of 1922 went a party, led by Calgary Power surveyor J.E. Spurling, to investigate the potential of a power project to tap the Spray Lakes water resources. (Decades later that survey would finally find fruition in the Spray-Rundle-Three Sisters development.)

And spreading out across the province went other teams of men to look for routes for transmission lines.

In 1925, Managing Director Gaherty took to the road himself to woo Alberta's towns, to negotiate contracts and franchises, to purchase existing power-producing equipment (however terrible!), to negotiate easements through farms and ranches.

And at night he'd drive his Model T back over the rutted roads to Calgary and spend hours with his engineers; drawing plans for the dream that was rapidly taking shape.

In 1926 — with the hard-working, hard-fighting construction crews of McGregor Telephone and Power Construction Company still throwing up poles and line across the province — the first towns of High River, Olds and Blackie agreed to Calgary Power service.

That trickle of three became a stream of 15 more the next year, and a flood of 46 in 1928.

And, by then, the third part of the Gaherty dream — rural electrification — was already taking shape.

Earlier in this account of the development of electric power in Alberta, we turned to Mary Ellen Bradley's account of the hardships faced by Alberta farm families before electricity. We'd like to turn to her again to see the effects of what Gaherty was bringing.

"Talk of organizing rural electrification areas began to circulate. Canvassers covered the district to see how many farmers were in favor of obtaining central station power.

"When asked for an opinion, Mr. Alberta Farmer said with sudden conviction, 'I've waited forty years for power!'

"Mr. Farmer and his neighbors found a new use for co-operative 'bees' — they grouped together to clear brush for power line right-of-way. They had their homes wired. They began to haunt appliance dealers' showrooms and scan mail-order catalogs for the electrical appliances they would buy.

"With initial organization complete, crews from Farm Electric Services Ltd. appeared in the district. Miles of poles and wires began to spring up. Then, at last, the awaited day arrived — their transformer was connected and now they had ELECTRICITY!"

The key to the success of Gaherty's plans was "dependability". The economy of the new service was obvious to customers, but they had to be convinced that, unlike the power they'd had before, this new service was always going to be there when it was needed. If the power went off, and with it the heaters in a chicken hatchery . . .

"No one," a Calgary Power veteran recalled recently with a shudder, "knows just how thin we were stretched in those early days.

"If, even just once, our luck had gone bad . . ."

But it didn't go bad. And today only three cities — Edmonton, Lethbridge and Medicine Hat — handle their own generating requirements. A handful of other communities, including Calgary, own distribution systems.

Calgary Power's operation has expanded to 12 hydro plants (a 13th is now under construction) and 2 thermal plants on Lake Wabamun.

Between Calgary Power and its northern neighbor, Canadian Utilities, 99 per cent of all the farms in Alberta have electricity. There are 74,000 miles of transmission and distribution line in the province.

In 1964, when G.A. Gaherty died, J. E. Oberholtzer of Alberta's department of industry and development engraved his name in Alberta history with a few simple words:

"There is no need for special memorials for some people. In the case of Dr. Gaherty the power projects throughout the province of Alberta stand as permanent records of his achievements."

* * * *

*

COMMUNICATION

Struggling into the Rocky Mountains in July, 1841, Governor Sir George Simpson of the Hudson's Bay Company brought his party to an abrupt halt and began examining tree trunks.

It wasn't a search for firewood or a peculiar outbreak of "bush-fever". It was a desperate hunt for a letter.

Within minutes, Sir George's party had found what they were looking for. Scrawled in charcoal on the bark of a thick pine was a "picture-letter" telling them their guide, Edward Berland, and 27 sorely-needed horses were waiting at a nearby lake.

Yelling, cursing, and swatting at clouds of mosquitoes, the party hurried on. What they left behind, for nature to erase, may well have been the first "letter" in Alberta.

It would be ten years — 1851 — before Canada would have its first postage stamp (the famous three penny beaver). And it would be many more long years before the pioneers of Alberta knew what it was like to have the benefits of mail service.

* * * *

Actually, for 20 years after that party of Sir George's passed through on its mad dash to the Pacific, it didn't much matter that there wasn't any mail in Alberta.

Like Sir George, the only white men who had seen Alberta in the early years of the 1800's were mostly just passing through — usually in search of a badly-needed pass that would let the Hudson's Bay Company or the rival Nor'westers carry trade to the Pacific.

But here and there the rival trading companies were putting up posts to trade with the Indians. And with those posts came our first "settlers."

For these men of the trading posts, life was lonely in the extreme. They knew there was a world outside, but they didn't know much about what was happening in it.

True, now and then there would be a packet of mail tucked into a shipment of trade goods. But usually that mail would be only business instructions from headquarters — or notice that a party of explorers (of which there seemed a never-ending stream in those days) was on its way west.

And Jasper Hawes of Jasper House would up his prices a few beaver-skins, or sigh and clear a space on the floor for the trail-weary party soon to appear over the eastern horizon.

* * * *

THE RUMORED WEST . . .

If early westerners were getting little news about the east, easterners were getting all too much about the west. And most of it was, well . . . slightly distorted.

Enthusiastic accounts from explorers brought ill-equipped adventurers hurrying west in search of gold that often wasn't there. And those accounts sometimes plunged them into mountain "passes" that all too often literally ended in a stone wall.

* * * * *

THE TRAGIC TRUTH . . .

Even while Palliser was probing the passes of the Rockies, gold was being found in the Fraser River. And news of the discovery brought easterners rushing west by the thousands.

The wiser made their way by boat, around the tip of South America and up the west coast. Others chose to go by land, confidently believing in reports that the way west was "an easy wagon road through a lovely country unequalled for its beauty and salubrity of climate," and that the Rockies could be crossed "with perfect safety."

In the spring of 1862, a party of more than 100 Overlanders left Ontario for the golden west. They travelled by train to St. Paul and then to Fort Garry.

There, equipped with carts and provisions for 60 days, they set out across the prairies. With them was a pregnant woman and her two children; the youngest only three.

None of the party, of course, had given any thought to settling in Alberta — and what they encountered when they reached it did nothing to change their minds.

The prairies they found were a virtual swamp. It was raining when the Overlanders hit the plains, and it was still raining when they left them behind.

Many of the streams and rivers had spilled over their banks and were unfordable. The party had to work waist-deep in water to build temporary bridges that barely held together long enough to rush wagons across.

Hour after hour, they waded across the flooded meadows of Alberta. There were frequent sarcastic queries about when they would find the "overland" route they'd heard about.

For the eleven days it took to reach Fort Edmonton, they were never dry. They staggered in to the post "toil-worn, jaded, forlorn and tattered."

Fort Edmonton, however, was a sight that brought loud cheering from the party. Not only did it mean shelter. It meant to the misinformed 100 that they were almost at their destination. As one recalled later, "We had full confidence in our ability to reach the El Dorado of our hopes."

Months later, the ragged, starving survivors of that party straggled into the Cariboo. Behind them, they had left the memories of slaughtered animals and lost possessions. Behind them, too, they had left those who had lost the strength or will to go on.

And behind them, in the Rockies, they left graves. How many graves is something that they, and history, never recorded.

For those whose strength had carried them to the Fraser, there was no reward. Fate sent all away empty-handed.

All, that is, but the woman who made it to the Cariboo in time to give birth to a baby girl; the same brave woman who set out from Fort Garry so many months before on the "easy wagon road" to a western dream.

* * * *

THE "WHISKEY" EXPRESS . . .

In 1860, eastern Canadians were enjoying the amenities of parcel-post, registered letters and postal money orders, and — in Toronto at least — street letter boxes.

Albertans weren't jealous, for the simple reason that, since they still didn't have any kind of postal service themselves, they just didn't know what was happening in the east.

But in 1860, for southern Albertans at least, the times were about to start changing. A wild and wicked crew of men was on its way to the southern plains to do some trading. And, with the compliments of the U.S.A. — and a native thirst for whiskey — southern Alberta was about to get mail delivery.

Officially, the Hudson's Bay Company would NEVER trade liquor to the Indians. (Unofficially, of course, everyone had a good idea where all that rum in Alberta was coming from.) The free-traders of the northwest United States weren't that coy. They were out to trade whiskey for fur — and they didn't care who knew it.

When these free-traders found the U.S. government didn't approve of their practice, they simply headed north and began plying their trade with the Blackfoot in Canada.

So enthusiastic were the Blackfoot and Peigans that the traders soon had a steady stream of bullcarts squeaking back and forth between forts like Whoop Up in southern Alberta and Fort Benton in Montana. Heading south, the big carts were stacked high with buffalo robes and furs. Heading north, the principal cargo was whiskey — but, to the benefit of Alberta pioneers, tucked in among the barrels were precious pouches of mail.

The bull-carts had opened a channel of communication with the south and east. Albertans, for the first time, could begin to send and receive mail with some semblance of regularity. There might even be an outdated but readable newspaper or two tucked in the letter pouch.

The appetite the traders created for whiskey was soon to be choked off by an angry Canadian government. But the second appetite they created was too great for any government to kill. Albertans had tasted communication, and they weren't prepared to do without it any more.

Finally, on July 1, 1871, the Canadian government gave in and opened Alberta's first post office at Fort Saskatchewan (north of Edmonton). Soon a network of post offices covered the west and the stagecoach and pony express had replaced the "whiskey" express forever.

Today, there's hardly a farm or ranch without a mailbox at the gate, or a city house without a slot in the door. And we even have parcel post and registered letters and money orders. And Toronto no longer has a monopoly on street letter boxes.

And if every now and then one of the letters you receive smells faintly of whiskey, don't let it bother you. It's just the ghost of an ill wind that blew us a little good.

* * * *

ROLL THE PRESSES . . .

"The great man of today in Canada is made up of one part achievement and nine parts printers' ink"—Bob Edwards.

* * * *

Hanging in the newsrooms of The Lethbridge Herald and The Edmonton Journal are certificates honoring the two newspapers as joint winners of the first Pulitzer Prize ever to be awarded outside the United States.

The award came for courage rather than fine writing. Given the history of journalism in Alberta, there may be some justice in that.

Alberta's pioneers were prepared to do without a lot of things: streetlighting, trolleys, running water, and all those other civilized frills.

And they were patient, those early pioneers. Why, they waited 25 years for the mails to come here from the east, and then there was the telegraph and . . .

Well, doing-without and being patient has its limits. And by 1880 Albertans had decided they'd waited more than long enough for one essential of civilized life: the newspaper.

The call was out, and before they knew what had hit them Albertans suddenly had newspapers. And more newspapers and more newspapers.

In fact, for a while it seemed that Alberta was going to have more newspapers than the constitution can stand. It seemed you couldn't open a tent-flap or the door of a box car without running smack into a printing press and a sweating, swearing publisher "bringing the news" to Alberta.

A good many of those self-made "publishers", of course, never stayed in business past their first editions. They lasted only until their first paper hit the muddy streets and the outraged eyes of their readers.

Fortunately, for every deadbeat there were ten dedicated journalists who had the vision to look ahead to the future, and the enterprise to work to become part of that future.

These pioneer newsmen were trying to bring legitimate journalism to a frontier. And, judging from some of the perils they faced, "trying" is the best word to describe the life of a pioneer publisher.

* * * *

A SERIOUS APHAIR . . .

Lost somewhere in history are the origin of the Rocky Mountain Cyclone and the name of the brave soul who published it. Which may be just as well.

Unlike some of his competitors, who were resorting to carving type from wooden blocks, this gentleman decided to go whole-hog and order a press and type from a supplier in the east.

As the lead article in the first (and only known) issue of the Cyclone demonstrates, he might have been better off if he'd stuck to whittling:

"We begin the publication ov the Cyclone with some phew diphiculties in the way. The type phounder phrom whom we bought the outphit phor this printing ophice phailed to supply any ephs or cays, and it will be phour or phive weex bephore we can get any. We have ordered the missing letters, and we will have to wait until they come. We don't lique the idea ov this variety ov spelling any better than our readers do, but mistax will happen in the best-regulated phamilies, and iph the c's, x's and q's hold out we shall ceep (sound the c hard) the Cyclone whirling, aphter a phasion, until the sorts arrive. It's no joque to us; it is a serious aphair."

* * * *

THE BIBLE AND THE BULLETIN . . .

The Edmonton Bulletin was Alberta's first real newspaper. And Frank Oliver was Alberta's first real publisher.

The paper blared into existence on December 6, 1880, with the slogan "Read The Bible And The Bulletin." To a lot of p e o p l e — particularly in Edmonton — the slogan made sense.

Frank Oliver, after all, was something most other publishers of the time were not, a professional newspaper-man. Even though he'd arrived in Edmonton to go into the grocery business, he'd first learned the newspaper trade working for the Winnipeg Free Press.

With credentials like that, it's easy to see why the people of Edmonton were willing to accept the Bulletin's slogan.

Credentials or not, it appears likely that Oliver would never have started the Bulletin had it not been for a want ad and a telegrapher with writer's cramp.

The advertisement was in Oliver's old paper, the Winnipeg Free Press, and pointed out that someone in Philadelphia had a printing press for sale for $20.

The writer's cramp belonged to Edmonton's over-worked telegrapher, Alec Taylor.

Taylor, for a long time, was the town's only source of news. So anxious were people for news of the rest of the world that Taylor used to write out, in long-hand, anything interesting that came over the wire and leave the bulletins on the counter of Frank Oliver's grocery store for the public to read.

Taylor was getting tired of the task, and the story goes that while he was delivering his bundle of telegraph news to Oliver's store one day, he spotted the advertisement in the Free Press.

"You worked on the Free Press, didn't you Frank?" he prodded Oliver. "If you know all about running a news-paper why don't you buy this press and start a paper? I'll give you all the news and I won't have to write it out my-self."

Oliver was hesitantly considering the idea when Donald Ross, owner of the Edmonton Hotel, walked in. Taylor told him of the idea he was trying to sell Oliver, and Ross was so taken with it, he offered one of his hotel outbuildings as a place to set up the press — free.

With offers of free news and a free building, how could Oliver refuse?

So, in a matter of days, the Philadelphia press was west-bound in a loaded freighter wagon.

At that time, the road to Edmonton involved a never-ending series of fords across the Saskatchewan River. No sooner would a traveller come dripping out of the Saskatchewan on one side than he'd go splashing into it again on the other.

On one of these crossings, the wagon carrying Oliver's press tipped over and dumped all the large type into the water. It was never retrieved.

The loss would have been enough to stop Oliver had it not been for the determined telegrapher, Alec Taylor. Taylor was so anxious to have the paper come out that he personally carved, from blocks of wood, the large letters to form the words "THE BULLETIN", and Oliver went to press.

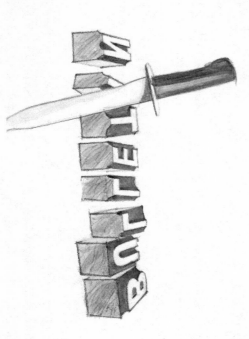

Frank Oliver, later, often said that those first editions were probably the smallest paper ever published. The Bulletin measured five inches wide by six inches deep (smaller than the page you're looking at!) and consisted of only four pages of printing when unfolded.

Alec Taylor, you'll recall, had promised Oliver free telegraph news. But, as luck would have it, the first issue of The Bulletin came out with its main headline reading: "No Telegrams."

The line had gone out the day before, and all Taylor's carving talent couldn't change that.

By the next week, however, the telegraph line was repaired and The Bulletin was in business. The paper was heady reading as a few samples from its first decade demonstrate:

—"George Gagnon lately killed a very large wolf, which, after disposing of one of his sheep, came back for another."

—"A Big Lake resident wants to know why the government potato contract was not awarded to him, seeing that his offer was 20 cents lower than that of the party who secured it."

—"Mr. Lucas, Government farmer at Peace Hills, has been supplied with his share of that band of cows. They are reported to be the sickest looking lot of animals in the county."

—"In New York City fully one half of the stage and cab horses are laid up with the epizootic."

—"Last Saturday morning the thermometers at Forts Edmonton and Saskatchewan registered 47 below zero."

Oliver's heart, however, was never really in the newspaper business. His real love was politics, particularly Liberal Party politics. In 1883, he won a seat on the North West Council. From then, until his death in 1933, Oliver was a politician first and a newspaper publisher only incidentally.

Despite the neglect, Liberal backing kept The Bulletin thriving for many years. It was only when the Liberals faded as a political force in Alberta in the 1930's that the paper began to suffer.

It struggled on until 1950, then quietly gave up and sold out to The Edmonton Journal.

If it died unhappily, The Bulletin could be proud that it had lived well. It had carried a city into the 20th Century. And, we mustn't forget, it also cured Edmonton's first telegrapher of what could have been the worst case of writer's cramp in Edmonton history.

* * * *

NOW AS I SEE IT . . .

Alberta's pioneer publishers had opinions on everything under the sun, and they considered it their divinely-inspired duty to share those opinions with their readers.

As a result, the pioneer newspaper seldom had an editorial page as we know it. It didn't need one. The whole paper was usually one long — and often outrageous — editorial.

That reader reaction often brought the not-so-delicate scent of bubbling tar and feathers wafting by the pressroom door didn't seem to deter these pioneer journalists a bit.

Indeed, so taken were they with the approach, that Alberta newspapers remained largely organs of opinion until well into this century.

But as Bob Edwards (the opinionated publisher to end all opinionated publishers) p o i n t e d out, this brand of journalism was, at best, a little risky. Writing in the Eye Opener on June 6, 1902, he lamented:

It is simply impossible to run a paper without an occasional error . . . As an example: "I've come," said the visitor with the club, "to see why you called me a political jobber in your paper today."

"I regret the error of the printer quite as much as you," replied the editor after opening a little drawer and taking out a gun.

"Ah, then you didn't mean to call me that."

"No sir. I wrote robber very distinctly."

* * * *

NOW THERE WAS A MAN . . .
Studying the microfilmed collection of the Eye Opener in the library of The Calgary Herald, a researcher felt someone at his shoulder and turned around to face a misty-eyed oldtimer.

"Ah, the Eye Opener," the oldtimer blinked. "Now there was a paper.

"And Bob Edwards. Now there was a man."

It would be hard to find an Albertan who'd disagree.

"The price of this paper is one dollar a year," Bob Edwards once remarked. "It ought to be five but we knock off four for irregularity."

The Eye Opener and its publisher were, indeed, irregular. But more than anything or anyone else they managed to put Alberta — and Calgary in particular — on the map of the world.

Drunk or sober, this Scot with the soft heart and the sharp pen managed to produce a newspaper guaranteed to provoke both laughter and indignation — with more of the former than the latter. And if he created an international incident while he was at it, or tore a strip from some shady politician's back, or took a jab at the Canadian Pacific Railway, so much the better as far as he and most of his readers were concerned.

"One reason the Eye Opener has so many high ideals," he once suggested, "is that Calgary is over 3,000 feet above the level of the sea."

Bob Edwards did have his detractors. Not everyone appreciated his wit and that, combined with his perpetual lack of funds, forced him to move his paper from town to town until finally, in 1904, he and Calgary discovered one another and began an affair that lasted until his death in 1922.

The story of Bob Edwards deserves a whole book (like Eye Opener Bob by Grant MacEwan), and it would be an injustice to try to tell his story in these few pages.

Instead, we'd like to offer a sample of the Eye Opener itself. Although it lacks an example of Edwards' letters from that fictitious remittance man, Albert Buzzard-Cholomondeley of Skookingham, Leicestershire, England, what follows is a pretty fair taste of the famous weekly's front pages.

Indeed, apart from some deletions made for space reasons, it is exactly the front page that faced his Calgary readers when they unfolded their Eye Opener on August 18, 1906:

EYEOPENERS...

Cheer up! Only 18 more weeks of the present council.

Over in Riverside last week, amongst the Germans, a very pretty wedding was solemnized between M a x Kahn the talented carpenter, and Miss Lena Katz. Considerable beer was licked up by the guests and the function, which otherwise would have passed off with great eclat, broke up in a free fight owing to a flippant remark made by someone present that the wedding seemed to him to be a case of catch as Katz Kahn.

It must make Lord's Day Alliance Shearer (who was no doubt immensely tickled at being invited by the cabinet to assist in framing the Lord's Day Bill) very sick at heart when he reads the Bill all over again in the quiet of his study. Instead of turning out, as the reverend gentleman and his longfaced friends fondly hoped, to be a compulsory insistence on the old Puritan Sunday of the well known Mayflower brand, the poor Bill got so changed around, amended, bent, twisted, and

banged about by the wicked men in the House that it is now but a ghost of its former self.

The situation so far as actual S u n d a y observance goes is not changed to any annoying extent.

If passed as first proposed, it would have been an infringement of the liberty of the subject such as the public, as a mass, would not have stood for a moment. But the Bill was happily juggled about and broadened out at the last minute when nobody was looking. One of the amiable peculiarities of the act is that its real meanings are in the n a t u r e of conundrums which, because it would cost a lot to try them out by legal process, will probably remain puzzles forever.

The act prohibits all manner of participation in any game, performance or meeting held for gain, or from which there are "gate receipts", except at church doors. Amateur golf, cricket, baseball, polo, footracing, or theatricals, on Sunday are permitted. Think of that, ye soreheads who have been kicking about the Lord's Day Act! The Lord's Day Act is all right, in spots.

As to working on the Sawbath. You can do any work of necessity and mercy on the Sawbath. Such works are specified, and include telegraph and telephone service, carrying travellers, renting and hiring carriages and small boats, preparing Monday morning newspapers, and, generally speaking, pretty much every sort of work that will not make capital lose some profit nor labor some employment.

Nothing the matter with that, is there?

Radcliffe, our genial hangman, has applied to the government for leave to augment his salary by travelling with a circus and giving exhibitions of his skill. If the permission is granted, which we very much doubt, Mr. Radcliffe proposes to "put on" Burchell's execution in all its detail, a cleverly prepared dummy of the famous murderer having already been secured from a well known Woodstock taxidermist. It is likely, also, that he may strive to amuse the children who stay for the concert with a comic representation of how he choked off a couple of Chinamen at Nanaimo last year.

In this connection, we might be permitted to suggest that Radcliffe be given the appointment of Official Foolkiller at a fair remuneration, his duties being to respond to calls from such towns as require his services. The only drawback to this suggestion is that he might, in order to save himself endless journeyings to and fro, decide to change his place of residence from Toronto to Calgary.

Do read the following astonishing incident which occurred at Olds (Cloakeyville) the other day.

It didn't occur exactly at Olds, but a lake four or five miles from town, where they have picnics, pleasure parties, and so forth.

Three Olds gentlemen were out for a sail in a boat. It was a very nice boat, but it had no keel. Consequently the sail had to be manipulated with the greatest care and skill.

Well, to make a long story short, a gust of wind struck the boat when about a quarter of a mile from shore and over she went. The three men floundered about in the water which was fifteen feet deep, and great was the panic and excitement among the pleasure-seekers picnicking along the beach.

A young Scots section-hand named Brown, a splendid swimmer, doft all his clothes to the buff and swam out to the rescue.

Another boat reached the drowners about the same time as he did, and pulled them aboard. Scotty Brown, however, decided to swim back.

When he reached the shore there was quite a crowd of ladies and gentlemen waiting for the rescued party. Among them was the wife of one of the men who were upset, a couple of school-mamms, and several others of the fair sex.

Scotty landed without a stitch of clothes on him, but the crowd was too much engrossed over the partially drowned men to pay very much attention to him. However, it appears that he did not go entirely unnoticed for, later on, one of the ladies was heard to exclaim in tones of intense admiration. "Well, I'll say this for Mr. Brown. He showed us he was a man anyhow!"

A newspaper has been started at the flourishing town of Midnapore, nine miles south of Calgary. It is called the Midnapore Gazette and is edited by a gentleman whose writings will never be mistaken for those of Mr. Goldwin Smith. One of the locals reads—

"Mrs. Jimmy Osborne, wife of our talented butcher, fell down the cellar steps last Tuesday and broke her knee-cap. The Gazette extends its sympathy to Mrs. Osborne in this her hour of bereavement."

The M.P.P.'s excursion appears to have been but a dreary affair. When will people who get up excursions intended specially for the amusement or instruction of a body of men engaged in some particular line of business, when will they tumble to the fact that any such excursion which includes "the women-folk" is bound to be a frost?

We never knew it fail yet. The wives and daughters act as a veritable wet blanket over the whole proceedings and effectively put a stopper on any fun and hilarity that might otherwise be indulged in by the men who are supposed to be off on a holiday.

The men are afraid to take a drink or to hit 'er up and strike a gait. If somebody starts to sing, the ladies conclude he is drunk. Poker is sidetracked, as is also the interchange of stories.

Then, again, ladies are prone to criticize. "Mr. So and So is such a charming man, while Mr. Toodleupteday is such a horrid man"—"Don't you think Mr. Joskins might dress a little better?" —"Where did Mr. McGonigle pick up that awful wife of his?"—"I think it very bad taste for the men to be always around the dining car conductor taking drinks when ladies are along," and so forth and so forth.

No, no! The Lord preserve us from an excursion where "the women-folk" are along. We have been there.

From all we can learn of the M.P.P.'s excursion it seems to have been a kind of juggernaut business from start to finish, the triumphant Liberals rolling in uncanny majesty over the hapless country crushing all Conservatives foolish enough to get in their path.

The two hapless members of the opposition, Robertson, and Don Hiebert were ignored most shabbily, neither being invited to speak nor even to show themselves as curiosities. This was all in exceedingly poor taste.

Nor was Mr. Young of the Herald, though a guest, invited to warble for the press. This was reserved for the great Liberal orator, Duncan Marshall, than whom there is no more fascinating talker in the west.

Liberalism was riotously triumphant. It was a grand missionary trip for the party, fall wheat and beet sugar being of secondary consideration.

Robertson and Don Hiebert should make the trip all over again by themselves and raise hell generally on behalf of the badly chewed-up Conservative party.

Let us draw a long breath and wait for the first despatch from London announcing Frank Oliver's presentation to King Edward's. His Majesty will no doubt be grief-stricken when he learns that Callahan has broken out of the new Edmonton jail.

After the next municipal election some of the present aldermen will put in an interesting half hour wondering why they ever took the trouble to stand as candidates again.

We heard a pretty good yarn the other day, happily free from all suggestion of double entendre, as so many good yarns are not—. It is about a visit to a sick bed.

Before being allowed to enter the chamber to have a chat with his sick friend, who was of a very stubborn, contumacious nature, he was handed the usual line of warning about cheering the odd fellow up and making light of his illness and so forth.

"Well, well, old chap," he cried cheerily to the patient, "you're looking fine. I don't believe you're sick at all."

"Me not sick! Great Scot! I'm awful sick."

"Not a bit of it, not a bit of it! Only imagination my dear boy. You are looking ever so much better since I was here."

"You are a liar."

"Why, old fellow, you are, upon my word! Eyes bright, good color, cheerful demen—"

"What are you giving me you blasted idiot! I tell you I am much worse."

"Oh nonsense!"

"Damned your eyes, I am!"

"Oh, pshaw!"

"Look here you fool, you chuckling head, you—you busted record. Look here! You see me lying here on the flat of my back! Well, the doctor tells me, and he is corroborated by four others, that if I turn over on my side I am a dead man."

"I don't believe a word of it my dear sir."

"You call me a liar?"

"Well, not exactly—"

"By God I'll show you!" roared the exasperated patient. And with that the old codger, to prove his point,

deliberately rolled over on his side and was dead inside of a minute. One last few seconds being devoted to a significant movement of his arm, as much as to say, "What did I tell you?"

*   *   *   *   *

It is easy to see why Bob Edward's readers looked forward so impatiently to every issue of the Eye Opener.

Edwards was rarely really vindictive. And even when he was being particularly "down" on someone, his wit had a way of making the victim grin while he squirmed. As in the following example from the Eye Opener while it was being published in High River in 1903:

"We read in A Book of Curious Facts that a pair of hogs owned 10 years have a progeny of 6,634,838 pigs, and yet Mike Moran and Peter McDermott, two talented citizens who are too fly for their own good, have each been married for a longer period than that and have only two children apiece. According to the above, they ought to have 6,634,838."

*   *   *   *

While Bob Edwards could fire his barbs into largely willing hides, most other Alberta publishers could not. Lacking Edwards' wit and wisdom, some newspaper owners turned the power of their presses loose in shrill, cruel and discriminatory attacks on those who couldn't fight back.

Anyone wanting to see the results of these kinds of attacks should find a copy of the Innesvale Freelance of Feb. 8, 1900.

There is hardly an item on the first page of that issue that can be reprinted. Certainly there is hardly an item that wouldn't land an editor in court on a libel or defamation charge if he dared to print it today.

This kind of mud-slinging journalism, combined with the newspapers' increasing interference in politics didn't take long to stir discontent among Alberta readers — and to draw the stern eye of political leaders. It wouldn't be too many years before this discontent and political disapproval took their toll.

* * * *

LET'S DILLY DAILY . . . .

For a long time Alberta was weekly newspaper country. It was hard enough to get out a paper once a week — what with rooting out advertisers and getting deliveries to subscribers — without trying the nightmare existence of daily publication.

But, inevitably, there were men among those early publishers who were bold enough and farsighted enough to see that Alberta's growing towns were ripe markets for daily papers.

The first to make the leap and survive was The Calgary Herald. Founded as a weekly on August 31, 1883 under the name "The Calgary Weekly Herald, Mining and Ranch Advocate," The Herald went daily on July 2, 1885 and has been at it ever since.

As other towns grew large enough to support the move, more and more papers followed the trend to daily publication.

Gradually, as the 1900's passed into their teens, then their twenties and thirties, Alberta's newspapers changed and began to look more and more the way they look today. But, in one important way, they didn't change quickly enough.

* * * *

FREEDOM OF THE PRESS . . .

The press tradition of freedom of opinion wasn't unique to Alberta. But, with the possible exception of some of the newspapers of the American southwest, nowhere was that tradition practised more fervently.

Today, the Alberta newspaper is careful to bundle most of its opinions onto one page under the warning label "Editorials." And, today, Alberta newspapers are careful not to let their political views color news reporting.

But, until well into the 1920's, that was seldom the case.

Anyone — especially politicians — were fair game for any kind of verbal attack. And many people — especially the smarting politicians — were beginning to feel the time was ripe to bring Alberta's newspapers into line.

The move to control the press came in 1937. And — as is so often the way — when it was made, it was made at the wrong time and in the wrong way.

By 1937, Alberta's newspapers, growing in size and in conscience, had already made the shift to "responsible" journalism.

But in 1937 there was a new political party in Alberta, the Social C r e d i t Party, and it had won control of the government two years earlier. Like all new parties — particularly when they find themselves running a government — this one felt a little insecure.

And there's nothing like the prospect of a hostile press to turn insecurity into reaction.

The attack started, not against one of the giants like The Edmonton Journal or The Calgary Herald, but against the small and quiet-spoken Lethbridge Herald.

The headline jolted every publisher in the province:

"Herald's Press Gallery Correspondent Threatened with Expulsion from House: Refuses to Reveal Sources of News."

The story The Lethbridge Herald ran under that headline made it plain what kind of war was coming:

EDMONTON — What may rightly be regarded as the big stick hangs over the veteran head of the Herald's legislative correspondent in the press gallery.

The Herald on several occasions has had stories some days in advance of the other daily newspapers on steps being considered by government and caucus for taxation, debt adjustment and other matters of policy. Prior to making his second budget speech in the House Friday afternoon, Provincial Treasurer Solon Low called the Herald correspondent to his office, where Chairman Glen MacLachlan and Commissioner L. D. Byrne of the Social Credit Board, and A. J. Hooke, government whip, were gathered. Mr. Low asked the correspondent where he obtained information for all the wild stories.

Recently, in caucus, it is reported, Hon. Mr. Low raised the same question and is said to have suggested a ruling that the Herald correspondent be denied the privilege of the press gallery. This the caucus declined to do.

At Friday's grilling, Mr. Low admitted there was a "kernel of truth" in the stories but insisted they were not in accord with the facts. The correspondent . . . flatly refused to divulge the source of such information . . . Mr. Low threatened expulsion from the press gallery might follow a repetition of the policy on the part of the correspondent, who replied that this was entirely up to Mr. Low.

* * * *

If anyone thought the incident just another political squabble, they were soon to learn differently.

Premier William Aberhart, only weeks later, was quoted in The Edmonton Journal as advocating licensing of newspapers and attacking the handling of news by the "so-called free press", charging they heeded the dictates of the "money barons" with r e s u l t a n t "false colouring" of dispatches.

What the government hopefully considered the final solution to the problem of the "so-called free press" was passage of a piece of legislation innocently titled: "An Act to Ensure the Publication of Accurate Information."

The act placed control of newspaper space under the Social Credit Board. It required publishers, d a i l y and weekly, to print the objects and policies of the government. And it decreed that a publisher must reveal the source by name and address of all information published and the identity of the writer of any editorial, article or news item.

Heavy penalties were provided; among other things, the suspension of any offending newspaper, and the outlawing of any newspaperman the Social Credit Board might specify.

The act touched off a furor that filled editorial pages from coast to coast.

In retrospect, one of the worst mistakes the government made was in opening its attack against The Lethbridge Herald.

The Herald might be small and quiet-spoken, but its publisher, W. A. Buchanan, was one of the toughest, most dedicated newspapermen in Canada.

Ontario-born, Buchanan had learned the newspaper business from the press-room up. He could set type, run a press, write a story, and do literally every job involved in newspaper production. He'd come west in search of a newspaper of his own; a newspaper he could run freely and well.

Buying in as a partner in the weekly Herald, he soon owned it outright, and not much later boldly moved it to daily status.

The legislation to control the press violated every principle he held, and he was out to fight it to the bitter end.

It was Buchanan, backed by John M. Imrie of The Edmonton Journal and F. P. Galbraith of The Red Deer Advocate, who was chosen by Alberta's newsmen to fight the act to defeat.

Actually, the controversial act was already in trouble. Before it could become law, it had to have Royal assent, the signature of Lieutenant-Governor Bowlen. Instead of signing, Bowlen sat on the bill for a while then — as was his constitutional right — handed it over to the Governor-General in Council at Ottawa for a decision.

The federal government, in turn, referred the bill to the Supreme Court of Canada for a ruling on its "constitutionality."

Before the Supreme Court, in N o v e m b e r, 1937, Buchanan fought the case for the Alberta publishers. Three months later, the court ruled the act ultra vires — and the Judicial Committee of the Privy Council in London backed the ruling.

The press bill was dead.

A year later, from New York, came a footnote that began:

THE TRUSTEES OF COLUMBIA UNIVERSITY

IN THE CITY OF NEW YORK

To All Persons to Whom

these Presents May Come Greetings

Be it known that

THE LETHBRIDGE HERALD

and

THE COLEMAN REVIEW

Have been Awarded Recognition with the EDMONTON JOURNAL, recipient of a special Pulitzer Prize for Distinguished and Meritous Public Service in 1937. In accordance with the provisions of . . .

It was Alberta Journalism's proudest moment.

* * * *

ORDINARY GARDEN VARIETY . . .

Looking over Alberta's newspapers today, some people — particularly oldtimers — are inclined to grumble that they "ain't like they used to be."

In some ways, they're right. But, in other ways, they're wrong.

True, it's only Fred Kennedy of The Albertan who makes the old-time claim that "I write as I please" and sticks to it (to the amusement and indignation of thousands of devoted readers).

But personal opinion was never really the mainstay of our newspapers. It was always the people of Alberta themselves. And the tradition of the people's newspaper is very much alive and growing, particularly among our weeklies.

The "typical" Alberta publisher today is very much like Neil Leatherdale of the Olds Gazette who points out proudly that his policy of printing "ordinary garden variety news" has raised his circulation in the 26 years he has run the paper from 1,200 to 5,000

Leaning back in a swivel chair in his crowded print shop, Mr. Leatherdale grumbles cheerfully that too many Alberta papers are "trying to get too darn sophisticated," instead of giving readers what they really want —news about themselves.

One of his proudest claims, and one that may point to the success of rural weeklies, is that his newspaper is mostly written by the people who read it.

"About 65 to 70 per cent of our material is sent in by people who want material published. We try to stick to what they say.

"If people have taken the time to write it, then my obligation is to take the time to read it, make sure it's understandable, and then make sure my boys set it in type the way they sent it in."

As far as Mr. Leatherdale is concerned, every Alberta newspaper is political. They always have been and they always will be. Personally — and most newsmen echo his feelings — he believes that there is nothing wrong in being political as long as you're honest about it, and as long as you're fair.

"I'm a Liberal and I make no bones about it. But at the same time I try to be fair. I think you have to. I don't think there's such a thing as being independent. I don't think this is possible.

"And, therefore, anybody who says they're independent is just kidding themselves.

"Everybody knows what my politics are, but, at the same time, I try to be fair about them. If a guy has done a good job, I'm willing to say that he's done a good job. And I think that's the most important part of the whole newspaper business today.

"Don't beat the bush just for the sake of beating the bush.

"Of course," he adds with a Bob Edwards' glitter in his eye, "it doesn't hurt to have a sense of humor, too."

* * * *

When a newspaper writer reaches the bottom of a page in a continuing story, he closes the page with the word "more."

And maybe that's the best place to leave Alberta journalism right now. With Neil Leatherdale and the word "more."

* * * *

POUNDING BRASS . . .

It was January, 1879 and Albertans had been getting mail service for nearly three years and were only a year away from their first newspaper.

And in Edmonton, a handful of people shivered near the door of a building at the Hudson's Bay post to listen anxiously for a flurry of clicks and clacks that would tell them the age of modern communication had arrived.

They didn't have to wait long. First there was a short burst of clicking, then another, and finally a nervous Alec Taylor started "pounding brass" in reply. The telegraph had come to Edmonton, and the cluster of people outside the door had the satisfaction of knowing they'd finally "caught up" with that unluckiest of companies, Dominion Telegraph.

Why unluckiest of companies? Well, because Dominion Telegraph had committed that deadliest of corporate errors: it guessed wrong.

In 1876, the company had hastily thrown up a telegraph line along what it (and the rest of Canada) had been led to believe would be the route of the new Canadian Pacific Railway. With a railroad line as mainstay, argued Dominion's directors, how could a telegraph company lose?

It could lose, as time would prove, all too easily. All it takes is for the Canadian Pacific Railway to change its mind — and its route.

But in 1879, Dominion Telegraph and the cluster of people in Edmonton didn't know anything about all that. All they knew was that the telegraph line, faithfully following the CPR map, ran through the present town of Leduc — 20 miles south of Edmonton.

Indignant at being left out of the modern age by Dominion T e l e g r a p h, Edmonton residents had been petitioning the federal government since 1878 in a bid to get the company to run a line north.

Indignation had got them nowhere. In the end, Edmonton had to find itself a contractor willing to supply material free of charge, and then make a generous offer to defray the expense of running the line north. Then, and only then, did Dominion bring the telegraph to Edmonton.

So the victory the people were celebrating outside Alec Taylor's shack was a little hollow (particularly in the region of the pocket-book).

It would seem even hollower as time went by and the people of Edmonton discovered that telegraph service, as offered by Dominion, wasn't all it was cracked up to be.

At its best, Dominion Telegraph's service meant instant communication with the whole world. But it was seldom at its best, thanks to poor wire, prairie fires — and itchy buffalo.

The line stretched nearly 1,000 miles west from Winnipeg, and it was 1,000 miles of pure trouble.

Poles were poplar, a wood whose only virtue is the accuracy with which it can be predicted how quickly it will rot at ground level. Wire was of such poor quality that, during wet weather in wooded areas, the signal wouldn't carry more than a few miles.

Even when poles weren't rotting off or wire wasn't out, Dominion could always count on a prairie fire or two to warm things up for them.

And then there were the buffalo. As low as Dominion Telegraph might rate on anyone else's popularity poll, the buffalo had them right on top of the list for being good enough to provide them with a thousand miles of back-scratchers.

The buffalo rubbed Dominion's poles smooth. In some places, they rubbed them right through. And every few days a really enthusiastic bull was guaranteed to actually knock down a pole—or a whole string of poles.

Alberta's first telegraph service wasn't, to say the least, all it might have been.

* * * *

CHECKERS AND CHECK-UPS . . .

Dominion Telegraph may not have brought its customers the best service in the world. But, in spite of that, it did bring some profound changes to pioneer life.

For one thing, it did much to bring peace. The North-West Mounted Police had come west in 1874 as a small force, and they counted on the telegraph to call them to the scene of trouble in a hurry.

So effective was the telegraph in this capacity that potentially troublesome Indians began speaking fearfully of it as the "speaking iron", a particularly potent form of white magic.

On one occasion, when a band of Indians rode up to a telegraph station and began to make abusive demands for free provisions, the operator wired for help then stalled for time.

Troops were there the next morning and the Indians fled in terror, convinced the police had come over the wire.

The telegraph also brought health service to a frontier where physicians were rare, and injury and illness were common.

Dominion Telegraph always had a doctor on call to handle emergency appeals for medical advice, and charged nothing for the service. It was a rough and ready form of doctoring, usually, but it saved countless lives.

And the telegraph also brought an entertainment bonus Dominion Telegraph hadn't counted on when it built its line.

When part of the line was out — which was often the case — operators on "live" sections would turn over their telegraph keys to the frontier checker experts for long-distance games in Morse code. Edmonton, ever aggressive in sports, was always on the wire challenging all comers in Battleford and Qu'Appelle.

* * * *

THE DOOMED DOMINION . . .

Dominion Telegraph had built its line on the gamble that the CPR would follow the same route west. When the gamble didn't pay off, and CPR ran its rail far to the south, it was only a matter of time before Dominion would have to settle its gambling debts.

The principal day of reckoning came in 1886 when the CPR started its own telegraph system, much more efficient than Dominion's, to carry messages back and forth across all of Canada.

Dominion struggled on for nearly two decades longer, surviving by filling the gap in telegraph service in northern Alberta. But then came the final blow.

In the early 1900's the Grand Trunk Pacific Railway pushed north through the province with rail — and a modern telegraph system.

By the time Grand Trunk reached Edmonton, Dominion was finished. Business dwindled and dwindled until finally, like the buffalo no longer there to rub against their rotting poles, Dominion Telegraph quietly disappeared.

* * *

THIS IS GOD SPEAKING....

It was Edmonton's Alec Taylor who persuaded Frank Oliver to start Alberta's first newspaper. It was Alec Taylor who served as Alberta's first telegrapher.

And it was the same Alec Taylor who started the first known telephone system in the province.

It wasn't, it must be pointed out right away, as big a project to start a telephone system in the 1880's as it would be today.

All it took was two sets, some wire, and a battery.

Like many others, Alec Taylor had read of Alexander Graham Bell's experiments with the telephone in 1874. And, like many others, Mr. Taylor was intrigued by the spread of telephone systems in the east.

When, in 1884, Mr. Taylor began to see advertisements in the periodicals touting an English-made telephone, he broke down and ordered two sets.

With the encouragement of the Hudson's Bay factor, Mr. Taylor ran a line between his telegraph office and the Hudson's Bay post. The idea was to cut out all the tiresome running back and forth with telegraph messages, and it almost worked out that way.

Early telephones were eccentric creatures at best, especially operating on lines as makeshift as the one between the telegraph office and Hudson's Bay post. At best it took a lot of yelling and hallooing — and a little cursing — to get the faintest of messages through. At worst, well, it was back to hand-delivering all those telegrams.

If the first two phones weren't too successful in the business field, Mr. Taylor did manage to put them to good use to solve an annoying personal problem.

Every day, punctually, as Mr. Taylor would open his telegraph office, an old Indian would shuffle in, squat down by the stove, and sit smoking until closing time. Alec Taylor tolerated the daily invasion for a long time, but he finally got fed up.

One day he arranged for a friend to come to the office, then hurried down to the Bay post. From there he telephoned back and had the friend call the Indian to the phone.

The Indian was horrified to hear an awesome, crackling voice address him with the message:

"This is God speaking. I want you to get out of that office and stay out!"

Mr. Taylor's office was Indian-free from that day forward.

* * * *

HELLO, OPERATOR? OPERATOR? . . .

Alec Taylor soon discovered that anyone in Edmonton with two telephones was in the telephone business — whether he wanted to be or not.

Slowly, lines spread from his office to service new customers, and by 1886 Alec Taylor had installed a switchboard — and a pretty, young lady to operate it.

Jane Lauder, later to become the wife of Sen. Griesbach, was Edmonton's — and Alberta's — first telephone operator. And she soon had, as Edmonton historian Naomi Radford points out, "all Edmonton at her fingertips."

There was nothing impersonal about Miss Jane's service. There couldn't be. Nearly every caller was a relative or a friend, and requests for information were made on a personal level.

"Janie dear, find Dr. Wilson for me, will you?" or "I want that little German butcher woman, please," were the forms the requests took. Naturally, Jane Lauder — with only 20 telephones on the line — was notably successful in tracking down the elusive Dr. Wilson, and in connecting callers to the happy, guttural voice of the proprietress of the meat store.

Thinking of Janie, one can't help but wonder what the reaction would be today if you asked the impersonal voice of the telephone operator to connect you with "that little German butcher lady, please."

* * * *

LONG DISTANCE, PLEASE . . .

Not content with all his other "firsts", Alec Taylor took it upon himself to arrange what seems to have been the west's first long-distance telephone call.

It was soon after Mr. Taylor's first two phones were hooked up, and there was a widespread debate taking place about the possibility or impossibility of long-distance voice communication.

Mr. Taylor said it could be done, and virtually everyone else in Edmonton said it couldn't.

So Mr. Taylor said somewhat heatedly that not only could it be done but he'd "d—n well prove it."

Taylor, as telegraph operator, had a thousand miles of wire at his disposal. He arranged for a cohort at Battleford to hook a telephone set onto the line there, and he did the same himself at Edmonton.

One midnight, with all the telegraph stations between the two points shut down, Taylor and his opposite in Battleford each cranked up tiny hand-operated generators and began making futile attempts to ring one another.

The little generators, however, weren't strong enough. But after three or four minutes, both men conceived the idea of screaming "hello" into the set, and made contact.

For 10 or 15 minutes — long enough to settle the sceptics — the two succeeded in making one another understand a few phrases.

* * * *

Having settled the hash of those who had disagreed with him, Taylor promptly turned his back on the whole issue of long-distance and returned to his perennial problem of trying to make contact with the Hudson's Bay post a few blocks away.

It wasn't until 1891 that the first true long-distance line in the province was installed between Cardston and Lethbridge. Unfortunately, according to contemporary reports, it spent most of its time being out of service.

* * * *

A LITTLE CHAOS . . . .

For a while after Edmonton started up the telephone bandwagon, every town in the province was hopping on and off; installing switchboards and tearing them out again, putting up lines and taking down lines.

In Calgary, where the city fathers had taken the precaution of calling in the Bell Telephone Company to install their system in 1887, service was so bad that the city's 40 customers refused to pay their bills.

* * * *

A WORD FROM THE CUCKOO . . .

Rural service, started by the Edmonton District Telephone Company in 1904, proved even more of a headache than city service.

It seems that some rural customers took quite a shine to the idea of eavesdropping on other people's calls — "rubbering in" as the practice was known.

In fact, it seems that so many rural customers liked to rubber-in that transmission often just gave out from the strain of having all those phones on the line at once.

The telephone company, naturally, took a dim view of the practice — threatening legal action and worse. But, of course, as customers knew all too well, it's a lot easier to threaten action than to take it in the case of so elusive a culprit as an eavesdropper.

In fact, the only recorded case of the company catching up with anyone was that of an unhappy gentleman who had the bad luck to own the only cuckoo clock in the district. And who had the misfortune to have his cuckoo clock "cuckoo" when he just happened to be listening in on a call.

* * * *

A CALL FROM THE LEGISLATURE . . .

Finally, in 1906, Alberta's government took a look at the world of telephone service and decided that it was just too chaotic.

There wasn't enough service to meet the mushrooming demands of the population, and what service there was spent most of its time out of order.

Alec Taylor had already sold out his Edmonton system to the city and wiped his hands of the whole business. Other private operators were doing the same in other towns.

So the legislature, pressed by private members, voted

$25,000 "for the purpose of investigating the advisability of government-owned telephones."

Two years later, Alberta Government Telephones was in business with the promise to "have a telephone system of its own connecting every part of this province, not only the towns, villages and cities of Alberta but also the rural portions where telephone communication is practicable and where the people desire to have it."

It is a promise that AGT, with more than half a million phones in service today, has kept singularly well. Even if the operator doesn't know who you mean by "that little German butcher lady."

* * * *

AND THIS IS CHBC, CALGARY . . .

Albertans, moving into the 1920's, had lost most of their sense of isolation.

After all, regular mail delivery was almost half a century old, telegraph lines criss-crossed the province, most homes had a telephone. What more could anyone want?

Well, there was this new-fangled something called radio. Not too many people in Alberta had actually heard a radio, but the newspapers were full of it and it seemed to be catching on like wildfire in the east and in the states. It would be nice, some people felt, to have a radio to listen to on those long winter nights.

By 1921, the Dominion air board had established a research station at High River, and an engineer named W. W. Grant was busy holding two-way radio conversations with other engineers in places like Denver, Colorado.

Then, in May, 1922, Mr. Grant came to Calgary and, with the backing of The Morning Albertan, brought CHBC to the airways. It was Alberta's first radio station.

By May, 1923, the Albertan could report:

"One year ago this week, CHBC, the radiophone broadcasting station of *The Morning Albertan*, officially commenced broadcasting concerts and news bulletins. Today, *The Morning Albertan* station, through its marvelous achievements, notably in long distance broadcasting, is known the continent over as one of the most powerful in the United States and Canada. In every city in every state in the United States and Canada, The Albertan station is known."

A little heavy on self-praise, perhaps, but true.

All over the province, people were plugging into crystal sets, and every businessman who could dig up a transmitter and an engineer was getting into the act.

* * * *

"BOMBING" IN EDMONTON . . .

Edmonton may have been a whisper short of beating its rival city to the south onto the air, but what it lacked in speed, it made up for in quantity. It soon had three stations running. To the confusion of listeners, all three ran on the same frequency.

Powerful U.S. stations were already plugging most available frequencies, and the few Canadian stations with high-powered transmitters had snatched up most of the rest. Edmonton had to be satisfied with the dregs.

Having three radio stations on the same frequency wasn't as confusing as it might seem. Radio in the 1920's was still very heavy on silence, broadcasting only a few hours a day. So it wasn't hard to work out a sharing arrangement.

Inevitably, of course, this "arrangement" led to a few mistakes. Like the night The Bible Students station,

CHCY, and the Journal station, CJCA, came on the air at the same time.

The combination of "Yes, Sir, That's My Baby" and divine prayer must have done strange things to listeners' ears and minds.

Edmonton, of course, also had to be more eccentric than Calgary.

In CJCA, for example, the announcer had to go off the air when he wanted to open a window, because the station's high-voltage cables ran across the studio window.

So, naturally, one night owner-announcer Dick Rice went to open the window. And, naturally, he didn't turn off the power. And, naturally, he was promptly knocked unconscious.

Rival station CHCY, equally exciting, recaptured the airwaves with a bomb scare.

Their transmitter was out in the wilderness, right in the middle of the present subdivision of Idylwylde. One Saturday night, an anonymous telephone tip warned the station control room that the transmitter was marked for a dynamite plot.

Technicians and friends rushed to the scene and found an appropriately ticking parcel. Frantic, they dumped the parcel in a pail of water until the ticking stopped. Then they opened it.

Inside was a clock wired to four batteries which, in turn, was wired to four giant firecrackers. It didn't turn out to be a complete fizzle, however. One of the firecrackers managed to go off with a loud roar.

It caused, one of those present recalled later, "a great amount of excitement."

* * * *

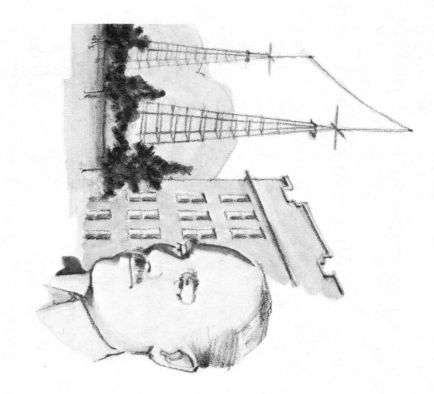

THE ELECTRONIC LECTURER . . .

The most frustrated man in Alberta radio had to be H. P. Brown, in charge of the visual aid department at the University of Alberta. And that's because, try as he might, he wasn't in Alberta radio.

As early as 1921, Mr. Brown was making earnest attempts to get U. of A. to set up an educational radio station. No luck.

Mr. Brown begged and pleaded, then begged and pleaded some more. But the university stood adamant. No radio for the University of Alberta.

Now, Mr. Brown was a persistent man. And a patient one. And he wasn't above using a little trickery to get what he wanted.

Somehow, the 1927 budget for the university contained, at Mr. Brown's instigation, $7,000 for a new lecturer in the department of extension.

Several months passed without anyone noticing that the new lecturer hadn't arrived on the scene — and without anyone becoming suspicious of an unusual amount of activity among electrical engineering students.

No one, unbelievably, even particularly noticed that the department of extension had graced the campus with two old windmill towers, 75 feet high, and topped with iron rods stretching up another 25 feet! (They stood around until 1966, by the way.)

All that took a powerful lot of not noticing.

By the time anyone did notice, it was too late. The "new lecturer" had turned into $2,000 worth of radio station, and CKUA was an accomplished fact. The patient Mr. Brown was the first announcer. Which just shows that you can't keep a determined man shut up forever.

* * * *

WITH A LOAN AND A LITTLE "LOVE" . . .

With the possible exception of Edmonton's Dick Rice, no man has played a larger role in Alberta broadcasting history than H. Gordon Love of Calgary.

Strangely enough, he got into the broadcasting business through the wrong end — by wanting to sell radios. In

1922, he and a partner started the Radio Corporation of Calgary as the sales outlet for an eastern radio manufacturer.

It didn't take the pair long to discover that they were going to have a powerful hard time selling radios to people unless there was something to hear on the radios. So the two approached The Calgary Herald and made a deal to erect a 500 watt station, CFAC, on top of the Herald building. The transmitter was in a small shack by the tower.

Love didn't stay stuck on top of the Herald building for long, however. Within a few years he had purchased the ailing CFCN and left radio sales behind forever.

By 1931, after bouncing from location to location in the city, Love put up a 10,000 watt transmitter at Strathmore and staked CFCN's claim as "The Voice of The Prairies," a claim that has never been relinquished.

He recalls those early years, when he was getting started, as tough ones — filled with bitter competition between radio and newspaper.

"At the time I started commercial radio broadcasting, Col. Wood at The Herald had every businessman on 8th Ave. owing him just enough money so they couldn't write a cheque for it.

"If any commercial was placed with us and Wood heard it, he would phone the advertiser and say: We've been real good to you, right? If the man didn't get the message, Wood would demand his money and the guy would have to cancel his commercials.

"Many times I had to lend guys money to pay off Wood just to stay on the air."

Under Gordon Love's direction, CFCN recorded a lot of "firsts", but none that makes him prouder than the fact

CFCN provided the first independent news service in Canada, in 1935.

The news came in by wireless from New York and was taken down, first by hand, then by typewriter. At one point it came in over a receiver in north Calgary and was rushed to the station by bicycle.

The west's first recreated sports broadcasts — of a World Series game in St. Louis — was sent over the airwaves by CFCN, with Gordon Love handling the broadcast himself.

Mr. Love, who had played professional baseball himself, called the game from dispatches that came in by telegraph and were handed to him while he was on the air.

He recalls with some amusement that, getting caught up in the game, he became quite liberal with description and atmosphere — provided solely by his imagination.

But, as it turned out, his imagination was in perfect working order. At one point in the broadcast, he told his listeners — purely on guesswork — that Babe Ruth had hit the ball right out of the catcher's hand.

"Later on," he grins, "a picture of that game came out and, sure enough, there was Ruth doing it just the way I described it."

* * * *

EAR PLUGS, PLEASE . . .

Most Albertans were enchanted with the arrival of radio. But not all. The Calgary Herald found room in its edition of Feb. 20, 1929, to express the quiet hope that new station, CJOC, would arrange its programs so that "radio fans will turn the dials for the local station and be able to hear interesting arrangements and that the use of phonograph records will be kept to a minimum."

On the same page, more pointedly, there was an "Otto Watt" cartoon that had Otto brooding over his bed and radio and muttering: "What to do, What to do." When a lady friend asked what was bothering him, he replied: "Oh I'm trying to decide which to get rid of — my bed or my radio. I don't need them both!"

* * * *

TRY THE HORIZONTAL HOLD . . . .

If Otto Watt had been around in October, 1953, he'd really have had something to worry about. That was the month Alberta's first five television station licences were issued. Less than a year later, CFRN in Edmonton and CHCT in Calgary were on the air.

In the process of setting up, Calgary finally outdid Edmonton in the showmanship department. A month before CHCT was to go on the air, it managed to have its huge transmission tower fall over.

* * * *

THE SOUNDS OF SILENCE . . . .

Today, in Alberta, communication — and the noise it makes — is everywhere. Where a hundred years ago people didn't really know what was happening a mile away, today they can see the whole world through the window of a television set.

Radios come in stereo and with ear plugs. Cars can be equipped with tape-decks. Newspapers can put out editions of more than 100 pages.

The old Morse key has been replaced with rattling teletype and broadband and satellite transmission, and telephones ring incessantly.

It's enough to make some who remember pioneer days think of Bill Peyto, the famous Rocky Mountain guide. Inevitably, when Bill found himself stuck with a particularly noisy party in a mountain camp, he'd grab his bedroll and head over the hill muttering something about finding "a little durn peace and quiet."

Wait up, Bill.

POLITICS AND A PROMISE

"Politics has not ceased to make strange bedfellows; at least the politicians continue to share the same bunk. You know the kind of bunk we mean." — Bob Edwards.

* * * *

It's not that pioneer Albertans didn't take politics seriously. They did. But they always took it with a grain of salt as well.

It was the rare pioneer who wouldn't agree with the view that Bob Edwards was to express later in his Calgary Eye Opener, that the main difference between the Liberal and Conservative parties was that "one is in and the other is out".

And what settled the issue of who was in and who was out, as the following accounts of early Alberta elections show, was often a matter of down-to-earth practicality.

* * * *

IF HE WAS TO "RARE UP ON HIS HIND LAIGS . . ."

Long before Alberta became a province on its own, it was part of the North West Territory and, by 1885, Alberta settlers were about to be given their first chance to choose part of the new government.

Pioneer E. N. Barker describes the process:

"Of course it was not long after the province (NWT) began to settle up that elections came along, and ever after it has been stated that the air became warmer, and the summer frosts grew less, because of the amount of sultry atmosphere pipe in and out at the time of our numerous elections.

"The first election came along in 1885, not so very long after the Riel rebellion. This rebellion stirred up the east from a long and continuous slumber. Word came out onto the range that a member for the North West Assembly was to be elected. . . .

"It was decided to run Lord Boyle, after the possibilities had been gone over. The real reason why His Lordship was chosen was that no one else knew anything about that sort of thing, and he, being a peer, was supposed to know something of parliamentary procedure.

"The canvassers who came out our way stated, 'He's the only man that can make a speech.'

"It seemed to be the general opinion that this was the great requisite, for, as one cow-puncher remarked, 'If we wuz to send a man down thar as our man, and he was to rare up on his hind laigs to say somethin' among them lawyers an' other fellers, an' he got himself rared up on his hind haunches an' dassen't say nothin' we'd look plumb foolish.'"

(As a matter of record, Lord Boyle was duly elected and, to the satisfaction of his constituents, he "rared up on his hind haunches" plumb good.)

* * * *

BREAD AND BUTTER VOTING . . .

One of the big problems in early Alberta elections, of course, was that so many of the settlers were too new to Canada to either understand what was happening or even much care.

We have a good example of this when, in 1891, the surprised pioneers of Cardston came up against their first federal election:

"One night," writes one of the Mormons, "we saw riding up the creek a bunch of horsemen who proved to be some Mounted Police, Arthur Harper, returning officer, and Jack Cowdray, the banker from Macleod, who was the scrutineer. Bob Giveen came along as scout and steerman.

"As soon as they stated their business, which was to hold an election, we cooked supper and put the whole bunch down on the floor to sleep.

"The next day, after breakfast, we all saddled up and rode over to the Ashe, Cotter and Derenzie Ranch to vote, for it was there that the poll was to be taken . . .

"A table was arranged in the house, at which sat the deputy returning officer and his poll clerk, and we stood up and said who we voted for. Whichever way a man voted, it must be known, as he had to announce in a loud voice who he voted for, so everyone around there knew and could go and tell about it.

"As Sir John MacDonald was in power, and D. W. Davis of Macleod was a Conservative, we four voters, all very young and not having had any previous experience in politics, concluded it was a waste of time trying to send one on the wrong side all the way down to Ottawa.

"So it was decided that as we all knew D.W. Davis, it would be better to vote for someone we knew and whom we could get at.

"Besides this, he was head of the I. G. Baker Co., at Macleod, and most of us dealt there, so that if we voted against him our credit in the future might be impaired. It was not considered good policy to go right against the firm that were the wholesale purveyors of this part of Alberta, were storekeepers, bankers et al for the whole of this section.

"We had been told that a man should not quarrel with his bread and butter, so of course D. W. Davis received a solid Conservative vote of four votes in the St. Mary's Polling Division."

* * * *

A MATTER OF TACTICS . . . .

For a long time in Alberta, politics continued to be almost a game; one that called for quick wits and a little well-intentioned deception.

So, when the Hon. Arthur Sifton made a bid for re-election in the NWT council, he called for help on Paddy Nolan — the Irish-born Calgary lawyer with the quickest wits in Alberta.

It was quite a challenge for Nolan. Sifton's riding was in southern Alberta's mining country — which would have been all right but for one small point. Sifton had become an ardent prohibitionist. He wouldn't take a drink, nor would he buy one for another man.

As Nolan knew all too well, Sifton's attitude was going to cost him votes.

Nolan arrived in one of the key mining towns a few hours ahead of Sifton and gathered as many miners together as he could fit inside the town's principal bar.

After setting up a few rounds, he heaved a massive sigh and shook his head.

"Boys," he said gloomily, "you know Sifton is to speak here tonight. He's a fine fellow, but he has one failing that I fear may cost him many votes." He tapped his glass. "It's this," he said sadly. "Yes, this.

"You see, he's been dreaming about a night with the boys ever since the campaign started, but he doesn't know when to stop, and I have a devil of a time keeping him straight."

Suddenly an idea seemed to hit Nolan, and he brightened.

"Say, if you boys will help, I think we may just manage to pull him through this meeting! I want you to see that no one asks him to take a drink, for if anyone asks him he can't refuse — and if he takes even one drink, the Lord knows where he'll stop."

The miners, of course, were delighted to help old Paddy out, and the meeting that followed was one of Sifton's best — though he never found out exactly why.

* * * *

SALT RUNS OUT . . .

By 1905, Alberta had become a province in its own right; named for the Princess Louise Alberta by her husband the Marquis of Lorne.

Albertans were still taking their politics with a grain of salt, but the salt was running out. There was war in Europe, then a post-war economic sag that sagged right into the great depression.

By the 1920's, the people of Alberta were taking politics seriously indeed. And the traditional rivalry between Liberal and Conservative as to which was in and which was out was soon to be settled in the provincial arena.

Neither was going to be "in" in Alberta for a long time.

* * * *

ABERHART FOR ALBERTA . . .

The staying power of Alberta's Social Credit government was as spectacular as was its first landslide victory.

Boasting a longer life-span in office than any other democratically-elected government the world has known, the Socred party held power for more than three and a half decades.

Behind it all was a big man with a Bible.

Portly, bald and bespectacled, William Aberhart became a high school principal when he arrived in Calgary in 1910.

It was a modest beginning for a man who would eventually mesmerize the population of the province.

Aberhart began his journey to political power along the straight and narrow road of religion. He taught Bible classes in Calgary churches for several years, then he organized a class of his own at Westbourne Baptist Church.

Few could guess that this class would become the nucleus of one of the most dynamic institutions in the province.

The Prophetic Bible Institute was founded in 1927 with William Aberhart as dean. Housed in a $65,000 building "with all modern conveniences" in the heart of Calgary, the PBI soon became the springboard for Aberhart's unparalleled evangelism.

His Sunday "Back to the Bible Hour" radio broadcasts captured the imagination of audiences nearing 350,000 people — half the entire population of the province.

* * * *

SOMETHING FOR EVERYONE . . .

Among those captivated by the radio broadcasts were the members of the fledgling Social Credit League, and soon league activities were revolving around the Bible institute and Aberhart its dynamic leader.

But Aberhart's message was not only spiritual. At a time when Alberta was writhing in the grips of depression, he came up with proposals for an economic cure-all.

He came upon his theories accidentally, while marking some examination papers in Edmonton in 1932. A friend had loaned him a book by British economist Major C.H. Douglas — the "founder of social credit". What Aberhart read in the book was to become the foundation of a political philosophy for Alberta.

At first, Bible Bill (as he was becoming widely known) tried to convince the members of the ruling United Farmers of Alberta party to adopt his ideas. But neither the UFA nor the traditional parties would have anything to do with this strange-sounding financial system.

So Aberhart returned to the pulpit and the airways to preach the message of social credit to the people.

Jobless and poverty-stricken, thousands of people heard him and took hope, while the business community reeled back with horror.

The social credit system, said Bible Bill, would provide a monthly "basic dividend" of $25 to every man, woman and child in the province.

The idea caught on like a prairie fire, and Alberta plunged into one of its bitterest election campaigns.

Not everyone, needless to say, was enthused by the possibility of a social credit government. Aberhart's single-mindedness had earned him powerful enemies in the whole political establishment of Alberta.

Conservative candidate Hugh C. Farthing (later an Alberta Supreme Court judge), for one, likened faith in social credit to "admitting to the world at large that we had got into our second childhood and still believed in Santa Claus."

But, on election day, Aug. 22, 1935, the Social Credit party swept 56 of the 63 seats in the Alberta legislature.

The overwhelming victory was, according to The Calgary Herald, "an uprising of a people demanding a new deal of some kind. It was a mass revolt against depression."

It was also an eloquent tribute to William Aberhart, the man whose booming voice and hell and brimstone speeches had penetrated to every corner of the province.

* * * *

PREDICAMENTS OF POWER . . .

Ironically, Aberhart was not a candidate in the 1935 election; it took a forced by-election to earn him a seat in the legislature, and his place as the new premier of Alberta.

But he had emerged triumphantly from the basement of the Bible Institute to take over the highest position in the province.

Before the election, Aberhart had swept aside all warnings about constitutional barriers to his radical reforms. But now the barriers seemed very real indeed.

Unable to fulfill an election pledge to establish social credit in Alberta within 18 months, Aberhart was even confronted with opposition from within his own party.

He managed to tame this, then went on to begin introducing his credit measures — the key to the total social security concept.

But the $25 dividends were not forthcoming.

One by one, Alberta's new government passed acts to control banks and bankers and the flow of credit. And, one by one, the federal government and the courts invalidated them.

The province was in an economic mire, but it is a tribute to the power of Aberhart that the people of Alberta never lost faith in him. His fiery personality and inexhaustible energy generated tremendous loyalty.

The economic boom that accompanied World War Two, and the major oil discoveries at Leduc finally turned the financial tide.

* * * *

THE VISION REMAINS . . .

Aberhart, right from the beginning, envisioned a brilliant future for Alberta. And he was convinced that this would be a future in which the Social Credit party played an unlimited role.

The vision was an accurate one. By 1970 the party had survived an unbroken string of nine elections.

And, when William Aberhart died in 1943, his carefully-groomed successor Ernest Manning carried the vision on — even succeeding Aberhart as the orator of the Back to the Bible Hour.

By the time Ernest Manning assumed power as premier, most of the far-fetched financial schemes of "Bible Bill" had faded into the past.

At least once in the Manning era, however, the Socreds found themselves doing battle with their time-honored enemy, the federal government. The Social Credit Bill of Rights, described by Manning as a new charter of freedom for Alberta, was declared unconstitutional by the Privy Council in 1946.

By 1964, with the economy booming, the Social Credit party had reached the heights Aberhart had dreamed of so many years before. It held 59 of the legislature's 63 seats, and a budget surplus of $50 million.

The third Socred premier, Harry Strom, saw his party

defeated August 30, 1971. Although re-elected himself, Strom resigned as party leader and the party's voice was split between the caucus and the grassroots organization.

Strom's successor as premier was the young Conservative, Peter Lougheed, whose grandfather was Alberta's first Lieutenant-Governor.

* * * *

BEYOND POLITICS . . .

"Statesman" is a dangerous word to use in Alberta. There are too many people around who remember Bob Edwards' definition of a **statesman** as "a dead politician".

But, at the risk of raising Edwards' ghostly mirth, there are some Albertans who deserve the designation "statesman", in the finest sense of the word. R. B. Bennett, for example, who became Canada's prime minister. And Roland Michener, our former Governor-General.

There are many others, and there is one, in particular, for whom even Bob Edwards would willingly have suspended his definition.

* * * *

CANADA'S "INDIAN" SENATOR . . .

James Gladstone, in a way, is the personification of all the history of Alberta.

His memories go back to a childhood when he lived in a tee-pee on the open prairie, when transportation was a horse and a travois, and when the buffalo still ran free.

Now in his eighties, he talks with easy familiarity of men we associate with the very beginnings of our heritage — Col. Macleod, Jerry Potts, the famous Indian chiefs, a grandfather who built Fort Whoop-Up.

"All this was open country then," he muses in his home in Cardston. "Wherever we went we camped, and there was nothing to disturb us and no one to chase us away. All this land was ours. It belonged to us."

By "us", of course, James Gladstone means Alberta's Indian people. And that "us" is, at the same time, his favorite private joke and the greatest honor of his life.

"What Indian is in me," he explains with a twinkle of his blue eyes, "is from Winnipeg. That's where my grandfather married this girl — French half-breed as far as I can learn, according to the name of her and all. Best I can do is about an eighth Indian — by blood."

But "blood" isn't what counts with Jim Gladstone. By choice — and by appointment — he is an Indian, and the greatest statesman his people have.

Raised as an Indian boy, he spoke Cree before he spoke English, and was fluent in Blackfoot by the time he was 12.

From childhood on, he made it his destiny to fight for the rights of his people; a fight he still continues, and which paid off in the unique honor at age 33 of being legally adopted as a full treaty Indian by the Blackfoot.

He remembers that day as the greatest of his life. Greater even, perhaps, than the day in the 1950's when he heard that John Diefenbaker had appointed him a member of the Canadian Senate — the only "Indian" ever to be elevated to such high status in the dominion.

And if anyone ever wants to question just how Indian Jim Gladstone really is, all they have to do is look back to the day he made his maiden speech in Canada's upper house — in Blackfoot.

"You think Indians got a good deal in this country?" he

demands abruptly. "Well they haven't. And I'm not going to stop fighting till they do."

Jim Gladstone makes that a determined promise.

But, then, Jim Gladstone has all Alberta history within his life-span.

And, in the end, that kind of determination and promise may very well be what our Alberta heritage is all about. . . .

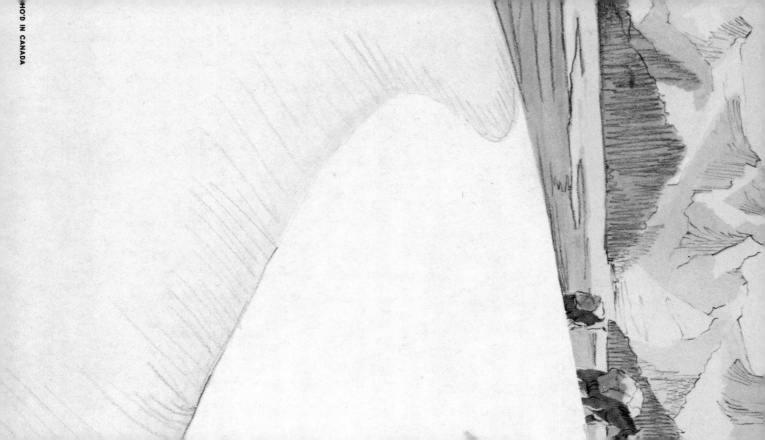

MOUNTAIN MEN

Our Alberta Heritage Series II

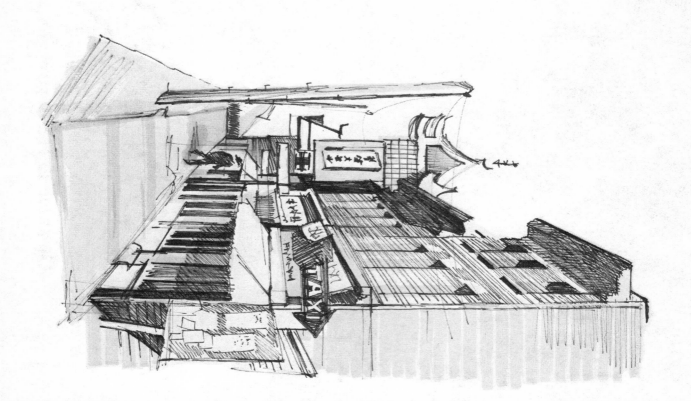

FOREWORD

"At last the Rocky Mountains came in sight like shining white clouds in the horizon."

— DAVID THOMPSON

* * *

Wong-Tai is an old man now. More than a hundred years old — though just how much older not even he can remember anymore.

Every day, when the weather lets him, he takes a short walk through the streets of downtown Calgary.

Few who see him know him. Fewer still recognize him as a frail, human link with a part of Alberta history that is far older than Alberta itself.

Wong-Tai is the last survivor of the Chinese laborers who struggled, and often died, to build the mountain section of the Canadian Pacific Railway.

All he remembers of those days is that the pay was 75 cents a day. And that when the job was finished he was given a gift of his pick and shovel.

Wong-Tai may seem a strange place to begin a selection of stories about Alberta's "Mountainmen." Much came before what he did and much came after.

But the rails that Wong-Tai helped lay became the fragile thread that finally bound Canada together as a nation.

Nothing that came before or after can quite equal that.

There was nothing particularly idealistic about Wong-Tai's reason for being in the Canadian Rockies. He was there for the 75 cents a day.

And, similarly, it was money rather than any offhand "because they were there" concept that led men to the first determined assault on the high west wall of the prairies.

The determination was displayed by two famous competitors—The Hudson's Bay Company and the North West Company. Both sought to be the first to open a route to the Pacific and to control Canada's fur trade.

What saved the conquest of the Rockies from being just a cold, commercial chapter in Canadian history were the men the rival companies chose for the job.

These men were hardheaded and businesslike enough, all right.

But, as the quotation from David Thompson at the opening of this introduction shows, these men saw something much more than money in the mountains.

That is what made them, and men and women like them, the "Mountainmen" of our title.

* * *

ADVENTURERS

High on one flank of Mt. Eisenhower lies a sloping alpine meadow. There, 7,000 feet above sea level, a person can sit beside the deep cut of a mountain stream and look up the last 3,000 feet to the towering summit of the famous "castle" of the Rockies.

Those 3,000 feet symbolize a great deal of the adventure of the Rockies.

Few could sit in that meadow without imagining the thrill of standing on that summit. And fewer still could bring themsleves to the task of the fearful climb up that final, vertical cliff.

Every quarter hour or so the summer sun cracks rocks free from the cliff. The rocks fall for long, silent seconds before booming and exploding into dust along the scree of the foot of the cliff.

Only 3,000 feet, but in those 3,000 feet lies the essence of the sublime danger that has always drawn — and always will draw — the adventurer to the Canadian Rockies.

Sometimes the 3,000 feet are a real, vertical obstacle to be surmounted. Sometimes they symbolize what it takes for a man to face "just one more season" of hunting for a gold mine that probably exists only in legend.

Sometimes they are the magic lure that draws a man back to the mountains after a lifetime of violence and danger and killing work.

Each of these "sometimes" has a man, and a story, that goes with it...

"The old instinct to ride after buffalo again came over me, and I have to admit I always have a keen appetite for any kind of good strong drink..."

—GEORGE 'KOOTENAI' BROWN

* * *

George Brown was a man who couldn't have existed outside the era of the opening of the Canadian west. And possibly that era couldn't have existed without George Brown.

He started out as a quick-triggered soldier of fortune and ended his days as an irritable old civil servant arguing with Ottawa about lost fire pails.

He was a law unto himself, and even that law was made only to be broken. Tall, powerful and fast, he went through life afflicted with the kind of temper that draws guns and sometimes pulls triggers.

His genteel British accent never managed to hide a tongue so rough that those who knew him said he invented a new curse every time he opened his mouth.

In later years, he wore his pale blonde hair hanging to his shoulders; some say in imitation of his friend Buffalo Bill, but perhaps it was only a wistful effort to cling to a fading era.

Poisoner of wolves, slaughterer of buffalo, gambler, Indian fighter, whisky trader — George 'Kootenai' Brown was all these things.

But he was also a man with a vision, a vision that led his life out in a long, looping circle from the Rockies and, in the end, brought him back to the Rockies again.

It was his determined following of that vision that redeemed him and that lets us remember him as one of our great mountain pioneers.

It was 1865 when George Brown first set foot in what is now Alberta. His education was behind him — Eton and Oxford — and so was the finishing school of a soldier's life in Panama and the life of a drifter in the western United States.

Behind him, too, was the darkest incident of his life. In Montana a fight had flared across a poker table and he had killed a man. No one, today, knows just what happened.

Brown himself kept the incident a secret and, although there is some evidence he was arrested for the shooting, there is no evidence he was ever brought to trial.

Probably the closest Brown ever came to talking about the incident was once, in his old age, when he told a friend that the sweetest words in the English language are "Not Guilty."

Whatever happened, he had headed north after the incident, lost himself in the gold fields of the Cariboo.

Now, two years later, he and four companions were riding down the east slope of the South Kootenai Pass and out onto the open prairie. They were bound for Edmonton where they had heard there was gold to be found.

As Brown recalled later, "We had no very clear knowledge of where Edmonton was, and there was no one to tell us."

Brown was convinced that the party should stick close to the mountains and head north, but his companions didn't agree. Reluctantly he followed their directions, and he almost didn't live to regret it.

Unknowingly, the party's looping route carried them into the heart of Blackfoot country.

At that time, the Blackfoot nation was at the peak of its power. Still uncrippled by white man's diseases, white man's whiskey and white man's bullets, the Blackfoot in 1865 were one of the fiercest and most efficient fighting forces in history.

Apart from Brown's party, there probably weren't more than a few white men in all Alberta at the time. And, learning from the experiences of tribes to the south, the

Blackfoot were anxious to see even these few white invaders driven out of their lands.

Years later, Brown remembered that trouble wasn't long in coming:

"One day, at a clump of cottonwood trees, we stopped to eat. Well, as we were eating we were suddenly surprised by a flight of arrows from the direction of the cottonwood trees and we knew that our first war party had begun.

"We all thought our time had come. The Indians had no firearms, but they were all young bucks, 32 of them, no old men or war women. All young warriors. A war party out for anything they could get. They had lots of arrows and they let them fly.

"We got up and started shooting at anything we could see. We had not much cover, only some brush, and the Indians had driven us away from the cottonwoods, many of which were two feet in diameter. If the Indians had guns they would have killed all five of us.

"It was at this time I received an arrow in the back, close to my kidneys. It was a miracle I was not killed—I thought my time had come—but I pulled it out, an arrow head two and a half inches long and the head out of sight. The jagged edges caught the flesh as I pulled it out, and it gave me great pain.

"I had a bottle of turpentine and, opening up the wound, one of my companions inserted the neck of the bottle and when I bent over about half a pint ran into the opening made by the arrow head. This was all the doctoring I ever got and in a few days I was well again.

"We were using old muzzle loaders with balls and caps and we carried bullets in our pockets and in our mouths. Two Indians fell victims to our intermittent fire and the rest, after about 20 minutes fighting, rode to the river and jumping *their horses into the stream, swam them across, taking one of my horses and another with them...*

Brown, in agony with the arrow wound, didn't take long to lose his famous temper. The result was what he later described as a "miniature civil war."

When the dust finally settled, the party had split up. Three of the men pushed on along their original route. Brown never heard of them again.

The fourth man, whose horse had been lost in the Indian raid, reluctantly decided to stay with Brown. No doubt the man, noting the fact that Brown still had two horses left, hoped that Brown would give him one. But Brown had all his worldly goods packed on the second animal and wasn't about to part with it under any circumstances.

Instead, he "helped" his companion by building him a bull boat (a circle of willow covered with a green buffalo hide), packing him into it with a load of raw buffalo meat, and shoving him off from the bank of the Saskatchewan River.

Brown's casual explanation of the act years later was that *"I thought I might run across him at Fort Garry if the river flowed in that direction, but I was not sure."*

(For the record, the man did survive. Brown met him again some time later — though not, it should be added, at Fort Garry.)

Now on his own, Brown struck out towards Edmonton. Or so he thought. The problem was that he had convinced himself that the Saskatchewan River would serve as the highway to his destination. "I reasoned that it must flow into the Atlantic Ocean or Hudson's Bay and that it would eventually bring us to the fringe of civilization."

In fact, the river would bring him to Duck Lake and a new chapter in his life.

After several weeks of wandering along the twisting river,

Brown came upon a small band of Cree Indians. From them, he learned that there was a "A-pit-hou-a-goo-es san," a "village of half-sons," nearby.

The "half-sons" were the Metis, and the village the Cree referred to was a settlement of 50 families of hunters who were preparing to winter at Duck Lake.

Brown pressed on to the settlement and was immediately accepted by the hunters. He spent the fall and winter living as part of one of the families, sharing the tasks of caring for the valuable buffalo ponies and of hunting for food. By the time spring came, Brown spoke the language and had learned the intricate social pattern of Metis life.

He spent several years with the Metis people, taking a Metis girl as his "wife" and building a reputation as one of the best buffalo hunters in a society that knew no peers as buffalo hunters.

In his later years, Brown made it plain that he could happily have spent the rest of his life as one of the Metis people.

But, sadly, by the time he met them history was already closing in on their way of life. The Metis had joined in the frenzied extermination of the buffalo, and when the buffalo disappeared so did the nomad hunters.

Brown had drifted far from the mountains, and he would drift further still in distance, in time, and in feeling.

After he left the Metis, he joined in the life of the whiskey traders and wolfers who were streaming north across the International Boundary.

His recollections of this period are defiant, filled with a refusal to apologize for things of which he obviously felt deeply ashamed. One of Brown's anecdotes in particular catches the feeling of his life at the time.

Brown was engaged in the dubious pursuit of hunting wolves with poisoned bait, and on this particular day had

brought in a load of pelts to a trader named Johnnie Gibbons.

He arrived at the post to find it crowded with about 30 Red Lake Indians. Gibbons had only two clerks and he persuaded Brown to help in the post for the day.

"In those days," Brown explains, "all traders sold rum and whiskey to the natives. Johnnie Gibbons was not any exception to the rule, and he put me in charge of dispensing the liquid. The Red Lakes would come in with a fur of some kind and hand it to me. It was my duty to give them as little whiskey as they would accept for it.

"There were no bottles, cups, or glasses in use in the west at the time, but the Hudson's Bay Company brought in *thousands of little copper kettles and these soon came into common use.*

It would be one of these kettles that an Indian would invariably push up to receive the whiskey in payment for his fur. Sometimes he would drink it where he stood and other times it was carried to his teepee.

"On this day the Red Lakes had run out of fur before their thirst for whiskey had been quenched. Chief Starving Wolf had come in and asked for a drink free gratis. By this time they were all very drunk and I didn't like to give them any more. So I said to him 'My friend and brother, you know I am not a man of two tongues. I'll give you one drink and that's the last you'll get.'

"So he drank his drink and left."

With the Indians gone, Gibbons sent an old man, Jimmie Clewitt, out to a storehouse behind the post to bring in a fresh jug of rum.

Brown was uneasy about the Indians and he was standing at the window. He saw Clewitt enter the storehouse and, an instant later, saw Chief Starving Wolf jump through the door after him, gun in hand.

"I yelled that the Indians had gone into the storehouse. Instantly we heard the report of a gun and saw Clewitt running for his life to the store. We also saw the Indian emerge with a large copper pot which we assumed was full of rum, and it was. Clewitt made for the house and falling into the porch groaned 'I'm done for.'"

One of the post's clerks, Billy Salmon, had been concerned about the old man going out to the storehouse alone and had followed. He was with him when the shot was fired. Like the old man, he had made a run for the porch, collapsing in front of the door. He had been badly wounded and later died.

Brown continues: *"The Indians immediately began peppering away at the store from their hiding places behind the storehouse. Odd bullets came through the chinking and there was rattling and clashing of all sorts of stuff on the shelves. (We) grabbed muzzle loaders and whenever the leg or wing of an Indian appeared around the corner he was nailed. Even Clewitt, whom we expected was dead, jumped up and, grabbing a rifle, began peppering through a window.*

"After several rounds had been fired, an Indian jumped out from behind the storehouse, probably to get a good aim, and Clewitt and myself both shot him. Another Red Laker ran out to pull in his dead body; but while getting over a fence he was shot in the leg and fled, dragging the broken member after him."

The other clerk, in the meantime, had managed to sneak away from the post and run for reinforcements. Just as the men in the post were running out of ammunition, the clerk returned with a party of 20 half-breeds and whites. The Red Lakers fled.

The men in the post took time to tend the wounded Clewitt and to tidy up, then:

"I need hardly say that after this narrow escape every one of us got drunk, and while in that state someone — perhaps I did it — cut the head off the dead Indian and, climbing to the roof of the store, stuck it on a stake standing up through the thatching.

"There the head remained for many weeks, a most weird and gruesome sight with its long hair blowing in every breeze..."

For a few years, Brown's life was a jumble of incidents like this. Finally he could stand it no longer.

Years earlier, when he had first come through the South Kootenai Pass to the prairies he had paused at a chain of lakes, the Kootenai Lakes (later to be known as the

Waterton Lakes). At the time he had been struck by the beauty of the lakes and by the deep conviction that his place in life was on their shores. He vowed that someday he would return and make his home there.

Now, 12 years later, he remembered the vow. He was finally on his way back to the mountains and to the lakes that would make "Kootenai" his middle name.

Brown made a partner of a man named Fred Kanouse and the two opened a store on what later became Brown's homestead at Waterton.

The store attracted many Indian customers. Brown and Kanouse, despite the attraction of huge profits, avoided trading in whiskey. It wasn't a matter of morality. As Brown pointed out later they had both seen too many drunken Indians on the rampage to want to chance the consequences.

Despite the absence of whiskey, business boomed. It was as much a matter of gambling as good trading sense. Both Brown and Kanouse loved a bet, and they knew that Indians would gamble on just about anything.

Brown explains: *"Someone taught the Flatheads and Kootenais to play poker and this became their great pastime when they visited the store. It took a card shark to beat them. Kanouse was an expert poker-player so he attended to that part of the business.*

"I was a foot-racer and a good shot, and in competition on the track or with the rifle I could always beat them.

"We had two good horses and in horse-racing we always got the best of them. In fact, we beat them at every turn."

Being a consistent winner is not without its risks and Brown, in his memoirs, tells of one incident where the partners showed a decided flare for diplomacy.

"I have a very distinct recollection of one very interesting race, not on account of the race so much as because of the big stakes we put up.

"We had just sold the Kootenais $500 worth of goods for furs they had delivered. They asked for a race and we asked 'What stakes?'.

"They had no furs and no money but they had the goods they just bought. So they took these goods — saddles, bridles, lasso ropes, blankets, dress lengths the squaws had bought for gaudy gowns — and piled them up in front of the store.

"Then they rounded up 40 head of Indian ponies valued at about $20 apiece. They then asked what we would put up. Fred Kanouse had $500 in greenbacks and he told them we would put up this against their pile of goods and horses. And the race was on.

*"Kanouse rode Honest John and the Indians had two or three horses in the field. Honest John won easily and

we carried the goods in and put them on the shelves again.

"The bucks took the loss quite philosophically but the squaws put up a howl. They said to their lords and masters: 'You are fools. You let these white dogs swindle you. It will soon be winter and we have no clothes, blankets, or anything else.'

"There were only three white men of us ... and there must have been nearly 70 full blooded Indians. So we had to go slow.

"Kanouse suggested giving every squaw a blanket which we did, and every buck a knife or plug of tobbaco or some small trinket he might ask for.

We also gave back the poorest of the horses we won, for some of the poor beggars were on foot and would have to double deck or walk back to the Flathead country. But we kept the best of the horses and all the saddles, bridles and other goods.

Every man, woman and child got some little present and away they went back to their stamping grounds quite happy."

Brown's most famous gambling story, of course, concerned the acquisition of his second wife, Nichamoose. Brown, a widower at this point, saw the girl when a band of her people came to trade at the store and he decided he would have her as his wife — at any price.

The price her family demanded was five horses and Brown paid cheerfully — which should have made them suspicious. No sooner was the transaction complete than Brown lured them into a bet and ended up with his five horses back and a new wife to boot.

Gambling and diplomacy nothwithstanding, the store was a short-lived proposition for Brown and Kanouse. Most of the Indians who traded with them came from what was officially the United States side of the international line.

As the border stiffened, more and more of the Indians traded in the U.S.

Brown and Kanouse decided to close up shop. Kanouse bought out Brown's share of the goods and headed out to set up a general store in the town of Macleod. Brown stayed behind to homestead by the lakes he knew and loved.

Long before anyone else, Brown considered the Waterton Lakes area a national park. He became the area's protector, stamping out careless or abandoned campfires, doing what he could to control irresponsible hunting. When the area was finally made a national park, George 'Kootenai' Brown was named its first superintendent.

Brown was aging and — very reluctantly — settling down. He had two homesteads on the go, and he was coming

to uneasy grips with the bureaucracy of park administration. He had even made his marriage to Nichamoose legal, with the famous missionary, Father Lacombe, performing the ceremony.

Kootenai Brown was always enough of a visionary to know that civilization would come rushing into the west. But even he was bewildered by the speed with which what had been his way of life for so many years disappeared overnight.

It must have seemed ironic to him to write Ottawa for authority to control gambling among the tourists who were flocking to the park.

And for a man of the open range it must have taken a great deal of soul-searching to lead the way towards fencing off the ranch land around Pincher Creek. He did it only because, in the winter of 1911, 4,000 head of cattle had drifted into the park, and 2,000 head had died from cold and starvation.

In time, Brown would even have his famous, flowing hair cut. The job of park superintendent, he felt, demanded a certain dignity.

Brown was prepared to accept the need for civilization but, short hair or not, he just didn't have it in him to become a civilized man himself. Although he learned to control his temper, he never lost the wild, free feeling of the pioneer mountainman.

Perhaps no story sums up the older Kootenai Brown better than the one of how, in 1910, at an unmellowed 70 years of age, he took part in his last buffalo hunt.

Although the buffalo were basically exterminated during the era of the hide-hunter, a few did survive. These were eventually built into the famous Pablo herd (later to be moved to Wainwright).

It was the Pablo herd that gave Brown his chance at a final hunt.

"A bunch (of buffalo from the herd) got away to the mountains," Brown writes. "They belonged to Pablo and he got an idea that he would finish up the days of real buffalo hunting with a party of old-timers to go after these. He began looking over the country for a few real old buffalo hunters that were left.

"One day I got a letter delivered to me by a long lanky half-breed cow-puncher. It was a letter someone had written for Pablo inviting me to be present at a buffalo hunt for a week.

"The half-breed told me of the preparations Pablo was making and the amount of good whiskey he was putting in store.

"I couldn't resist the invitation. The old instinct to ride after buffalo again came over me, and I have to admit I always have a keen appetite for any kind of good strong drink. We are not getting nearly as good whiskey as we used to....

"Anyway I accepted the invitation of Pablo and I rode my old buck-skin over the border to Montana.

"The most distinguished guest was Buffalo Bill, and to him fell the honor of killing three of the remaining buffalo. He was a great hunter. I have heard his wife tell of contests where he beat his opponents by killing nearly double the number of buffalo they could kill in the same time.

"Pablo himself got two, I got one, and several others got one each. Pablo presented each of us with the hides we killed and with as much meat as we could pack home.

"It was a tame meeting compared to the days when we hunted herds of thousands of animals....

"I have never seen a buffalo since, either wild or in captivity."

Ten years later George Kootenai Brown was dead. His grave is on a high point overlooking the park that is his legacy.

       *   *

There has never been another man quite like him — "either wild or in captivity."

       *   *

"In the name of Almighty God, by Whose strength I have climbed here, I capture this peak, Mt. Robson, for my own country, and for the Alpine Club of Canada."

—REV. GEORGE B. KINNEY

When, in 1909, the bareheaded Rev. Kinney staked his claim to the roof of the Canadian Rockies, he was claiming it for more than country or club. He was also claiming it for the "grand old man" of Canadian mountaineering — Arthur O. Wheeler.

It was Wheeler who created Canada's Alpine Club, and it was Wheeler who stood, in spirit if not always in fact, with every Canadian pioneer climber on the peak of every Canadian mountain they conquered.

On so many trails in the Canadian Rockies there comes a point where mere mortals can go no farther, where the trail guide says "experienced climbers only" and means it.

Beyond that point is a whole world of towering cliffs and cornices, a world of ropes and ice-axes and pitons and climbing ladders; the world of Arthur Wheeler and men like him.

Wheeler came to mountaineering relatively late, at the age of 40, and he came to it more out of necessity than out of choice. A trained surveyor, Wheeler had been with the federal topographical surveys branch off and on since 1885, and was an expert in phototopography.

In 1900, assigned to help map the Canadian Rockies, he discovered that the only way he was going to get his camera equipment to the tops of the mountains was to carry it there, and he set to work on a crash course in mountaineering.

What started out as a labor of necessity, however, soon turned into a labor of love. Alone in the high, wild world of the Selkirk range, Wheeler discovered, like so many men before him, the place where he belonged.

By 1905, when he published his survey of the Selkirks, Wheeler was as thoroughly a man of the mountains as if he'd drawn his first breath there.

In fact, Wheeler was born to the comparative levelness of Kilkenny, Ireland, and lived there until his parents brought him to Canada at the age of 16.

Right from the time of his arrival Wheeler "burned" to explore the vast and largely untamed country in which he found himself. And, in 1876, the best avenue to exploration for a young immigrant boy was to become a surveyor. Five years later, in 1881, Wheeler's apprenticeship was behind him and he had qualified as an Ontario Land Surveyor.

By 1885 he was in uniform with the Dominion Land Surveyors' Intelligence Corps and played a part in suppressing the Riel Rebellion.

By 1900, Wheeler's list of survey accomplishments stretched on an on: work on the CPR, settlement surveys for the North West Territories, summers alone in a birch-bark canoe on the Great Lakes.

But then came the Selkirks and Wheeler's rendezvous with Alberta history.

If Wheeler had climbed out of the Selkirks in 1905 as just another man in love with the mountains, his name would be forgotten — or at best little known — today.

What he came out with, in fact, was an urgent vision. Alone, looking out over the sea of peaks, Wheeler had been struck by the realization that most of the mountains he saw had never been named, never been climbed. The Canadian Rockies were one of the last great frontiers of mountaineering.

Wheeler knew it was inevitable that all these mountains would soon be conquered, and he was determined that they would be conquered in the name of Canada.

In 1906, with the help of Mrs. H. J. Parker of the Manitoba Free Press and of Calgary's Rev. J. C. Herdman, he founded the Alpine Club of Canada. The next year he started the Canadian Alpine Journal and became its first editor.

Wheeler's Alpine Club quickly became the focal point for the efforts to conquer Canada's peaks. Climber after climber came to Wheeler for advice as they planned their assaults.

At some point in this period Wheeler seems to have made a decision about the role he would play in the campaign to claim Canada's mountains for Canada. Another man might have been tempted to make it a personal campaign, turn it into personal triumph, but Wheeler chose another course.

Although he continued to climb enthusiastically, and although he took part in many expeditions, he deliberately moved himself into the background. He became the man who organized, who encouraged, who applauded, but never the man who stood triumphant in the spotlight.

The decision has a curious effect on his story. Increasingly, his contribution to Canadian alpine history tended to blend into the stories of other men, and increasingly it is in these other stories that Wheeler is to be found.

One of the best illustrations of this is the story of the efforts to conquer Mt. Robson. In the early 1900's Mt. Robson, standing at 13,700 feet, was considered the highest mountain in the Canadian Rockies.

In 1906, shaping plans for the new alpine club, Wheeler suddenly realized that, though many had seen and passed the giant of the mountains, no one had actually attempted to climb it.

Wheeler immediately seized on the idea of an attack on Robson by Canadians as the most appropriate way to set the club on its way.

Ever enthusiastic and ever persuasive, Wheeler cornered the famous brothers of Canadian climbing, L.Q. Coleman and Prof. A. P. Coleman, and urged them to try the climb. By the winter of 1906, Wheeler had the Colemans convinced and they began making plans for an expedition the next summer.

In August, 1907, the Colemans were on their way to the mountain. At the last moment they had recruited a promising young climber, Rev. George Kinney, as the third member of their team.

One of the greatest difficulties the team faced, apart from the climb itself, was the problem of getting to the mountain. Mt. Robson stands west and north of Jasper and, in 1907, there was no Jasper Highway nor even a clear-cut passable route.

The Colemans and Kinney chose to go north from Laggan (Lake Louise). It was probably as good a way as any, but it wasn't good enough. It took them 41 days, weeks longer than they had expected, to reach the base of Robson.

They had one tantalizing glimpse of the peak, then storms moved in to shroud the mountain in clouds. The clouds and the storms stayed.

The party had arrived to late in the season and the frustrated trio finally had to return to civilization, without having gone any higher on Robson than the timberline.

The next year the three were back again, and again too late in the season to be sure of good climbing.

The too-familiar clouds were in place when they arrived, and they settled down to wait. Two days later the weather cleared. But two days later it was Sunday, and Rev. Kinney was quite emphatic about "no climbing on Sunday." The weather closed in again by Monday morning.

Five days later it cleared enough for the party to climb. The Colemans and Kinney made it to 10,000 feet, then were driven back by rain and darkness. Another day of storm and then the weather cleared. Sunday again. The Colemans must have been sorely tempted by atheism.

Snow moved in the next day and stayed for three weeks. The Colemans and Kinney tried to climb anyway, from time to time, but were always driven back by storms.

Finally, with the food supply nearly exhausted, they decided they had to admit defeat. But Kinney insisted on one final — solo — attempt on the mountain.

It took until nightfall to reach the 7,000 foot level and he spent the night shivering in a blanket, unable to light a fire.

At dawn he was climbing, inching his way up to 10,500 feet. Floundering in deep snow and pounded by a mounting gale that literally blew him off his feet on repeated occasions, he finally had to give up. Later he insisted he would have continued his attempt the next day if he hadn't promised the Colemans that he would be out only one night.

The next day, as the party was packing to leave for home, the weather cleared again and they decided on one last climb. They made it to within 1,200 feet of the summit but had to turn back, frustrated, when darkness closed in.

It was the end of another year. The three parted company, agreeing to meet in Edmonton for another attempt on Robson the next August.

The next May, however, Kinney heard rumors that a "party of foreigners" was on its way to attempt the elusive peak. He rushed into action, Determined to head off the foreign attempt, he hurried from his home in Victoria to Edmonton to stage his own assault.

In Edmonton he contacted John Yates, the packer who had been with the expedition the two previous years. But Yates refused to have anything to do with an attempt on Robson so early in the season. Spring had been late and the mountains were hidden under heavy snow — with the threat of avalanche increasing daily.

Kinney, however, had made up his mind to climb Robson and he was going to do it, Yates or no Yates.

On June 11 he set off alone, his three horses packed with provisions and with only a couple of dollars and some loose change in his pocket.

He wasn't particularly worried about being alone, having, as he explained later, vague hopes of meeting someone on the trail "who would share fortune with me."

He was deep in the Athabasca Valley, drying out after being stranded for several days by the flooding Rocky River, before he met the fortune-sharer he had been hoping for.

It was Donald (Curly) Phillips, who was later to become one of the more famous Rocky Mountain guides, but who was at this time on his first trip into the mountains.

Phillips had never climbed a mountain before, but the eager Kinney somehow persuaded him he could learn all about mountaineering — on Mt. Robson.

It wasn't until he stood, craning his neck back to try to see the top of the forbidding mountain, that Phillips realized what he had got himself into.

Curly Phillips, however, wasn't a man to back off from anything. So, tied behind Kinney with a length of ordinary rope, and with a piece of stick for a mountain axe, he set off to climb his first mountain.

In three days, with Kinney forced to cut ice-steps much of the way, the pair had made it to 11,000 feet. Yates, the packer, had been right about avalanches. They whistled by Kinney and Phillips with frightening regularity.

The pair retreated and brought up supplies to establish a camp at the 10,000 foot mark. Then Kinney cut steps up to the 12,000 foot point. There, however, the two were pummelled by falls of ice and stones and were forced to flee for their lives.

During the flight, Kinney noted later, "the now-melting snow masses that covered every ledge threatened to slide from under our weight and drag us over the cliffs.

"Phillips," he added wryly, "was fast becoming an expert in climbing."

They were forced all the way back to the base and had to wait out eight days of storms before they could climb again.

On the ninth day, at first light, they were hurrying up the mountain. On the west shoulder, at 10,500 feet, they dug through the snow covering a ledge, built a little wall of stones to keep themselves from rolling off the mountain, and settled down to shiver out the night.

Kinney and Phillips both knew that the next day would have to be their final attempt on the summit.

At dawn, stiff with cold, they started to climb again. The morning was clear but only briefly. Soon they were struggling up through clouds of sleet and mist. Kinney later said the conditions were "a blessing, in a way, for they shut out the view of the fearful depths below."

Hours later they were on the icecap of the summit, so surrounded by swirling snow that they could hardly see their hands in front of their faces.

Kinney swung his ice axe at the lip of snow in front of him and ... "it cut into my very feet, and through the little gap that I had made in the cornice, I was looking down a sheer wall of precipice that reached to the glacier at the foot of Berg Lake, thousands of feet below. I was on a needle peak that rose so abruptly that even cornices cannot build out very far from it.

"Baring my head, I said, 'In the name of Almighty God, by Whose strength I have climbed here, I capture this peak Mt. Robson for my own country, and for the Alpine Club of Canada'."

On their way back, just outside Jasper, they met the "foreigners" Kinney had been so anxious to beat. In fact, the "foreigners" were a collection of the most brilliant climbers in the world: Sir Edward Whymper, Arnold Mumm, Geoffrey Hastings and Leopold Amery — the last three of the British Alpine Club, and all four with conquests of more than 20,000 feet on their records.

The four British climbers heaped praise on Kinney,

writing later that "no mountaineering success was ever more richly deserved, or won by a finer exhibition of courage, skill and indomitable perseverance."

Kinney's triumph was complete — or so it seemed.

His fellows in the Canadian Alpine Club — particularly the sharp-eyed A. O. Wheeler — were the first to notice it. There was an elusive something wrong with Kinney's triumph, something vaguely dissatisfying in the way he talked of it.

Soon rumor was circulating even outside the clubrooms: Somehow, by accident, Kinney had turned back a few feet short of the summit of Mt. Robson. The mountain was still unclimbed.

Kinney denied the suggestion hotly. But suspicion nagged on, troubling Wheeler and a few of the other club members.

Some members felt the mountain should be climbed again to confirm the club's claim of its conquest. But they hesitated to do anything, however indirectly, that would suggest Kinney had been lying.

It was A. O. Wheeler, finally, who stepped in to do what had to be done. It had been his suggestion that had launched the Colemans and Kinney on their three-year struggle with Robson. He had brooded over their efforts, urged them on, encouraged them when frustration seemed to gain the upper hand.

He had cheered Kinney's triumph, and now he was prepared to do whatever was necessary to keep that triumph from turning hollow.

In the summer of 1813, under Wheeler's personal supervision, the Canadian Alpine Club set up camp at the base of Mt. Robson. Wheeler hand-picked the team for the assault: Albert MacCarthy and William Foster, two of Canada's best climbers, and Conrad Kain, indisputably the best alpine guide in Canadian mountain history. Wheeler spent hours with the team, plotting the best line to the summit.

The day came for the climb and the three moved out at dawn. Kain cut ice-steps at a furious rate, refusing to let up even for a moment. At some points the three had to wade through hip-deep snow.

Eight hours later they saw, just above them "great masses of ice and rock, dome upon dome, swept clear by raging storms to reveal clear green ice scintillating in the sun." And just above that was the summit.

A short while later, squeezed together on the slim, top-most spire of Mt. Robson, they cemented the Canadian Alpine Club's claim on the peak.

On their way back down, they noted the route Kinney and Phillips had taken in 1909.

Conrad Kain described it as "quite the most dangerous way that could be chosen up the peak" and insisted that Kinney and Phillips "deserve far more credit than we…"

Bit by bit, in the years that followed, the truth of what happened during Kinney's attempt on Robson came out.

The main information came from Curly Phillips who said that, climbing in the blinding storm, he and Kinney "had reached on our ascent an ice-dome 50 or 60 feet high, which we took for the peak. The danger was too great to ascend the dome."

It would be half a century before Kinney himself, now an elderly man, provided the final word. He conceded that he had probably been "mistaken" in his claim and had actually stopped a few feet short of the summit.

One wonders how Wheeler, if he had still been alive, would have felt to hear the wisdom of the decision he made in 1913 finally confirmed.

Firmly planted on a slope overlooking Banff, on the

site Wheeler picked for them, are the headquarters of the Canadian Alpine Club. Wheeler designed the building and personally supervised its construction.

It makes a fine landmark. The kind to guide the way for all the other young boys who "burn" to be explorers.

* * *

"I've decided to give it maybe one more try…"

MIKE CZECH

* * *

It takes a few minutes for a visitor to realize that the far-away gleam in Mike Czech's eye is the gleam of gold.

Sitting in his perpetually half-finished house in Coleman, Czech displays a talent for avoiding questions that would do credit to a cabinet minister.

He has a habit of staring off into the distance and stirring uneasily in his seat as though he wished the annoying questions would go away — or as though he wishes he were somewhere else.

When forced to answer, he is liable to say vaguely that: *"Well, maybe I'll tell you about that one of these days. Why don't you come back in…"*

All this becomes understandable when you realize that Mike Czech is in the grips of that legendary, lost, cursed gold mine: the Lost Lemon.

Czech is not an old man (somewhere in his 40's by appearance, but even here he remains vague) but he has devoted most of his adult life to the search for the mine.

It doesn't bother him that many have died on the same quest. Or that all the evidence available suggests the mine never existed, that it was all a grotesque hoax on the part of the claim-seeder.

"It's there all right," Czech insists with a half-smile. He will say no more.

"There" to Czech and to most of the others who spent their lives searching for the mine, is the Livingstone Range, that massive forbidding block of mountain stretching north from the Crowsnest Pass almost to Rocky Mountain House.

The legend of the Lost Lemon is easily told.

In 1870 a party of prospectors came north from Montana to scour the North Saskatchewan River for gold.

With them were two men named Lemon and Black Jack who split away from the main party to search the Highwood River.

Working upstream they found traces of gold and followed the traces toward the headwaters.

Somewhere along the way they struck paydirt, rich diggings and a ledge that was the source of the gold.

(One supposed sample of the find made its way to Fort Benton in Montana where traders described it as "a body of solid gold with little rock shot in it.")

In camp the night of the find the partners quarrelled and Lemon, waiting until after his companion was asleep, split Black Jack's head open with an axe.

Thrown into a panic by realization of the enormity of his murderous act, Lemon built up the fire and spent the rest of the night pacing back and forth like a caged beast, rifle in hand.

His panic wasn't eased by the sound of ghastly moaning and twittering that filled the air around the camp.

Unknown to Lemon, the murder had been witnessed by two Stoney braves, William and Daniel Bendow. It was they who were providing the sound effects that were driving Lemon to terror and that sent him fleeing on horseback at first light.

Fearful that news of a gold find would draw an army of prospectors into their hunting grounds, the Stoney chief Bearspaw swore the two braves to secrecy when they told him what they had seen.

Lemon made it back to Tobacco Plains in Montana. There he confessed the murder to a priest who was an old friend of his, and he showed the priest a bag of the gold he said he and Black Jack had found the day of the crime.

The priest sent another man, John MacDougall, to the scene of crime. MacDougall buried Black Jack and piled stones over the grave to keep off wolves and to act as a landmark.

As soon as MacDougall left, the Stoneys tore down the cairn and scattered all traces of the grave and the camp.

All winter Lemon remained with the priest, hovering always on the edge of insanity.

By spring, however, he was apparently well and, with the organization of the priest, led a large party of miners north to find the mine.

Lemon, however, was unable to find the site. After days of searching, the miners became convinced Lemon was trying to mislead them, keep them from the gold.

They threatened Lemon with death and he promptly became violently insane. Although he would have lucid periods from time to time, he remained insane for the rest of his life.

The miners had to turn back.

The next spring another expedition, again organized by the priest, set out. The guide was to be MacDougall, the man who had buried Black Jack.

But on his way to join the search party, MacDougall stopped at the whiskey post of Fort Pitt and drank himself to death. Again a hunt for the mine had to be called off.

Every year another party would set out and every year fate – or tragedy – would frustrate it.

The most notable hunter was a man named Lafayette French who claimed to have a map drawn by Lemon.

For 15 years he scoured the hills in search of the mine. One night, in the early 1890's, French sat down and wrote an excited letter to a friend at Fort Benton. He had, the letter said, finally found "IT."

Later that night the cabin burned to the ground.

French escaped, but so badly burned he couldn't speak before he died.

Searchers later found, melted in the ruins of French's cabin, what was rumored to be "thousands of dollars" worth of gold.

With French's death, the search for the Lost Lemon lost most of its steam. Also, there was the growing conviction that the mine was guarded by an Indian curse.

And from time to time there would be found in the range the remains of cabins with food, rusted rifles, cooking kits, rat-eaten bedrolls. Men don't abandon these things in the wilderness — unless tragedy strikes.

Gradually the hunt for the mine became the mission of "foolhardy" men like Mike Czech. And finally it has become the mission of Mike Czech himself.

So much for the legend. But what are the facts?

Late in the 1960s, Glenbow historian Hugh Dempsey probed the legend and took it apart piece by piece.

He found Black Jack was a real man and a well-known prospector — the only problem, in terms of the legend, being that he was alive and in a hospital in Victoria 13 years after he was supposedly murdered by Lemon.

Lemon's friend the priest was identified in early accounts as Father LeRoux. Church records showed no priest of that name ever served in the area.

But Dempsey found the LeRoux of the legend suspiciously like a French-Candian adventurer named Jean L'Heureux, particularly since the names LeRoux and L'Heureux are identical in sound.

L'Heureux had studied for the priesthood but, after a

scandal, fled to the Montana gold fields where he posed as a priest and missionary.

In 1862, he was connected with a gold-seeding scheme which sent an expedition of miners rushing north to Fort Edmonton.

Dempsey asks if it is "mere coincidence" that a phoney priese named L'Heureux started a false gold hunt in 1862 and that a mysterious priest named Father LaRoux sent out search parties in search of the Lost Lemon in 1871? The matter of Lafayette French's gold is also cleared up.

It turns out the gold was discovered in the cabin years after French's death — and that it had been planted there by its finder as part of a cover story to explain some gold illegally smuggled in from the United States.

The Stoney braves, the Bendow brothers, who witnessed the murder of Black Jack also proved a shaky part of the legend: The name Bendow appears on no treaty lists and Stoneys, questioned later, said they had never heard of the existence of the name in their tribe.

Finally, there is Lemon himself. Dempsey found an American prospector named Frank Lemon who, on an expedition into "Lost Lemon" territory, had lost his partner — known as Old George — in a shooting. Whether he was shot by Indians or in a quarrel with Lemon was never explained.

Lemon also claimed to have found gold on the trip — not a jackpot but a good showing that "got as high as $15 or $20 in the pan in a gulch."

The find, it turned out, wasn't even on the same side of the mountains as the supposed Lost Lemon.

Add to this grim little tale the meddling of the adventurer L'Heureux and the legend takes shape. And becomes no more than legend.

Still, Senator Dan Riley — who knew French, and L'Heureux both — continued to finance searches for the mine right up to the time of his death.

And the Stoneys, to this day, remain determinedly silent on the subject of the Lost Lemon and refuse to assist in the hunt for it — for reasons that have never been given.

The Lost Lemon. The name is well-chosen since lemons are gold — and bitter.

But Mike Czech, despite discouraging years of searching, is convinced the mine is there to find.

In the end, what difference does it make if the mine exists or not?

Mountainmen have followed more futile dreams into a place in the history of the Canadian Rockies.

EXPLORERS

"*I thought we were not keeping close enough to the mountains.*"

—George 'Kootenai' Brown

* * *

It took more than half a century for the white man to find a "road" through the Canadian Rockies.

For the men who took part in the search, it was an exercise in frustration. After all, it is one thing to be searching for something you only "think" is there. It is quite another to be searching for something you "know" is there.

And the early explorers "knew" the road they sought through the mountains existed; the Indians of the Canadian Rockies were using it — or, as it turned out, "them" — all the time.

For a number of reasons, Indians were determined that the explorers and traders weren't going to find any easy way through the mountains.

For the Indians, it was a last chance to retain control of part of their shrinking world.

It was also a matter, in the case of the Peigan Indians for example, of keeping enemy tribes deep in the mountain interior from getting their hands on guns that traders would provide.

It was one of the longer and more successful conspiracies in the history of Indian-white relations, and it wasn't without its humorous side.

Traders and explorers were often able to persuade Indians to guide them to one of the mysterious routes, but somehow these searches always ended up in a blind canyon or at the foot of a cliff, with the Indian guide scratching his head in feigned perplexity.

Not the kind of thing to improve the temper of an impatient explorer.

Of all the men who set out in search of the elusive road to the western sea, four names stand out above the others: Alexander Mackenzie, Simon Fraser, David Thompson and Sir George Simpson.

Alexander Mackenzie, in his expedition of 1793, wasn't really out to find an "easy" road to the Pacific. His was basically a scouting trip, to spy out land for a fur trade that was running short of fur east of the mountains.

But his push into the interior of the Rockies laid much vital groundwork for the two explorers who would follow him.

And perhaps Sir George Simpson, that crusty baron of the fur business, shouldn't be on the list at all.

Except that when the road was finally found he painted one of the most flamboyant white lines in history right down the middle of it.

* * *

"The judge had a nephew in need of an occupation; the North West Company was in need of sturdy young clerks who seemed to have talents..."

—FROM AN INTRODUCTION
TO THE JOURNALS OF SIMON FRASER.

* * *

Simon Fraser has been described as the most neglected of Canada's major explorers. As one historian notes, even the majority of his journals and letters have been published in forms that were "without exception inaccurate."

With the help of his uncle-judge, Fraser was apprenticed to the North West Company at the age of 16.

That was in 1792. From that time until he emerged in his famous expeditions that ended with the conquest of the Fraser River in 1808, he remains an historic enigma.

Almost nothing is known of his career.

There were at least four Frasers with the North West Company at the same time and Simon Fraser's name stands out with certainty in the company records only once.

That was in 1801 when a unanimous vote made him a partner, with a 46th share in the profits of the Nor'westers.

If nothing else, that acceptance to partnership at the early age of 25 demonstrated that Fraser had become a man the company valued.

Fraser's concern as a partner was the operation of North West's Athabasca Department and it led him directly to his assignment as the company's mountain explorer.

By the early 1800s, both the North West Company and The Hudson's Bay Company were suffering from over-extended supply routes.

The fierce competition between the companies was pushing trade farther and farther west as Indians over-trapped in efforts to meet the demands of the rivals.

By the time of Fraser's acceptance as a partner, the forests east of the Rockies were virtually trapped out and the companies were both operating deep into the mountain interior.

The North West Company was suffering most from the move westward.

The Hudson's Bay Company was bringing in supplies and shipping out furs through its ports on Hudson Bay and James Bay — no short trip, but certainly shorter than that of the Nor'westers who had to ship back and forth between the Rockies and Montreal.

The Nor'wester line was simply too long to stand the strain. The answer was a route through the mountains to the Pacific and Simon Fraser was given the job of finding it.

What made the task of Fraser and the other fur company explorers particularly difficult was that the road they were seeking had to be one made out of water. A portage here and there was acceptable, but with the loads made up in bundles of 90 pounds — and the usual assignment of two bundles to a man — a dry route was out of the question.

The Nor'westers were particularly intrigued by the Columbia River. They knew it came out at the Pacific, and Mackenzie's explorations in 1793 had created the belief (mistaken) that he had found the upper reaches of the Columbia.

So, in 1805, Simon Fraser was instructed by his company to advance up the Peace River, cross the Rockies, establish trading posts in what is now the interior of British Columbia, and endeavor to trace the Columbia River to its mouth.

Those instructions resulted in two expeditions, the last in 1808 finally taking Fraser and his men down the river that would later bear his name, a river that even today is described as "one of the most difficult and dangerous in the world."

That final journey was, in terms of what he had set out to do, a failure. The river hadn't been the Columbia. And it hadn't by any stretch of the imagination turned out to be a river that would serve as a trade route through the Rockies.

Still, even in his own day and even among the men in the North West Company who suffered most by the failure, Fraser's journey was considered a triumph of human courage and endurance.

And the very enormity of what he had done set the stage for those who would follow, those who would finally find the watery road to the sea.

History is always particularly good at describing the ends of things — the disaster of final failure, the triumph of victory over great obstacles.

But what about the beginnings of things?

In Fraser's case, the tale of his final terrible trip to the sea has been told many times and in many ways.

More important, in his rough, impatiently written journal, he does what few men remember to do: he records how it began.

And that story, of the first stage of the first journey, is every bit as exciting as the final tale of the thrust to the sea.

Fraser received his instructions in the summer of 1805 and by the fall of that year he had led a party of 20 men up the Peace River to the foot of the turbulent Peace River Canyon.

There he established a base camp and, being a good businessman, he also established a trading post.

All winter, waiting impatiently for spring break-up, he and his men restlessly expanded outward from that first trading post to gain firm control of fur trade in the district.

Two men in Fraser's party stand out particularly — though in distinctly different ways.

The first was his second-in-command, John Stuart, who would be at Fraser's side on all three of his journeys of exploration. It was often Stuart, as the excerpts that follow from Fraser's journal show, who kept the expedition — and its men — alive.

The second man was probably one of the most aptly named men in Canadian history: La Malice.

La Malice was Fraser's senior voyageur, and time and time again he lived up to his name with displays of incredibly shifty, mean and unreliable behavior.

By late spring in 1806, Fraser was ready to begin and La Malice wasn't the only problem he faced in making that beginning.

John Stuart was Fraser's only capable canoe-maker and Stuart was much to busy with other duties during the early spring to devote much time to the work.

The result was that Fraser was left to begin the journey in three canoes that were ill-made and in constant need of repair.

Worse yet, the men he had available were a sorry lot, largely incompetent and in ill-health.

A typical birchbark canoe of the type Fraser used needed a crew of three: a bowman, a steersman and a middle man. The most important man in each canoe was the steersman. And, as Fraser would note with dismay in his journal, none of his steersmen were any good.

Fraser himself took charge of the first canoe, Stuart of the second and, to the eternal woe of all concerned, La Malice became the fourth man in the third.

We pick up Fraser's journal on the first day of the journey.*

WEDNESDAY, MAY 21: *"About sunset Mr. Stuart and I took our departure with two canoes, and encamped at the first point. La Malice will follow tomorrow as soon as the canoe will be arranged. Mr. Stuart's canoe made a great deal* of water, and is so rude and ill-made that they were every moment in danger of over-setting it, for which reason we will be obliged to pass a couple of days at this place to arrange it. It is the worst-made that ever I saw and is more like a trough than a canoe … It would be more easy to make a new one than to arrange it."

FRIDAY, MAY 23: "Fine warm weather. A strong head wind all day. At noon we were obliged to put ashore to gum (gum from evergreen trees was used to seal leaks in the fragile bark canoes), the canoes being so leaky that we could not prevent the property from getting wet. Here we lost four hours … Little Gervais, who steers Mr. Stuart's canoe, is not able to keep it straight. Indeed, the want of a steersman will greatly retard our progress up this strong current."

*Some editing, to correct spelling and replace archaic or unclear words, has been done in these excerpts. Certain deletions have also been made for reasons of space.

SUNDAY, MAY 25: "Set off early, and soon after came to the foot of the strongest rapid we saw yet. The canoes were towed up with the line but one of them struck upon a stem which broke a small hole in the bottom and it took us near an hour to repair it."

TUESDAY, MAY 27: "...the water rises very fast. Indeed it has risen upwards of three feet since we left ... We came to and encamped at the last rapid ... La Malice, who was before us, attempted to ascend this rapid with the pole, but Mr. Stuart, who was the nearest to him, called to him to desist ... It was really difficult to come up this rapid, and we were obliged to take out the load and carry it over a rocky point of 400 yards, and the canoes were taken up light (paddled up unloaded). La Malice, who was first up, left his canoe with only the bow of it on shore, and while he was busy at the lower end it went off and ran down the rapid ... they went for it with another canoe. I was much displeased with La Malice on this occasion, as well as with his attempting to go up with a full load, and threatened him severely if he was not more careful in the future."

WEDNESDAY, MAY 28: (At this point, Fraser's party, still following Mackenzie's route, has turned east to follow the Parsnip River) "... which is overflown, and the current was so very strong that it was with much difficulty we could advance. No use can be made of the poles on account of the depth of the water, excepting some times against the banks and drift wood, and the current runs with such velocity that it cannot be stemmed with three paddles, and not easily with four ... and the banks are so thickly interwoven with trees and shrubs that it is seldom they can be approached, so there is no method left except that of going up by pulling the branches, and the canoes are in continual danger of being broke to pieces by the drift wood."

THURSDAY, MAY 29: "The water still rising and wood continually drifting down the river. My canoe was very near cut in two."

FRIDAY, MAY 30: "We set off at half past 4 a.m. ... a stump (a few hours later) ran through my canoe, which obliged us to push ashore, and we lost two hours ... We encountered more misery today than any day yet, and were obliged to cut several logs and obstructions to open a passage. My canoe through the awkwardness of the bowman and steersman was very much endangered and every soul on board near perishing."

MONDAY, JUNE 2: (The expedition this day reaches the lake that is today identified on the map as McLeod Lake.) "Here we left one of the canoes and separated its load on the other two, on account of all the men being nearly exhausted with fatigue, and especially La Garde, who steered my canoe since the 26th of last month, has such a sore wrist that he is no more able to."

TUESDAY, JUNE 3: (The party is once again moving but is brought up short about noon.) "Both canoes have become so heavy and shattered that they cannot be taken out of the water by less than four men."

(Finally, on June 8, the party reaches Fort McLeod, one of the posts which Fraser had established earlier. There Stuart and La Malice supervise the construction of two new canoes, the old ones now being beyond repair. It isn't until June 23 that the expedition is able to move on along the Nechako River. Two days later, the expedition is once again in difficulty — though of a different sort.)

WEDNESDAY, JUNE 25: "La Malice paddled only at intervals

today; he being unwell, and in the evening he declared himself disabled ... What ever it is, he appears to suffer very much and is quite disabled. It is really vexing ..."

FRIDAY, JUNE 27: "... we went on well, but was obliged to put ashore on account of La Malice, where we lost four hours. As he could not sleep for several nights past, last night Mr. Stuart gave him 30 drops laudnum, and he complains of being worse since ... La Malice seems very weak and often delirious, and yet he eats as well as the others."

SATURDAY, JUNE 28: "We were not above half an hour gone when La Malice jumped on shore, we being near the bank, and fell down senseless. This obliged us to put ashore and pitch our tents for the night ... By all appearances, if he (La Malice) is really as bad as he pretends, he will not live long. We are all really ill off in regard to the men. Saucier is sick, Gagnon complains of his side, Blais of having a pain and a lump upon his stomach, and Gervaise is not well, and La Londe is not able to steer his canoe."

SUNDAY, JUNE 29: "About noon we were obliged to put ashore and light a fire to warm La Malice and cook for him. He will eat nothing but cakes and pemmican boiled up with flour and sweetened with sugar."

TUESDAY, JULY 1: (La Malice, complaining of being treated like a dog in his illness, claims Fraser and Stuart have a grudge against him. News of this reaches Fraser.) "This assertion of his, La Malice, is entirely false. We have been attentive and kind to him ... and nothwithstanding his complaints he used more than one half of the medicines (God knows good or bad)we possessed, and destroyed more flour and sugar than both of us did since we left ... I recollect when St. Pierre (one of the men) fell in a fit he was abandoned by La Malice, and scarcely drawn out of the water, and when I afterwards reprimanded him for his apparent disregard of his duty as a Christian, even if he was indifferent to the feelings of humanity, he told me laughing that as he thought he (St. Pierre) was dying, he left him to die alone, and set about mending his canoe, but now it is his turn to suffer and he complains."

THURSDAY, JULY 3: (The two canoes are now on the James River.) "Our progress will be very slow now, as we will be continuously compelled to put the people of both canoes in one on account of the current and rapids being too strong to be managed by four men, and none of them adroit. The navigation of the river is very dangerous on account of it being narrow, the current running so swift and many trees and obstructions laid across."

FRIDAY, JULY 4: "We set off early, with both canoes ... and through the awkwardness of the men mine was run against a large obstruction in the middle of the river, which broke the bow and smashed all the pieces to the second bar (rib). all hands jumped out and pulled the wreck on shore before it had time to fill and sink. We lost the most part of the day to mend it ... This labor always falls to Mr. Stuart's lot, there being no other person that can do it."

MONDAY, JULY 7: "Gave all hands a dram to cheer up their spirits after their violent exertion during the whole day. All hands worked hard and Mr. Stuart and my share of the labor is the most difficult, as we not only work in the canoes the same as the others, but are obliged either one or the other to examine the river on foot before we risk the canoes, so that as soon as we arrive with the canoe at the place we return from on foot, we embark again to examine farther on."

WEDNESDAY, JULY 9: "All the goods are entirely wet and

the provisions are spoiling. When we arrived at this place the canoes were no more able to float, their bottoms being entirely hashed, and after getting bark and gathering some gum we patched them up for the present. The weather was cloudy all day and towards the evening it rained."

THURSDAY, JULY 10: *"Fine weather. After the canoes were gummed a little we continued on and had better going than we had reason to expect ... At 10 a.m. we arrived at the large river, opposite an island, without encountering any other difficulty than cutting several trees that laid across the channel ... This is a fine river ..."*

Fraser thought he was finally on the upper reaches of the Columbia. Instead, he was on the river that would later be given his name. And it would be two years before he discovered it wasn't such a "fine river" at all, even if it did — finally — take him to the sea.

Sixteen days later, on July 26, the first stage of Fraser's expedition ended.

During those 16 days, Fraser had to cope with a guide who, as it turned out, didn't know where he was going. He had to cope with starvation as supplies ran out and game and fish became elusive.

He even had to cope with the mauling of one of his voyageurs by a bear.

The first stage ended at what is now called Stuart Lake. There — in a frustrating illustration of just how desperately long the Nor'wester supply line had become — he had to wait until the fall of the next year for supplies and fresh men.

What the first part of Fraser's journal shows, the part that appears in fragments here, is something of the incredible hardships that had to be faced by the men who set out to conquer the Rockies.

The image left of Fraser himself is much the same as

that of the river he conquered — an image that commands respect.

Although he had his detractors, not even his most severe critic ever called him unfair, dishonest, or without honor.

Indeed, the character sketch written by Fraser-scholar E.O.S. Scholefield in 1908 probably best sums up the "most neglected" of our Mountainmen:

"... *a well-built active man, with heavy, almost dour, face, whose distinguishing features are a determined chin, firm, large-lipped mouth, prominent somewhat snubbed nose, light-blue eyes, broad receding brow, overhung with a mass of tousled hair of reddish tinge — a strong, honest face, indeed, but one giving more the idea of determination and physical robustness than of intellectuality or refinement.*

"*A man inured to hardship; versed in woodcraft and the lore of the savage; strong in danger; of inconquerable will and energy; unlettered, not polished, it may be, but true to his friends and honourable in his dealings; somewhat eccentric if we judge aright; a man typical of his age and calling.*

"*An heroic spirit truly, if case in the not altogether heroic mould of a fur-trader.*

"*He stands there a commanding figure.*"

* * *

From the ocean they expected a more boundless view, a something beyond power of their senses which they could not describe ..."

—DAVID THOMPSON ON HIS MEN'S FIRST REACTION
TO THE PACIFIC.

* * *

News that Simon Fraser's river had turned out to be neither the Columbia — nor navigable — frustrated the North West Company, as had other explorations before.

For two years, they let the project of the route to the Pacific sit.

Then, late in 1810, came news of a development that made finding the route imperative. American traders, under the leadership of John Jacob Astor, had landed at the mouth of the Columbia River and built a fort and trading post.

Unless something was done quickly, the Indian fur trade that had been coming east through the Rockies would reverse direction and go to the Americans waiting in the west.

For one Nor'wester at least, there was no question of what had to be done.

"Everything was changed," he noted in his journal when he heard the news of Astor. "I was now obliged to take four canoes and to proceed to the mouth of the Columbia to oppose them. Accordingly, I set off from Lac la Pluie."

The man who made that note was David Thompson, and his determination was about to put the second "sea" in Canada's "sea to sea."

In 1810, Thompson was nearly 30 years old, and his career had reached the point where he could well afford to rest on his laurels.

He had come to Canada at 14, apprenticed to the Hudson's Bay Company. Later, he had moved to the competition, the Nor'wester, and now like Fraser he was a partner in the company.

By training and by instinct, Thompson was a shrewd and gifted trader. But he was gifted in a far more important way as well: As a surveyor and map-maker.

It was only by accident that this second gift was ever discovered — accident in more ways than one. In his late teens, while still with the Hudson's Bay Company, Thompson suffered a very bad fracture of his right leg. The injury left him an invalid for more than a year.

In the winter of 1789-90, towards the end of this period

of recovery, he encountered a man named Philip Turnor, the chief surveyor for the Hudson's Bay Company. Turnor and Thompson were stranded together in Cumberland House for most of the winter.

To pass the time, Turnor taught the youth the rudiments of geography and astronomy. David Thompson proved to be an exceptional student.

By the time winter was over, he was skilled in mathematics, astronomy, and field surveying. He knew the survey use of the compass, the telescope, the thermometer and chronometer. He had learned to use the Nautical Almanak, the sextant and the artificial horizon.

From that point on, David Thompson would be as much explorer as he was trader and, during the next 22 years of his life, he would personally survey and map almost two million square miles of Canadian wilderness.

To understand what he accomplished, one has to realize that before he started the entire map of western Canada was blank. When he finished, it was filled.

In 1810, when he set off to oust Astor from the mouth of the Columbia, Thompson was only two years from retiring from the west and, by standards of his day, far too old and tired for so difficult a mission.

And the mission was far more difficult than even Thompson could imagine. While there are many passes in the Canadian Rockies, there are only four real breaches in the 1,000-mile wall. And only one of these, the Peace River route, has what the early traders were looking for: a waterway that pierces the entire mountain chain.

Thompson knew nothing of the Peace route. He did know, however, that many rivers had been followed from the Pacific far up into the mountains. It was the link with the same river that had eluded Fraser that Thompson was determined to find — the link with the Columbia.

Thompson knew he had no reason to be optimistic of finding it. Three times before — in 1800, 1801 and 1806 — he had set off on the same search, and three times he had failed. And he had watched the stubborn and capable Simon Fraser fail as well.

Thompson, however, was not a man to accept failure.

In November, 1810, he set off from Rocky Mountain House with a party of men. Heavily burdened with supplies and trade goods, the party spent four weeks hacking through thick bush as it pushed northward towards the Athabasca River, which Thompson believed to be the first link in the chain to the Pacific.

When the party emerged from the timber onto the flats and marshland near the Athabasca, the going got easier, but away from the protection of the trees the men felt the full impact of the winter cold. It was a steady 30 degrees below zero. The punishing cold drained strength away, left the men bitterly weary and clumsy.

Thompson's party was immobilized for days, the men barely able to muster the energy needed to hunt for the game they needed to supplement their food supplies.

It was the end of December before they were finally able to push on, following the Athabasca into the mountains. Most of the party's pack horses were too weak to carry a load, so supplies were transferred to improvised dog sleds. With game scarce and supplies running low, Thompson had to slaughter several of the horses for food.

He had to send some of his men back to Rocky Mountain House. A few others deserted. Thompson made the rest continue against their will.

By the end of the first week of January the party was just south of the present site of Jasper and almost hopelessly bogged down in deep snow. Thompson was forced to lighten the sleds and to leave a large quantity of supplies cached under the care of one of the party. The few remaining horses were exhausted and Thompson turned them loose. The men added the horses' loads to what they were already carrying on their backs.

With 13 men and 8 dogsleds left, Thompson pushed on 15 more miles south along the Athabasca valley to the juncture of the Whirlpool River. Thompson decided to turn to follow the frozen Whirlpool.

Toiling up the 5,000-foot climb, Thompson couldn't know he had finally found the key to what men had been seeking for half a century: a road to the Pacific.

Nor could he know that the route he was pioneering would open up the whole inland range—the last frontier of the fur trade—to eager Hudson's Bay men and Nor'westers.

On the night of January 10, the party was camped on an icefield, high in the mountains. Thompson was worried and restless. For the previous few days the weather had been bad; snow and mist making it impossible to judge where they were or the condition of the country around them. Tonight, finally, the weather had cleared and Thompson left the circle for an anxious, solitary walk.

It was an exceptionally clear night, and Thompson soon pulled up short. For the first time he saw where he was: on the western edge of a deep cut through the mountains.

Far below him, curving off the southwest, was a river that looked vaguely familiar. If the river was the one he knew as the Kootenae ... He forced the exciting idea from his mind and returned to camp.

Thompson had been right, however. The river was the Kootenae, and soon it and a network of small waterways were leading the party westward until finally, on January 26, Thompson reached the shore of the Columbia River.

The days from the 10th to the 26th of January, however, had been costly ones for Thompson.

Most of his men were voyageurs, used to canoes and rivers. They were superstitious, and frankly terrified by the strangeness and loneliness of the mountains.

In his journal, Thompson mentioned one instance of this superstition and terror — an instance that reminds one of the legend of the Sasquatch:

"Strange to say," Thompson wrote, "here is a strong belief that the haunt of the mammoth is about this defile. I questioned several of the men. None could positively say they had seen him, but their belief I found firm and not to be shaken.

"I remarked to them that such an enormous heavy animal must leave indelible marks of his feet and his feeding. This they all acknowledged, and that they had never seen any marks of him and therefore could show me none.

"All I could say did not shake their belief in his existence."

Thompson might have wanted to treat this display of superstition lightly, but he couldn't. He had too-vivid evidence that this fear was combining in the worst way with the effects of weeks of physical hardship.

He was losing men steadily; some because he had to send them back for supplies, but more from simple desertion.

The real crisis came on the morning of January 26, the day he was finally to reach the Columbia. Thompson decided he had to send three of his remaining eight men back to pick up stores that had been cached on the trail. They had hardly left when four other men deserted. Of his original party of 13, Thompson now had only one man left.

Together they pushed on the last few miles to the Columbia. But here Thompson's luck seems to have gone astray.

He didn't realize the river was the Columbia. He guessed again – wrongly this time – that he was on the Kootenae.

Although he was impatient to push on, Thompson realized he had no choice but to wait here until he had supplies and reinforcements and – most importantly – some kind of boat.

With the help of his companion, Thompson constructed a rude cabin by the river and settled down to wait.

It was more than a month before reinforcements arrived: three voyageurs, an Indian guide, and two dogsleds of trade goods and dried provisions.

Thompson immediately set his party to work on the problem of a boat, only to find that birchbark, the usual material, wasn't going to work. Birch in this location was too thin-skinned for canoe construction.

"We had to turn our thoughts to some other material,"

he writes, "and cedar wood being the lightest and most pliable for a canoe, we split out thin boards of cedar wood of about six inches in breadth and builded a canoe of twenty-five feet in length by fifty inches in breadth, of the same form of a common canoe, using cedar boards instead of birch rind, which proved to be equally light and much stronger than birch rind.

"The greatest difficulty we had was sewing the boards to each round the timbers. And we had no nails, we had to make use of the fine roots of the pine."

It was mid-April before Thompson was ready to continue his trip. By this time, however, he had decided his party was still too small and too low on provisions and trade goods (these to bribe whatever hostile Indians they might meet). So Thompson led his men off towards the Nor'wester posts already established in what are now the states of Montana and Washington.

The detour lasted nearly three months, with Thompson dividing his time between rebuilding his party and practising diplomacy among the Indians of the interior.

It was July 3 before Thompson was once more on the Columbia (and aware of it this time) and on the stretch-run to the Pacific.

On July 10 he met Indians who had encountered the Astor party and he saw seals playing in the river. On July 15, Thompson finally saw the Pacific itself.

Thompson notes the sighting in his journal as "a great pleasure," but he adds wryly that: *"my men seemed disappointed. They had been accustomed to the boundless horizon of the great lakes of Canada and their high rolling waves.*

"From the ocean they expected a more boundless view, a something beyond the power of their senses which they could not describe; and my informing them that directly

opposite to us, at the distance of five thousand miles, was the empire of Japan added nothing to their ideas…"

Late on the morning of July 15, the astonished men of Astor's post looked out across the water in time to see history bearing down on them.

"We saw a large canoe with a flag displayed at her stern rounding the point we called Tongue Point," one of the Astor men wrote later. *"The flag she bore was the British, and her crew was composed of eight Canadian boatmen or voyageurs. A well-dressed man, who appeared to be the commander, was the first to leap ashore…"*

* * *

A FEW YEARS LATER

"At a season when the water was very high, one of the Company's boats was descending the river; and, through the rashness of an American who happened to be on board, the crew were induced to run this rapid, while the gentleman in charge more prudently resolved to prefer the portage.

"Hurled madly along by the boiling waters, the boat was just emerging into a place of safety, when she was sucked, stern foremost, into a whirlpool; and, in a single instant, a tide, that told no tales, was foaming over the spot where eleven men, a woman, and a child, had found a watery grave."

The above account of an accident on the Columbia River is from the records of The Hudson's Bay Company. The accident occurred about 15 years after Thompson's discovery of the road to the sea and it shows just how unsafe that road would always be.

* * *

"As we had more of the sun in the boat than on horseback,

three baths a day were scarcely sufficient to make the heat endurable...."

—Sir George Simpson

* * *

The three men who did most to conquer the Rockies — Mackenzie, Fraser and Thompson — were all from the North West Company.

It is one of the ironies of Western Canadian history that, in the end, it was The Hudson's Bay Company — the Nor'westers arch rival — that reaped the benefits of the conquest.

In the years that followed Thompson's journey to the mouth of the Columbia, Hudson's Bay men poured into the Rockies. Everywhere the Nor'westers turned, they found Bay men opposing them.

It was a bitter struggle for control and the Nor'westers were the weaker side.

The Hudson's Bay Company had made powerful allies — including the same Jacob Astor that Thompson had been sent to the Pacific to oust. The combined wealth of Astor and Bay was too much to withstand.

The struggle went on for 10 years, finally ending with the absorbtion of the North West Company by its rival.

During those 10 years, Bay men and Nor'westers wrestled, and often fought, over control of the mountain trade.

Wherever the post of one company went up the post of the other was soon facing it. Indeed, in one case, the rivals shared a common stockade.

Violence was common. So were arson and theft. Even the Indians — torn between the two companies and perhaps inspired by their tactics — became increasingly hostile.

To add the violence of man against man to an environment where man already faced a desperate day-to-day struggle for survival was tragic.

The surrender of the Nor'westers in 1821 ended the battles of the traders. It also brought into prominence a man named George Simpson, who soon would earn himself the title of the "Little Emperor" of the fur trade.

Simpson (later Sir George Simpson) was given control of the Hudson's Bay Company a year before the Nor'westers surrender and it was Simpson who shaped the final campaign that resulted in that surrender.

Following the take-over, Simpson hurled back and forth through the Bay holdings in the west, showing a ruthless capacity for organization and an equally ruthless firmness in bringing an end to the violence that still lingered in the mountains.

Elegantly dressed, linen stock at throat and personal piper leading the way, Simpson would march into a camp of hostile Indians and immediately humble them — or browbeat them — into an agreement of peace.

Just how badly that peace was needed is shown by an extract from Simpson's own journals, an extract that comes from a time long after "tranquility" had supposedly returned to the Rockies.

"At Okanagan," he writes, "we were concerned to learn that the Indians of the interior, as far back as New Caledonia, principally the Schouschwaps, were in a state of considerable excitement. The cause was as follows.

"In the month of February last, a chief of the name of Kootlepat visited Mr. Black, the gentleman in charge of Thompson's River, at this post of Kamloops, when a trivial dispute took place between them.

"Immediately on returning to his camp, at a place called the Pavilion, Kootlepat sickened and died, enjoining his people with his last breath to keep on good terms with the whites.

"Whether or not the chief's dying injunction was interpreted into an insinuation that he had perished in consequence of having quarrelled with his white brother, the Indians came to the conclusion that Kootlepat's death had been caused by Mr. Black's magic or medicine.

"In pursuance of this idea, the widow of the deceased worked upon the feelings of her nephew, till he undertook to revenge her husband's untimely fate.

"The avenger of the blood forthwith set out for Kamloops; and, when he arrived, both cold and hungry, he was by the orders of his destined victim, placed before a good fire and supplied with food.

"During the whole day, Mr. Black, who was a hard student, remained writing in his own apartment; but, having gone out towards evening, he was returning through the room where his guest was sitting, and had just reached the door of his chamber when he fell down dead, with the contents of the savage's gun in his back.

"In the appalling confusion that ensued, the murderer was allowed to escape from the fort, betaking himself immediately to the mountains.

"He was chased from place to place like a wild beast, being obliged to abandon first his horses and lastly his wife and family; but it was not till after eight months of vigilant pursuit, that he was finally hunted down on the banks of Fraser's River by some of his own people.

"As a proof of his comparative estimate of civilization and barbarism, this miserable being, with the blood of Mr. Black on his conscience, earnestly begged to be delivered up to the whites; and on being refused this last boon, he leaped into the stream, swimming away for his life, till he was despatched, just like a sea otter, by arrow after arrow…"

Such incidents were common, and common, too, was the way this one had started in suspicion and distrust.

But it is significant to note that it was the slayer's own people who pursued him and executed him. The influence of the Little Emperor was already showing.

By 1841, the empire of The Hudson's Bay Company stretched around the world, with outposts in the south seas, the Orient and Russia.

Simpson, as the organizing genius behind the empire, decided it was time to make his own mark as a conqueror of the mountains and set out to find his own route through the Rockies to the mouth of the Columbia.

It was to be part of a spectacular dash around the world, with Simpson visiting every part of the international trade empire of which he was governor.

His journal of that global voyage fills two volumes and the section dealing with the trip between Fort Edmonton and the Pacific has close to 70 pages to itself.

Despite his discovery of the pass that today bears his name, Simpson's journey through the mountains doesn't really stand out as a key event in the exploration of the mountains.

It does stand out, though, as an example of how much the style of exploration had changed since Thompson's day — particularly the style of an explorer who had the resources that went with being governor of one of the world's great trading monopolies.

Simpson was not a patient man. He didn't like to dally when he travelled and his organizational demands rode down all obstacles to speed.

By sending out advance parties to await him with fresh horses and with boats, and by travelling with the best party of packers and guides and boatmen in the company, he was able to average 40 to 50 miles a day where Tomppson and others had been lucky to make 10 or 15 miles a day.

Simpson habitually had his party moving by three or four in the morning and thought nothing of "getting a start on the day" by having them race 20 or 30 miles before breakfast, ending the race by having them carry him ashore from the boat to his meal.

But then, a few short excerpts from his journal can sum up the man and his journey better than the words of another:

"... *Leaving our old band of horses under the charge of the Indians, we immediately started with thirty-two fresh steeds. After crossing a prairie of two or three miles in length, we spent two hours in ascending a steep mountain, from whose summit we gained an extensive view of ranges of rocky hills; and, while the shadows of evening had already fallen on the valley at our feet, the rays of the setting sun were still tinging the highest peaks with a golden hue.*

"We encamped at the foot of the mountain with wolfish appetites, for, though we had a good deal of exercise during the day, yet we had eaten nothing since seven in the morning; but what was our disappointment to find that six horses— one of them, as a matter of course, being the commissariat steed — were missing!

"Having exhausted our patience, we went supperless to bed about midnight; but hardly had we turned in, when a distant shout made us turn out again in better spirits.

"The horses quickly arrived; and before an hour had

elapsed, we had despatched a very tolerable allowance of venison-steaks and buffalo tongues."

Elsewhere, Simpson describes another meal, this one drawn from the supplies of one of the company posts along his route:

"Just fancy, at the base of the Rocky Mountains, a roasted turkey, a suckling pig, new bread, fresh butter, eggs, ale, &c.; and then contrast all these dainties with short allowance of pemmican and water.

"No wonder that some of our party ate more than was good for them..."

Whatever else he did, the Little Emperor set a style for mountain travel that would later be echoed in the linen, crystal and silver of dining cars, and he created a demand for speed that only the coming of the trains could meet.

After Sir George Simpson, the Rockies would never seem the same again...

* * *

AN EXPLORATION FOOTNOTE — ON THE LIGHTER SIDE.

"He nursed a great desire to be attacked by a vampire, simply so he could be in a position to say it had happened to him."

—KEN LIDDELL

* * *

Nothing could be less like the man for whom they were named than Alberta's Waterton Lakes.

Whatever the season the Lakes area is always predictably serene. Charles Waterton was never predictably anything — least of all serene.

As a consequence, though he never even set foot in the province, Waterton has managed to win himself a place in Alberta history as our most "oddball" explorer.

The son of an English squire, Waterton was a naturalist, and a good one. Indeed, it was his reputation as a naturalist that led a member of the Palliser expedition to name the lakes for him.

Unfortunately, Waterton's professional reputation was often obscured by his bizarre techniques.

Very few scientists other than Waterton, for example, ever chose to capture a full-grown boa constrictor by the simple expedient of knocking it out with a right hook to the jaw.

Nor have many other scientists let their curiosity lead them to a ride on the back of an alligator. Waterton did this, vaulting onto the napping alligator and twisting its forelegs up behind its back to use as a bridle.

He chose never to repeat the twisting, bucketing experiment because, as he explained, he had found the seat decidedly "uncomfortable."

Waterton built a wall, ten feet high and three miles long, around his English home. Within the wall he created a sanctuary for buzzards, crows and magpies because, he contended, these birds were victims of discrimination.

Even outside the scientific community, Waterton had the reputation of being ... well ... slightly unusual.

He never wore shoes outdoors, even when tramping through the jungles of South America.

At home, he slept on the bare wooden floor.

And he greeted friends by growling and biting them affectionately on the ankle.

On one occasion, in Rome, after a wild reunion with an old schoolmate, Waterton was sighted perched on one foot on the head of a marble angel – a hundred feet up the face of a building.

When it came to personal health, Waterton was very much an advocate on the do-it-yourself approach.

On the rare occasions when he fell ill, or when he had an unfortunate encounter with a wild animal, Waterton's response was to dose himself with "laudanum, calomel, jalep and bark," and to draw from his arm "twenty-seven ounces of blood."

Since he lived to a ripe 83 years of age, it is hard to fault this otherwise dubious approach to medical science.

Although he did make one trip to Canada, Waterton never came as far west as the lakes named for him. Which, from his performance in the east, was probably just as well.

Spraining his ankle while jumping down from a train, Waterton remembered that one cured a sprain by pumping cold water over it. The pump which happened to be handiest at the time was Niagara Falls.

"I descended the winding staircase and hobbled to the scene of the action," he wrote later. "As I held my leg under the falls I tried to meditate on the immense difference there was betwixt a house pump and this tremendous cascade of nature, and what effect it might have upon the sprain; but the magnitude of the subject was too over-whelming and I was obliged to drop it."

In the end, Waterton's eccentricity has outlived his repu-tation as a scientist. His works are lost and his grave hidden by weeds.

All that is left is a collection of anecdotes and a string of peaceful lakes; lakes far too calm for the memory of so uncalm a man.

* * *

TAMERS

"On the mountaintops we stand, all the world at our command..."

—GORDON LIGHTFOOT

* * *

For more than 40 years after Sir George Simpson's flat-out race through the Rockies, a kind of stillness settled over the mountains.

Traders and Indians came and went in the routine traffic of fur trade. An occasional, unusually adventurous hunter would make the arduous trek west in search of big game.

But, somehow, the Rockies had become only a nice place to visit — and the trip was too much trouble to make the visit worthwhile.

All that changed with the coming of the railway.

This book is not the place for the great — and lengthy — story of the building of the CPR. That subject is dealt with well, and at due length, in other books.

But with the driving of the last spike in 1885, Donald Smith was also hammering home the first nail in the settlement of Alberta's mountain region.

Even before the last spike was in, William Van Horne

had renamed Siding 29 "Banff" and engaged an American architect to design for the mountain setting a hotel he could advertise as "the Finest Hotel on the North American Continent."

The hotel was designed to resemble a French chateau, in tribute to the French-Canadian voyageurs who had quietly contributed so much to the conquest of the Rockies.

At other sidings small chalets sprung up to accommodate passengers on the CPR's transcontinental trains.

Van Horne launched a massive advertising campaign, lauding the Rockies as "the Mountain Playground of the World," a description in use even today.

Van Horne's objective, of course, was to create passengers for the company's trains. And like the company's similarly-motivated campaign to bring settlers to the prairies, it worked and worked well.

A growing stream of people came to the Rockies. Some came to hunt or fish or climb. Some came for the healing powers of the hot springs in the Banff region (an area made a national park at the urging of the CPR). Some came simply for the peace and quiet and the clarity of the mountain air.

Around the railroad, and around the business of providing service to the visitors, sprang up a host of companies to supply food and supplies, guides for would-be climbers, carriages and horses for leisurely touring.

The people who provided the service built and often stayed to make their homes in the Rockies.

One of the first of note was an Irishman named John Brewster who saw the hot springs of Sulphur Mountain and anticipated the tourist boom that would follow the railway west.

Others, like Bill Peyto and Jim Simpson, were guides and packers who found tourism turning their trades into small industries, and who settled down to let civilization sneak up on them.

And there was one lady who settled down simply to paint ... and a churchman who wrote books ... and a man who strung a clothesline to a mountain...

There was nothing ordinary about the settlers of the Canadian Rockies.

* * *

"Most people are hemmed in by clocks and timetables and their molehills become mountains. The first time they see a real mountain they put the molehill in its proper place."

—JOHN BREWSTER.

* * *

Probably no single family has played a greater part in settlement — and development — of the Alberta part of the Rockies than the Brewster family.

Since the day John Brewster set foot in the mountains in 1887, the family's interests have grown to include Banff's Mount Royal Hotel, the Columbia Icefield Chalet and a string of motels and lodges that stretches from far north on the Alaska Highway south to the U.S. border.

Then there is the Brewster Transport Co. operating bus and taxi service throughout the Rockies. And Brewster Pack Trains Ltd. And the Kananaskis dude ranch and Devil's Head ranch.

Within a year of coming to Banff, John Brewster — a blacksmith by trade — had rounded up a herd of wild cows and was operating a milk route to the new Banff Springs Hotel.

His two oldest sons, Bill and Jim (Jim was six then) took care of the actual delivery.

Six years later the two older Brewster boys were in business on their own, at the ages of 12 and 11.

"Tourist attention!" their advertisement read, "Complete camping and packing outfits and experienced guides to any part of the Rocky Mountains Furnished on short notice at reasonable rates! Special facilities offered to fishing parties. W. & J. Brewster — Guides and Packers."

By that time the boys' father had taken a loan urged

on him by CPR and was well-established in the livery business.

In time there would be six Brewster sons, all actively involved in some aspect of the family business.

Of them all, perhaps the best-known was Jim Brewster. By the time he was seven, Jim as an experienced horseman, hunter and guide, and he could speak Cree as well as he spoke English.

Like all the family, he developed a shrewd business sense. But in him it was mixed with a flair for adventure and showmanship that was to make him famous.

In 1904, at the age of 22, he and a friend duplicated the exploits of the early explorers and travelled the Columbia River in a canoe.

The next year he was leading one of the major hunting expeditions of the era, guiding a party to the Arctic to hunt muskox.

A tireless booster of the mountains, he travelled extensively in Europe and the United States to promote the Canadian Rockies. In time he became a friend of royalty and, in the process, a special protector of the remittance men who were banished to the anonymity of the Rockies.

"He showed them the mountains," one observer writes; "He showed them the game on which they could vent their spite; and if necessary he could drink them under the nearest icecap.

Another person who knew the young Jim Brewster writes of seeing him in town buying supplies for a hunting party — six loaves of bread and four bottles of whiskey. Asked what he was doing, he replied he'd just bought the supplies for the week.

"But what," asked the friend, "do you want with all that bread?"

Anecdotes tended to grow up around Jim Brewster.

Like the time he stalled the schedule of visiting royalty by detouring the king and queen of England by his house to meet his wife.

"I may forget a lot of things about the royal visit," he chortled later, but never my wife's face as we walked in the door. She was so excited she nearly fainted, and her face was as white as a sheet.

"However, it wasn't two minutes till the Queen and she were chatting away like old friends."

And when Brewster wasn't providing the ingredients for stories, he was telling them.

One of his stories, in particular, sums up the quality of his tale-telling.

In England in 1907 to promote travel in the Rockies, Brewster looked up an earl he had met in Canada and was invited to visit the earl's estate.

Brewster accepted and went off to catch the train.

"I had a crock with me and got into a first-class compartment. The train stopped once and the guard came to see me. 'As you are his lordship's guest, I just wanted to see you were all right,' he said.

"At the local station there was a car for me and another for my bag, and when I got to the castle a butler came to the door and said, 'I will announce you to his lordship,' or some such twaddle.

"When I got in the hall, there was a line of flunkies with sideburns and I went into a room like St. Paul's Cathedral to meet his lordship.

"We got on fine, but the effect of the crock was beginning to wear off and we had some port. Now, I'm only used to California port, and this tasted like satin, and I maybe thought it was harmless.

"Anyway, when I got upstairs into a bedroom that looked like Grand Central Station without the steam heat, I couldn't find my clothes.

"The bag had been emptied and I thought I'd probably brought it down empty.

"Then there was a tent on the bed and steps up to it.

"When I began to get desperate, a valet came in and I tried to make friends with him, but it was no good.

"He held my pants for me to step into, and I found somebody had provided me with a tuxedo."

The next morning, Brewster found that someone had also provided him with a suit of hunting pinks and that he was off to the hunt.

"I was a real comedian, with a top hat and a red coat, a horse seventeen hands high, and three flunkies to help me up.

"The saddle had no pommel, and that worried me for a bit, but soon I got the hang of it.

"The dogs started to bark and I made the first fence all right, and that horse was the finest horse I ever knew.

"I passed the Duke of Beaufort, who was the Master of the Hunt, and then I passed the whips, who look after the dogs.

"I passed the hounds without stepping on any of them, and we were getting on fine when the thing was called off and a fresh lot of flunkies appeared with fresh horses.

"They loaded me onto another horse, and after a time I found the saddle bag had flasks of whiskey in them and we spent a fine afternoon…"

Jim Brewster went on through the years, telling stories and doing business and watching the communities of Banff and Jasper and Lake Louise grow and grow.

In later years he would lament a little that people no longer knew him on the street, and make the slight admission to age that the rear sight of his rifle looked "a bit feathery."

Jim Brewster and the rest of the Brewster family opened the wilderness of the Rockies to everyone.

And, thanks to them, no one is likely ever to mistake the mountains for molehills again.

* * *

"I may not be able to write, but, by George, I can preach!"
—C. W. GORDON

* * *

It was the summer of 1917, near the end of a terrible war, and there were few tourists among the crowd that streamed out of Banff one Sunday to the foot of Mt. Rundle.

There, on a rock by a lake known — appropriately enough as The Devil's Cauldron, a stocky dark-haired man in kilt and service jacket stood and began speaking.

He began hesitantly enough, as he always did, but as time passed his voice and words gained strength.

Rev. C. W. Gordon had just come back from the war in Europe. He had seen most of the men of his regiment perish in the horror that was France. At Somme, he had said the funeral rites for his colonel and friend.

In all truth, many of those who had come to the foot of Mt. Rundle that day hadn't come to hear the strong, solemn words of this preacher. In all truth, to many of the people before him, Rev. C. W. Gordon wasn't even C. W. Gordon; he was the most famous Canadian writer of the day: Ralph Connor.

So popular were his books that it was estimated at the time that one of every sixty Canadians had a copy of the famous "The Man from Glengarry."

In all, the novels he wrote sold a total of five million copies.

Even today, most people are familiar with such titles as The Sky Pilot, Glengarry School Days and Black Rock. What those who listened to him that day at The Devil's Cauldron couldn't know was that the man facing them, the best and most successful Canadian writer of his day, was dead broke, ruined by the illegal acts of those he had left in trust of his wealth while he was away to war.

He said nothing of that in the sermon he preached. Instead he spoke of temperance, of courage and, above all, of forgiveness.

And, as was his habit, he spoke at great length. Those with Sunday roasts at home in the oven shifted uneasily before the vision of good roast beef shrivelling to charred leather.

Though much of his life was spent away from the mountains of Canada, Gordon was considered one of Banff's own sons.

What made this man, born in a small eastern town, a man of the Rockies? And what, even stranger, turned a committed missionary and minister into a popular novelist?

Gordon was born in Glengarry County in what was then Upper Canada in 1860, the same year his Presbyterian-minister father came to Canada from the Highlands of Scotland to escape the confines of the established Church of Scotland.

The father was a fearsome, evangelical preacher and his influence on his son was enormous. The younger Gordon never gave serious thought to any other way of life than that of a churchman — despite the fact that his father's exhortations to the good life were often accompanied by the banshee wailing of a bagpipe with which he used to shake the walls of the house for hours on end.

Gordon was later to admit that he spent his life intensely disliking the instrument and would flee at the very thought of it being played.

Little is known of Gordon's relationship with his mother, but it is significant to note that he said the gentle, long-suffering heroines of his novels were all based on her.

The boy was taught to work for everything. Even as a child of ten he hired himself out as a laborer and he worked his way through the University of Toronto, paying every cent of his tuition and expenses from his own pocket.

He spent some time at the university after graduating, teaching classics, then put himself through Knox College Divinity School and through two years at Edinburgh University in Scotland.

He was ordained as a minister in 1890 and called to missionary service in the Northwest Territories.

His first mission parish was Banff and he immediately fell in love with the mountain community.

Banff, in the 1890s, was far from being the pleasant tourist and resort town it is today. Rather it was a tough, hard-boozing settlement with more than its share of troublemakers.

A perfect town, as Gordon later noted tongue-in-cheek, "for an Evangelist."

A single man of 30, particularly one of such unquestionably sterling character, was an unusual attraction in a frontier town and Gordon was quickly drawn into the modest social life of the settlement.

Every evening, in one home or another, the young people of the settlement gathered to sing around a piano or to chat and sip tea. Gordon was one of the more faithful at these gatherings and, until recently, there were still old-timers in Banff who could recall that he would occasionally sing, in a fine tenor, for these parties.

Unfortunately, the old-timers pointed out, he usually accompanied himself on a guitar which he played exceptionally badly.

Ah well, a man can't be single, moral, a good singer and a good musician all at the same time. The girls of Banff took him to their hearts anyway and it looked for a long time as though he would find a bride among them.

But Gordon finally left Banff still a bachelor and it wasn't until he was 45 that a young Winnipeg girl, Helen King, won his heart and became his wife. He and Helen had six daughters and a son, King, who became a Rhodes Scholar and later an active figure in the United Nations.

In his long career with the church, Gordon would go on to become head of the Presbyterian Church in Canada and one of the leaders in the fight against booze, prostitution and conscription.

All this became overshadowed, however, by the emergence of his alter-ego.

Gordon was 36 and he had just made a futile trip to

Toronto to try to get church officials to raise money for missionary work in the west.

He had come away empty-handed but with an incidental set of instructions from the editor of the church's weekly magazine to write a story "to illustrate the need" of mission work in the west.

At the time Gordon was the over-worked minister of a run-down church on the outskirts of Winnipeg. Night after night, after prayer-meeting had ended, Gordon would go home and toil at the task of coming up with the required story.

The result, published first in 1896, was called Christmas Eve in a Lumber Camp.

The story was a fictionalized sermon about how a Presbyterian minister moved a camp of hard-drinking lumbermen to prayer.

Its name would later be changed to Black Rock and become one of the main stories in the first anthology of Ralph Connor's work.

The first story behind him, Gordon began to write and write and write still more. Being a fiction writer was not a respectable occupation for a minister so he was asked to come up with a pen-name. There was a sheet of mission letterhead on his desk when the request came and he compressed the first syllables in two of its words to come up with Cannor.

The publisher read Cannor as Connor and added Ralph because it seemed to go with the name. And so Ralph Connor — a non-existent being whom Gordon would later say had grown to become a "second person inside me" — was casually born.

Ralph Connor was prolific, his books came out at a rate of one a year, and wildly popular.

By the time his second novel appeared public curiousity over his real identity had reached a fever pitch and Gordon came — briefly — from behind the mask.

Much of the clamor for his true identity came in the United States where his work was so popular that it was made part of many high school reading lists. "The world will insist on knowing it," the St. Louis Democrat editorialized in its plea for the true identity of the author.

Connor's work is "so intense that one grinds his teeth lest his sinews snap ere the strain is released," The Chicago Tribune added.

And "his passionate writing appeals to all that is best in human nature," summed up the San Francisco Chronicle.

His identity out in the open, Gordon made lecture tours and, in the U.S., police had to be called out to hold back the crowds that gathered to hear and see him. President Woodrow Wilson was a well-publicized fan of Ralph Connor. And Henry Ford collected a complete set of autographed volumes of Ralph Connor's work.

In Detroit, when Gordon was asked to deliver a sermon

in a church, he rose to begin a prayer and the congregation spontaneously broke in with the singing of "For He's a Jolly Good Fellow."

Few men could stand so startling a thrust into fame and fortune without changing. In Gordon's case, it is to his tribute that all the fuss did was heighten his affection for the simple life and increase his sense of humor.

His New York publisher once described a visit to Gordon. He arrived at the house to find Connor was out.

"I was guided through a trail in the woods," he recalled, "to where he stood, bareheaded and alone, in sweater and old clothes, whittling a cane from roots of trees."

Carving canes — walking sticks — from the roots of trees was one of Gordon's ways of staying in physical touch with nature. So were riding a horse and paddling a canoe.

"I should have been born an Indian," he once lamented.

As for his sense of humor, a long-time friend once wrote that: *"He could unbend more completely than any man of his age that I have known."*

His favorite practical joke was one he reserved for the first time a new guest sat down to the Gordon's dinner table.

The guest would be placed at the end of the table, opposite his host, and at a signal from Gordon the people on either side would lift the oilcloth table covering to form a trough down which Gordon would solemnly pour his drinking water and then howl with laughter as the astonished guest received the watery cargo right in the lap.

After the guest was wrung out, fed and installed in the drawing room, Gordon would entertain him by an evening of singing as badly as he could while accompanying himself on a banjo he proudly claimed he could play worse than anyone he knew.

In fact, though, despite the recollection of his early

inability on the guitar, Gordon was an accomplished musician who could perform on the guitar, banjo or flute. Late in life he enhanced a natural singing voice by taking lessons.

He became so fussy on the subject of vocalizing that he thought nothing of stopping his congregation in mid-hymn to demonstrate how they could be singing better than they were.

By the time the First World War appeared on the horizon, Gordon's writing had made him a millionare. He had built a large home for his family in Winnipeg and a summer home in the resort community of Kenora, Ontario.

When Canada entered the war he went overseas as a chaplain.

A careful man, he left his financial affairs in order before he left. There was a $100,000 insurance policy and all his cash assets were turned over to a lawyer-associate to invest in the booming Winnipeg real-estate market.

The real-estate boom never materialized and the market collapsed in 1915, but Gordon was assured by his friend that his money had been protected and was divided among eight land companies the lawyer had set up.

It was only with the death of the lawyer, while Gordon was still overseas, that it was learned that the money had been misused and that Gordon had been left virtually penniless.

Connor's publisher recalled that it was almost impossible to convince him that he had been the victim of a criminal; and that, when he was finally convinced, his decision was to forgive the act and to do everything in his power to have it forgotten.

Nor did he allow the loss of his wealth to influence a life-long habit of open-handed charity. He gave everything he could to those in need during the depression years that followed the war, even though he was often as badly off as those he aided.

His financial disaster, however, seemed to open the door to a host of other troubles. Although he would go on writing and writing, in retrospect, better than he ever had before, his work began to lose its popularity.

Unable to recover from the loss of his money, he gradually had to give up the life-insurance policy he had hoped would provide for his family after his death. The same was true of the taxes on his homes and these too had to be given up, finally.

The only thing that never failed was Gordon's determined Christianity. He worked on and on, creating hostels for the homeless, acting as an advocate for the working poor.

But all that was still ahead, unknown to any of those who sat on the grassy slope by The Devil's Cauldron and listened to Canada's most famous author and best-known churchman.

This man, after all, was a brave minister who had gone to a terrible war to ease the misery of their sons and brothers and husbands. That made him part of them all.

And this man, too, was Ralph Connor: the author who had thrilled them with his adventures and fanned their courage with the examples of the firm-hearted characters he created.

When all is said and done, what they felt, sitting on the grass by a mountain lake, was right. There were two men before them.

It is the same judgement that history wrote on his gravestone when he died in 1937:

GORDON AND CONNOR
MINISTER OF GOSPEL

Author Canadian

* * *

"He just loved that mountain and that view so much he wanted to share it with everyone."

—Recollection of a friend of John Jaeggi.

* * *

Mountain tops are usually the private reserve of the special few who have the courage and the strength to climb to them.

In the Canadian Rockies, however, there is one mountain top that belongs to everyone, thanks to a Swiss-born guide named John Jaeggi.

Many of the thousands of visitors to the Rockies every year ride the gondola lift to the top of Sulphur Mountain to gaze out across the roof of Canada's mountain world. The lift is almost taken for granted. So is the teahouse on the summit. So, for that matter, is a bronze plaque outside the teahouse that few bother to read.

John Jaeggi came to Canada in 1924 and went to work as a guide for the Canadian Alpine Club. In his work, he became familiar with most of the peaks of the Rockies and, for some reason never fully explained he became enchanted with Sulphur Mountain.

It was a rather curious enchantment. Sitting too close to the edge of the Banff townsite to attract particular attention from mountaineers, Sulphur had been notable, until Jaeggi entered the picture, only as the source of the sulphur springs whose hot waters were one of Banff's tourist attractions.

As years went by and John Jaeggi expanded from guide to outfitter and packer he kept his eye on Sulphur Mountain. Sulphur, unlike most other peaks in the area, was relatively easy to climb and the federal government finally built a trail to its summit.

Jaeggi watched people using that trail and decided that they should have something more waiting for them at the top than the view.

John announced he was going to build a teahouse at the summit and then set out to do just that. The plan was greeted with widespread amusement in the community, and he was kidded that he would sell a lot more tea if he put the teahouse at the bottom of the mountain instead of at the top.

Jaeggi ignored the jibes but, indeed, as he started work on the project it must have seemed occasionally that there was something to the idea of sticking to the bottom.

All the materials and supplies for the project had to be packed on horseback. Even the most basic ingredient for the tea — the water — had to be carried in tanks from a spring halfway up the trail.

By 1940, however, the teahouse was finished. Everything it it was built of logs, including the furnishings. And if John Jaeggi charged five cents a glass for water, visitors were glad to pay it after they learned what effort was needed to get it to them.

For those who made it to the teahouse there was the added bonus, too, of a signed certificate testifying to their feat.

Jaeggi realized, of course, that not everyone had the strength or inclination for the long climb so he built a way-station halfway up the mountain where people could rest — and drink tea — and discuss how they would tackle the full climb to the summit "some other day."

For those who were unable to make even the halfway climb, John outfitted a tractor with a platform and drove them to the way-station.

By 1945 his ideas were proving so successful he doubled the size of the cabin on the summit, creating a panoramic view for his visitors.

When, in 1949, he married Edith Ashton who owned a hotel near one of Sulphur's hot springs, he found a fellow-dreamer and the encouragement to pursue his dream of sharing the mountain with still more people.

Jaeggi made a trip back to Switzerland, then another and another until he had been there 12 times. The trips were no sentimental journeys; they were study trips to investigate the idea of installing a European-type gondola lift on Sulphur Mountain.

He became convinced the idea was practical and that it would make money. But, unhappily, he couldn't find a Canadian investor with the same convictions.

From 1953 to 1957, detailed plans in hand, he made the round of money-men and got turned down cold.

In 1957, frustrated by the indifference of Canadian investors, he turned to Europe and it was finally a group of Swiss businessmen who came up with the money to build the lift.

It was completed in 1958, but Jaeggi himself was to see his dream in action for only three years. In 1961, while on holidays, he was struck by a car and killed.

The gondola, of course, has justified all Jaeggi's dreams. Hundreds of thousands of people have ridden it in the years since it began operation.

It has made it possible for everyone — the aged, the disabled, the very young — to stand on a mountain top. That was what Jaeggi wanted all along.

And the thick cables that hook base to summit serve as a good example for those who would scoff at dreamers.

It took a dreamer, after all, to tie down a mountain.

DANGER AND DISASTER

"He died on the way, in terrible torments — just as had happened to so many of his victims"

—MARIUS BARBEAU,
SPEAKING OF TCHATKA, A STONEY MEDICINE MAN.

* * * *

From time to time, earlier in this book, there have been hints that the Indians of the Canadian Rockies were less than friendly, and much less than helpful, to the white men trying to find their way through the mountains.

The truth is that, for many years of the period during which the west was being settled, the Indians of the mountains hated the white men and would kill anytime they could get away with it. Indeed, at least one trader had to resort to terrible threats to turn smallpox loose among the tribes before his posts could operate in peace.

The reason for the Indians' hatred of the whites sprang from the way the white trader upset the natural balance among the western tribes.

The Stoneys, the Kootenays, the other Indians of the mountains all depended, like the plains Indians, on the buffalo for their main source of food and skins. Tribes like the Stoneys would make at least two expeditions a year down to the plains to hunt the buffalo.

Such expeditions, of course, meant invasions of the traditional territory of the Blackfoot and the Cree — and such violations of frontiers were a challenge to battle.

"Frontiers were not an idle question for the contenders," notes Marius Barbeau, Canada's foremost expert on early Indian life. "They meant safety within their borders where the hunters could scatter at random according to the needs of the chase. In the pursuits of nomadic life, the welfare of all hinged upon the success of the hunt.

"Parties of hunters from various tribes would clash over conflicting claims. No redress could be found but in violence. The security of frontiers once abolished, might have proved the only protection, numbers and cunning, the only pledge of victory."

And it is here, with Barbeau's guidance, that we begin to understand the seeds of the mountain Indians' hatred of the white man. For the coming of the white man tipped the scales of battle. The white man moved in from east to west, bringing the rifle and bullet and gunpowder with him. The Indians of the mountains were the last to get the modern weaponry.

Barbeau paints the painful results:

"In the earlier encounters, the Crees, and then the Blackfoot, had the upper hand. They had secured the coveted firearms from the traders.

"The Blackfoot were the Bedouins of the prairies. Their numbers and boldness gave them the ascendency over other nations, and they never relented in the defence of their vast domains, which extended from the Red River to the Rocky Mountains and from the sources of the Missouri to the Saskatchewan.

"Their war and hunting parties were the terror of the land. In their innumberable encounters with the scattered parties of Cree, Stoney and Kootenay poachers, they were generally victorious. And bitterness sank deep everywhere. The toll of lives grew heavier as time went by. The confused threads of murder and revenge could no longer be unravelled.

"Neither were the territorial claims of the Blackfoot beyond dispute. Were they not themselves intruders from the east long ago?

"The Kootenays and the Flatheads, among others, claimed that the privilege of hunting the buffalo had come down to them from their forefathers. Though they now lived across the mountains, they had always largely depended upon it for subsistence. From childhood they had migrated twice a year in family groups down the mountain passes for the same pursuit.

"The mountain tribes as a last resort might have renounced their pretensions, for they were fighting a losing battle, with only bows and arrows to oppose the guns of the marauders of the plains. Game could be found on their own mountain slopes — deer, mountain sheep and goat, bear, wild-fowl and fish.

"But even the tragedy of their dwindling numbers failed to curb their hereditary bias. The buffalo was at stake, and if anyone hinted at withdrawal from the bad lands, they stubbornly replied that while a single one of their warriors remained alive they should do as their forefathers had done. No right should be relinquished.

"Firearms were the cause of all their misfortunes, since only the Blackfoot could procure them from the North West Company at Fort-des-Prairies, east of the mountains.

"The Kootenays and their allies, the Flatheads, the Coeur-d'Alenes and the Shuswaps, entertained the most violent hatred against the white men for their harmful if unintentional favouritism."

This situation continued until about 1812, when Thompson and other white explorers and traders managed to break trails into the country of the mountain tribes.

These tribes decided to swallow their hatred for the time being — because the white men wanted beaver and were willing to give firearms in return. With these firearms, the mountain tribes believed, vengeance could be taken at last against the Blackfoot.

It was Thompson who recorded the reaction of one Salish chief to the new situation:

"We have now twenty tents of women who have no husbands, with their children, whose fathers are in the Land of Spirits, and as many tents of aged women whose sons have fallen in battle.

"We have all noticed the arrival of the white man among us for these three years bringing us guns, ammunition and shods of iron for the heads of our arrows.

"Before their arrival we were pitiful and could not defend ourselves. But we are now as well armed as our enemies and our last great battle has obliged them to give up to us great parts of our lands for hunting the bison.

"Now we do not fear to war with them."

The Indian of the mountains would not learn to love the white intruder, but he would tolerate him in exchange for the tools of long-awaited revenge.

And revenge there was, bloody revenge that caught the Blackfoot by surprise, produced bloody and brutal battle from which fewer and fewer warriors — on either side — returned to sing by the fires of their own people.

The hatred of the mountain tribes and the brutality of the Blackfoot produced horrors of conflict and torture that almost exceed human imagination.

Ross Cox, a trader, recorded a grim example of the horrors of this war of bloody revenge. It was Christmas Day in 1812 and the Flatheads were torturing a Blackfoot captured in battle. The behavior of the Flatheads and the Blackfoot alike are typical of many similar — and equally horrible — incidents of the time.

"The Flatheads had gathered around the fire to witness the spectacle. Some of them heated an old gun barrel until it had turned red and then burnt stripes as if to make a pattern on the legs, the thighs, the cheeks and the neck of the prisoner, who stood perfectly motionless against a tree to which he was tied.

"Then they cut the flesh about his nails and separated his finger joints one by one. The Blackfoot never winced. Instead he laughed and goaded them on to further efforts.

"'My heart is strong,' he would say; 'you cannot hurt me, you are like fools. Try it again; you don't know how to do it. We torture your relatives far better, because we make them cry aloud like children.'

"A Flathead, who had lost one eye in an encounter years before, was standing sullenly near the fire. So the prisoner taunted him: 'It was by my arrow that you lost your eye. Do you remember?' Thereupon the one-eyed brave darted at him and gouged one of his eyes out of its socket for revenge.

"Undisturbed the Blackfoot now looked with his remaining eye at another of his tormentors and said, 'It was

I who killed your brother and scalped your father. Have you so soon forgotten?' At this provocation the Flathead warrior sprung up like a panther, scalped his insulter and would have plunged his knife into his heart had he not been advised to desist.

"It was now the turn of the head-chief to be insulted by the bleeding prisoner at the stake. 'It was I that made your wife a slave last year. We put out her eyes, tore out her tongue and treated her like a dog.'

"A shriek of rage greeted these words. The chief seized his gun and before the sentence was complete shot a ball through the prisoner's heart, thus ending his frightful torments."

From the need for weapons, the mountain Indians developed a respect — of sorts — for the power of the white man, whose mysterious allies across the seas could supply more and more of what was needed.

"This 'respect,' coupled with the blood-hatred the mountain Indians had for their enemies of the plains, combined — seemed to distill itself — in the veins of one man, a Stoney named Tchatka, whose grim ghost must still haunt the passes of the Canadian Rockies.

* * * *

Tchatka was many things in his life and left many legacies to his own people, the Stoney Indians of the Canadian Rockies. The legacies are mixed.

He left, on the positive side, a return to respect and pride for the Stoney at a time when the Blackfoot were humiliating them on all fronts.

On the negative side, he left a reputation for treachery, cowardice and disgrace that haunts his name to the present day.

As a youth, Tchatka travelled with his people onto the

prairies in their search for the buffalo. On these expeditions, as the 1700's were turning into the 1800's, the Stoney began to encounter the white man, the traders who were establishing posts along the fringes of the foothills.

Tchatka fell in awe of the white man, felt the pull of their ways.

In the months between the expeditions, he would spend his time day-dreaming of the whites and their powers. On the expeditions themselves, he spent less and less time on the hunt and more and more time at the posts, hanging around the counters where the goods were displayed, feeling in his hands the strange shapes and 'medicine' of the white man's goods.

Most Indians were curious about the white man and his ways, but usually such curiosity soon passed off. But in Tchatka, the curiosity only grew stronger day by day.

This young Stoney and his curiosity were soon noticed by the traders. They found his interest ingratiating and his manner both clever and polite.

Tchatka was particularly liked by the French-Canadian voyageurs, who found his attempts to learn to speak their language both impressive and amusing. They named him Le Gaucher, "the left-handed one," and gave him as much friendship as voyageurs ever gave to Indians.

The young Stoney's preoccupation with the ways of the whites was noticed by his own people and met with their strong disapproval.

Tchatka was a son of a large and powerful family, destined by birth and ability both, to be a leader of his people. This concern for the ways of the still-hated white man displeased his elders.

By tradition, Tchatka should have gone into the wilds, braved the hardships alone and emerged a hunter and a warrior. His uncles pressed him to follow tradition, to develop through toil and privation the ability and courage to be a leader of his people.

Tchatka refused and was branded both lazy and a coward, though — at this time — he really was neither.

"The truth is," says Marius Barbeau of Tchatka, "that he cared little for pelts and scalping, the ruling ambition of the time. He had notions of his own. His imagination was ablaze with the new ways of life, the ways of the white strangers from the land of sunrise.

"He often resorted to the nearest trading post, forsaking his relatives for prolonged periods. By sheer persistence he managed to learn many truths, many lies, and to unravel many puzzles.

"He finally penetrated the mysteries of the gun casting death at a distance, of powder tearing things to bits when it explodes, and of poison slowly bringing death when it is consumed with foods.

"Above all, he never tired of listening to the tales of another world. The French servants around the stores were fond of telling stories. He sat gaping at what they said of vast wars across the seas, of boundless armies, of guns the size of trees, of generals commanding thunder and lightning, of witchcraft producing wonders, and of kings and princes of fairyland basking in splendor and glory.

"The ambition some day to contemplate all these marvels with his own eyes deeply aroused him. But it also dawned upon his, after many disappointments, that the trail to the home of the mighty was long, almost endless, and strewn with pitfalls.

"He could not very long entertain the hope of becoming a white man himself or, even, living like a white man. Indians, it was easy to see, were not really wanted at the forts, except to procure furs, fish and buffalo meat from their own hunting grounds. And his services as a messenger and guide did not seem sufficiently appreciated. He finally gambled on his last chance one day."

The gamble, as Barbeau records, was disastrous.

"A chief's daughter in his own country always married a chief's son. That was the custom. He himself was of good lineage, the nephew of Walking Bow, whose fame as a powerful warrior had spread from the lakes to the mountains. And the chief-trader's daughter, he knew well, was still unwed. More than once he had seen her, watched her; he had gazed lovingly at her as she smiled to him. That is why he made up his mind.

"She would be his bride and thereafter he would live at the post, with the white men. So he came with presents for the would-be father-in-law. His proposal was listened to according to etiquette. But the bridal presents were returned before the morrow, to his utter dismay. He had thus courted defeat.

"In the face of humiliation he managed to curb his wounded pride; he stayed on at the post for a while. So deep had been his childish hope that it could be smothered only by stages. Then a feeling of revenge crept into his heart, only to be silenced. An Indian is never in a hurry.

"He turned away from the land of promise, slowly, very slowly. His uncles were still waiting for him on the prairies. To them he would return. He started off at night, unseen, disheartened. The heavy bundle on his back contained what was left of his former hopes, rich possessions for his life to come — tobacco, a beaver hat, a red sash, a bright calico shirt, pills of slow and deadly poison, a double-bladed knife in a sheath, gun powder in buffalo horns and a prayer-book full of magic signs."

Despite the disaster and humiliation of his foolish at-tempt to enter the white man's world by marriage, Tchatka had not lost his ambition for greatness.

All that had changed was that he would seek another road, another kind of greatness. The contents of the pack on his back would play an important part in the new plan he had formed in his mind during the long days at the post after his failure there.

When Tchatka returned to his own people, Barbeau points out, "he was no longer an inexperienced youth.

"The cunning exploitation of his new knowledge and strange crafts helped to enhance his prestige among his nomadic folk.

"Shrewdness was his supreme gift, if ever it was in an Indian. He possessed the white man's 'power' every one could see. Charms and amulets worked miracles in his hands. He muttered incantations at night and communed with the spirits above, the powerful Manitous from the east. The potency of his magic bundle in itself was enough to inspire respect of friend and foe alike.

"Prophecy had always induced timid believers to submit in advance to the dictates of fate. No one dared resist the supernatural powers. To Tchatka it appealed as the easiest means for him to achieve domination. So he became a seer and sorcerer."

Tchatka courted the seers and other medicine men of the Stoney people. He learned what he could of their secrets and supplemented them with the bag of tricks he had brought back with him from the post. He sought out and won to his cause young men who were willing to serve him unquestioningly as disciples — and as spies.

All during this period while he was building a base for his power, he was careful not to risk his life in the too-frequent battles with the Blackfoot. He always stayed on the sidelines, a fast horse ready to carry him away if the tide of battle turned against the Stoney.

To any who dared mutter "cowardice" at this, Tchatka would simply reply that: "I am not a fighter, I never will be. My power is in my medicine."

Soon there were few who questioned the strength of this "medicine" for Tchatka had become a great sorcerer. As Barbeau explains:

"Future events he could foretell as if reading them out of his prayer-book. His uncanny wisdom knew no bounds. He could see far away beyond the skyline. What the others failed to detect were the means at his command, the young spies who served him as secret messengers to get wind of news. Fair probabilities were a safe guide to his foresight; so his predictions seldom failed."

The main obstacle that faced Tchatka now, in his search for power, was that rigid custom dictated who would rule the Stoney. This custom depended hugely on a man's ability as a warrior, the scalps he had taken, the wounds he had suffered and afflicted. Tchatka had taken no scalps and had neither suffered wound nor given it.

Tchatka set out to overcome this obstacle, to win his way onto the ruling council, not by valor but by guile. The tool he chose to use was his aging uncle, Walking Bow.

It took a long campaign of diplomacy and guile, but finally Tchatka won his uncle to his cause. And such was the prestige of Walking Bow that when he proposed that precedent be defied and his nephew admitted to the ruling circle, none questioned and all agreed.

Tchatka, of course, wasn't out simply to sit among the rulers, he wanted to be the ruler of the rulers. And there were many ahead of him, men who had won precedent with time, courage and wisdom. Many excelled him in matters of both war and peace.

Again, however, Tchatka had a plan – this time a cruel

plan. He would combine his 'gift' for foretelling the future and the pills of poison he had in his medicine bag.

Again, Barbeau details the results.

"Thus it came about that in prophetic spells he would say: 'This chief has not long to live; so my Manitou has told me.' And the unfortunate leader whose name had been uttered would fall the victim of a mysterious ailment after weeks, sometimes months, of mental agony. All his rivals disappeared in the same way, one after another.

"Suspicion and the desire of retaliation more than once brought peril near him. Anger smouldered in many breasts. But he inspired fear, as one who can dispose of life. Many were they who thought it best to propitiate him by the offer of presents, buffalo meat, horses and trophies.

"Walking Bow, the head-chief, at times had to shield him against rivals and foes at home. He used his influence to help him in his rapid rise to power. No one dared oppose his will, for his lofty stature, his bravery and violence defied resistance. Scalps taken from the enemy adorned his head-dress, his robe, his spear and the saddle of his steed.

"Tchatka more than any other feared his anger. By flattery and deceit, by subservience to all his desires and fancies, he succeeded in winning his confidence and friendship. They often travelled together and gave one another feasts and banquets in which the greatest harmony always prevailed.

"Jealous as Tchatka was of Walking Bow's rank, he could not dispense with him until all those opposing his march to the supreme power in the tribe had been removed…"

For Tchatka, grown now powerful and cruel, was out to supplant his benefactor as head chief.

Walking Bow did not know his peril and Tchatka was careful to give no sign. His long practice at the trading post, in hiding his true feelings and disappointment, was being put to deadly use.

Finally, the day came when Tchatka saw his chance to make a deadly move.

"His emissaries," writes Barbeau, "sighted a camp of Blackfoot hunters one day. From their description he knew that the warriors of his own tribe could surprise them and win a decisive victory. The moment had come for him to fortell the event and to strike a supreme blow.

"He invited his uncle to a feast and presented him with a poisoned dish of buffalo tongues. The fatal meal having been consumed to the last mouthful according to the custom, it could not fail to produce its effect after a few hours. Thus would be removed the last obstacle left in his path."

Tchatka, having made the key move, now had to act quickly and daringly to gain control — for in poisoning Walking Bow he was not only removing his last obstacle to power, he was also removing his main defence against his enemies.

Barbeau documents Tchatka's cunning — and extraordinary luck — in vivid terms:

"Walking Bow had no sooner departed after the banquet than his nephew summoned all the leading warriors to his lodge in great haste. Word went round that grave events impended, for the Manitous had given warning.

Tchatka appeared before them attired for the first time with all his finery — the flowing calico shirt, the red sash around his waist, the tall beaver hat on his head and the open prayer book in his hand.

"His Manitou, the Thunder, stood in the centre of the lodge near the fire, under the shape of a magic stone painted red and surrounded by a fence of short sticks.

"At the sight of these strange objects, the assembly sat dumb with awe, and the inspired seer delivered his prophecy as if under a spell.

"He could see far away and tell what was to happen. A camp of the enemy stood near a river, a few days' journey. The Stoneys could take it by surprise and capture many scalps. Time had come for them at last to avenge previous defeats.

"But that was not all. A most valiant brave present at the assembly would fall this very night never to rise again, and at the very moment of his death the Thunder Manitou would blow up to pieces with a dreadful noise to accompany the departing soul into the world of spirits. Another chief, more favoured by the Manitous, would step into his place for the good of all the nation.

"A dismal silence greeted these prophetic words. Victory and revenge naturally aroused their expectations, but in spite of it all dread appeared on every countenance.

"Who was to fall that very night? No one could tell, as many leaders were almost the equals of the head-chief. Not even Walking Bow had any clear idea of his own doom.

"But no doubt could be entertained as to the prophecy; too many others had already proved true. The warriors withdrew in silence and gloom. Dark apprehension invaded the camp with the shades of night.

"At midnight a messenger came running to Tchatka's lodge. 'Come, come! Walking Bow is ill, very ill.'

"But the wily seer could not so easily be induced to affront danger. His uncle, he knew, now suspected his treachery. He would stretch him dead at his feet while he still possessed enough strength.

"So he replied, 'Go and tell him my visit would not help him. And I could not at this moment leave my Manitou alone.'

"The prey of terrible convulsions, Walking Bow declared

to the friends and relatives surrounding him, 'I suspect him, my nephew.'

"Consternation and tumult spread to every lodge. Some warriors uttered frightful yells, vowed speedy revenge and resorted to Tchatka's quarters.

"The seer, still attired in his finery, stood alone near the fire, facing his Thunder Manitou. At the news of his uncle's ordeal he pretended real sorrow, and trembling at the sight of uplifted tomahawks he enjoined the avengers to stay their arm and listen once more to his words.

"'Relatives and friends,' he said, 'Walking Bow is my uncle and my friend; we are of the same blood and eat from the same dish. How could I injure him who has always given me his help and confidence?

"'He was the strongest of warriors at sunset and now is grappling with death. This shows how powerful are the Manitous. What could I do? If I predicted his death it is because the very spirit of Thunder was speaking through my mouth.'

"As the tomahawks were still threatening him, he pleaded again, 'You disbelieve my words? If you do, look at my Manitou, the red stone; look at it closely, for what I have predicted will happen. It will blow up in bits with a terrible noise when the great warrior dies. And when it has happened, will you again lift your arms against me? Will you distrust me as you do now?'

"The sullen warriors drew inside the lodge hesitatingly, one by one. Like mute sentinels they sat around the mysterious red stone. As they waited in dread for its disappearance the fire grew dim and the feeble light shivered on their sinister faces. Ghost-like shadows danced on the sloping sides of the lodge.

"Runners from Walking Bow's tent came by at intervals, shouting, 'The chief utters naught but shrieks of rage against his nephew ... He is in convulsions ... He is growing more feeble ... His speech is gone ... He is in agony ...'

"Cries of despair responded to the last message: 'He is dead!'

"And the red stone by the fire burst into a thousand fragments with the noise of thunder. It filled the lodge with fire and cinders, severely wounding those who sat near and frightening the others into a wild stampede.

"Tchatka's powers once more stood vindicated in the eyes of all. The feeling of revenge gave way to one of terror and reverence. No one approached him but with respect. His Manitou, being the Thunder, he now received the name of 'Great Medicine.'"

What Tchatka had done involved no magic at all — just a good sense of stage management and a healthy dose of the gunpowder he had carried from the trading post inside a horn.

Days before, in total secrecy, Tchatka had drilled a hole in the stone and packed it with close to a pound of black powder. When the Manitou was set up in his lodge, he had left an inconspicuous trail of powder leading to the stone, and when the news of his uncle's death came he was waiting in the shadows with a glowing ember to touch off the fuse.

He had accomplished the first part of his prediction. Now it was up to him to bring off the second — the victory over the Blackfoot hunters — and his grasp on the control of the Stoneys would be complete.

There were still many, particularly among the close relatives and friends of Walking Bow, who would have moved against Tchatka if they had dared. And, as Tchatka knew, they would move if he couldn't make his prediction of victory over the Blackfoot come true.

Tchatka again began an elaborate production. He went

into seclusion in his lodge the day after Walking Bow's death. No one but his 'disciples' dared approach him and no one else in the tribe suspected that these disciples were bringing him updated reports on the Blackfoots' movements.

The second day saw the isolation continue and so did the third day. Tchatka's enemies began to see this inaction as a sign of failure and slowly started agitating for revenge against Tchatka.

Before they could muster enough power to move, however, word was circled through the camp to 'Watch the Great-Medicine Lodge!'

Tchatka was getting ready to go into action on the decisive phase of his plan and, on sunset of the third day, nature intervened to give his stage management a hand. A storm began building from the northeast. Dark clouds moved in, lightning flashed and thunder rumbled.

The Stoneys stirred uneasily, remembering that Tchatka's Manitou was the Thunder.

Tchatka, like the others, was watching the approach of the storm and playing its timing for full dramatic effect.

As the time came to move, Barbeau notes, Tchatka showed all the sense of a veteran Broadway director.

"When the storm was about to break out, at midnight, a deep sound from the seer's lodge startled the people, a sound like that of a large water drum. It was loud enough to be heard throughout the camp. Tchatka's voice rose gradually and the meaningless syllables he uttered were those of a new incantation.

"Runners now summoned the warriors to the Great-Medicine lodge, and while the assembly gathered according to etiquette, wind, rain and thunder roared mightily in unison.

"At the back of the lodge stood Tchatka, a headress

of swan's down on his head. His left hand deftly beat a tchantcheega – a huge drum made of a hollow tree, about three feet high, with a goat skin tightly stretched and pegged at one end. Powerful new Manitous, Grizzly-Bear and Buffalo-Bull were painted yellow and red on the bleached skin, and on the wood all around a large number of small human faces were traced in black outline to represent Blackfoot heads.

"Apparently unaware of the warriors' entry into the lodge he continued his incantation for a while, and then, when all were seated in a half-circle opposite him, he kneeled down in the manner of a Christian and offered thanksgivings to the Great Spirit and his new protectors, the Grizzly and the Buffalo, for their many favors.

"Standing up defiantly while thunder and storm raged outside, he intoned a vehement war song. His lips were dyed red with vermillion to indicate that the spirit of war was in his breath and that his thirst was only for blood, the blood of the enemy…"

Satisfied that his audience was properly primed, Tchatka began a speech designed to stir their hottest emotions. For the past three days, he claimed, he had left this world and gone to the world of the spirits and ghosts.

"There, I have beheld frightful scenes, I have heard sighs, moans and lamentations. I have walked among the dead…"

Among the dead, he told the warriors, were those of the Stoney warriors, women and children who had been slain by the Blackfoot. To the trembling warriors, he told the tale of the dead:

"Let those who have ears listen once for all. There is no time to lose. The souls of our massacred relatives cannot go to the land of rest until they are avenged in blood. They wander up and down in the dark through barren deserts, without food for subsistence. They are cold, thirsty and hungry.

"We are the cause of their torments, since we dare not start on the war path against our foes, and they complain of our forgetfulness.

"A friendly soul touched my hand and said, 'Tchatka, we know you. You are a great sorcerer. It is in your power to bring our deliverance. When you return to our people tell them what you have seen. In your teepee you will find your new Manitou, the drum Tchantcheega. Arise and beat it when the storm breaks out, at night. We shall be near. Tell the warriors to be ready, to start on the war-path at daybreak, for thirty Blackfeet tents stand at the source of the Milk River, not far away. Victory shall be yours. Revenge will end our sufferings.'

"Thus the ghosts have spoken, and when I recovered

my senses I found the drum Tchantcheega at my feet. Now you have heard the truth, friends and relatives. What shall you do?"

It was a question that need hardly have been asked. Tchatka had cunningly touched the vein of deep hatred and longing for revenge that the Stoney had inside them. To a man, the warriors leapt to their feet and screamed the war cry and soon were circling the fire in the scalp dance.

By daybreak, 400 Stoney warriors, war-painted and their arrows sharpened, were ready to set out. They waited by their saddled horses for Tchatka to appear and lead them into battle, but he did not come.

A delegate was sent to his lodge to ask him to take the lead as the vision had foreseen. But he refused, reminding the delegate that only yesterday they were ready to slay him, and besides he was a seer, not a warrior. Choose someone else, he suggested.

Delegate followed delegate to plead with him and Tchatka toyed with each. It was only when the rest of the elders of the tribe had pledged him unquestioning confidence and accepted him as head-chief of the whole tribe that he agreed to go — which had been his plan all along.

The war party was on the trail for some days, Tchatka at the lead with his drum Tchantcheega fastened behind the saddle.

On the trail, he bragged that "If my predictions come true we shall tear from the enemy as many scalps as there are on my drum. We shall see the great chief of the Blackfoot as he appears here, without scalp and without hands."

Tchatka's scouts finally located the Blackfoot encampment and the whole force of Stoneys encircled it by night.

At daybreak, the bloodbath began — but all the Blackfoot warriors were away. There were only women and children and old men to slay, but to the worked-up Stoneys a scalp was a scalp.

The war party, hands bloody and scalps dangling from their saddles, was soon on the trail again. They had killed many, but where were the Blackfoot warriors — particularly the "great chief" Tchatka had predicted would be slain?

As it turned out, it was the Blackfoot who found the Stoneys, not the other way around. There was a shower overnight and, as the party took up the trail again, the way was obscured in fog.

Out of the fog, suddenly, came the Blackfoot and, as Barbeau records it, "Before Tchatka had time to think of his own safety, he found himself enveloped in the midst of fighters, unable to seek shelter anywhere.

"His horse tumbled under him and he fell to the ground. A Blackfoot of lofty stature and great strength hurled his spear at him. The weapon grazed his head and sank quivering into the earth. Then he dashed for him, knife in hand.

"Tchatka by then had had time to jump to his feet and draw his double-bladed knife from its sheath.

"Coward as he was he was he found himself compelled against his own choice to fight for his life. And he did fight with great boldness and skill. He seized the wrist of his adversary and managed to hold the knife off his own body.

"When the battle in the front line had ceased, the Stoneys returned to look for their chief, whom they had lost sight of. They found him struggling arm in arm, on the ground, with a powerful enemy. The Blackfoot at this moment disengaged his arm and lifted his knife for a fatal thrust.

"But a tomahawk from behind stretched him unconscious, and Tchatka in his turn raised his own knife, shouting, 'Friends, behold the chief of the Blackfoot!' and he plunged the blade into his heart. With the same blood-stained knife he scalped him and cut his hands off, to fulfil the prophecy which has ever been retold among the Stoneys.

"Then he said, 'Here was Bear's Foot, the terror of our own people for so many years,' and he pulled off the white man's medal which hung from his neck as a mark of distinction. His warriors, in commemoration of this, now conferred upon him the name of Minayonka, 'the Knife-holder'.

"After so swift and overwhelming a victory they all returned home loaded with trophies. The exultation of the whole tribe ran so high that public rejoicing lasted for a whole moon; scalp dances, songs and thanksgivings were repeated a hundred times.

"Tchatka's new name Minayonka, 'the Knife-holder', was celebrated in every mouth. Never had the nation known such a famous leader, warrior and sorcerer all at once. His ambition was fulfilled at last, for he was entrusted with the supreme, undivided authority over the affairs of the nation."

Tchatka, true to his character, was not content to let mere glory and power suffice. As Barbeau remarks:

"To mark his triumph in his own way, Tchatka selected three wives on the same day, without even considering that two of them were already betrothed to two of his influential warriors. Protests were not heeded, and the parents of the brides felt so honoured by the head chief's choice that they forgot their former pledges and took their daughters to his lodge as soon as an invitation was received.

"To curb discontent and restore peace in every household Tchatka decided to start for the hunt, but not without leaving orders to the most trusted of his partisans to poison his two rival pretenders in his absence.

"Upon his return he feigned surprise at the news of the mysterious death of the pretenders, and only concluded, 'So it always happens. The Manitous have done it. Let those who contradict me, who despise my power, remember it. Their danger is near.'"

For 40 years, Tchatka held the Stoney people under his complete domination — both by fear and by his skill at warfare. From the stories he had heard at the trading-post so many years before, he had developed a keen understanding of warfare: the need for intelligence-gathering and the way in which forces can be used in mass attacks.

Memories of his humiliation at the trading post, now called Fort Union, haunted him constantly, but he kept swallowing the taste of revenge out of fear of the white man's power.

But the day finally came when this fear gave way to a pressing need and he set forth on the path to his final undoing.

What set him on the path was an unexpected defeat at the hands of the Blackfoot. For once, Tchatka's spies had failed and the Stoney were taken by surprise on a war raid in 1830. More than 60 of his warriors were slain and another 60 were taken prisoner, to be returned to torture and death at the hands of the Blackfoot.

It didn't help that Tchatka himself had fled the scene of the battle when the tide turned against the Stoney and his excuse that his new Manitou, the Badger, had carried him away, fell feebly on the ears of the many Stoney who were mourning the death of husbands and sons.

Tchatka decided that he had to act — and quickly — to "cover the dead" with a victory of some kind, so that the defeat would be forgotten. As usual, his love of the theatrical played a strong part in his new strategy. Again it is Barbeau who offers the best description of the incident

— and of the human compassion that brought Tchatka to disaster instead of treacherous victory.

"He retired to his sacred lodge in anticipation of new dreams, new visions of victory. This time his inner determination moved against the white traders at Fort Union, the post where his early ambitions had encountered defeat. Badger, his Manitou, had ceased to serve his purpose, so he called back his old-time protectors, Thunder, Grizzly-Bear and Buffalo-Bull. The mere allusion to their familiar names would spur confidence and instil new vigour in faltering hearts.

"Summoned to his lodge in the name of powerful Manitous, the tribal leaders and the warriors heard of a new war adventure, to the east. Untold riches were to fall into their hands without bloodshed, in a single night. Spoils would be so abundant that the horses of the whole tribe could not drag them all on their travois. The new prophecy was bound to be true, for Tchatka's reliable Manitous of old now had returned from their prolonged retreat.

"The raid contemplated against the trading establishment, Fort Union, was entirely devoid of risk. The occupants had no reason to be suspicious of standing on their guard, since the friendliest relations with all natives had always prevailed.

"The prize lay within the grasp of the Stoneys, but on one condition only: they must unreservedly agree with the plan of their chief and remain blindly faithful to the very end. They all pledged themselves to the most servile obedience. Brighter days were in sight.

"Escorted by three hundred of his best warriors, Tchatka started in the direction of the fort, which stood on the prairie not many days off. His scheme was to approach the traders with the customary amenities, then overwhelm their small force at night and take possession of the two years' stock of goods which had just arrived for the needs of the fur trade.

"The Stoneys were greeted at the fort as on former occasions. The calumet was lit and handed over by the chief trader to the leading visitor, Tchatka, who passed it on to his followers without drawing a whiff of the white smoke like the others.

"This apparent oversight was barely noticeable, and the usual precaution of disarming the native visitors for the night and placing their weapons under lock and key was not even resorted to; Tchatka's old-time friendship for the white people sufficed to remove all suspicion...

"By a shrewdly concerted plan, the dusky warriors had arranged to retire to the various rooms of the establishment for the night. To Tchatka and a faithful follower was reserved the keeping of a small detached dwelling within the fort's enclosure. In that house resided a white woman whose life he wanted to spare, for he remembered her from the time of his youth. She was to be his prisoner, perhaps his wife in spite of the fact that she was married — for he had never forgotten her as the late chief-factor's daughter, the very one who had been ignominiously refused him at the time of his juvenile illusions, long ago. All the other residents were to be massacred at a given signal before the break of day.

"A Stoney runner whose sister was married to a white servant at the fort could not silence his brotherly feelings. He invited her in deep secrecy to resort to his room for the night. But, as she could not understand his meaning, he explained that all her white friends were to perish before sunrise. She promised to follow him, but instead hastened to confide in her husband, whom she wanted to save from death.

"The plot at this stage could no longer remain a secret.

It reached the authorities in the twinkle of an eye.

"Orders from headquarters were whispered around quietly and swiftly. Every white man was armed to the teeth, the guns were loaded, and the two bastions were made ready for siege. All hopes for a successful resistance might have been vain but for a singularly fortunate coincidence; a number of Canadian employees (voyageurs), altogether about eighty, had arrived a few days before from the northern posts to receive their share of the newly arrived trading goods. Their presence now made a great difference; it offered the only safeguard of the moment.

"Mr. Denig, the chief trader, summoned Tchatka and a few of his accomplices to appear before him, as soon as all preparations were complete. He reproached them with their treachery. They wanted to stab their own friends and protectors in the back. How could he place further reliance in them, since they acted as liars and traitors? They deserved only contempt.

Their choice now was either to quit the fort forthwith or be destroyed by the big guns that were levelled at them from every side. Dumbfounded, the warriors instantly decided to withdraw, even without consulting their guilty leader, who was deeply vexed and confused at the failure of his wonderful plot.

"The blow to the great seer's prestige among his own people was decisive, final. Anger and defiance could no longer be suppressed, particularly since the supply of poison in his medicine bag was nearly exhausted."

Tchatka was to make one final bid to restore his prestige, an ill-conceived raid on the Mandans which resulted in the loss of all the Stoney war party except Tchatka himself, who managed to flee the carnage on foot.

It was his last attempt to reverse the downhill curve his cruel career had taken. He was now an old man and, if the Stoney still held his past deeds in esteem, the man who did them was no longer a power among his people.

In the autumn of 1843, the old man made a choice. He could not go on living without power and there was no way left to grasp power. He reached into his old medicine bag for the little poison he had left.

Even in this final act, however, Tchatka could not resist the appeal of the theatrical. It was the time of the fall gathering, the time when all the tribes brought in their furs to the trading posts. As the Stoney prepared to leave their village, Tchatka reported a vision:

"My end is fast approaching. Before many sunsets my soul shall depart for the unseen prairies of our dead relatives."

The Stoney came once again to the gates of Fort Union and the old seer shook Denig by the hand.

"Friend," said Tchatka, "here is the place where I have always wanted to live, to die, among the friends of my youth. Never again shall I visit your wonderful fort. Never shall I see the country of the white man across the sea. My time is passed."

Denig was curious and uncomfortable at these statements. The old chief seemed in good health and inquiries among the Stoney confirmed the impression that Tchatka had not been ill.

That night, when the Stoney gathered to feast, Tchatka prepared his own dish and ate it to the last drop. Then, while the others were dancing by the fire, he retired alone to his lodge.

By morning he was spitting blood. By afternoon he was in terrible convulsions. By night he was dead.

It was a cruel but fitting end for a man who had tried to seize the power of both the white and Indian world in so ruthless a way.

There were many before Tchatka who had been evil, and there would be many men after — thieves and murderers who would also be evil. But in the mountains of our west, no man so distilled the essence of the worst of the encounter of the two cultures.

It is an ironic footnote that Tchatka's own people decided, in the end, to forget his murdering and treachery and remember instead that he had led them to many victories and much revenge.

To this day, the place where he is buried is venerated by his people and his name is venerated as "the greatest man that ever visited our nation."

* * * *

NEW PIONEERS

Our Alberta Heritage Series II

FOREWORD

"I'd do it all over again if I had the chance."

— CON FARRELL

* * * *

Alberta, today, is a hand stretching to the north and, somewhere out there at the very fingertips, are this province's new pioneers.

They're homesteading "back" of Manning, or prospecting the fringes of remote lakes, or wrestling with oil rigs on the edge of the Arctic circle.

Amazingly — and wonderfully — these "new" pioneers are no different in courage, resourcefulness and humor than the first hardy souls who pushed north from Fort Edmonton so very long ago.

These people have always had a character all their own.

Who but a member for Peace River would arrive for the first sitting of Alberta's new legislature with two pet moose trotting happily along behind his rig?

And who but a Punch Dickins would fly 2,200 miles down the Mackenzie to dole out fresh oranges to startled Eskimos who had never even seen an airplane before?

For that matter, who but a northern Alberta sheriff

would react to a railroad being behind on the property taxes for its station land by chaining one of the railroad's locomotives to the track?

There is, even today, a 200-mile strip of forest that divides north from south in this province. There's a differ-ence in those on the northern side, and it is this "differ-ence" that this book is about.

* * * *

EXPLORERS

"We're the People, the worthwhile people. Around us live the less favored people …"

—A BEAVER INDIAN

* * *

* * *

The opening of the north was, once again, the accomplishment of the men of the fur trade. Indeed, in Alberta, the development of the north (in terms of the presence of white people) came far earlier than did the development of any other part of the province.

The traders were interested in two things, beaver and moose. The fur of the beaver was what they had to sell to the rest of the world. And the moose was the staple food that kept them alive while they worked.

Both beaver and moose are creatures of the forest and the waterway and it was through the forests and along the waterways that the fur trade moved westward. In Alberta, that line of development was, in the early stages, along the 200-mile-wide strip of forest that divides the province north of Edmonton.

The first traders were the men of the Hudson's Bay Company. In time the competition of the Nor'westers

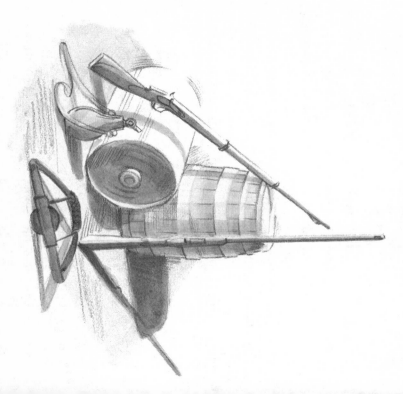

would thrust the fur trade north and west. And the incursions of the American free-traders would thrust it southward.

Indeed, in time, the north would become the focal point of the struggle between Hudson's Bay men and Nor'westers and control of it was control of the centre of the entire industry.

It is hard to believe today that Fort Chipewyan, which still lacks a road link with the rest of the world, was once considered the most important fur post in the west. It is also hard to accept that it was one of the first, being constructed by the Nor'westers in 1788. (The first northern post was Athabasca House, built in 1778.)

It was from Fort Chipewyan that Mackenzie set off to explore the river that bears his name. It was from there, also, that Sir John Franklin set off on his exploration of the barren lands.

In the Athabasca district, as northern Alberta was then known, one finds all the key figures of the history of the fur trade: George Simpson, Mackenzie, Thompson . . .

But it is there, too, that the fur traders built the least-proud part of their history and where their exploitation of the Indian was most severe.

As they moved into the district from the east, the traders carelessly upset a delicate social balance and destroyed the foundation on which the northern Indian had built his life for thousands of years.

To the trader the northern Indian was simply a fur-gathering machine and a hunter of meat for his hungry posts.

Looked at in those terms, it made sense to "improve" the machines by replacing old-fashioned bow-and-arrow-and-deadfall parts with modern rifles and steel traps.

That is what the fur trader did in the north and the machine that resulted was, in the end, too efficient for its own good.

Countless thousands of beaver pelts were shipped out of the Athabasca district. As for moose, well, a full-grown moose fed one man for a month, and there were many men to feed through the long, cold Athabasca years. In one winter, along the Peace River posts alone, a traveller casually counted the slaying of 3,000 moose for food.

Everyone – even those who knew better – acted as though they believed the supply of beaver and moose would never run out. But, of course, it did run out. And when the supplies of the two commodities became too small to make it economical to remain, the fur traders moved on and the Indians were left to perish or to move on as well.

And, as he first moved across the west, the trader threw into chaos the already violently strained relations among the northern tribes.

There were four principal tribes in the northern forests. The Cree ruled from Churchill, on Hudson Bay, to about Edmonton. North of the Cree were the Chipewyans. West of both the Cree and Chipewyans, controlling country to the watersheds of the Athabasca and Peace rivers, were the Beaver Indians. And west of them were Sekanais.

It takes many square miles of territory to provide enough game and fur to feed, clothe and shelter an Indian family. It takes many hundreds of square miles to meet the needs of a tribe.

And as areas are hunted out, tribes need to expand into new hunting territories. This process of constant expansion brought the tribes of the northern forests into competition for territory.

Expansion was literally a matter of life and death to the northern tribes and the fighting was bloody and the truces uneasy and short-lived.

Violence always lay close to the surface and, as the following story shows, the violence sometimes erupted within a tribe as well as between tribes.

Within the Beaver tribe, well before the coming of the white man, there was a struggle for power going on between two factions, one led by the family of the hereditary chief.

The outcome of that struggle was uncovered and recorded in the middle of the last century by Capt. W. F. Baker, a northern traveller of whom we will hear in detail later. Of the Beaver struggle he writes:

"One day a young chief shot his arrow through a dog belonging to another brave. The brave revenged the death

of his dog, and instantly a hundred bows were drawn. Ere night had fallen some eighty warriors lay dead around the camp, the pine woods rang with lamentations of the women, the tribe had lost its bravest men.

"There was a temporary truce – the friends of the chief whose arrow had killed the dog yet numbered some sixty people – and it was agreed that they should separate from the tribe and seek their fortune in the vast wilderness lying to the south.

"In the night they commenced their march; sullenly their brethren saw them depart never to return. They went their way by the shores of the Lesser Slave Lake, towards the great plains which were said to be far southward by the banks of the swift-rolling Saskatchewan.

"The tribe of Beavers never saw again this exiled band, but a hundred years later a Beaver Indian, who followed the fortunes of a white fur-hunter, found himself in one of the forts of the Saskatchewan. Strange Indians were camped around the palisades, they were portions of the great Black-foot tribe whose hunting-grounds lay south of the Saskatchewan; among them were a few braves who, when they conversed together spoke a language different from the other Blackfoot; in this language the Beaver Indian recog-nized his own tongue.

"The fortunes of the exiled branch were then traced, they had reached the great plains, the Blackfoot had protected them, and they had joined the tribe as allies in war against Crees or Assiniboines. Today the Sarcees still speak the guttural language ..."

Thus the violent beginning of the Sarcees who, today, are generally considered – even among themselves – as native plains Indians.

In the north, among the rival tribes, an uneasy peace finally came into being. It was based on the delicate balance of their relative strengths and numbers.

But then the white trader entered the area and with his arrival the peace crumpled. For the white trader had brought with him those things designed to improve the fur and food gathering machinery and one of these things, the gun, changed the definition of strength for the Indians.

Since the trader came in from the east, the Cree were the first to get the rifle and they quickly turned it on the Chipewyan to the north and the Beaver to the west. Victory was easy and great territory was gained, but the victories and the gains were to be short-lived.

Despite the best efforts of the Cree to prevent it, the fur traders went on northward and westward and soon the Chipewyan and Beaver, too, had the gun and the chance to wreak vengeance on the Cree and the chance to loose bullets at their other rivals.

In time, of course, a new balance of power was struck and peace restored, but in all the tribes there were fewer warriors and hunters than there had been before.

The principal tribes, the ones already mentioned, were numerous enough and strong enough to survive the warfare that came with the gun.

But some of the smaller tribes were not. Perhaps the grimmest illustration is that of the fate of the Snake Indians.

The Snakes, at the height of their strength, never numbered more than about 20 families and they stayed close to the small rivers running into the Athabasca River. The Snakes, like all the northern tribes, had their traditional enemies; in their case the Wood Assiniboines.

By 1840 both tribes had the gun and were using it on one another. Since neither was a large tribe to begin with, neither could stand the loss of mature men that came with this new form of warfare.

So, in 1840, at a place close to the post of Jasper House, the Wood Assiniboines proposed a peace. All the warriors of both tribes would come unarmed to a pre-arranged meeting place and smoke the pipe that would end war between them forever.

The Snakes agreed and here we pick up the consequences as they were recorded in the late W. B. Cameron's "When Fur Was King":

"... the men of the (Snakes) band, leaving their guns, arrived and were placed in the inner circle around the council fire. The Assiniboines, however, concealed their guns under their blankets and at a pre-arranged signal drew them and shot down in cold blood every man of their ancient enemies. They then rushed to the Snake camp and wiped out the rest of the band, with the exception of three young women whom they brought as prisoners to Fort Assiniboine. Here they were stripped, bound and placed in a tent, to be tortured and finally dispatched at a great scalp dance to be held the next day.

"During the night a French half-breed, Bellerose by name, crept into the lodge where the prisoners lay and cut their bonds. All he could provide them with was his scalping knife and a fire bag containing flint, steel and punk. The women made their escape and followed the Athabasca River to its junction with the Baptiste. Here they could not agree to their further course. Two decided to follow the Athabasca, the third the Baptiste. The two, making a raft and taking with them the fire bag, crossed the Baptiste and were never afterwards heard of.

"The third, left only with the knife, travelled up the Baptiste some thirty miles and there made preparations for wintering. Berries were still to be had, she managed to kill a few squirrels and with the sinews from their tails made snares for rabbits. She killed some porcupines and groundhogs, too, dried them and out of the rabbit skins made herself a dress. She kindled a fire in the primitive way, by revolving the point of one dry stick rapidly in a hole made in another, and collected a large pile of dry wood. By the time winter set in she was prepared for it.

"Thus she lived until midsummer, gathering gum from the poplars and making dried meat from rabbits and other small animals she killed."

Cameron goes on to tell that, on one of the occasions when she was away from camp on a hunting trip, another Indian ran across her trail in the woods.

The Indian was an Iroquois, one of the many who came west with the fur traders and decided to stay in this new land. The man was puzzled by the strange tracks and was unable to decide "what kind of animal" might have made them. He was superstitious, however, and there were tales of strange beings — "weetigoes" — who wandered these western woods. He decided to leave well enough alone.

"The next summer, however," Cameron continues, "when the hunters were in camp some little distance from the Baptiste, this man decided to return to the spot and try to find out what animal had made the mystifying tracks. he struck the river where the Snake woman was living, saw snares set, trees barked and fresh prints in the ground that resembled those of a human being . . .

"Creeping round cautiously, with his gun at full cock and prepared at any moment to be pounced upon, he came to a high bank where an immense collection of dry wood with a little fire near it was piled not far from the entrance of a small cave. He could see no other sign of life.

"He hid himself close to the cave, and presently a wild creature in a short skirt of rabbit skins approached with a load of rabbits. Throwing down the pack, this grotesque object picked up some sticks with which to replenish the

fire, and ... the hunter knew at once that she must be one of the three women who had escaped two years before from the Assiniboines.

"Noticing him at length she made a frenzied effort to escape but was soon overtaken. She had become perfectly wild and he had much difficulty in bringing her to the camp. Then the officer in Jasper House kept her with his family for two years. She remained as a servant to his wife, for another two years as at the end of which time she married a Shushwap.

"She was the only survivor of her tribe."

As if the gun wasn't a cruel enough gift to the Indian, the white trader brought with him one even deadlier: disease.

Smallpox was the deadliest, wiping out thousands of northern Indians. Whole villages were left lifeless by the disease. In one winter alone, smallpox claimed the lives of one-fifth of the Beaver tribe.

And, too, the traders were uneasy about the violent record of these Indians of the Athabasca. While all the traders had firm instructions about striving to make their Indian suppliers feel friendly and grateful towards the fur companies, in this district there were too many dealings that took on the air of exchanges between potential enemies.

In such an atmosphere, the Indians quickly became suspicious and quick to take offence at any hint, even if only imagined, that they were being cheated.

Most of the traders were scrupulously fair, particularly those of the Hudson's Bay and North West companies. In time they won the confidence of the Indians who traded with them.

But some of the traders, a handful of them, were not fair. And sometimes they ignored the rule that said the Indian had to be treated as a human being.

The Indians in these cases reacted with the swift violence that was instinctive to men whose people had been schooled to a life of war by centuries of it.

One case, where a cruel and stupid act was followed by slaughter then by administrative short-sightedness, stands as a low point in the history of trading in the north.

Traders and their voyageurs, being men and lonely, often made arrangements to take Indian "wives," though wives these women often were in name only. Sometimes these relationships lasted a lifetime, as we shall see later in this book, and sometimes they were concluded when the trader left the country in which he had been working.

Generally, these relationships were approved by the

Indians. They served to strengthen the bonds between their people and the traders on whom they were growing to depend for many of the necessities of life.

Occasionally, though, a white man would resort to cunning or force to capture an Indian woman and hold her in virtual slavery.

It appears, though details are naturally cloudy, that this is what happened at Fort St. John in 1823.

The official explanation, given in company records, blames what happened to the men of that post on a decision to relocate the post "to the Rocky Mountain Portage, for the convenience of the Tsekanies, who were excellent hunters, but who could not be well supplied from this post, on account of the distance."

"Unfortunately, a quarrel had arisen about this time between the Indians of St. John's and the Tsekanies. The former viewed the removal of the post from their lands as an insult, and a measure that gave their enemies a decided superiority over them, and they took a very effectual method of disappointing them."

Such was the explanation offered by John McLean of the Hudson's Bay Company of what set the scene for tragedy. But another source, Capt. W. F. Butler, gives a different account based on what he was told on one of his trips in the area: The men of the post had seized some Beaver woman and the Beavers were out to avenge the kidnapping.

In any event, in November of 1823, the leader of the post at St. John's sent his men away with goods for the new post, remaining alone to keep an eye on what was left behind.

"This," John McLean writes, "was the opportunity the Indians sought for, and they did not fail to take advantage of it.

"The unfortunate man had been in the habit of walking daily by the river side and was taking his usual promenade the day after the departure of his men, when he was shot down by two of the assassins.

"They then carried his body to his room and left it and his blood still marks the floor.

The men, altogether unconscious of the fate that awaited them, came paddling toward the landing place, singing a voyageur's song, and just as the canoe touched the shore a volley of bullets was discharged at them, which silenced them forever. They were all killed on the spot."

News of the slaying of the five reached Chipewyan and

sent shock waves through the company. A prominent company man, William McGillivray, was recruited to lead a punitive expedition against the Indians of St. John's.

Sixteen men were chosen to follow him, most of them Cree warriors.

Before the expedition could leave, however, cooler heads intervened and called it off. Such reprisals could touch off fighting across the north and ruin the fur trade.

Besides, there was a better way to take revenge of the savages who had dared to raise their weapons against white men.

The company, in 1825, simply closed all the posts on the Peace River upstream from Fort Vermilion and kept them closed for three years.

In his book, The Land of Twelve-Foot Davis, J. G. MacGregor records the effect of that decision:

"Closing these posts was a much more drastic punishment than killing a few Indians in retaliation would have been. This measure had the effect of starving to death most of the Beavers in the vicinity.

"A scant thirty years only had elapsed since the traders had come among the Beavers. Before that, from time immemorial, they had hunted with primitive weapons and were wholly independent of the white man.

"In a short thirty years' period they had become so dependent on the white man's traps and guns and ammunition that many starved when the traders closed their posts and thus denied these things to them."

In those 30 years, too, the Beavers had been so efficient in meeting the white traders' demands for meat and fur that there simply wasn't enough game left to keep the Indians alive.

Three years later the traders re-opened the posts. Revenge had been accomplished and, besides, the economics

of the fur trade made it logical to tap the fur resources of the Peace.

The Beaver had paid a bitter price for the incident at Fort St. John. But so had the traders. Burning inside the surviving Indians was a hatred that, if rarely surfacing, would still never end. Never again would these people give themselves totally to the white men, and this was the white man's loss.

It was the Beavers and their neighbors who, during the rush of 1898 to the gold fields of the Klondike, played a major part in the fact that only two per cent of the would-be prospectors ever got through on the overland route.

The prospectors, the Indians said, were trespassers and were to be treated as such.

It was in 1898, at Fort St. John, that the Beavers gave one of the displays of the hatred they had borne for so many years.

That year a large party of Klondikers struggled north from Edmonton, bringing with them horses and wagons and carts filled with goods and supplies.

Along the trail there were incidents with Indians, but none bad enough to cause serious worry to these gold-hungry tenderfeet.

At Fort St. John, when they had crossed the river, they faced one of the major obstacles of their trip, the steep 900-foot wall of the Peace canyon.

It took a full day of hauling and pushing and back-breaking effort for men and horses to struggle to the top of that obstacle. At the very top, they halted, too exhausted to go any farther.

The camp went to sleep early and soundly that night. But as soon as full darkness came, the camp was thrown awake by yells and shrieks of laughter as a party of Beavers, backed by their Sikannie neighbors, struck the party.

The Indians weren't out to touch any of these white men; they knew the consequences of that.

Instead, they cut loose their horses and stampeded them, in a frenzy, back down the river.

Then it was the turn of the wagons and carts. All were hurled down the face of the 900-foot hill, tumbling end over end to rest, just so much splintered timber, at the edge of the river.

All the prospectors goods and supples — and chances of making it to the Klondike — had rested in those wagons and carts. Now the chance was gone.

For 20 years, the remains of those wagons lay at the foot of the hill at Fort St. John, and for 20 years the Beavers could look down, satisfied, at the evidence of their venge-ance.

All this may seem a bit too grim. The opening of the north, after all, was really a mixture of grimness and good-ness and there were times of joy as often as there were times of sorrow.

But at least what grim things have just been said will help to set the stage for the experiences of the happy wanderer we are about to meet...

"If today we are what we are, it is because a thousand men in bygone times did not stop to count the cost."

— CAPT. W. F. BUTLER

* * * *

* * * *

Many and mighty were the men who explored and opened up the northland. But it isn't one of the many and mighty who bring down to us the best of the explorers' pictures of northern Alberta.

Rather it is an Englishman named Capt. W. F. Butler who was one of those rare breed of men who explore for the sake of exploring, who take on the hardship and

dangers of a strange land simply, well, for the sheer joy of it.

It was such a mood of sheer joy that moved Capt. Butler, in the mid-1800s, to attempt a trip across the north, across the Rockies, and to the sea.

He made a record of that trip, called it Wild North Land, and had it published. Sadly, few copies remain of that chronicle today.

Butler had the Victorian flair for description and since he was not obligated to, or employed by, any of the companies in the north, he is able to provide a clear and largely unbiased picture of the land and people he encountered.

In the excerpts that follow, taken from the part of his journal dealing with what is now northern Alberta, we get perhaps the fairest picture available of life there in the day of the fur trader. And, far from incidentally, we get a delightful look at what it was to be an explorer in that day and age.*

"Figures convey but a poor idea of cold, yet they are the only means we have, and by a comparison of figures some persons, at least, will understand the cold of an Athabasca winter. The mean temperature of the month of January, 1844, at Fort Chipewyan, was (minus) 22 degrees, 74'; and during the preceding month of December the wind blew with a total pressure of one thousand one hundred and sixty pounds to the square foot.

"It is perhaps needless to say more about the rigour of an Athabascan winter."

---

*Most of the excerpts have been sharply condensed. Spelling, however, has been left untouched on the theory that the reader should share the private joy a researcher finds in the quaint arrangements that ornament the words of another era.

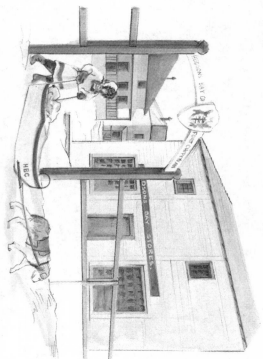

Butler, who was stalled at Chipewyan while waiting to get his travelling party together, goes on to describe the typical Hudson's Bay post:

"The term 'Fort' which so frequently occurs in these pages may perhaps convey an erroneous impression to the reader's mind. An imposing array of rampart and bastion, a loop-holed wall or formidable fortalice may arise before his mind's eye as he reads the oft-recurring word. Built generally upon the lower bank of a large river or lake, but sometimes perched upon the loftier out bank, stands the Hudson's Bay Fort. A square palisade, ten to twenty feet high, surrounds the buildings; in the prairie region this defence is stout and lofty, but in the wooded country it is frequently dispensed with altogether.

"Inside the stockade some half-dozen houses are grouped together in square or oblong form. The house of the Bourgeois and Clerks, the store wherein are kept the blankets, coloured cloths, guns, ammunition, bright handkerchiefs, ribbons, beads, &c., the staple commodities of the Indian trade;

another store for furs and peltries, a building from the beams of which hang myriads of skins worth many a gold piece in the marts of far-away London city; — martens and minks, and dark otters, fishers and black foxes, to say nothing of bears and beavers and a host of less valuable furs. Then came the houses of the men.

"Lounging at the gate, or on the shore in front, one sees a half-breed in tasselated cap, or a group of Indians in blanket robes or dirty-white capotes; everybody is smoking; the pointed poles of a wigwam or two rise on either side of the outer palisades, and over all there is the tapering flagstaff. A horse is in the distant river meadow. Around the great silent hills stand bare, or fringed with jagged pine tops, and some few hundred yards away on either side, a rude cross or wooden railing blown over by the tempest, discoloured by rain or snow-drift, marks the lonely resting-place of the dead.

"Wild, desolate and remote are these isolated trading spots, yet it is difficult to describe the feelings with which one beholds them across some ice-bound lake, or silent river, as the dog trains wind slowly amidst the snow. Coming in from the wilderness, from the wrack of tempest, and the bitter cold, wearied with long marches, footsore or frozen, one looks upon the wooden house as some palace of rest and contentment."

Butler waited at Chipewyan with his lead sled dog, a husky named Cerf-vola that made the entire trip with him, first as a worker then as a pet.

Impatient as he was, it was March before he was able to get a party together and set out for the Peace.

It didn't take Butler long to decide that the men who had hired on as guides and packers weren't all they might have been:

"On the evening of the 12th of March I camped alone

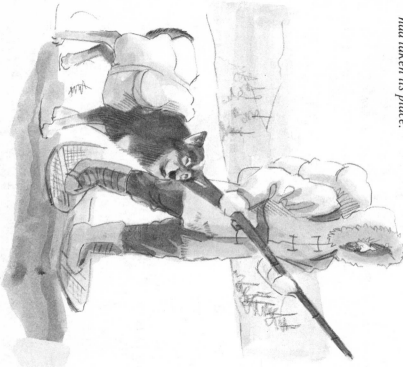

in the wilderness. The three or four men were busy scraping the deep snow from the lee side of some low willow bushes, but they were alien in every thought and feeling; and we were separated by a gulf impossible to bridge; so that I was quite alone. I will not say on whose side the fault lay . . . I found a far stronger tie of companionship with the dogs that drew my load, than for the men with whom I now found myself in company.

"They were by no means wild; far from it, they were eminently tame. One of them was a scoundrel of a very low type, as some of his actions will hereafter show. In him the wild animal had been long since destroyed, the tame brute had taken its place.

"The man was a French half-breed; strong, active, and handsome, he was still a sulky, good-for-nothing fellow. One might as well have tried to make friends with a fish to which one cast a worm, as with this good-looking, good-for-nothing man.

"He had depth sufficient to tell a lie which might wear the semblance of truth for a day; and cunning enough to cheat without being caught in the actual fact. I think he was the most impudent liar I have ever met.

"The motive which had induced him to accept service in this long journey was, I believe, a domestic one. He had run away with a young English half-breed girl, and then ran away from her. If she had only known the object of her affections as well as I did, she would have regarded the last feat of activity as a far less serious evil than the first."

Butler then turns to a description of another of the party, "a Swampy Indian of the class one frequently meets in the English-speaking settlement on Red River. Taken by himself, he was negatively good; but placed with others worse than himself, he was positively bad. He was, however, a fair traveller, and used his dogs with a degree of care and attention seldom seen amongst the half-breeds.

"Small wonder, then, that with these worthies who, though strangers, now met upon a base of common rascality, that I should feel myself more completely alone than if nothing but the waste had spread around me. Full thirty days of travel must elapse ere the mountains . . ."

There is much that smacks of racial prejudice in his description of two of his companions, but as an appraiser of character, he turns out, as we shall in time see, not to be too far wrong.

The party is travelling with dog sleds, reserved for their supplies and goods, and the men are on snowshoes. Butler, with the passage of days on the trail, falls victim to "mal-de-raquette," an infliction caused by the constant bite of part of the snowshoe into the sole of mocassined foot:

"I have endured no little misery; and each day now further increased them. The muscles of ancles and instep had become painfully inflamed, to raise the snow-shoe from the ground was frequently no easy matter, and at last every step was taken in pain. There was nothing for me but to tramp on in spite of aching ancles.

"At the camp I tried my remedies, but all were useless. From pain-killer, moose fat, laudanum and porpoise oil I concocted a mixture, which I feel convinced contains a vast fortune for any enterprising professor in the next century, and which even in these infant ages of 'puffing' might still be made to realize some few millions of dollars; but nevertheless, my poor puffed foot resisted every attempt to reduce it to symmetry, or what was more important, to induce it to resume work.

"That sixteen-hour day had inflamed its worst passions, and it had struck for an 'eight-hour movement.' One can afford to laugh over it all now, but then it was gloomy work enough; to make one step off the old hidden dog-track of the early winter was to sink instantly into the soft snow to the depth of three or four feet, and when we camped at night on the wooded shore, our blankets were laid in a deep furrow between lofty snow walls, which it had taken us a full hour to scoop out."

Days later, Butler and his party reached a trading post on the Peace:

"Weary limbs and aching ancles pleaded for delay at this little post, but advancing spring, and still more the repeated assaults of my servant and his comrades upon my stock of luxuries, urged movement as the only means of saving some little portion of those good things put away for me by my kind host at Chipewyan.

"It seems positively ridiculous now, how one could regard the possession of flour and sugar, of sweet cake and sweet pemmican, as some of the most essential requisites of life. And yet so it was.

"With the grocer in the neighbouring street, and the baker round the corner, we can afford to look upon flour and sugar as very common-place articles indeed; but if any person wishes to arrive at a correct notion of their true value in the philosophy of life let him eliminate them from his daily bill of fare, and restrict himself solely to moose meat, grease, and milkless tea. For a day or two he will get on well enough, then he will begin to ponder long upon bread, cakes and other kindred subjects; until one day he learns to long for bread . . .

"My servitor, not content with living as his master lived, was helping the other rascals to the precious fare. English half-breed, French ditto, and full Christian Swampy had apparently formed an offensive and defensive alliance upon the basis of a common rascality. Article I of the treaty having reference to the furtive partition of my best white sugar, flour, and Souchong tea; things which, when they have to be 'portaged' far on men's shoulders in a savage land, are not usually deemed fitted for savage stomachs too.

"One night's delay, and again we were on the endless trail . . ."

The party struggles on past Fort Vermilion and adds another dog team and driver to its number:

"For 200 miles above Vermilion the course of the Peace River is north-west; it winds in long, serpentine curves between banks which gradually become more lofty as the traveller ascends the stream. To cut the long curve to the south by an overland portage now became our work; and for three days we followed a trail through mingled prairie and forest-land, all lying deep in snow. Four trains of dogs

now formed our line. An Ojibbeway named White Bear, led the advance and the trails took in turn the work of breaking the road after him.

"Mal de Raquette had at last proved more than a match for me, and walking had become impossible; but the trains returning to Dunvegan were lightly loaded and the various dogs take their turn in hauling my cariole.

"Our trail led towards the foot of the Buffalo Hills. I was now in the country of the Beaver Indians . . .

"No men in this land of hunters hunt better than the Beavers. It is not uncommon for a single Indian to render from his winter trapping 200 marten skins, and not less than 20,000 beavers are annually killed by the tribe on the waters of the Peace River.

"On the morning of the third day after leaving Vermilion we fell in with a band of Beavers. Five wigwams stood pitched upon a pretty rising knoll, backed by pine woods, which skirted the banks of the stream, upon the channel of which the lodges of the animal beaver rose cone-like above the snow.

"When we reached the camp, At-tal-loo, the chief, came forth. A stranger was a rare sight; and At-tal-loo was bound to make a speech; three of his warriors, half a dozen children, and a few women filled up the background. Leaning upon a long single-barrelled gun At-tal-loo began.

"The mayor and corporation of that thriving borough of Porkingham could not have been more solicitous to interrupt a royal progress to the north, than was this Beaver Indian anxious to address the traveller; but there was this difference between them, whereas Mayor Tomkins had chiefly in view the excellent opportunity of hearing his own voice, utterly unmindful of what a horrid bore he was making himself to his sovereign, At-tal-loo had in view more practical results:

his frequent iteration of the word 'tea,' in his guttural
harangue, told at once the story of his wants:—

"This winter had been a severe one; death had struck
heavily into the tribe; in these three wigwams six women
had died. It was true each brave still had three or four wives
left, but moose were plenty, and a man with six helpmates

could be rich in dry meat and moose leather. Tea was the pressing want. Without tea the meat of the moose was insipid; without tea and tobacco the loss of even the fifth or sixth rib became a serious affair.'

"I endeavoured to find out the cause of this mortality among the poor hunters, and it was not far to seek. Constitutions enfeebled by close intermarriage, and by the hardships attending upon wild life in these northern regions, were fast wearing out. At the present rate of mortality the tribe of the Beavers will soon be extinct, and with them will have disappeared the best and the simplest of the nomad tribes of the north.

"At-tal-loo was made happy with tea and tobacco and we went our way . . .

"About noon one day we reached a camp of Crees on the south shore of the river. Moose meat was getting scarce, so I asked my yellow rascal to procure some tit-bits from the camp in exchange for tea. The whole party at once vanished into the tents, while I remained with the dogs upon the river. Presently my friend re-appeared; he 'could only get a rib-piece or a touch leg.' 'Then don't take them,' I said. I saw the rascal was at his old work, so taking some tea and tobacco, I went up myself to the tents; meantime the men, women and children had all come out to the shore. I held up the tea and pointed to the moose meat; in an instant the scene changed — briskets, tongues, and moose-noses were brought out, and I could have loaded my dogs with tit-bits had I wished; still I pretended to find another motive for my henchman's conduct. 'See,' I said to him, 'I make a better trader with Indians than you do. They would only give you the tough bits; I can get noses enough to load my dogs with.'

"But the camp posessed an attraction still more enticing; early that morning I had observed the Indians and half-breeds *arraying themselves in their gayest trappings. The half-breed usually in dressing himself devotes the largest share of attention to the decoration of his legs; beads, buckles, and embroidered ribbons flutter from his leggings, and his garters are resplendent with coloured worsted or porcupine-quill work.*

"These items of finery had all been donned this morning in camp, the long hair had been carefully smeared with bear's fat, and then I had not long to wait for an explanation of all this adornment. In one of the three Cree tents there dwelt two good-looking squaws; we entered this tent, the mats were unrolled, the fire replenished, and the squaws set to work to cook a moose nose and tongue for my dinner. Dinner over, the difficulty began; the quarters were excellent in the estimation of my men. It would be the wildest insanity to think of quitting such a paradise of love and food under at least a twenty-four hours' delay.

"So they announced their intention of 'bideing a wee.' I endeavoured to expostulate, I spoke of the lateness of the season, the distance I had yet to travel, the necessity of bringing to Dunvegan the train of dogs destined for that post at the earliest period; all was of no avail. Their snow-shoes were broken and they must wait. Very good; put my four dogs into harness, and I will go on alone. So the dogs were put in harness, and taking with me my most lootable effects, I set out alone into the wilderness.

"It still wanted some four hours of sunset when I left the Indian lodges on the south shore, and held my way along the far-reaching river.

"My poor old dog, after a few glances back to see why he should be alone, settled himself to work, and despite a lameness, the result of long travel, he led the advance so gamely that when night fell some dozen miles lay between us and the Cree lodges.

"At the foot of a high ridge whose summit still caught

the glow from the low-set sun, while the river valley grew dark in the twilight, I turned the dogs towards the south shore, and looked about for a camping-place. The lower bank sloped down to the ice abruptly; but dogs going to camp will drag a load up, over, or through anything, and the prospect of rest above is even a greater incentive to exertion than the fluent imprecations of the half-breed below.

"So by dint of hauling we reached the top, and then I made my camp in a pine-clump on the brink. When the dogs had been unharnessed, and the snow dug away, the pine brush laid upon the ground and the wood cut, when the fire was made, the kettle filled with snow and boiled, the dogs fed with a good hearty meal of dry moose meat, and my own hunger satisfied; then, it was time to think, while the fire lit up the pine stems, and the last glint of daylight gleamed in the western sky. A jagged pine top laid its black cone against what had been the sunset. An owl from the opposite shore sounded at intervals his lonely call; now and again a passing breeze bent the fir trees until they whispered forth that mournful song which seems to echo from the abyss of the past.

"I felt at last at home. The great silent river, the lofty ridge darkening against the twilight, yon star burning like a beacon above the precipice — all these were friends, and midst them one could rest in peace . . .

"I awoke with the dawn. Soft snow was falling on river and ridge, and the opposite shore lay hid in mist and gloom. A breakfast, which consists of pemmican, tea, and biscuit, takes but a short time to prepare or to discuss, and by sunrise I was on the river.

"About noon I camped on the south shore. I had still two meals for myself, but none remained for the dogs; the men had, however, assured me that they would not fail to make an early start, and I determined to await their coming in this camp. The day passed and night closed again, but no figure darkened the long stretch of river, and my poor dogs went supperless to sleep. Cerf-vola, it is true, had some scraps of sweet pemmican, but they were mere drops in the ocean of his appetite.

"The hauling-dog of the North is a queer animal about food; when it is there he likes to have it, but when it isn't there, like his Indian master, he can do without it.

"I had been asleep some hours, and midnight had come, when the sound of voices roused me, and my recreant band approached the dying campfire. They had at length torn themselves away from the abode of bliss and moose meat, but either the memory of its vanished pleasures, or a stray feeling of shame, kept them still sullen and morose. They, however, announced their readiness to go on at once, as the crust upon the snow was now hard. I rose from my robe, gave the dogs a late supper, and once more we set out.

At Dunvegan, Butler got rid of his unsatisfactory helpers and took on new ones. He then pushed on, westward along the Peace, trying to beat spring to the mountains. At one point, he again runs into a party of Indians, and uses the occasion to contrast the life of the Indian woman with that of the woman back in England.

"In some instincts the savage mother might teach her civilized sister a lesson of womanity," he concludes.

The trip remains largely without incident until the party reaches the site of the original Fort St. John, that fateful place where Beaver and traders had clashed so tragically years before:

"On the north shore of the river, directly facing the tumble-down fort, a new log-house was in the course of erection by the Hudson's Bay Company. Work moves slowly in the North, and this log-house lay long unfinished. One fine day a canoe came floating down the lonely river; it held a solitary *negro — pioneer, cook, trapper, vagrant, idler, or squatter, as chance suited him.*

"This time the black paddler determined to squat by the half-finished log-house of the Company. Four years earlier he had dwelt for a season on this same spot.

"There were dark rumours afloat about him; he had killed his man it was averred; nay, he had repeated the pastime, and killed two men. He had robbed several mining shanties, and had to shift his residence more than once beyond the mountains on account of his mode of life.

"Altogether Nigger Dan, as he was called, bore an indifferent reputation among the solitary white man and his half-breed helpers at the post of St. John's. By the Indians he was regarded as something between a beaver and an American bear, and, had his head been tradeable as a matter of fur, I believe they would have trapped him to a certainty.

"But despite the hostile feelings of the entire community, Nigger Dan held stout possession of his shanty, and claimed, in addition to his hut, all the land adjoining it, as well as the Hudson's Bay Fort in course of erection.

"From his lair he issued manifestoes of a very violent nature. He planted stakes in the gound along the river-bank, upon which he painted in red ochre hieroglyphics of a menacing character.

"At night he could be heard across the silent river indulging in loud and uncalled-for curses, and at times he varied this employment by reciting portions of the Bible . . . .

"On the 12th of April, four days after my arrival at St. John's, my young host was the recipient of the following ultimatum: —

April 12

KENEDY   I hear by Worne you that Com and Gett your
persnol property if eny you
have Got of my prmeeis In 24 hours And then keep away
from me because I shal Not betrubbld Nor trod on only
by her most Noble
    Majesty
    Government

(Sgd)   D. T. WILLIAMS.

"On the back appeared, —

I have wated longe A-day for an ancer from that Notis you toer Down and now It is my turn to tore down ———

"*Although the spirit of loyalty which breathed through the latter portion of this document was most admirable, it is nevertheless matter for regret that Dan's views of the subject of 'persnol property' were not those of a law-abiding citizen; unfortunately for me, both the Hudson's Bay claimant and the negro occupant appealed to me in support of their rival rights. What was to be done? It is true that by virtue of a commission conferred upon me some years earlier I had been elevated to the lofty title of justice of the peace for Rupert's Land and the North-West Territories, my brother justices consisting, I believe, of two Hudson Bay officials and three half-breed buffalo runners, whose collective wisdom was deemed amply sufficient to dispense justice over something like two million square miles.*

"*Nevertheless, it occurred to me that this matter of disputed ownership was one outside even the wide limits of my jurisdiction. To admit such a want of jurisdiction would never have answered. 'Rupert's Land and the North-West' carried with them a sense of vast indefinite power, that if it were once shaken by an ad;ion of non-competency, two million square miles, containing a population of one -wy-fourth of* a wild man to each square mile, might have instantly become prey to chaotic crime.

"Feeling the inutility of my lofty office to deal with the matter in question, I decided upon adopting a middle course, one which I have every reason to believe upheld the full majesty of the law in the eyes of the eight representatives of the Canadian, African, and American races of man, now assembled around me. I therefore issued a document which ran thus: —

JUDICIAL MEMORANDUM

Various circumstances having occurred in the neighbourhood of the Hudson's Bay Fort known as St. John's, on the Peace River, of a nature to lead to the assumption that a breach of the peace is liable to arise out of the question of disputed ownership, in a plot of land on the north shore of the river, on which the Hudson's Bay Company have erected buildings to serve as their future place of business, and on which it is asserted one Daniel Williams, a person of colour, formerly lived, this is to notify all persons concerned in this question, that no belief of ownership, no former or present possession, will be held in any way to excuse or palliate the slightest infringement of the law, or to sanction any act of violence being committed, or to occasion any threats being made use of by any of the said parties which might lead to a breach of the peace.

Executed by me, as Justice of the Peace for Rupert's Land and the North-West, this 22nd day of April . . .

"I claim for this memorandum or manifesto some slight degree of praise. It bears, I think, a striking analogy to diplomatic documents, for which of late years the British Government has been conspicuous in times of grave foreign complications; but in one important respect my judicial memorandum was very much more successful than any of the political papers upon which it was framed; for whereas they had been received by the respective belligerents to whom they had been addressed in a manner not at all flattering to our national dignity; my very lucid statement that, diplomatically speaking, two and two made four, had a marked impression on the minds of my audience.

"On the one hand, I clearly pointed out that murder, arson, and robbery were not singly or collectively in unison with the true interpretation of British law; and on the other, I carefully abstained from giving any indication of what would result from the infringement of that law in the persons of any of the belligerents.

"I have reason to believe that the negro was deeply impressed by the general tenour of the document; and that a lengthened perusal of the word 'executed', in the last sentence, carried with it a sense of profound strangulation under which he long laboured.

"And now it was time to think of moving again towards the setting sun . . ."

And that, for the time being, is what we shall leave him doing: heading out towards the setting sun. In time he came successfully to the mountains and over them and to the Pacific, his dog, Cerf-vola finally free and at his side.

If he showed himself to be a bit of a bigot, this explorer we've chosen, well, at least he was a bigot with a sense of humor.

And, however much he may appear no more than a careless wanderer, he proved himself to be as much an explorer as any of the men whose names appear elsewhere in these books.

After all, Capt. Butler drew a word map of a particular time among particular men in a particular place. Can any explorer really claim to have done more?

* * * *

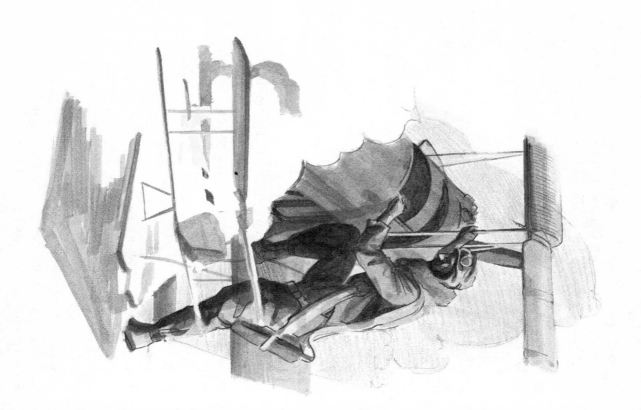

ADVENTURERS

"The funny thing about history is that you don't realize you've been making it until you have."

—PUNCH DICKINS.

* * *

* *

*

The bush pilot was flying an old trapper into his wintering grounds and listened to the man, who was staring down at the ground below, mutter something every few minutes: *"There's one day,"* then, a few moments later, *"There's another day."* And on it went.

The old trapper, counting away in minutes what had once been for him days of fighting on foot through the dense bush, is probably one of the best examples of the difference the airplane has made to life in the north.

Ever since the day Wop May flew the mayor of Edmonton under the low-level bridge, leaving the poor man vowing never to fly again, airplanes and the men who fly them have held a legendary place in Alberta history.

It was these tiny airplanes and the bush pilots who did the detailed mapping of the north.

It was these men who made it possible to tap the mineral wealth, flying in everything from prospectors to bulldozers.

They carried in food and mail and brought out fish and furs. They performed incredible feats of heroism, often risking their own lives, to bring medical attention to people seriously ill or badly injured.

And they did it all in a characteristic, zany way, that has led to countless stories that begin with a grin and a shake of the head and a "Say, did you hear about...?"

In 1967, in Yellowknife, many of the old-time bush pilots were flown in for the commemoration of a cairn to their exploits and for a reunion.

An interviewer for the provincial archives went along, armed with tape recorder, to preserve the occasion.

Unfortunately for the interviewer, he caught up with the pilots as they were unwinding in a hospitality suite. The tape that resulted, if one has the patience to sit down and listen to it long enough to decipher the words hidden among the laughter and rattling of ice-cubes, is a classic of hilarity as the pilots yarned and tall-taled their way through their experiences in the north.

There are stories about a pilot who liked to read in the cockpit while he was flying and who, as a consequence, flew over a stranded fellow-pilot at least twice without seeing his signals or plane – or shaking fist.

There are stories about monumental drunks that filled cabins with spilled pails of honey or cockpits with splitting headaches.

There are all kinds of stories on that tape, most of the best of them unprintable.

Fortunately, for the sake of more sober historians, the interviewer later was able to take on some of the pilots one at a time and get something like organized information out of them.

But he had been given an illustration of the axiom that any time you put more than one bush pilot in one place they'll talk you to death.

On their own, the old-timer bush pilots tend to make little of their exploits. These men flew in open-cockpit planes, in all weather, over unmapped territory, without radios and with compasses that, being so close to the magnetic north pole, often spun like useless tops.

"Oh, it was just a job," they'll say, as though anyone would do what they had done for $100 or $150 a month and a few cents a mile in flight pay.

"I never had any, you know, what you'd call real adventures," will be what you get from a man like Con Farrell, who had more adventures and hair-raising incidents in each week than most of us would run into in a lifetime.

Probably as good an example of what a bush pilot sounds like on his own is the following account given by Scotty Moir to an interviewer:

"I started flying in 1917 with the Royal Flying Corps. I flew for about a year, a year and a half, during the First World War — that is, I was in a year and a half; but I only lasted about six months until they knocked me down and put me in the hospital for about eight months, and by the time I got out of the hospital the war was over.

"Well, I came back from overseas in 1919 and I was supposed to go back to university to complete my course in medicine. But I was rather unsettled and I thought I'd take a year off or so and see what was going on.

"I landed up in a little town in Manitoba, where I had gone to school, and the bank manager there talked me into going into the bank.

"Spent eight years with the bank ... ended up in Lima, Peru, of all places, for two years. And when my stretch was up I came back to Canada, which would have been around 1926, and I poked around and said, well, I'm too old to go back to school now.

"Flying was starting to go, so I arranged to take a course at Camp Borden in 1928 and I took my instructor's course and ended up as the assistant instructor at the Winnipeg Flying Club. And from there I went to the Brandon Flying Club, I went to the Saskatoon Flying Club, and from there I went to the bush — in 1930.

"I started in the bush as a pilot with Star Airways and my career then varied from one company to another and ended up as one of the first pilots with Air Canada — Trans Canada Airlines in those days. Retired in 1951."

Did he have any adventures in his bush-flying career? Well, no adventures, really, although there were a few "incidents."

"The one that stands out in my mind as far as danger is concerned is one when I was coming out from Edmonton one day in the wintertime and everything was going fine.

"I made a few stops, one at McMurray, one at Fort Smith, and I was getting on for Yellowknife when I ran into a lot of turbulence and I had quite a heavy load on board. One of the pieces of freight was a big 1,200 pound roll of cable and it was right behind my seat.

(Moir was flying a Bianca Airbus, a heavy-freight machine, and had a mechanic and helper on board.)

"All of a sudden I felt a tremendous drag on the airplane as though someone had taken a hand and just pulled it around. I looked out and here one of the skis had fallen down. Now, the skis on a Bianca are a pretty fair size."

(Normally the skis, fitted over the wheels, are held in line by a combination of springs and cables. In this case, a cable was the wrong size and it had failed, allowing the tip of the ski to hang down and create a massive drag against the air.)

"I had to increase to full power to gain altitude and we were down to 1,500 feet and I kept putting on the power and managed to hold it to that altitude.

"I radioed ahead — we had radios in those days — to Yellowknife, and I told them what had happened.

"I tried everything I could to try to get the ski back up but it was no go and I told them in Yellowknife to get some fire extinguishers out to the landing place in the middle of the bay.

"I made one circle around and then I came in.

"I cut the power and the gas. What I hoped to do, you

see, was drop her in from about 20 feet and hope the ski would come up.

"Well, the funny part of it was that, as I reduced speed for the landing, the tension on the bindings on the ski was enough that it pulled the ski back up in place. And the result was I made the best landing I ever made — but that was a very trying hour."

Accomplishments?

"I think just starting in the bush (at the time he did) was accomplishment enough. We didn't really think of it at the time, it was just a job, but really all the boys who were flying then were assisting to open up the north.

"And there is no doubt about it, the airplane did open the north country up. And now we can look back and feel a certain satisfaction in saying, well, I was part of that."

* * * *

"I'm game."

—JACK CAMERON, A TRAPPER.

* * * *

The "very trying hour" that Scotty Moir described was similar to countless other trying hours experienced by the men who flew north from Edmonton.

But, of all the incidents recorded, there are three that stand out and all concern propellors.

The first of these stories came about as the result of Imperial Oil's determination to beat the rush to Fort Norman, 900 miles north of Peace River, to stake claim to the oil fields that had been discovered there.

The airplane was already recognized as the fastest way to travel in the north and, if it wasn't always the most reliable way, well, that was a chance you just had to take. The planes chosen for Imperial's race to Fort Norman were both new Junkers, all-metal aircraft, able to operate on float, wheel or ski, and considered the most promising of the newer designs to adapt to the north.

Peace River was chosen as the base camp for the operation and the planes were lifted from the ice there early one spring by two veteran bush pilots, George Gorman and Elmer Fullerton.

They had plotted their course over largely-unexplored territory with an ordinary ruler on a sketchy map.

The first flight was bound for Upper Hay River, halfway to Great Slave Lake, to cache aviation fuel there for use in the try for Fort Norman. North of Peace River there weren't even telegraph lines, let alone aviation fuel, so it was a trip of necessity.

It was a trip, too, that proved to be near-fatal. The Indians at Upper Hay River had never seen an airplane before and, as the two fully-loaded Junkers made their landing approach, the Indians seized every rifle they could lay hand on and began blasting away at these threatening monsters soaring down at them.

Fullerton and Gorman had both seen service as combat pilots during the First World War and, startled though they were, instinctively took evasive action.

They returned to Peace River and, examining their aircraft, found a number of bullet holes, some of them uncomfortably close to the cockpit.

It took a careful, diplomatic excursion to the Indians before that particular spot found its way into their flight plans again.

The actual expedition, once preliminary plans were completed, left Peace River on March 24. With the pilots went mechanics, William Hill and Pete Derbyshire. William Waddell, a surveyor, was along to stake claims and there was an RCMP Sergeant, Hubert Thorn, returning to his post at Fort Simpson.

They were on route to their refueling stop when a blizzard grounded them at Fort Vermilion for two days.

When the weather cleared it was on to Hay River for fuel then off to Fort Simpson.

There, they circled, looking for a landing place. Gorman took his plane down first and, as Fullerton watched from the air, the machine ran along the snow then jerked, rocked, and pitched nose-down before skidding to a halt with one wing high in the air.

Fullerton quickly brought his plane down, by good luck missing the hidden rut of a dog trail that had been the undoing of the other plane.

Gorman and his passengers were shaken up but uninjured. The airplane itself, however, was another story. The crash had broken the propeller and destroyed one of the plane's skis.

The aircraft would have to stay where it was until replacement parts could be brought in and the second plane would go on alone.

The only problem was that the landing spot was too small for Fullerton's fully-loaded aircraft to take off. It had to be unloaded and the plan was to fly it to a nearby inlet, sled the cargo to that point, and take off from there.

On the half-mile flight, however, Fullerton discovered the plane's engine had developed problems.

When he rejoined the party back at the fort, they made a careful review of the situation.

Since Gorman's plane had flown fewer hours and its engine was in better condition, the propeller and one ski would be transferred to it from Fullerton's plane. Gorman's plane, then, would be the one to push on while Fullerton and one of the mechanics tried an overhaul on his engine and waited for a prop and ski.

The prop and ski were fitted to Gorman's plane and it was flown to join the now-disabled second craft on the inlet.

The cargo was sledded over and the plane loaded. Gorman and his passengers climbed on board, the engine started and the plane went speeding along the ice. It lifted and climbed then, at 50 feet, the engine died and the airplane came crashing down.

Those on board were bruised and battered but otherwise okay. This crash, however, had put an end to Gorman's plane and with it — it appeared — to the expedition.

One wing was broken, propeller shattered and undercarriage wrecked.

They were a thousand miles from replacement parts, breakup was coming, and however often pilots and mechanics added up the surviving parts of the two aircraft, they came up short a propeller.

A propeller is a very carefully engineered part of an airplane. Every curve has to be perfect, every line, and it has to be in perfect balance. One iota of fault in any of these things and a propeller can tear itself, or an airplane engine, to pieces with vibration.

The bush flight mechanic is a resourceful man. He can improvise just about anything and patch together just about anything. But not a propeller. That, no one had been able to do so far.

But, the more the two crews looked at the situation, the more it looked as though that was exactly what they would have to do if they were to avoid calling off the expedition and avoid being stranded for months.

At least they had to try. They had the parts of a broken propeller to use for a pattern and they began scouring the resources of the remote trading post for the necessary materials.

The Roman Catholic mission had a workshop they could use and a supply of glue boiled down from moose hoofs. The Hudson's Bay post had oak boards, 10 feet long and about six of seven inches wide. At the post, too, was an expert cabinet-maker named Walter Johnson.

One of the mechanics, Bill Hill, and Johnson gathered these dubious resources together and set to work.

The broken propeller was glued together and a pattern made from it. They cut pieces of tin to match every contour of the original prop. These would be the templates they would follow in making the new one.

Boards were stacked and slightly fanned to give the needed width. The boards were scraped and gouged, glued heavily and clamped together.

Thirty-six hours later, they cut a piece from the end

of the glued assembly and attacked it with hammer and chisel to see if they could force the boards apart. If they could, the assembly wouldn't be strong enough for a prop; if they couldn't, it would be. The glue job held.

So, hour upon hour, the two men carefully worked at the delicate job of carving a propeller. They started with the edge of an axe, moved on to adze, spokeshave, file and finally sandpaper.

In the end, when the new propeller was matched against pattern and templates, it fitted perfectly.

Then came the test of balance. It was hung horizontally on a nail. A mere fraction of an inch out of balance that was soon corrected with careful filing and sandpapering.

There was no varnish at the post, so they gave the prop a coat of red paint. When it dried, the prop was fitted to the patched-together airplane that had been assembled by the others in the crews.

Fullerton started the engine. It and the new prop ran smoothly. He ran the engine up to speed for 30 seconds. The prop was examined again. Still apparently perfect.

Fullerton taxied the plane to one end of a cleared landing area, turned it, taxied as far as he could then gave the plane full power and pulled back on the stick.

The plane climbed smoothly into the air and he kept it aloft long enough for a flight check.

He landed, grinning, and soon everyone was congratulating Hill and Johnson and celebrating the performance of their new red propeller.

There was one pressing concern, however. It was April 23. Break-up was already starting and the plane was fitted with skis. They couldn't risk going on to Fort Norman because the ice on the Mackenzie would be breaking up. In fact, all they would be able to do, if they were lucky, was make a dash back to civilization and hope there was some ice left around to land on.

A good night's rest, they decided, then they would load up and get out while the getting was good.

Before dawn an Indian was at the door of their cabin, pounding and yelling at them to wake up. The ice on the inlet had started to move out.

By the time the party could prepare itself and the plane for take-off, there were only 200 yards of ice left, too little to get into the air with cargo and passengers — if not too little to get into the air at all.

Fullerton climbed into the cockpit with a trapper named Jack Cameron.

Fullerton would get the plane into the air and bring it down on one of the small lakes nearby where the ice was still solid. Cameron would guide him back.

"Sure you want to take the chance?," Fullerton asked the trapper.

"I'm game," Cameron grinned back.

They were down to 100 yards of sticky ice as Fullerton hurled the plane forward for take-off. At the very edge of the open water Fullerton pulled back the stick and the craft, its skis skimming the water, slowly floundered into flight.

Cameron guided Fullerton to the small lake then led him back through the sticky snow to the post. It took the party all day to haul their equipment back to the airplane and load.

They camped overnight on the shore, then took off at first light; deciding in favor of a straight dash to Peace river instead of the longer route from post to post.

Even at that, the fear nagged them all day that there would be no ice left at Peace River no matter how quickly they flew.

The spinning red prop ahead was forgotten, at least for the moment. Besides, it was performing so well, everyone (except, certainly, Bill Hill) may have forgotten its home-made origins.

As they moved south, their worry increased. There was less and less snow. Rivers were opening. Small lakes had islands of thin ice left in their centres. Where would they land?

They decided in favor of Little Bear Lake, a few miles from Peace River, but first they circled over Peace River and dropped a message at the field stating their intentions. Fullerton brought the airplane over the lake with 20 minutes of gas left. Ice had melted out from the shoreline here, as well, but there was no choice left. He had to try it.

He decided to bring the plane down under power and bounce the skis on the ice a few times to test it. That way, if the ice broke under them, they could still get the plane back into the air.

Down they came and bounced, bounced, then bounced again. The ice held. Fullerton cut power, sighed with relief, and landed.

Almost immediately, they heard another plane approaching, bringing them gas and wheels so that they could get to base.

They were surprised to see it was another Junkers. An official from the company had come north to see how well the two planes they had sold had performed.

And when the official saw that bright red propeller ...

To this day, that propeller remains a legend. Anytime a flight mechanic finds himself facing the impossible, he closes his eyes and sees it spinning away. Then he opens his eyes and improvises like hell.

* * * * *

"What time do you want the ruddy beast ready to go?"

—Chris "Limey" Green, air mechanic

* * * *

It was October, 1932, and two brothers, who patrolled line 150 miles north of Edmonton for the army signal corps, returned to their cabin after a day of work.

The Sen brothers, after a day in the cold air, decided to light their stove which they had rigged so that it was fed by line from a nearby pocket of natural gas.

The stove, unknown to them, had sprung a leak and, when they went to light it, it exploded in their faces.

Both were blinded and burned badly about the face, chest, arms and hands. They were critically injured and knew it. Fighting against the pain, one of the brothers used his elbow to tap out a message on the telegraph key, telling headquarters in Edmonton of their situation.

A trapper, who lived nearby and who had rushed over

when he heard the explosion, arrived and, following the directions of the brothers, rigged a telephone onto the line so that he could talk to Edmonton.

The man on the other end of the line was Maj. James Burwash, commanding officer of the corps in Edmonton, and he didn't need much of a description to realize how seriously hurt the brothers were.

But what he also realized, that they didn't yet, was that there was no way to save them.

By 1932, the airplane was already firmly entrenched as the ambulance of the north. Its speed in getting medical help to the injured and in getting the injured out to hospital, had already been demonstrated many times.

But there are two times in the year when the bush plane can't fly. In the bush, the plane has to rely on skis to land on ice or on floats to land on water. During spring break-up and the fall freeze, when rivers and lakes were neither open water nor firm ice, the bush plane was grounded.

And it was fall freeze-up now. Any pilot who tried to land to help the Sens would crack up his airplane and stand a good chance of losing his own life.

Still, Maj. Burwash couldn't just stand by and listen while the two men died. He put out a call for a bush pilot, any bush pilot.

"At least we can talk about it," he decided.

The man who answered his summons wasn't just any bush pilot, he was the youngest and wildest of them all, a man named Grant McConachie.

No account of northern aviation, or of Canadian aviation for that matter, could leave out Grant McConachie. He started out as one of the most reckless of the barn-stormers and ended up as president of CP Air, pioneering that company's service to Australia and the Orient.

He was a visionary, one of the first to see the possibilities of commercial air service in the north and one of the first to pursue it.

Many months ago, while doing research for these books, I was directed to a writer in Vancouver named Ron Keith who had just finished a book on McConachie. It was still unreleased and he let me read it in manuscript. That book, Bush Pilot with a Briefcase, is one of the best and most compelling ever written about Canadian aviation.

It was in the manuscript for this book that I first saw

the story of our second "propeller" and of what followed McConachie's meeting with Maj. Burwash that night.

There wasn't enough ice to land on any of the rivers or lakes near the Sen cabin; the trapper confirmed that.

Then what about beach space? McConachie asked. No, the trapper replied, bush right to the edge of the water.

McConachie was dogged. Wasn't there, anywhere nearby, a lake with some kind of beach space?

It seemed there was, 10 miles from the cabin. It wasn't much of a beach but water was low at this time of year and there might be enough level area to get a plane down.

McConachie outlined his scheme to the major. He had a plane, a Fokker he used on the barn-storming circuit, sitting in a hangar nearby. It was still on wheels.

Get him a doctor and medical supplies, get the trapper to move the Sens to the lake and light a smoky fire to define wind direction, and he and his mechanic would go in.

If they banged up the plane on landing, well, the doctor was there for the Sens and the whole party could just sit it out until enough ice formed to send in a ski-equipped plane for them.

Burwash considered. There was no way he was going to risk a doctor on a hair-brained borderline expedition like this. But he would get a doctor to instruct McConachie on what to do and provide him with the needed medical supplies.

If McConachie and his mechanic wanted to risk it on that basis, fine and thank you — even if it does sound insane.

McConachie got on the improvised telephone and gave the trapper the instructions. Get them over there at daybreak, he said, and make sure that fire gives enough smoke.

The trapper promised to follow instructions.

At dawn the next day, McConachie's mechanic, Limey Green, climbed into the enclosed "cabin" inside the fuselage of the Fokker and listened as McConachie, in the open cockpit ahead of him, ran up the engine and taxied out for take-off. Inside the cabin, already lashed firmly to the floor, was a box of medical supplies. Not that the Sens were likely to get the benefit of them, as Limey gloomily saw it.

As the plane gained speed and lifted into the air, he considered the major drawback to McConachie's scheme, a drawback the 23-year-old pilot hadn't mentioned to Burwash the night before, but that he had been considering ever since.

The wood-and-canvas Fokker was a beautifully responsive flying machine. It moved along with the greatest of ease. Stopping, however, was another matter.

It had no wheel brakes. Instead, it had a tail hook that was supposed to catch in the ground on landing and drag the plane to a halt. On frozen beach and shore ice, that hook would simply skid along the surface.

The lack of wheel brakes also posed a problem in steering. In the air and during the early stages of a landing, a plane is moving quickly enough to be guided around by its rudder. But as speed drops, the rudder becomes ineffective and the pilot steers by touching one or the other or both of the wheel brakes.

If and when the Fokker slowed below the point of rudder response, it was going to go where it wanted, which might possibly not be where McConachie or Green wanted.

These problems, McConachie decided, would solve themselves. He was a superb pilot and he knew it. He was also a superbly confident man. Even if they piled up he was sure he and Limey and that precious box of medicine would get through unharmed.

Limey may or may not have shared these optimistic visions, but at least he was along and that was what counted.

McConachie spotted the lake and glided down towards it.

"It was a big lake covered with thin ice," he recalled later. "I could see the trapper's cabin and the three men on the shore.

"The shore line, which appeared to be clear of obstructions, was frozen marsh overgrown with bullrushes, and there was a narrow margin of sand, just enough for one wheel, between the overgrowth and the lake ice. I figured if I could set one wheel down along that sand margin, the other on the flat shore ice, there was just enough room for the wing tip to clear the trees. Nothing to spare, though.

"The trapper had followed my instructions and had a fire going so the smoke would give me the wind direction, but he got a little overenthusiastic and there was so much smoke that it blinded me completely as I flew in low over the beach on the landing approach.

"After two attempts I had to give up that idea and decided that, instead of landing into the wind, which is normal so the head-wind will give you the slowest possible ground speed, I would have to try a landing down-wind. This, of course, stacked the odds higher against me because the wind would be pushing me along faster instead of acting as an air brake.

"However, there was no choice, so I had to rely on my experience with this particular aircraft to bring it in at the lowest possible airspeed. It was like treading an invisible tightrope. Just a shade slower and I knew the plane would stall and drop from the sky out of control. I kept the nose high, with a lot of power on, so we were actually wallowing down through the air in a power stall, practically hanging on the propeller.

"Then, just as the wheels were rattling over the first of the bullrushes on the shore, I chopped back the throttle completely. I cut the ignition switches to minimize the danger of fire if we cracked up, and pulled the control column full back to complete the stall and uttered a small prayer.

"It was pretty rough as we plopped down into those bullrushes. I thought the first impact would drive the undercart right up through the floor. Then we bounced and jolted along the beach. There was a frightful moment when I thought we would keep on going right through the trapper's cabin. Without brakes, and with the tail-skid hook dragging uselessly on the rock-hard surface, there was nothing I could do to slow the landing run. Luckily, we rolled right up to the door of the cabin and came to a stop almost beside the bug-eyed trapper and his two patients."

McConachie saw immediately that the Sen brothers were in very bad shape. As Limey began inspecting the plane for damage, McConachie pulled out the box of lotions and ointments and bandages and began giving the injured men first-aid.

But he could see from their condition that, if he waited for the lake to freeze before he took off again, they would both die.

He asked Limey for the results of the inspection. Visibly, Limey told him, the only damage was that the fabric underbelly of the plane was split from end to end, apparently from passing over the stake of an otter trap on the beach.

Limey began sewing and McConachie turned his mind to the problem of taking off along the beach.

Again the lack of wheel brakes faced him. Without them, there was no way to hold the plane back and push up to full throttle and make a short take-off. The Fokker was built to run along, gaining speed, until it was going fast enough to become airborne. There wasn't room enough for that on this beach.

Finally he found the solution:

"We hauled the aircraft back as far as we could up a slight slope and tied the tail to a tree, running the rope over a stump we could use as a chopping block. I told the trapper to stand by with his axe while I ran up the engine to full power, then to chop the rope when I waved my hand.

"Meanwhile Chris had loaded the heavily bandaged patients into the cabin and made them as secure and as comfortable as he could.

"We were taking off into the wind, and I figured that with the down-slope and starting with full power we had a good chance of making it. I pushed the throttle wide open, waited for the engine to pick up full revs, then gave the signal. The trapper swung his axe, the rope parted and away we went rumbling through the bullrushes.

"With full power from the start, the blast of the slip-stream over the rudder gave me full control, so it was not too difficult to thread the needle of the narrow beach between the trees and the lake. We didn't seem to hit any obstructions, but suddenly, just before the wheels left the ground, there was the most terrible vibration. I thought it would shake the plane to pieces.

"I throttled back as much as I dared but by this time there was no other choice. We had to either take off or crash, so I manoeuvred the Fokker out over the lake, just skimming over the tree tops, figuring it was better to crash through the ice than into the trees if we had to go in.

"The shuddering continued. It increased when I put on

more power, diminishing as I pulled the throttle back, but I couldn't figure out what it was. The engine seemed to be working all right. Chris couldn't find any damage to the fuselage. However, we were able to gain some altitude and continue the flight."

To the worried McConachie and to his agonized patients, the trip back to Edmonton seemed endless. But finally they landed and the Sen brothers were whisked away in waiting ambulances.

Reporters and photographers who had got wind of the flight were also waiting. Under normal circumstances, McConachie was a man who didn't mind a little publicity, but on this occasion he forgot all about the newsmen as soon as a pale Chris Green called him around to the front of the aircraft and pointed at the propeller.

It was split in two, end to end. All that was holding it together, and all that had kept it from flying off the shaft during the flight, was a thin metal strip. Possibly aided by the kind of luck that rewards those who perform the impossible.

* * * *

"Well, I'm glad if I've made some contribution to the development of the country and to the welfare of the people who live and work in the north country."

—Punch Dickins

* * * *

Grant McConachie, for all he represented the epitome of the skill and daring and "What the hell, let's give it a try" breed of bush flier, was much more important in the end as a visionary.

His conviction that the airplane had an important, commercial role to play in the north led to the development of an industry and played a large part in making it possible

for people to live normal lives in country where they would otherwise perish.

Clennell H. "Punch" Dickins is another kind of visionary and, though his appraoch to flying was the opposite of McConachie's, he, too, pursued a vision into aviation history.

And, as McConachie himself would gladly yield in later years, Punch Dickins was "the" pioneer flier of the north.

Columnist Jim Coleman once wrote of Dickins that he is "as modest and unassuming a gent as ever pulled on leather helmet and goggles."

That holds true even today. Whether sitting over coffee in his Victoria apartment or standing at the podium making one of his few public speeches, Dickins is a hard man to get to talk about himself.

He has, for example, never told the story of how he won the Distinguished Flying Cross during the First World War.

"The war is over," he says and quickly changes the subject.

But a quick glance through the headlines of the past half-century gives some idea of his place in aviation history:

"*DICKINS TOOK LIFE IN HANDS FLYING TO WATERWAYS AFTER HIS PLANE HAD BEEN DAMAGED . . . DICKINS FLIES 74,630 MILES IN SINGLE YEAR'S PIONEERING OVER BLEAK NORTHERN TRAILS . . . FLIES INJURED MAN HERE: HAZARDOUS MERCY FLIGHT . . . PUNCH DICKINS BRINGS BACK GREAT DAYS OF BUSH FLYING . . . DICKINS AWARDED O.B.E. . . .*"

And what the headlines don't add is the part he played in development of great bush planes like the Beaver and Otter. Or the many flight-safety practices that he created.

It was Dickins who pioneered the northern pilot's rule that you always carry enough emergency equipment and food to feed and shelter those on board in the event of a forced landing.

The first emergency radio to go into the air in the north went in Dickins' plane.

And for all the risks he took on his many flights he had only one minor crash in his whole career.

Dickins has earned many names for himself during his flying career, "Snow Eagle," "White Eagle," "Flying Knight of the Northland" and (in Greece) "Ponts Ntikins."

The "Punch" he earned as a child when an aunt described him as a "fat little punch."

Like virtually all the early bush pilots, Dickins learned to fly during the First World War.

He was 17, with one year of university behind him, when he left Edmonton to fight in France. There, in combat, he listed seven kills and won his unexplained DFC.

In the years that followed, his aerial survey flights filled in the map of the north. He set off on search flights that routinely carried him to the North Pole and back.

He was the pilot for the expedition that discovered the huge uranium deposits on Great Bear Lake.

It was during this period that Punch Dickins had his vision and decided to pursue it.

His vision was a simple one by today's standards: air mail for the north.

At the time his idea was generally considered extravagant and impractical.

Dickins felt otherwise. He had already pioneered air mail flights across the prairies and he knew, from personal experience, what was involved in extending it to the north.

He also knew better than most what the mail means to those in the north. When you live a thousand miles back in the bush, with no normal contact with the outside world, mail becomes as precious as gold. To get it only once or twice a year is simply not enough and Dickins saw that.

In 1924 he prepared a report on the feasibility of the idea, but the postal department was unmoved. He refused to give up the idea and used every opportunity to badger the post office to try it.

Finally, in 1929, the post office relented and a test-flight was authorized.

Dickins set off on the flight in January, 1929. On board his Fokker with him were his engineer, Lew Parmenter, postal inspector T. J. Reilly and Fred Lundy of Western Canada Airways.

They were in the air only 20 minutes when ice particles in the carburetor caused engine trouble and they had to turn back.

It took two days in Edmonton to remedy the fault, then they set off again. They were forced by a blizzard to land at Lac la Biche, only half-way to the first day's goal of Fort McMurray. The next day they took off again and made it to McMurray.

Lundy left the party and remained at McMurray to set up a company base.

Dickins prepared to set out again. The journey from this point on, he knew, would be the real test of the experiment and he laid his plans carefully.

From post to tiny post they flew, leaving precious mail for the residents and picking up the letters they had written. Word of the flight had been radioed ahead and, in every settlement, there was an enthusiastic crowd waiting.

Fort Chipewyan was the first, then on to Fort Smith. Fort Fitzgerald, only 16 miles from Smith, was to be saved for the trip back as they were to pick up a heavy cargo of furs there before again touching down at Smith.

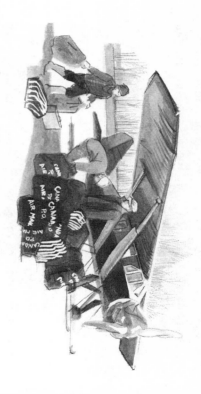

But at Fort Smith, Dickins characteristic caution changed the plan.

The river level had dropped early in the freeze and the surface of the ice was dangerously rough.

After bumping in for a landing, Dickins turned to Parmenter: "*I think this calls for a change of plans,*" he commented. "*We're to bring back a heavy cargo of furs and I wouldn't want to land on this with a loaded plane. Better go to Fitzgerald now and miss them both on the way back.*"

The decision made, they took to the air for Fort Fitzgerald. But the ice there looked even worse.

"*I'm not going to take the chance,*" Dickins decided. "*It will put airmail back 10 years if we crash.*"

So they flew on to Fort Resolution on Great Slave Lake. There, Reilly stayed to handle some post office business.

Dickins and Parmenter pushed on, fighting through snow and fog to Hay River, Fort Providence and, finally, Fort Simpson.

It was time for the return journey and they took to the air again with a heavy cargo of fur and mail. Their first stop on the way back would be Fort Resolution.

The wind was blowing snow across the ice there and, unseen by Dickins, piling it into hummocks.

Landing, the Fokker struck one of these and the undercarriage buckled. As the plane pitched forward the propeller struck the ice and twisted and bent.

There on the ice Dickins and Parmenter stood and gloomily surveyed our third propeller.

They had no spare parts and no radio communications at Resolution. An Indian set out by dogsled for Fort Smith, where there was a radio, with an appeal for a flight with the needed parts.

Dickins watched the Indian leave and knew it would be a long time before any spare parts could arrive. He was driven by a sense of urgency; this was what he meant by the comment that a crash could set northern airmail service back a decade.

Like the builders of the red propeller, Dickins and Parmenter scoured the post in the hope of finding some way to get the plane flying again.

At the Roman Catholic mission, they found a piece of waterpipe that, on inspection, proved good enough to make the needed repairs to the undercarriage.

But what about the propeller?

They stood, at 40 below zero, and examined it. One tip was bent. Carefully they bent it back, hopefully to its original configuration.

The other blade was a serious problem. It was curled around and they lacked the proper tools to straighten it.

"Well, we have nothing to lose, so let's give it a try," Parmenter said. Dickins nodded and they slowly started to pull the blade around.

The metal was strained and brittle with cold and, though they pulled gently, it snapped under their gloves, leaving the blade nine inches shorter than the other.

When their initial dismay passed, Dickins asked: "Do you think the old bus would fly if we cut off the other end to match the broken one?"

Parmenter lifted his shoulders. "Again we have nothing to lose," he answered.

So they started to saw. It took five days of work in the bitter cold before the two ends matched.

The other repairs finished, Dickins taxied the plane out for a test. He built speed, everything seemed okay, so he added speed and the plane lifted easily into the air.

The plane flew, but Dickins and Parmenter didn't want to risk an attempt to fly out fully loaded and lacking those nine inches on either end of the propeller.

They took off empty and headed to Smith, arriving only a day later than the Indian they had sent out with the message. From Smith they flew to McMurray where a new plane was waiting for them.

With it they returned to Resolution and picked up the cargo of mail and furs, then completed the historic experiment.

Confronted by Dickins and by his shrinking propeller, the post office had to admit that, with these kind of men and machines around, airmail might just work in the north after all.

Regular service started with the Christmas flight of 1929. Dickins returned to his "ordinary" work. Like making the "ordinary" first flight down the length of the Mackenzie to the Arctic Ocean. Or the "ordinary" year when he piled up that record 74,630 miles of travelling.

In the introduction to this section we mentioned Wop May flying the mayor of Edmonton under the low-level bridge.

Well, Dickins once landed on the river by going under the high-level bridge.

"It wasn't for the thrill", he explains. "It was a necessity. When I take a plane up it's purely for business."

Grant McConachie once said Punch Dickins has piled up enough "firsts" to fill an airplane.

That's the plane Dickins takes up "purely for business."

* * *

* * * *

"Welcome to northern Alberta." — A PWA STEWARDESS

The old-time bush pilots like to say that the real "bush-flying era" ended with the Second World War when proper landing strips and facilities were built in the north.

But the truth is that it still goes on and on. Float planes still wag their wings as they come into Chipewyan from

a flight into the barren-lands. Young men in red baseball caps still fly deep into the Arctic in small planes.

And if Pacific Western Airlines now flies jets into Mc-Murray and big turbo-prop Electras into Chipewyan, there is still a special "bush-flying" feel to that service.

Like the day the southbound Electra was delayed by engine trouble and the passengers waiting at Chipewyan groaned as the loudspeaker in the airport announced it would be yet another "30 minutes" before the plane arrived there.

"You know what PWA stands for up here?" one regular passenger asked. "It stands for Please Wait Awhile."

But when the drone of the Electra was finally heard, he smiled and added: *"To tell you the truth, the waiting is worth it."*

On board and airborne, the passengers settled back and watched the stewardess pour out cups of coffe and load them onto a tray.

The plane hit an airpocket and dropped. So did the coffee, all over the stewardess and the floor.

She sighed and wiped at the front of her uniform. "Welcome to northern Alberta," she grumbled.

Then she grinned broadly and poured fresh coffee for everyone.

TAMERS

*"As the weather begins to be cold we have taken our vege-
tables out of the ground, which we find to have been very
productive."*

— DANIEL WILLIAMS HARMON.

* * *

* * *

"Thursday, October 10. This day, a Canadian's daughter,
a girl of about fourteen years of age, was offered me; and
after mature consideration, concerning the step which I
ought to take, i have finally concluded to accept her, as
it is customary for all gentlemen who remain, for any length
of time, in this part of the world, to have a female companion, with whom they can pass their time more socially
and agreeably, than to live a lonely life, as they must do,
if single.

"If we can live in harmony together, my intention now
is, to keep her as long as I remain in this uncivilized part
of the world; and when I return to my native land, I shall
endeavour to place her under the protection of some honest
man, with whom she can pass the remainder of her days
in this country, much more agreeably than it would be
possible for her to do, were she to be taken down into

the civilized world, to the manners, customs and language of which, she would be an entire stranger.

"Her mother is of the tribe of the Snake Indians, whose country lies along the Rocky Mountain. The girl is said to have a mild disposition and an even temper, which are qualities very necessary to make an agreeable woman, and an affectionate partner."

The man who penned that entry in his diary in 1806 was a trader named Daniel William Harmon and the arrangement he was entering was, if immoral, the common one of the north. A man took an Indian or half-breed girl and kept her until he tired of her or until — as Harmon proposed — it came time to leave the country and return to civilization.

The woman herself recognized her status as being little more than a chattel and accepted it. As hard a life as it may be, such an arrangement was at least a little less hard than the life she would find by remaining among her own people.

The girl whom Harmon "accepted" crops up from time to time in his faithfully-kept diary.

On Feb. 25, 1810, for instance, he wrote: *"On the evening of the 15th inst. my woman was delivered of two living boys. They appear, however, to have been prematurely born; and from the first, little hope was entertained that they would long survive."*

The woman remained at his side all through his years in the north. She cooked for him, cleaned for him, bore him other children. As was the way of this savage wilderness some of them lived and some of them died.

In 1819, 13 years after he had taken in the girl, the time for him to leave to return to civilization and to live up to the promise he made himself "to endeavour to place her under the protection of some honest man."

Instead, however, he sat down to make the following entry in his diary:

"My intention is, during the next summer, to visit my native land. The mother of my children will accompany me; and, if she shall be satisfied to remain in that part of the world, I design to make her regularly my wife by a formal marriage. It will be seen by this remark, that my intentions have materially changed, since the time that I first took her to live with me.

"Having lived with this woman as my wife, though we were never formally contracted to each other, during life, and having children by her, I consider that I am under a moral obligation not to dissolve the connexion, if she is willing to continue it.

"The union which has been formed between us, in the providence of God, has not only been cemented by a long and mutual performance of kind offices, but, also, by a more sacred consideration.

"We have wept together over the early departure of several children, and especially, over the death of a beloved son. We have children still living, who are equally dear to us both."

A story with a loving ending … and, still, it is more than that. Of all the recorded incidents of that period in our northern history, it seems to be the one that best illustrates a subtle change that was taking place.

The white man had come to exploit the north and its people and, having accomplished that, leave them. But, as Harmon discovered, in a wilderness a man may discover ways to meet deeper needs.

Traders like Harmon were discovering other things as well. Along the Peace, and especially on the flat prairies north of it, the soil was rich and if you had cleared a bit of it, and planted things in it, those things grew, and grew marvellously well.

Even among fur traders there were men who considered the significance of this.

But, even as they were considering it, history was mixing together the ingredients of a new age that would outrace their dreams. It would take fire, gold, war, the scream of a steam-whistle and the drone of an airplane propeller, but the north was about to be hurled into the 20th century.

* * * *

"Cheeseburger Deluxe (served with tomato, onion, relish and a generous side-order of golden French fries) ... $1.25."
— FROM A MENU IN FORT CHIPEWYAN

* * * *

In many ways, Fort Chipewyan looks like what it once was: the hub of the fur trade in the northwest. The Hudson's Bay Company is still there. So is the old school established by French-speaking missionaries. Sled dogs sprawl and doze in the summer sun.

But it is only an illusion. The Bay post carries popsicles. The mission school has a truck parked outside its door. And the sled dogs don't face a winter of work, but a winter of racing.

On the steep shore, where voyageurs once patched birchbark canoes, a mechanic in orange overalls is tuning a helicopter engine.

There is a hotel and restaurants where fresh milk, flown in from Edmonton that morning, is poured over brand-name breakfast flakes.

Jukeboxes brawl out the latest and loudest hits. There are electricity and telephones and, to complete the disillusionment, the contrail of a jet overhead.

Fort Chipewyan's curious mixture of present and past

is, in many senses, the mixture of the whole northern part of Alberta.

The 20th Century came rushing in so quickly that it had — and still has — a little trouble catching up with itself.

What happened? What took place between the day Harmon stood contemplating a handful of soil and the day of the northern Alberta we know?

The first change was fairly subtle and not that uncommon wherever the fur trade was practised. A few white men decided that, if the Indians could trap fur to sell, so could they.

They set up trap lines and, with the instincts of their settled backgrounds, made themselves a base — a home — from which to operate. Initially, if anyone had suggested to those men that their rude, thrown-together shanties were homes, they'd have thrown their heads back and hooted with laughter. These shacks were no more than minimal

shelter and a place to keep a few rags of clothes and a little gunpowder dry.

But gradually the shanties became more sophisticated — and more permanent. And, it should be noted, the areas of land they hunted and trapped became more permanent as well.

The white man's sense of property is far different from that of the Indian.

The Hudson's Bay Company itself, in the process of solving its supply problems, unconsciously and unintentionally played its part in thrusting northern Alberta into the modern age. The company began to organize and refine its methods of river travel and the process would lead to steam boats plying the northern rivers and lakes and to a barge service that still handles the bulk of the freight that moves in and out of the north.

Then there was gold, a tiny sparkle in 1870 and a broad, tragic gleam in 1898, to bring people into the north by the thousands.

And, in 1894, there was fire. It began with a careless campfire and spread to wipe out the forest barrier that had, up to then, separated the north from civilization . . .

* * * *

"It was that darned two set me wrong."
— HENRY FULLER (12-foot) DAVIS

* * * *

Henry Fuller Davis was one of those men who decided to take the personal approach to the fur-trapping business. But he went one step farther. He was also one of the men who decided to take the personal approach to the gold-seeking business. And went one step farther.

It was the combination of these two extra steps that earned him his place in the history of the west.

The first time anyone hears the name 12-foot Davis, there always comes with it the vision of a great physical giant of a man.

It is a little disillusioning to find out that Davis was actually quite short and far from physically imposing.

But his stock goes up again quickly when one learns how he did earn his name: through a combination of sharp eyes and sharper wits that still reminds miners everywhere to double-check their measurements.

There are many versions of the story about how Davis acquired his legendary nickname. The one that is probably most accurate is that told to a Peace River pioneer by Peace River Jim Cornwall, a contemporary of Davis and a legend in his own right.

The pioneer was a passenger on the river boat of which Cornwall was captain:

"It was on this trip," he writes, "that Jim Cornwall told me all he knew about a man who he said went under the name of Twelve Foot Davis and explained to me that this man Davis had been a prospector and had wandered into the Cariboo, and knowing his stuff started measuring out claims as permitted by the government of B.C. from the Discovery stake (the stake from which all other measurements of claims are made), and located a 12-foot strip of overlapping ground that adjoined the Guggenheim interests.

"In the ensuing argument the government had sent out one of their qualified engineers who ruled that Davis was entitled to the 12-foot strip, which was, according to Cornwall, taken over by the Guggenheims for some thousands of dollars.

"Davis then hightailed it over the mountains . . ."

The story of Davis' 12-foot claim spread all over the north and followed him as, over a period of time, he made his way to settle in the Peace River country.

The story generated a great deal of admiration for Davis. At the same time, however, it also generated some distrust and resentment of him as a man who was a little too slippery for other people's good.

From this mixed reaction grew most of the confusion that surrounds the history of the man.

There are those who pictured him as a cruel and brutal man who drove a train of Chinese coolies back and forth through the north like packhorses, carrying furs and trade goods for Davis to sell. In these stories Davis is always unscrupulous and quick to take financial advantage of the unwary.

On the other hand, such a well-informed historian as J. G. MacGregor pictures him as one of the better and bigger-hearted citizens of the north.

"Like all men in lonely places," he writes, "where each enters into the joys and sorrows of his few neighbors, Davis too was blessed with much of the milk of human kindness."

MacGregor and others paint a picture of Davis as a short, wiry man, totally illiterate and a thoroughly addicted chewer of tobacco.

Far from being a man who used others as beasts of burden, they note, he habitually carried 200 pounds on his own back — twice as much as he asked anyone who worked for him to carry.

And the description of him given by MacGregor offsets any rumors that Davis was a man to take advantage of others:

"Many a traveller and pioneer had reason to bless the hard-bitten old tobacco-chewing trader for his open-handedness and for his ever open door. They blessed him, too, for his pumpkin pies. For a short period during his youth he had been a pastry cook in Boston.

"At Dunvegan he applied his old-time skill to the pumpkins grown in the mission garden there; the result was lauded up and down the Peace River as 'Davis' Pumpkin Pies.'"

On one occasion, Davis' generosity combined with his illiteracy to create a storyteller's delight.

It was New Year, 1892, and Davis was alone is his post at Hudson Hope. A servant showed up with a message from the manager of the nearby Hudson's Bay post.

Davis was in a quandry. The servant couldn't read and neither could he — though he wasn't about to admit that to the servant.

So Davis squinted wisely at the writing on the page. The only character he could identify on it was the figure 2.

Davis reasoned that the only reason anyone would write anyone else in the north was because something was seriously wrong. He concluded the manager must be sick. His unfailing remedy for sickness was whiskey. People might not get better on it, but they sure felt better on it.

So he wrapped two bottles and sent them along with the servant to deliver to the Hudson's Bay manager with his hopes for a speedy recovery.

It wasn't until one of his partners returned to read the letter for him that Davis learned it had only been a routine invitation to dinner — not an appeal for Davis' precious whiskey.

"It was that darned two set me wrong," he lamented every time someone brought up — as they frequently did — the story of his mission of mercy.

Was Davis a good man or a bad one? After the years that have passed, it is hard to know for sure. But it is tempting to believe in the verdict that Davis finally passed on himself.

In 1900, after being blind and sickly for five years, Davis was on his death bed. He was asked by a friend, an Anglican sister, if he were afraid to die.

"No, miss," he replied, "why should I be afraid to die? I never killed nobody, I never stole from nobody, I never wilfully harmed nobody and I always kept open-house for all travellers all my life.

"No, miss, I ain't afraid to die!"

* * * *

"By fall the land was beautiful again, that is, beautiful under the circumstances."

— J. G. MacGregor

In 1893, the railroad reached Edmonton and tied it firmly to the rest of Canada. But north of Edmonton, all was still wilderness. It was a wilderness that was attracting settlers, but only in small numbers because only the most

hardy could brave the long, difficult path called the Athabasca Trail.

That trail, carved with great difficulty and even greater
disregard for comfort, led far north through the forest

barrier to the Peace River country and the rich prairie waiting to be turned into propserous farms. Those who had the strength to complete the journey usually found the rigors of the trail were exceeded only by the rigors of taming the land and by the difficulties and expense of surviving in the tiny settlements of the north.

The hardships of the trail persisted well into this century and are vividly painted by the wife of a young telegraph operator named Gauvreau who made the trip only three years before the First World War.

"In early September, 1911," she writes, "we journeyed into the Peace River country from Edmonton. We were picked up by the government lineman, driving a team of horses and a democrat.

"All we could bring with us was a bedroll, a grub box, a small trunk of personal belongings. I had two kittens in a shoe box I was taking with me for company.

"We drove up to the Edmonton Journal Building, and all came out to wish us luck on our long, hard, treacherous journey. It was a beautiful, warm sunny day, and I was so excited, everything was so new to me.

"Pierre (her husband) was born and raised in Edmonton, and was anxious to get away from the city.

"Later the next day the Edmonton Journal came out with headlines 'Sturdy Telegraph Operator and young wife going into the cold, north unsettled Peace River Country.'

"We drove from Edmonton to Athabasca Landing, 90 miles, took us three days, we camped in the open, made a campfire and cooked our meals.

"We had to lay over in Athabasca Landing for three days, but we were comfortable, stayed at the Dominion Telegraph office with Mr. and Mrs. McKernan, telegraph operator.

"Then we went by boat up the Athabasca River to Mirror

Landing, 75 miles. A wagon portage of 16 miles to Salteau Landing brought us to the river, and lake boat — which wormed its tortuous and slow way up the Little Slave River to Sawridge, 50 miles at the outlet of Lesser Slave Lake — then across 75 miles of lake to what was then known as Lesser Slave Lake settlement (now Grouard).

"The last lap of 85 miles from there to Peace River Crossing was made by team and took four days — that was the toughest part of the journey, just one big mud hole. It was bog the whole distance owing to such heavy bush that it never dried out.

"Pierre came in to take charge of the Dominion Government Telegraphs, the terminus of that time of the only means of communication from far out posts to what was generally termed the civilized world.

"The Peace River Country at that time was a land of very few settlers, a few trading posts, Indians, half-breeds, and an occasional traveller.

"Everything was very high priced — $2.50 for a dozen eggs, $9.00 for 100 lbs of flour, $12.00 for 100 lbs of sugar, $1.70 for butter, and only wild meat.

"Peace River Crossing had only a few buildings and the main street was only a narrow wagon road with brush piled on the sides. Natives and Indians living in teepees were lined along the road.

"Our home was a two storey log building owned by John Wright, a kindly old man but a dirty bachelor. A native girl told me one day 'Old John is sick, he has a cold. He must have washed his face or changed his underwear.' For sure, he wore the same clothes week in, week out, day and night. He lived in the kitchen, which was a lean-to to the house built on after the government rented the place for the government telegraph office.

"Our part was a big living-dining room-kitchen all in

one, a bed room, and the front part was the office. We had home-made furniture, benches and table. The bed was boards, nailed together and on stilts. Was is ever a cold place!

"The telegraph instruments were on a large packing box, and a big iron stove to heat the house.

"It was a hard, cold winter, 72 below. The people that had to take horses out had to blanket them and put chest pads on. One would often see horses bleed from the nose, and sometimes drop dead in harness."

That is the way it was in 1911, in the 20th Century. In 1893, it was much worse and most people felt that the country of the Peace was never going to be properly settled, let alone civilized. But for carelessness and fate, they might have been right.

The trouble with the Peace River country, as even its most enthusiastic boosters admitted, was that it was too darn far away. The normal course of settlement would have been a steady development northward from Edmonton. But there was a barrier of forest wilderness, never less than 200 miles deep, in the way. So the prospective farmer had to think in terms of cutting and clearing — which didn't appeal to many — or in terms of taking his chances beyond the barrier — which didn't appeal to many either.

Then, in 1894, on the far, northwest edge of the forest barrier, someone let a campfire run wild. It was late summer, the forest was bone dry, most of the streams dried up, and the fire swept south and east like an explosion.

"This was the great fire of 1894," writes J. G. MacGregor. "Seen from a distance, it showed as a cloud of greyish black smoke. At night, it appeared as an ominous red glow in the northern sky. Near at hand, it presented a magnificent but terrifying spectacle. After the main fire had passed, there remained blackened hillsides and smoking stumps. Even these were beautiful at night. The darkness of night hid the devastation, and the first night after the fire made a thing of beauty out of the scarred stumps and tree-trunks that were left standing. For each was still burning in various places up and down the blackened trunk. What had once been a forest was now a circle of torches, tall and short, their flames flickering in the breeze. Occasionally the flames would burn through a tall trunk and the upper twenty feet would crash to the ground in a sea of sparks that flared for a while and died out as they passed down the wind. It was beautiful but tragic."

The sense of tragedy passed, however. It didn't take long to realize that the fire had done an incredible service to the north. It had cleared, in a few days, land it would have taken settlers years of toil to get access to in a normal way.

The flow of people northward became stronger and stronger. Within a few years, the prospect of the north was so enticing that it was even attracting speculators, who filled Edmonton papers with lavish — and often improbable — advertisements.

The speculators were not known for always sticking strictly to the truth and one of the most popular jokes in Edmonton became that about an oldtimer who went north to Peace River to examine the land he had bought from a speculator.

"Did you get a chance to stand on your land?" a friend asked him when he returned.

"No," the man replied ruefully, "but I leaned against it for a while."

* * * *

"Due north, Dawson City; starvation and death. Due south, Home Sweet Home and a warm bed."

— A SIGN ON THE KLONDIKE TRAIL.

* * * *

Even today, after close to a century has passed, it is hard to know whether to regard the gold rushes of the 1890's as tragedies or Godsends for northern Alberta.

Certainly they turned Edmonton from a quiet town of 2,000 into a major city. And certainly they left behind many who could not reach the Klondike to settle the sparse settlements of the Peace River country.

But when you consider that of the 2,000 people who set north from Edmonton in the rush of '98, less than two per cent made it to the Klondike, and consider that many of those who failed also lost their lives, the story of the rushes begin to take on the atmosphere of tragedy.

The Overlanders, in 1892, wrote the lessons for those among the people who came after that had sense enough to learn it. The Overlanders, hundreds strong, set out from Ontario on the touted "overland" route to the goldfields. All but a handful of those who passed Edmonton died in the Rockies and the few who made it arrived in the Klondike after the rush had ended.

By 1893, however, rail had reached Edmonton and its benefits were touted and exaggerated beyond all reason. Growing numbers of would-be gold seekers fell for the advertisements that urged them to get to the Yukon by way of Edmonton instead of using the longer but surer sea route up the west coast of the United States.

"Edmonton, the back door to the Yukon," the advertisements said. What they didn't say was that the Yukon lay close to 2,000 miles of wilderness and muskeg away from that back door.

From 1895 through 1898, in growing numbers, prospectors poured through Edmonton and headed north. Some of them got no farther than the outskirts of town where a glimpse of the wilderness that awaited was enough to make them turn back. Others pushed along the Athabasca Trail.

Beyond Athabasca Landing, those (about half) who chose the MacKenzie River faced the Grand Rapids and, if they hadn't the sense to portage around them, almost certain death. If they survived that, other rapids waited before Fort McMurray to take their toll. Those who chose the Athabasca River route into the Peace River country fared a little better, but not much.

And, in the end, all had to face the mountains and

wilderness and deadly winters in the interior of British Columbia.

The rushes provided occasional funny moments, like those given by some of the vehicles designed to overcome the hardships of the trail. One was a steam-powered sled constructed vaguely along the lines of a modern steamroller, its main drum studded with spikes. It was called the "I will" until it dug its own grave in the mud a hundred yards into its maiden voyage and became the "I didn't."

Another was called "The Duck." Constructed along the lines of modern soft-terrain vehicles, it used huge wine barrels on axles for wheels to support it on muskeg. It made it three miles north of Edmonton before the rocks and washboard trail battered it to pieces.

Apart from the prospective settlers brought into the north, the rushes created demands for transportation that hastened the coming of rail and that created a steamboat industry on the northern rivers and lakes. They also provided much of the demand that gave the northern barge system the strength it carried into the modern day.

The rushes even led to the first attempt to push a modern road through to the Yukon. Cut by Mounties and hired crews from 1896 onward, the eight-foot-wide swath stretched to the middle of British Columbia before the rush for gold died and the project with it.

In truth, the itch of gold is still there and there are those who scratch at it in the north. Today, though, they no longer rely on trails and steamboats and footpower to reach the northern wilderness.

Instead, they reach it suspended on the wings that, more than any other single development, carried northern Alberta into this century . . . .

*   *   *

*   *

PEOPLE

"Pioneer, trader and pathfinder, he was every man's friend and never locked his cabin door."

— P. R. GAUVREAU

* * * *

Much has been said about the people and characters of northern Alberta. A lot has been impossible, improbable or just downright false.

All the same, the idea that the people in the northern part of our province are a little different from anyone else persists. And maybe it should persist.

The demands of the north do have their effect on the people who go there. It takes an adventurer, still, to take on the north country and it takes a particular blend of courage and stubborness to stick it out.

What is the truth about the people who opened the north and who live there?

The answer to that question, fortunately, is a matter of history.

Earlier in this book, we mentioned the experiences of the wife of a telegrapher named Gauvreau and her first impressions of the Peace River country. It is time to turn to Gauvreau himself.

The Gauvreaus came into the north from Edmonton in 1911, eventually settling at Peace River. Over the years, Gauvreau managed to make the acquaintance of nearly everyone — notorious or otherwise — in the remote reaches of the province.

Fortunately for us, Gauvreau not only knew these people, he wrote about them. In his later years he became a regular contributor to a host of magazines and newspapers, pouring out thousands of words about the people and tales (often tall) of the north.

The largest and most important body of his work, though, never was published. Hundreds of pages long and tracing his life from childhood on, it rests in the provincial archives in Edmonton in a box simply labelled "Gauvreau Papers."

This is no place for a major "expedition" into those papers, but it is a good place for a "hike," at least, along a trail where you can meet the characters, good and bad, who made the north what it is.

"When I left Edmonton," Gauvreau writes, "it was with team and democrat, a bedroll, grub-box and a couple of trunks.

"It took me three days to get to Athabasca Landing; hung around there a couple of days, then caught the steamer upstream on the Athabasca River. A day and a half later we were at Mirror Landing.

"Stops had to be made to pile on cordwood, which was contracted for during the winter months.

"From there to Salteaux Landing on Little Slave River was 16 miles. The women rode in the wagons or democrats. The men walked, as there were too many to get accommodation on the horse-drawn vehicles, which also carried the freight loaded on the Midnight Sun, the steamer which traversed the upper waters of the Little Slave on to Lesser Slave Lake.

"The lake was 75 miles of rough going, but we finally arrived at Slave Lake (Grouard now) and I was met there by Charlie Gibbs, who was acting as telegraph lineman at Peace River Crossing.

"That 85 miles was really rough going. That, too, was three days, but at that time nobody seemed to care or even think of time as an element, distances either. Twenty-five miles a day with a load was considered a really good day."

Gauvreau and his wife used the Hudson Bay post in Slave Lake to stock up on household goods.

"I bought an HB four-point blanket – 14 pounds, 14 dollars. Yes, that's right, one dollar a pound and that thing lasted for years.

"We also bought some knives and forks, spoons, tin plates, cups, etc. The silverware was 40 cents each.

"Have you ever sat down and used one of those pieces of silverware where eggs stuck like glue, the tines felt like they were covered with sheep tallow, cold? Well that was it. Stir your cup of tea and lick off the spoon and the tongue almost stuck. Nothing but lead that would bend if dropped on the floor.

"Well, we arrived in Peace River Crossing. There was the Peace Hotel, a two-storey log-hewn building, erected early that same spring of 1911. It was run by Allie Brick, first MLA for the Peace River, who also had a big farm 12 miles up the Peace.

"There were only two bedrooms in the hotel, upstairs, to the right of the stairway, while to the left was the ram pasture. Everyone slept in there, just took up enough space on the floor for his or her bedroll, standard equipment then, and everybody was happy."

It didn't take Gauvreau long to settle into the life of the settlement — or into its mischief.

Gauvreau fell in with a group of lively practical jokers, including a young Englishman known as Phil Godsell. Godsell, in later years, was to become famous as a writer of crime stories and as a recorder of the life of northern Indians and the Eskimo.

But, at the time Gauvreau made his acquaintance, he was simply a clerk in a trading post and his lively imagination was not bent on writing but on livening up Peace River Crossing.

Together with another five men, Godsell and Gauvreau formed an organization called the "Seven 'P' Society," which Gauvreau later described as a "secret organization which only held one single meeting and that was for the purpose initiating a new member, a recent arrival from Fort Vermillion."

That initiation brought Gauvreau his first contact with Sgt. Jack Anderson, the legendary mountie of the north.

The new arrival was a man named Lawrence and, as Gauvreau notes, it was quite an initiation.

"No one but Godsell," he writes, "could have conceived such an initiation as Lawrence was put through. His $10 fee was used for a bottle of brandy. Beef and wine, etc. were contributed.

"When the grog started to run low in the wee small hours, the initiation was proceeded with by Lawrence being placed on an ordinary chair, on top of an ordinary table.

"He was as long as a well-rope and the ceiling was only seven feet high, so with a pearl grey thundermug on his head, which he had to hold by the handle, and doubled over like a jack-knife, he had to repeat the mumbo-jumbo thought up by Godsell, which the rest of us took turns to put just another stick of wood in the airtight heater, which was opened full-blast — which meant we all had to sit on the floor on account of the heat.

"Outside, sitting on a woodpile at 30 below zero was Sgt. Anderson with handcuffs in his pocket, waiting for the first one that stepped outside. But we had been tipped off, so after freezing for hours he gave it up as a bad job and went home, over half a mile away to the barracks, and contented himself with ruminating about our conduct the next day. The entire population at that time was about 15 or 20, scattered over three miles.

"Well, anyway, after a few gallons of water had been sweated out of the victim and he was dead sober, so the doors were opened to let in fresh air. Nothing has been heard since of the society."

Recalling the incident years later, Gauvreau mused over the career of Godsell and lamented the fact he had lost touch with him.

"At this writing," he said, "I am wondering where he is. I taught him to swear and wonder how he is progressing after the last time I saw him many years ago."

Of Sgt. Jack Anderson, Gauvreau had no need for such wonderings. He saw Anderson frequently and under conditions that shed needed human light on the iron-willed policeman who pounded the entire north for a beat.

Anderson has been made out to be many things — some cruel, some almost superhuman.

"Much has been written about him," Gauvreau recalls, "some good, some not of the calibre that should be attributed to him.

"He was rough, you bet, and tough, and God pity the poor fellow he hired to go with him on foot, whether it was on snowshoes or bare ground. I used to have to dogtrot to keep up with him and he never changed his pace all day.

"I heard so much of him before I came here that I was wondering whether I should come or not.

"When I came in I had brought two cases of Three Star Hennessy Brandy, and had them hidden in the old cellar in the house I occupied as the Government Telegraphs.

"I was awakened one hideously cold night, at least 50 below, when there was a pounding at the door, which I had plugged up to keep out the cold. No one else in the world would make so much noise, so I guessed it was Sgt. Anderson."

It was, as Gauvreau had guessed, Sgt. Anderson. Anderson stopped just long enough to tell him that he was on his way to Green Island, 40 miles away, to pick up two newcomers who had been carrying on with the female population there and needed to be brought into line.

"During the middle of the next night," Gauvreau continues, "there was more pounding and sure enough there was old Andy, covered with ice where his moustache stuck out of his buffalo coat.

"As soon as I opened the door, he blurted out 'Gauvreau, give me a good drink. I haven't had any sleep since I was here last night and only stopped long enough to change horses along the road.'

"I told him I didn't have any liquor, thought he was just fishing as I didn't know him any too well — except what was bad, and that I had only heard.

"'Come on, open that cellar door and get a bottle. I need something to warm me up as sitting in a sleigh is rough going after hours of it in the cold.'

"That settled the matter. I knew then that he knew all along that I had booze in the cellar, so I went down and got a bottle and poured out two-thirds of a tumbler full. He gulped it down like plain water, so I suggested he take the bottle with him as he was hitting for Lesser Slave Lake because the miscreants had come back by another road and he was on their trail.

"I can't do that Gauvreau, I'm on duty, can't carry liquor with me, just give me another drink and I'll be on my way, catch them buggers by morning.'

"They had, in the meantime, stolen a grindstone, a heinous offence.

"He flipped the bottle and filled the tumbler and down it went, hell for leather. That would have knocked an ordinary man cuckoo.

"He just buttoned up his buffalo coat and was away. When I looked, there was barely half a bottle left. Those glasses were big.

"The next evening a wire came through from him. He had reached Lesser Slave Lake and he had his prisoners with him. They got six months imprisonment. He got the grindstone.

"I have gone to some lengths to illustrate what that man could endure."

Adding up the mileage Anderson covered to get his men, Gauvreau made the total close to 200 miles in little more than 48 hours – all at 50 below zero.

"It was only a matter of another 45 miles to where the larger barracks were, so as soon as he relieved himself of his charges there he hit the hay – then back to his own bailiwick without undue delay."

The incident of the midnight brandy drew Anderson and Gauvreau together and they soon became fast friends.

Anderson, as often as his duty permitted, took to spending his time in the Gauvreau kitchen, indulging in his passion for cribbage and devouring cocoa and Mrs. Gauvreau's home-made cake.

During those long evenings, Anderson told Gauvreau

painkiller, Florida water, etc. coming into the country, as well as liquor permits, so he undertook to go around amongst the halfbreeds, and what few whites there were, with a petition to the Government to stop the flow of intoxicants into the country."

Holmes was a black-coated and imposing figure and there were few, including Gauvreau himself, who withstood the demand to sign in favor of prohibition – whatever secret thirsts this may have violated.

Indeed, according to Gauvreau, the north might have gone dry but for the doings of already-mentioned Bill Doherty.

Doherty was a big Irishman, both witty and bad-tempered.

He was also the manager of one of the two trading posts in the area and, at the time when Rev. Holmes descended on him with the famous petition in August of 1912, Doherty was painfully recovering from the effects of a prolonged bender.

"I happened to be in the store when the Rev. Holmes walked in," writes Gauvreau, "with his frock coat bulging and old Bill noticed it right off the bat and winked at me, as we had been discussing the petition and wondering how far Holmes would get with it.

"As was customary, Holmes was very polite and, by way of breaking in on the interview, asked Bill if he kept any of those gallon cans of apples the Hudson Bay Co. used to have. Bill shook his head slowly back and forth. 'But said the Rev., pointing to a shelf, 'there they are right up there.'

"Bill never looked around at all and said: 'I know where they are; we don't keep them, we sell them.'

"That got the Rev. gentleman in good humor and gave me the petition.

much about himself and about the tribulations of trying to preserve the law in thousands of square miles of wilderness.

He spoke offhandedly of the forced marches on snowshoe or behind a dogsled, of the danger of facing armed and dangerous men alone. Sometimes, he would lament the quirks of the law which let men he knew to be killers go free.

On one occasion, he casually recounted the tale that has brought Anderson down through history as something of a grim figure.

The 'mocassin telegraph' had brought him news of a possible murder in the Pouce Coupe territory.

"He told me about having to hit for Pouce Coupe overland, the short cut, on snowshoes. He only had two dogs for his cariole, which had to contain his bedroll, feed for himself and dogs, and extra clothing as the snow was very deep that year. He had to walk ahead of the dogs most of the time to save their strength.

"He ultimately got to his destination where he found a trapper by the name of Coleman, an old man, with his head lying in the open fireplace, cindered at the back and the body frozen stiff.

"He sized up the situation, arrested an American by the name of Trumper or Trotter when he found that individual had struck Coleman over the head after an argument and who stated that when Coleman went down he ran for his life as Coleman was after the rifle hanging on the wall. Anderson couldn't see it that way."

Anderson came up with evidence. There was the nature of the injury to the back of Coleman's head and the fact he had been dragged into the fireplace. More than that, he was able to prove that some gold coins the American had in his possession had been Coleman's.

The coins and the prisoner posed no problems. B...
of the body, the evidence of the head wounds? Th...
was frozen stiff and impossible to transport throug...
snow on a sled with only two dogs.

Anderson's solution was one that has haunted
tation ever since. He took a bucksaw and cut off C...
head, transporting the "evidence" in a lard can.

Anderson, in telling the tale to Gauvreau, pa...
incident as a matter of grisly necessity. And, 1...
the result was that the American was duly fou...
of murder by a jury in Edmonton.

Gauvreau, himself, never commented on th...
last word on Anderson was that "He was m...
even if we did have the odd fight."

* * * *

In his reminiscences about Anderson, Gauvr...
a talent for noticing the small doings of larg...
fondness for cocoa and a passion for cri...
examples.

In his dealings with some of the other char...
north, Gauvreau showed an equal talent f...
opposite: the ability to notice the large doi...
men. The result was, in the case of a man...
Doherty, a precious and pleasant addition to...

In the years just before World War One,...
were at work in the world. The Peace River...
still have been a wilderness dotted with tin...
but civilization was on the march in the sout...

Civilization inevitably reared its ugly h...
River Crossing in 1912 — in the form of...
to prohibit the sale and consumption of al...
ages.

A certain Rev. Holmes, Gauvreau recal...
the notion that there was too much beef-...

"Now Doherty's dad was a preacher man in Ireland and, as Bill told me on many occasions, a good one. He found him smoking a cigarette in the house when he was 26 years old and walked up and slugged him on the chin.

"Consequently, Bill knew the Bible inside out and backwards, so when Holmes asked him if he would put his signature on, like a lot of the rest, Bill told him only on one condition — that if he could name the dog that licked Lazarus' hand. Holmes was mystified. The Bible makes no mention of any name.

"Bill was adamant: 'Oh yes it does, oh yes it does.'

"Says Holmes, 'I wish I had my Bible with me, I could prove it to you.'

"So Bill gave me the nod, told me to go upstairs and pick up his Bible, which was on the dresser.

"From here on I am a bit lost, because when I gave it to Bill he handed it to Holmes and said something about Matthew, Mark, Luke and John — or whoever it was.

"However, Holmes turned to the subject at hand and said 'There you are, read that.'

"'You read it yourself, out loud', came back Bill.

"So Rev. Holmes went on about some crumbs on the floor and the sores on Lazarus — I just forget the proper lingo — but finally he came to the spot where it said 'and moreover the dog licked Lazarus' hand.

"'There you are!' hollers old Bill, 'There you are — it does so give the name!'

"There was a bit of an argument and Bill reached over and took the Bible and pointed: 'and moreover the dog licked Lazarus's hand.'

"MOREOVER, that was the name of the dog — at least so Bill said and stayed with that and did not sign the petition."

* * * *

Gauvreau and his wife had come to northern Alberta with many trepidations and, for the first year or so, there was no question that life was hard indeed.

For all Gauvreau's lively recollection of the characters they found at Peace River Crossing, life in the tiny settlement was harsh. The couple had left the hotel a couple of months after their arrival in the settlement, moving into one half of a log house owned by a settler known as Old John.

The house was ill-built, with many cracks and chinks for the wind to blow through — which left the Gauvreaus huddled near the fire or bundled under their Hudson Bay blanket and rabbit robe most of their first winter in Peace River.

To make matters worse, Old John was a member of the legion known as the "great unwashed." The Gauvreaus never knew him to change his clothing or to use soap and water. And, Mrs. Gauvreau would note often after, Old John had the same attitude towards housecleaning as he did towards Old-John cleaning.

The Gauvreaus stuck it out until May, 1912, when they finally were able to make a home of their own.

Old John's house, however, was not without fond memories.

"While there," Gauvreau writes, "my first son and heir was born, on my birthday, March 5th, 1912, without benefit of doctor or nurse.

"Old Nancy Brick and Laura Doherty, wife of the post manager Revillion's were the big help — with Three Star Hennessy as an anaesthetic, taken internally."

At about this time, too, fate handed Gauvreau an economic bonus in the strange form of a pool table.

The table was freighted in the same month Gauvreau's son was born.

"Charlie Banford and I set the thing up," recalls Gauvreau, "and that was the sign of better things to come as everyone wanted to play pool for money.

"That was the only gold mine I ever struck pay dirt on, as I was far better than a green hand at pool when I left Edmonton."

The chance to pick up money from the table was a welcome one for Gauvreau:

"I was only getting $75 a month from the Government — with Eagle Brand milk 50 cents for a small can; flour $20; Sugar $33. The great and only CPR Strawberries that the Hudson Bay Co. called Prunes were three pounds for a dollar. Even the little white bean that had so much to say for itself was four pounds for a buck.

"And me with a new baby, paying 25 cents a yard for cheesecloth to make a mosquito bar — standard equipment at all times.

"Flannellette was 50 cents a yard, while a four-pound pail of jam was $4.50, strawberry jam was $5.50 and coal oil $7.50 for a five-gallon can.

"I still have the Gillette Safety Razor, got it at a bargain as the only one left after a few years on the shelf, but the gold plating was stressed and I got it for $5.

"High freight rates were always claimed as the cause of the high prices — even to a package of sewing machine needles."

The pool-table income alone wasn't enough to offset the expense of finding a new home well upwind of Old John. It was here that Gauvreau's employer, the telegraph company, stepped in. The company decided to construct a combination office and living quarters for its operator at Peace River Crossing. As a blessing, Gauvreau recalls, it was definitely mixed:

"It was some building. The logs were taken out of the

Smokey in January, sleighed down to the Catholic Mission Sawmill, eight miles up the Shaftesbury Flat, and sawn into rough lumber.

"Do you get me? I said 'rough' and that's what it was.

"But beggars can't be choosers, and lumber of any kind was not available, so anyone can imagine what a two-storey house was like built of green lumber and occupied before the end of May the same year.

"Boy, when I think of walking up to that new home as it was nearing completion and finding the inside full of steam from a hot fire inside and real cold weather outside, no insulating, and building-paper popping like the war was on.

"The studding was put up of two-by-four on its flat — there was a shortage of it — and it was over two feet apart and a heavy person could walk fast upstairs and shake the whole works like jelly as the ceilings were only felt paper.

"It took me two years to get an appropriation for a lumber ceiling and that sort of steadied the whole works.

"However, downstairs the floor had cracks from half to an inch wide. There was some heat coming from the small cellar where the batteries were kept, wet batteries. Frank Anderson, the lineman, had to keep a good fire down there all the time.

"Later on I saved a lot of heat by sending out to Edmonton for a full roll of heavy linoleum, 12-foot wide, that cost me in Edmonton at that time $1.10 a linear foot, wholesale.

"So with a house 36 by 22 and a kitchen 16 by 18, it took a lot of covering, but we had a bit of comfort in the winter after that, provided we kept the wood heaters loaded with wood. The upstairs was heated by holes cut in the floor and grates put on. Them was the days."

* * * *

With new son, new home and the constant task of avoiding the vigilant Sgt. Anderson's attempts to stop the betting at the pool table, Gauvreau was living a full life.

It was not too full, however, to keep him from continuing his career as a watcher of people and a muser about human nature.

Gauvreau recalls one incident with particular fondness.

By 1911, the realization was spreading that the Peace River Country had potential as farming and ranching land. One of those who had the vision — and the guts to pursue it — was a freighter named Bill Smith and known as Little Billy.

Little Billy wanted to go into the cattle business and, while still freighting, was slowly moving stock into the Peace River area.

He was about to head on a regular freighting trip westward in the spring of 1911 when he heard of a chance for a good buy on some calves. Being temporarily short of funds, he borrowed $50 from Gauvreau.

"He never came back from that trip for nearly a year," Gauvreau writes. "Nevertheless, it was in July of 1912 when I awakened in the late afternoon. I was asleep on a bench in the shade with the mercury 105 — beastly hot.

"There at the counter stood a stranger. I got up rather shakily and asked him what he wanted. He retorted 'The operator.'

"'That's me, says I.

"'Okay, I was coming through Spirit River last week and a fellow stopped me and asked me if I would give the operator at Peace River Crossing $50,' was his reply.

"All right, I said, that must have been Little Billy Smith.

"'I don't know what his name was and I didn't ask him, so here is the $50 he gave me.'"

"Thanks a lot, I guess I better give you a receipt.

"He looked at me and said, 'What for? This $50? Never mind, I never gave him a receipt and, anyway, I'll probably never see him or you again.'

"Well, I said, my name is Gauvreau. What's yours?

"'Just Johnston, stranger in these parts, just looking over the country — and you can have it.'

"That was the last time I saw him and wouldn't know him if I saw him now.

"In the late fall, just before Christmas 1912, Little Billy pops out from somewhere up west and the first thing he asked me when unloaded from the sleigh was: 'Did you ever get the $50 I owed you?'

"I looked him square in the eye, without a blush. No Billy, I think the least you could have done was to have sent me some of it just to let me know you were alive.

"He went on to explain he had hit it here and there, then reached down in his pistol pocket and pulled out $50 and handed it to me."

Gauvreau kept up the joke through supper, through a few games of pool at the hotel and a few snorts out of a handy brandy bottle.

When he figured the suspense had gone on long enough, "I got a change of heart and hauled out the $50 and handed it to him.

"He looked at me with a queer glint in his eye. 'I didn't think that guy was a crook, he looked honest to me, but when you told me he hadn't given it to you, I just figured I had missed my hunch.'

"Then I asked him, what was that guy's name?' 'Damned if I know — I didn't ask him. I was putting up hay and he was driving by on his way to the outside so I flagged him down and handed him the money.'"

This episode of honesty stuck fast in Gaurveau's memory

and almost half a century later he would ponder the mysterious Johnston and say:

"We took most people at face value and I hope if he ever hears of this episode he will get in touch with me. Not too many of that kind of hombre in this world of make-believe and money madness…"

* * * *

In 1912, Gauvreau began to notice the slow march of civilization on the Peace River country. Real-estate speculators began to appear and with them rumors of railroad service and better roads. Soon prospective settlers — and a strong mix of opportunists — were trickling into the wilderness of the Peace.

Gauvreau, by now a veteran of the country, recalls with something close to glee the "welcome" the Peace River country of the time extended to the greenhorns.

"1912," he writes, "saw a big rush of homesteaders. In order to file on a homestead one had to look over the land and then either walk or drive over to Lesser Slave Lake where old Pete Tompkins was the land agent and there file on the quarter."

West of the Peace, he notes, government land surveyors had already been in and marked out the land. These surveyors, each backed by a crew of 20 workers, were an object of admiration for Gauvreau, as he knew what hardships they had to face in the wilderness.

"If any of those early birds are alive today, they will tell the same story, it was no country for a human being.

"A lot of them nearly died from the effects of bites of no-see-ems, blackflies, mosquitoes, bulldogs (a particularly vicious fly) — hordes and myriads of them, terrible to behold and devilishly poisonous.

"The banks of the Peace and all tributaries, as well as islands, were bedecked with evergreens" — ideal home for the "hordes and myriads" of insect life.

"There was no remedy to protect oneself except a cheese cloth that could be fitted to a wide-brimmed hat.

"Over the bed and under the mattress or rabbit robe, the cheese cloth was tucked in — or no sleep.

"The whine of the mosquitoes was terrific and no sleep for a night or two until the tired brain refused to function, from there on sleep was easy.

"Horses had to have earmuffs; over their noses from the bridle hung strips of leather about one-eighth of an inch wide to keep the horses breathing and keep the flies out of their nostrils, as these strings of leather would bob with the motion of the horse as it plodded along. On their sheaths was burned bacon grease and on their backs was a net, effective in a way but not complete protection.

"Smudges, they had to be so smoky it almost killed the animals and, as horses will do unless the smudge was fenced, they would stand in the fire, burn their hooves.

That seems fantastic, nevertheless it is absolutely true. Many a horse was shot, even though he was valuable, as he cooked his own feet beyond redemption.

"Cattle were not so bad. They would lie in a huddle and kick up dust as well as the smoke, but they went through a lot of suffering…

"When the big thunder occurred in June, that was the death knell of the bulldog — the most vicious of the flies as he took out a three-cornered chunk each time he decided to molest someone or something.

"The heat of the day got rid of the mosquito, but his place was admirably taken by the sand fly and the little black fly, who would eat a forehead of a human raw in short time, under a cap or hat.

"He was the guy that cut the horses on the sheath, back of front legs, nose and eyes. They were bad on hot days. If it was cool and raining, he gave way for daylight raids by the mosquito.

"I have seen moose, in late June when the river was in flood, run right off the high bank into the raging water and float with only the big nubbin of his nose and nostrils above water — and bulldogs that looked like a post hovering above."

Gauvreau returns to the subject of the homesteaders, this time with some bitterness towards the government that was luring them in:

"*As I said before, they would hike over the heavily-wooded terrain, pick up a couple of pieces of their choice, then go over to Lesser Slave Lake to file — pay their $10 which the government of the day demanded as sort of bet that they would not take the 160 acres of land at the end of three years.*

"*The government won a terrific lot of those bets, but those they lost were from the stalwarts that remained to build up an inland empire which, after only 40 years, has started to come into its own — not because of any government but in spite of it or them."*

* * * *

The movement into the country brought with it a lot of undesirables, types who would give police and settlers alike a hard, and sometimes dangerous, time.

Sgt. Jack Anderson was still, despite the assistance of occasional squads of other mounties, largely on his own as far as dealing with the dangerous types — the robbers, gunmen and murderers. He managed to do the job in his usual superhuman way, but his pre-occupation with serious offenders left it up to the people of Peace River Crossing themselves to cope with the, well, lesser evils...

"1913 was a hectic year in Peace River Crossing," writes Gauvreau. "The woods were full of the white ladies of easy virtue. The town was full of bootleggers, including Grand Trunk Dempsey (one of the most arrogant and unscrupulous bootleggers in the west), and the native ladies were already here in number."

To cope with this combination, the settlers finally set up a vigilante committee of five of the toughest men in town.

"These men pledged law and order, without fear or favor, and seven days notice was posted in various places about the town that in seven days the raid would be made, and giving everyone a chance to hit the trail."

Most of the undesireables — and particularly Grand Trunk Dempsey — sneered at the warnings and goaded the vigilantes, convinced that nothing would come of the effort to clean up the town.

What Dempsey and the others weren't counting on was the fact that the notice had been carefully timed — and that Sgt. Anderson would be waiting in the wings when

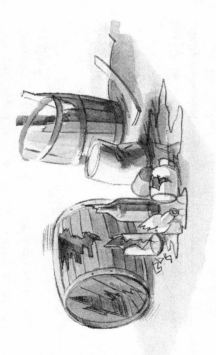

the day arrived.

The vigilantes avoided head-on confrontations. Instead they gathered evidence and sniffed out the hidden sites of the bootlegging operations.

"Only they," records Gauvreau, "knew what they found until the fatal day arrived when old Sgt. Anderson was given the blueprint at 5 p.m.

"Before 6 p.m. Dempsey and a lot more were in the clink. They were fined pretty heavily and left the country.

"But their booze, in galvanized cans, cases, stray jackets, in sacks, in hay stacks, under brush piles, well it was all picked up and it was a real collection.

"When the smoke of battle cleared away, Old Andy was right on the job. He had two men in the barracks cracking bottles together in a washtub, so glass and booze were carried over and dropped in the Peace.

"I happened up with a telegraph for the Sergeant. He was supervising every break. He went out for a couple of minutes and one of the boys handed me two bottles of Peter Dawson, which I cached in my hip pockets and sat and talked with the boys as they went about their business of protecting the government from any double-dealing.

"After a short time, I decided to go back to the office, a matter of a little better than half a mile, so I put my hands in my pants pockets so my elbows would hold out my coat as I trudged out, so everything was fine and dandy.

"I took the liquor home and told my wife about how we slipped up on Old Andy and how I would bet the other two boys would be around to collect their pound of flesh, so to speak.

"Nothing doing. Who showed up about eight o'clock that night for a game of cribbage but Old Andy himself.

"As usual, everything went fine until about midnight when my wife suggested a cup of cocoa and a piece of cake, the usual deterrent from further cribbage proceedings, but this time it was different.

"'How about a good drink of booze,' says Old Andy, 'I haven't got a drop, am waiting for my permit which is somewhere along the road.'

"'The old boy looked at me and as soon as he did I knew the jig was up. 'The bulge in your clothes when you left the barracks this afternoon was the real tip-off. When I told you I was going out behind, I did that to give you and the boys a chance to put something over on me and, as far as I know, you were the only one that tumbled. So dig it out and we'll celebrate the occasion before the boys come down to blackmail you.'

"Well, that was that. I got out a bottle and we had a snort or two..."

* * * *

Gauvreau, from this experience, should have known better than to think he would ever be able to slip one over on Old Andy when it came to hiding liquor from him, but he kept on trying. It was, after all, one of the forms of "sport" the settlement offered.

During one period, counting on Anderson's respect for his semi-official position as telegraph operator, coupled with part-time activities as postmaster, he took to having another operator ship him the odd bottle in the registered-mail sacks.

Gauvreau figured this scheme was foolproof "and yet that old son-of-a-gun of an Old Andy told me years afterwards that he knew, or had an idea, of what was going on.

"So he landed one night after dark, about an hour after the mail came in, and I had hidden a small case of liquor under the pile of mail bags upon which he had parked himself, and he was telling me — while I was working overtime to get the huge pile of mail sorted out, that he wasn't going to play any favorites. Liquor was liquor and the law was law.

"As for me, I was keeping him getting on his feet so I could throw another sack on the pile. And yet that old evil had a hunch — in fact I'm certain now — that he was laughing behind his poker face and knew all the time there was more than empty mail sacks under him. He did not admit this to me until many years after..."

* * * * *

Gauvreau's attention was to be turned away, at least for a period of many years, from the simple life of a telegraph operator and the joys of joking with a circle of friends.

With the influx of settlement was coming "civilization" and civilization meant government and bureaucracy.

Gauvreau, as some of his remarks have already shown, hadn't much use for either politicians or bureaucrats and he soon ran afoul of both.

The first conflict came when Gauvreau decided to get in on the homestead rush and filed on a piece of property. Although his claim was accepted and registered, two months later he was told there had been an "error" and someone else already had the rights to the homestead. Would he please choose another parcel?

Gauvreau did some checking and uncovered the fact that the error was a fiction and the whole exercise nothing more than "patronage," a bid to get good piece of land for someone who had status with the government.

Fighting the issue, since he depended on the government for his job, didn't seem like a wise idea, but Gauvreau decided to fight anyway — and he fought and fought and fought — working in the settlement by day and squatting on the property at night to keep it secure. It was a fight that dragged on for a decade and it was a fight he inevitably lost.

The worst part of the loss came long before he had to relinquish the property. It came almost at the beginning of the battle. He was fired from his job as operator.

Gauvreau had to choose yet another homestead location and work it with a passion to keep his family going.

Worst of all, both Mrs. Gauvreau and their infant son fell sick. Gauvreau never spells out what was wrong, except to say that it wasn't too serious. It was serious enough, however, to require hospitalization — and that was a project that consigned the woman and child to a terrible trip to the south:

"In June I had to send my wife and son out to Edmonton for hospitalization.

"That was about the last of June, so it was a two-day trip to Grouard — which was celebrating the first of July as the 60th anniversary of the priesthood for Bishop Grouard. That meant a party was on all the time — hoedowns, lots of whoopee, lots of Indians and half breeds and, as Grouard was growing, also lots of whites.

"That meant the boats were tied up until the festivities were over with, a whole week of them.

"Finally, the boat started out and two days later my wife was in Athabasca and a pretty sick woman. There she met Emily Murphy, the original woman Police Magistrate, so they teamed up together and hired a Model T for quick transportation to Edmonton.

"They got stuck in a slough and had to wade to shore and something went 'boom' with the Model T and just about when the world was at its blackest along comes the mail man with his team and democrat, so the Model T was abandoned and that night was spent at Half-Way Lakes, run by the family of Egge's.

"The next night they were in Edmonton and my wife in the hospital, right pronto. The Model T never caught up with them.

"The CNR was getting its right-of-way in shape for train movements, so in September my wife and son caught the first passenger coach on a work train, but it got derailed near Morinville and that was two or three days layover in a badly bed-bug infested hotel.

"All hotels were bed-buggy, couldn't be anything else, but if one slept on an old camping site instead, they got their bedding and clothes full of lice.

Being inside a building had its advantages — you could keep the lights burning and keep the bed bug in his lair. Blowing out the light was the signal for his dropping on the floors and beds in countless numbers..."

It was a trying experience for Gauvreau. Communication between the settlement and Edmonton at that time was still largely dependent on the telegraph and that summer a continuing wave of brush fires burned out that service.

"I had gotten word my wife and kid were in the hospital, but in the meantime those big brush fires had eaten up miles of telegraphs, so there was no communication of any kind except mocassin telegraph."

* * * *

Gauvreau, his wife and son finally back with him, settled down to work his homestead and make the necessary extra money on the side "doing this and that" to keep the family's collective head above water.

It was a grueling existence: cutting and clearing, planting and nursing a farm into existence. For most men, it would have been all they could do to keep up.

Gauvreau, however, always managed to find time to keep his eyes on the people and world around him and to muse over the changes that were taking place.

He watched the fires — including the one written of elsewhere in this book — clear away the barrier of forests and brush faster than an army of settlers ever could. He watched this army of settlers come marching in.

He also watched another army go marching out, gone to the "Great War" that took so terrible a toll of human life.

By 1918, he recalled sadly, he was the only one left of the men who had originally settled at Peace River Crossing.

It was with definitely mixed feelings that he saw how the influx of settlers was "civilizing" Peace River Crossing. His journals contain page after page describing the steady, block-by-block development of the settlement into a town and finally into a city.

He even watched — this time with amazement and amusement — as his old office-cum-home was physically carted across town by an ambitious developer too much in a hurry to build.

Throughout, he retained his gift for making friends with

people and for keeping track of their doings.

Peace River Jim Cornwall, the steamboat operator who became the biggest single booster of the Peace River Country, was one of Gauvreau's friends. It was Gauvreau who gave much of the needed support when Cornwall took on the project of putting the grave of 12-foot Davis on the heights over the town.

In later years, long after Cornwall had died, Gauvreau kept his wary eye on the monument, constantly battling the "morons" who vandalized it and scorning the "goody-goody" ladies whose answer to the vandalism was to surround the site with so much fencing "that a man can't read what it says on the thing at all."

He delighted in keeping track of the doings of the pioneers of the north — great and not-so-great.

It is in Gauvreau's papers that you discover that Charles Major, author of **When Knighthood Was In Flower**, once spent a pleasant morning fishing for greylings on the Peace River.

It is here, too, that you meet people like Johnny Gullion, captain of the first steamer the Hudson Bay Company put on the Athabasca.

Gauvreau's tantalizing sketch of Gullion: "a huge man that didn't look so big. Six feet tall, shoulders like a buffalo bull and strong fine type of leg, not the bulky kind that went into that frame. And he was as strong as a bull. He had pitted his strength against everything on the Athabasca River for years as he had run the gauntlet of the Grand Rapids without mishap for several years, and I never heard of him having been bested in weight lifting. He weighed slightly over 200 pounds, but was as light on his feet as a ballet dancer and could roll off the **Red River Jig** endlessly."

Gauvreau, like many of the other early settlers, never ceased to be puzzled by the way in which the Indians always knew when a steam boat was due. Suddenly, without warning, Gauvreau and the others would simply find that wagon-loads of Indians were in the settlement and patiently waiting by the river.

"I asked one or two of them what they were all coming into town for, since it was not treaty time.

"They all had the same answer — 'Steamboat come, anooch tipisgow' — and sure enough it never failed. The old steamer whistled loud and long and it would the long summer night...

"The teepees were lighted up with bonfires, the pass-the-buck game was on and the tom-toms- beat out their rhythmic (or otherwise) beat all through the night. The boat was in. There was no doubt about that.

"Can anyone tell me how those native knew? There was no radio, no telephones, no telegraphs, no road of any kind except the river, but they were here on time and usually stayed a week, when their money, credit and grub supply ran out.

"That didn't happen only once. It happened until the whites began to be on the increase and the natural taciturnity of the native resolved itself into the stay-at-home type."

Gauvreau had many Indian friends, but his favorite was Akenum, who took the white man's name of Felix Show.

"That little old fellow must have been around 108 years of age when he died. It was uncanny to listen to him talk of the old days when he was head boatman for George Simpson, governor of the Hudson Bay Company.

"He knew where Fort Garry was, Fort Agustus, the Clear Water and Athabasca Rivers, the Saskatchewan — the lakes and rivers of the entire north — but he never heard of Winnipeg or Edmonton. Anything he told me was from nothing else than what he actually knew from experience.

"He knew his stuff. He used to describe how the canoes were tracked up the Peace by brute force, how they crossed from one channel to the other in order to get footing on the shore, building a small raft and taking a rope across, and if one of the trackers got drowned, he just had to stay drowned."

* * * *

The Gauvreau papers are filled with images like these. They are filled, too, with the man's growing realization that those of whom he wrote were rapidly fading away.

In time, he realized that the "fading away" was catching up with him, too, and in the 1950's he finally abandoned the homestead life and moved into **Peace River**.

Before he did, though, he had time for one last visit with the best of his old friends — Sgt. Anderson.

Gauvreau had been on vacation in California in February of 1944, and on his way back detoured to see the now-retired policeman.

"I stopped long enough at Jasper to race down and give him a snort of **Kentucky** bourbon I had carried across the line with the seal broken by the customs inspector, and it was there we threshed a thousand things over in the short space of time available. I nearly missed my train that time.

"That was the last time I was ever to see the old sport alive. God bless his old heart."

Settled into **Peace River**, Gauvreau figured he would be living a life of oblivion, anonymous to all the strangers around him.

To his surprise, he found he was famous and respected. Letters began to arrive, begging him for stories for magazines and newspapers. There were other letters, from a new generation asking him politely if he had remembered their fathers or grandfathers and could tell any tales of them. Gauvreau, to his credit, was able to oblige all sources of inquiry.

With "nothing to do but write," Gauvreau found still more time to contemplate the life he had chosen for himself so many years before, the "life of the north."

One day, not long before he died, he sat down and pounded out on his old typewriter his summing-up of the country the **Peace** had become.

"It is indeed a changed country, but the magnetism has not waned for thousands of visitors who annually tour through in wonderment and awe. All vow to return.

"The scenic grandeur cannot be surpassed, as all agree

who view it. There is variety fit for the most fastidious.

"The lure of the north cannot be defined, suffice to say, but the oldtimer, the pioneer in every sense of the word, remains to watch the result of his work and faith unfold itself before his very eyes.

"As the onward march of civilization breaks forth in one fell swoop to snatch the last vestige of the primitive moods and whims that so long held sway over a land, that has made its bid for supremacy through the lean years of struggle and toil by cold, unvarnished facts forced upon an unsentimental world by dint of perseverance until the facts could not further be denied and the onward march of progress becomes an army of invasion.

"There has never been a complete failure, unless of course these failures could be put into another category and referred to as individuals who expected to pick gold coins off the berry bushes and who slackened at the extra courage required...

"Times were hard and many left for greener fields, but in the main the distant green fields were only a mirage and many have returned to start all over again.

"Those that remained fought all adversity with a stoicism and courage that could not be denied, and these are the ones who can now sit back and review their long struggle with a feeling that perhaps, after all, their happiest days were those while the struggle was at its peak.

"And there are no regrets expressed now that time, that great healer of all wounds, has laid its flourishing hand on the men that knew no defeat and who, today, lay their hand on the shoulder of the newcomer and feelingly say 'You have a cinch on what we had my boy. Dig in — sweat a bit — and you'll have a stake in three years that it took us almost 20 years to realize.'

"To some, this is the last Great West, but many generations must pass before this can be quoted as a fact, for far to the west of the Peace River Country lies a vast territory that must someday come in for its call as the Last Great West. When that time comes, the Peace River Country must give way and to its younger generation say 'Go west, young man, go west.'"

* * * *

At the opening of this section of the book, we quoted from Gauvreau, Peace River Jim Cornwall's epitaph for 12-foot-Davis:

"Pioneer, trader and pathfinder, he was every man's friend and never locked his cabin door."

It is the measure of a man's humbleness that Gauvreau never realized that the same words could have been applied to him.

BIBLIOGRAPHY

This is a selected bibliography on Alberta and Western Canadian History. For the most part only works which are in print have been included. Some of the best works on Alberta History are now out of print and hence not included in this list. Some of the items included may be out of print by the time of publication of this volume. All of them should, however, be available in larger public libraries in the province.

GENERAL WESTERN CANADIAN HISTORY

Cashman, A. W. *An Illustrated History of Western Canada.* Edmonton: Hurtig. 1971.

Hill, Douglas. *The Opening of the Canadian West.* Don Mills: Longman. 1972.

Macdonald, Norman. *Canada, Immigration, and Colonization, 1841-1903.* Toronto: Macmillan. 1966.

MacEwan. J. W. Grant. *West to the Sea.* Scarborough: McGraw-Hill. 1968.

Morton, A. S. *A History of the Canadian West to 1870-71.* Toronto: Univ. of Toronto Press. 1973.

Thomas, L. G., ed. *The Prairie West to 1905.* Don Mills: Oxford Univ. Press. 1975.

FUR TRADE

Ballantyne, R. M. *Hudson's Bay, or Every-day Life in the Wilds of North America.* Edmonton: Hurtig. 1972. (Reprint edition).

Campbell, Marjorie W. *The Fur Trade.* Toronto: Clarke Irwin. 1973. (Canadian Jack-daw series).

Campbell, Marjorie W. *The North West Company.* Toronto: Macmillan. 1973.

Campbell, Marjorie W. *The Nor'Westers: the Fight for the Fur Trade.* Toronto: Macmillan. 1973.

Campbell, Marjorie W. *Push to the Pacific.* Toronto: Clarke Irwin. 1968. (Canadian Jack-daw series).

Canada. Dept. of Indian Affairs. *Fur Trade Canoe Routes Then and Now.* Ottawa: Publishing Centre. Supplies and Services. 1969.

Innis, Harold A. *The Fur Trade in Canada: an Introduction to Canadian Economic History.* Toronto: Univ. of Toronto Press. 1956.

McKay, Douglas. *The Honourable Company.* Toronto: McClelland & Stewart. 1966.

Marsh, James H. *The Fur Trade.* Don Mills: Collier-Macmillan. 1971.

Neering, Rosemary. *Fur Trade.* Don Mills: Fitzhenry & Whiteside. 1974.

Ray, A. J. *Indians in the Fur Trade: their Role as Trappers, Hunters, and Middlemen in the Lands Southwest of Hudson Bay, 1660-1860.* Toronto: Univ. of Toronto Press. 1974.

Rich, E. E. *The Fur Trade and the Northwest to 1857.* Toronto: McClelland & Stewart. 1967.

Williams, Glyndwyr. *Highlights of the First 200 Years of the Hudson's Bay Company.* Winnipeg: Peguis. 1977.

Woodcock, George. *The Hudson's Bay Company*. New York: Crowell-Collier, 1970.

ACCOUNTS OF FUR TRADERS AND EARLY WESTERN TRAVELLERS

Butler, William. *The Great Lone Land*. Edmonton: Hurtig, 1968. (Reprint).

Cheadle, W. B. *Journal of a Trip Across Canada, 1862-63*. Edmonton: Hurtig, 1970. (Reprint).

Cheadle, W. B. & Viscount Milton. *The North-West Passage by Land*. Toronto: Coles, 1969. (Reprint).

Erasmus, Peter. *Buffalo Days and Nights*. Calgary: Glenbow, 1977.

Henry, Alexander. *Travels and Adventures in Canada and the Indian Territories, 1760-1776*. Edmonton: Hurtig, 1969. (Reprint).

Kane, Paul. *Wanderings of an Artist Among the Indians of North America*. Edmonton: Hurtig, 1967. (Reprint).

MacGregor, J. G. *Peter Fidler: Canada's Forgotten Surveyor*. Toronto: McClelland & Stewart, 1966.

Palliser, John. *The Papers of the Palliser Expedition, 1857-60*. Toronto: Champlain Society, 1968.

Smith, J. K. *David Thompson*. Don Mills: Fitzhenry & Whiteside, 1975.

Southesk, James, Earl of. *Saskatchewan and the Rocky Mountains*. Edmonton: Hurtig, 1969. (Reprint).

Spry, Irene. *The Palliser Expedition*. Toronto: Macmillan, 1973.

Thompson, David. *David Thompson's Narrative, 1784-1812*. Toronto: Champlain Society, 1962.

Wood, Kerry. *The Map-Maker: the Story of David Thompson*. Toronto: Macmillan, 1955.

RIEL REBELLIONS

Anderson, Frank W. *1885 — The Riel Rebellion*. Calgary: Frontier, 1962.

Anderson, Frank W. *Riel's Manitoba Uprising*. Calgary: Frontier, 1974.

Bowsfield, Hartwell, ed. *Louis Riel: Rebel of the Western Frontier or Victim of Politics and Prejudice?* Toronto: Copp Clark, 1969.

Flanagan, Thomas. *The Diaries of Louis Riel*. Edmonton: Hurtig, 1976.

Howard, Joseph. *Strange Empire*. New York: Morrow, 1959.

McCourt, Edward. *Revolt in the West: the Story of the Riel Rebellion*. Toronto: Macmillan, 1958.

Morton, Desmond. *The Last War Drum*. Toronto: Hakkert, 1974.

Morton, Desmond. *The Queen vs. Louis Riel*. Toronto: Univ. of Toronto Press, 1974.

Neering, Rosemary. *Louis Riel*. Don Mills: Fitzhenry & Whiteside, 1976.

Stanley, George F. G. *The Birth of Western Canada: a History of the Riel Rebellions*. Toronto: Univ. of Toronto Press, 1960.

Stanley, George F. G. *Louis Riel*. Scarborough: McGraw-Hill, 1972.

Woodcock, George. *Gabriel Dumont*. Edmonton: Hurtig, 1975.

MOUNTED POLICE

Atkin, Ronald. *Maintain the Right*. Toronto: Macmillan, 1973.

Chambers, Ernest J. *The Royal North-West Mounted Police*. Toronto: Coles, 1972.

D'Artigue, Jean. *Six Years in the Canadian North-West*. Belleville: Mika, 1973. (Reprint).

Dempsey, Hugh A., ed. *Men in Scarlet*. Calgary: Historical Society of Alberta, 1974.

Dempsey, Hugh A. *William Parker: Mounted Policeman*. Edmonton: Hurtig, 1973.

Denny, Cecil. *The Law Marches West*. Don Mills: Dent, 1972.

Donkin, J. G. *Trooper and Redskin, 1884-1888*. Toronto: Coles, 1973. (Reprint).

Haydon, A. L. *The Riders of the Plains*. Edmonton: Hurtig, 1970.

Kelly, Nora & William. *The Royal Canadian Mounted Police*. Edmonton: Hurtig, 1971.

Longstreth, T. M. *The Scarlet Force*. Toronto: Macmillan, 1974. (Reprint).

RAILROADS

Berton, Pierre. *The Last Spike; the Great Railway, 1881-85*. Toronto, McClelland & Stewart, 1971.

Berton, Pierre. *The National Dream; the Great Railway, 1871-1881*. Toronto: McClelland & Stewart, 1972.

Bowman, R. F. *Railways in Southern Alberta*. Lethbridge, Historical Society of Alberta, 1973.

Innis, H. A. *A History of the Canadian Pacific Railway*. Toronto: Univ. of Toronto Press, 1970. (Reprint).

Lavallee, Omer. *Van Horne's Road; a Picture Story of the C.P.R.* Montreal; Railfare Enterprises, 1974.

McDougall, John L. *Canadian Pacific; A Brief History*. Montreal; McGill Univ. Press, 1968.

Regehr, T. D. *The Canadian Northern Railway*. Toronto, Macmillan, 1976.

Shipley, Nan. *The Railway Builders*. Scarborough, McGraw-Hill, 1965.

INDIANS AND METIS

Ahenakew, Edward. *Voices of the Plains Cree*. Toronto; McClelland & Stewart, 1973.

Bearon, Daphne. *Indian Legends*. Agincourt; Gage, 1971.

Cardinal, Harold. *The Unjust Society*. Edmonton; Hurtig, 1969.

Clark, Ella E. *Indian Legends of Canada*. Toronto; McClelland & Stewart, 1960.

Campbell, Maria. *Halfbreed*. Toronto; McClelland & Stewart, 1973.

Canada. Dept. of Indian Affairs. *A Survey of the Contemporary Indians*. Ottawa: Publishing Centre, Supplies & Services, 1968.

Dempsey, Hugh A. *Blackfoot Ghost Dance*. Calgary; Glenbow, 1968.

Dempsey, Hugh A. *A Blackfoot Winter Count*. Calgary; Glenbow, 1965.

Dempsey, Hugh A. *Crowfoot; Chief of the Blackfeet*. Edmonton; Hurtig, 1972.

Dempsey, Hugh A. *Tailfeathers; Indian Artist*. Calgary; Glenbow, 1970.

Ewers, John C. *Blackfeet; Raiders on the Northwestern Plains*. Norman; Univ. of Oklahoma Press, 1967.

Ewers, John C. *The Horse in Blackfoot Indian Culture*. Washington; Smithsonian Institute, 1969.

Ewers, John C. *Indian Life on the Upper Missouri*. Norman; Univ. of Oklahoma Press, 1968.

Fine Day. *My Cree People*. Invermere; Good Medicine Books, 1973.

Hall, A. *Indians of the Plains*. Don Mills; Fitzhenry & Whiteside, 1972.

Hungry Wolf, Adolph. *The Blackfoot People*. Invermere; Good Medicine Books, 1975.

Hungry Wolf, Adolph. *Indian Summer; a Good Medicine Book Created in the Canadian Rockies*. Invermere; Good Medicine Books, 1975.

Hungry Wolf, Adolph. *Teachings of Nature*. Invermere; Good Medicine Books, 1975.

Jenness, Diamond. *The Indians of Canada*. Ottawa; Publishing Centre, Supplies & Services, 1969.

Jenness, Eileen. *The Indian Tribes of Canada*. Scarborough; McGraw-Hill, 1966.

Leechman, Douglas. *The Native Tribes of Canada*. Agincourt; Gage, 1956.

Light, Douglas W. *Tattooing Practices of the Cree Indians*. Calgary; Glenbow, 1972.

MacEwan, J. W. Grant. *Portraits from the Plains*. Scarborough; McGraw-Hill, 1971.

MacEwan, J. W. Grant. *Sitting Bull; the Years in Canada*. Edmonton; Hurtig, 1973.

MacEwan, J. W. Grant. *Tatanga Mani; Walking Buffalo of the Stonies*. Edmonton; Hurtig, 1969.

Maclean, Hope. *Indians; an Introduction to Canada's Nature People*. Ottawa; Canadian Association in Support of the Native People, 1977.

Melacon, Claude. *Indian Legends of Canada*. Agincourt; Gage, 1974.

Morris, Alexander. *The Treaties of Canada with the Indians*. Toronto; Coles, 1971. (Reprint).

Patterson, E. Palmer. *The Canadian Indian; a History Since 1500*. Don Mills; Collier-Macmillan, 1971.

Sealey, D. B., ed. *Indians Without Tipis; a Resource Book By Indians and Metis*. Agincourt; Book Society of Canada, 1974.

Sealey, D. B. *The Metis; Canada's Forgotten People*. Winnipeg; Manitoba Metis Federation, 1975.

Shipley, Nan. *Almighty Voice and the Red Coats*. Don Mills; Burns & MacEachern, 1967.

Schaeffer, Claude E. *Blackfoot Shaking Tent*. Calgary; Glenbow, 1969.

Sluman, Norma. *Poundmaker.* Scarborough: McGraw-Hill, 1967.

Smith, Derek. *Canadian Indians and the Law.* Toronto; McClelland & Stewart, 1975.

Surtees, Robert J. *The Original People.* Toronto: Holt, Rinehart & Winston, 1971.

Symington, D. F. *The Canadian Indian; the Illustrated History of the Great Tribes of Canada.* Toronto: McClelland & Stewart, 1969.

Walsh, Gerald. *Indians in Transition; an Inquiry Approach.* Toronto: McClelland & Stewart, 1971.

MISSIONARIES

McDougall, John. *Opening the Great West.* Calgary; Glenbow, 1970.

McDougall, John. *Pathfinding on Plain and Prairie.* Toronto; Coles, 1971.

MacGregor, J. G. *Father Lacombe.* Edmonton; Hurtig, 1975.

Pritchett, John P. *Black Robe and Buckskin; the Story of Catholic Pioneering in Northern North America.* New York: College & Univ. Press Services, 1960.

Stocken, H. W. G. *Among the Blackfoot and Sarcee.* Calgary; Glenbow, 1976.

PIONEER LIFE

This subject is also covered in many other works in the bibliography.

Broadfoot, Barry. *The Pioneer Years, 1895-1914.* Toronto: Doubleday, 1976.

Bruce, Jean. *The Last Best West.* Don Mills: Fitzhenry & Whiteside, 1976.

Robertson, Heather. *Grassroots.* Toronto: James Lorimer, 1973.

Robertson, Heather. *Salt of the Earth.* Toronto: James Lorimer, 1974.

Roberts, Sarah Ellen. *Of Us and Oxen.* Saskatoon: Modern Press, 1968.

AGRICULTURE IN THE WEST

Gray, James. *Men Against the Desert.* Saskatoon: Modern Press, 1967.

MacEwan, J. W. Grant. *Power for Prairie Plows.* Saskatoon: Western Producer, 1971.

RANCHING IN THE WEST

De Leeuw, Gary. *Alberta Foothills.* Toronto: Holt, Rinehart & Winston, 1971.

Long, Philip S. *The Great Canadian Range.* Calgary; Bonanza Books, 1974.

MacEwan, J. W. Grant. *Between the Red and the Rockies.* Toronto; Univ. of Toronto Press, 1952.

MacEwan, J. W. Grant. *Blazing the Old Cattle Trail.* Saskatoon: Western Producer, 1966.

Russell, Andy. *Trails of a Wilderness Wanderer.* New York: Random House, 1971.

OIL INDUSTRY

Gould, Ed. *Oil; the History of Canada's Oil and Gas Industry.* Saanichton; Hancock House, 1976.

Gray, Earle. *The Great Canadian Oil Patch.* Toronto: Maclean-Hunter, 1970.

Massey, D. L. *An Oil Well Near Edmonton.* Scarborough; Ginn, 1969.

THE 1920'S — PROHIBITION

Anderson, Frank W. *The Rum Runners.* Calgary; Frontier, 1968.

Gray, James. *Booze; the Impact of Whiskey on the Prairie West.* Toronto; Macmillan, 1972.

Gray, James. *The Roar of the Twenties.* Toronto; Macmillan, 1975.

THE DEPRESSION

Broadfoot, Barry. *Ten Lost Years, 1929-1939.* Toronto; Doubleday, 1973.

Gray, James. *Men Against the Desert.* Saskatoon, Modern Press, 1967.

Gray, James. *The Winter Years.* Toronto; Macmillan, 1976.

Grayson, L. M. *The Wretched of Canada; Letters to R. B. Bennett, 1930-35.* Toronto; Univ. of Toronto Press, 1971.

Hoar, Victor. *The On to Ottawa Trek.* Vancouver; Copp Clark, 1970.

Long, Philip S. *Dreams, Dust and Depression.* Calgary; Cypress, 1972.

EDUCATION

Chalmers, John W. *Schools of the Foothills Province.* Toronto; Univ. of Toronto Press, 1967.

Charyk, John. *The Little White Schoolhouse.* Saskatoon; Prairie Books, 1968.

Charyk, John. *The Pulse of the Community.* Saskatoon; Prairie Books, 1970.

ETHNIC GROUPS

Bennett, John W. *Hutterian Brethren; the Agricultural Economy and Social Organization of a Communal.* Stanford; Stanford Univ. Press, 1967.

Flint, David. *The Hutterites; a Study in Prejudice.* Don Mills; Oxford Univ. Press, 1975.

Hostetler, John. *Hutterites in North America.* New York; Holt, Rinehart & Winston, 1967.

Hostetler, John. *Hutterite Life.* New York, Herald Press, 1965.

Hostetler, John. *Mennonite Life.* New York; Herald Press, 1959.

MacGregor, James G. *Vilni Zemli; the Ukrainian Settlement in Alberta.* Toronto; McClelland & Stewart, 1969.

Marunchak, Michail H. *Studies in the History of Ukrainians in Canada.* Edmonton; Ukrainian Free Academy, 1966-. (Series).

Palmer, Howard. *Land of the Second Chance; a History of Ethnic Groups in Southern Alberta.* Lethbridge; Lethbridge Herald, 1972.

Tarasoff, Koozma. *A Pictorial History of the Doukhobors.* Saskatoon; Western Producer, 1969.

Woodcock, George. *The Doukhobors.* Don Mills; Oxford Univ. Press, 1968.

Woycenko, Ol'ha. *The Ukrainians in Canada.* Winnipeg; Trident Press, 1968.

MISCELLANEOUS WORKS ON ALBERTA HISTORY

Anderson, Frank W. (All titles available from Frontier Publishing, Calgary).

Anderson, Frank W. *Almighty Voice.* 1971.

Anderson, Frank W. *Calgary-Banff Highway.* 1968.

Anderson, Frank W. *Calgary-Medicine Hat Highway.* 1970.

Anderson, Frank W. *The Carbon Murders Mystery.* 1973.

Anderson, Frank W. *The Dynamic Crowsnest Pass.* 1963.

Anderson, Frank W. *Enchanted Banff and Lake Louise,* 1965.

Anderson, Frank W. *The Frank Slide Story.* 1961.

Anderson, Frank W. *Ghost Towns Journal.* 1973.

Anderson, Frank W. *Mystic Jasper.* 1973.

Anderson, Frank W. *Sheriffs and Outlaws of Western Canada.* 1973.

Anderson, Frank W. *Waterton: Land of Leisure.* 1973.

Barnett, Don & Mogen, Pat. *Alberta: A People and A Province.* Don Mills; Fitzhenry & Whiteside, 1975.

Bickersteth, J. B. *The Land of Open Doors.* Toronto; Univ. of Toronto Press, 1976.

Boudreau, Joseph A. *Alberta, Aberhart and Social Credit.* Toronto; Holt, Rinehart & Winston, 1975.

Cashman, Anthony W. *The Best Edmonton Stories.* Edmonton; Hurtig, 1976.

Cashman, Anthony W. *Heritage of Service: the History of Nursing in Alberta.* Edmonton; Alta. Assoc. of Registered Nurses, 1966.

Cashman, Anthony W. *A History of Motoring in Alberta.* Edmonton; Spartan Press, 1976.

Cashman, Anthony W. *Singing Wires; the Telephone in Alberta.* Edmonton; Alberta Government Telephones, 1972.

Cunniffe, Richard. *Calgary — In Sandstone.* Calgary; Historical Society of Alberta, 1969.

Dempsey, Hugh A. *The Best of Bob Edwards.* Edmonton; Hurtig, 1975.

Dempsey, Hugh A. *Indian Names for Alberta Communities.* Calgary; Glenbow, 1969.

Dempsey, Hugh A. *Jerry Potts; Plainsman.* Calgary; Glenbow, 1966.

Drinkwater, T. A. et al. *Atlas of Alberta.* Toronto; Univ. of Toronto Press, 1973.

Fraser, Esther. *The Canadian Rockies; Early Travels and Explorations.* Edmonton; Hurtig, 1969.

Holmgren, Pat & Eric. *Over 2,000 Place Names of Alberta.* Saskatoon; Western Producer, 1976.

Irving, John. *The Social Credit Movement in Alberta.* Toronto; Univ. of Toronto Press, 1950.

Kelly, L. V. *North With Peace River Jim.* Calgary; Glenbow, 1972.

Kennedy, Fred. *Alberta Was My Beat; Memoirs of a Western Newspaperman.* Calgary; The Albertan, 1975.

Kroetsch, Robert. *Alberta.* Toronto; Macmillan, 1968.

Liddell, Kenneth. *Southern Alberta's Roamin Empire.* Calgary: Frontier Publishing, 1963.

Luxton, Eleanor. *Banff; Canada's First National Park.* Banff; Summerthought, 1975.

MacEwan. J. W. Grant. *Calgary Cavalcade; From Fort to Fortune.* Saskatoon; Western Producer, 1966.

MacEwan. J. W. Grant. *Eye-Opener Bob.* Saskatoon; Western Producer, 1974.

MacEwan. J. W. Grant. *Fifty Mighty Men.* Saskatoon; Western Producer, 1974.

MacEwan. J. W. Grant. *Memory Meadows; Horse Stories from Canada's Past.* Saskatoon; Western Producer, 1976.

MacEwan. J. W. Grant. *Poking into Politics.* Saskatoon; Western Producer, 1966.

MacGregor, James G. *Edmonton; a History.* Edmonton; Hurtig, 1975.

MacGregor, James G. *A History of Alberta.* Edmonton; Hurtig, 1972.

MacGregor, James G. *The Klondike Rush through Edmonton, 1897-98.* Toronto; McClelland & Stewart, 1970.

MacGregor, James G. *Overland by the Yellowhead.* Saskatoon; Western Producer, 1974.

MacGregor, James G. *Pack Saddles to Tete Jaune Cache.* Edmonton; Hurtig, 1973.

MacGregor, James G. *Paddle-Wheels to Bucket Wheels on the Athabasca.* Toronto; McClelland & Stewart, 1974.

MacPherson, C. B. *Democracy in Alberta.* Toronto; Univ. of Toronto Press, 1953.

Mann, William E. *Sect, Cult and Church in Alberta.* Toronto; Univ. of Toronto Press, 1955.

Mardon, E. G. *Names on the Face of Alberta Communities.* Lethbridge; U. of Leth. Press, 1973.

Peel, Bruce. *Steamboats on the Saskatchewan.* Saskatoon; Western Producer, 1972.

Rodney, William. *Kootenai Brown; His Life and Times.* Sidney; Gray's Publishing, 1969.

Sharp, Paul. *Whoop-Up Country; the Canadian-American West, 1865-1885.* Norman; Univ. of Oklahoma Press, 1973.

Wormington. H. M. *An Introduction to the Archaeology of Alberta.* Denver; Denver Museum of Natural History, 1965.